The Languages of the World

'All will delight in the extensive linguistic buffet presented in *The Languages of the World*'. *Times Literary Supplement* review of the first edition.

This, the Third Edition of Kenneth Katzner's best-selling guide to the world's languages, is essential reading for linguists and language students. It will also fascinate anyone interested in the origin and interrelationship of languages, in alphabets, writing systems, small ethnic groups, or linguistic minorities. It has been thoroughly revised and updated to include more languages, more countries, new extracts, and up-to-date information on populations and the numbers of people speaking each language.

Features include:

- nearly 600 languages identified as to where they are spoken and the family to which they belong
- over 200 languages individually described, with sample passages and English translation
- fascinating insights into the history and development of individual languages and useful information about the alphabet, pronunciation, and vocabulary
- a listing of every country in the world, showing its principal languages and the number of speakers of each
- a description of each of the world's language families

Written specifically for the non-specialist and avoiding technical linguistic terms, *The Languages of the World* is an indispensable handbook on the subject of languages, peoples, and language families. Its user-friendly style and layout, delightful original passages, and exotic scripts will now delight a new generation.

Prior to his recent retirement, **Kenneth Katzner** worked for the US government and also served as an editor on a number of international encyclopedias and English dictionaries. He has authored a large English–Russian/Russian–English dictionary.

For Betty

The Languages of the World

Third Edition

Kenneth Katzner

London and New York

First published in 1977, revised edition 1986 by Routledge and Kegan Paul Ltd, 2002
by Routledge

Reprinted in 1989, 1990 and 1992
by Routledge
11 New Fetter Lane, London EC4P 4EE

Simultaneously published in the USA and Canada
by Routledge
29 West 35th Street, New York, NY 10001

New Edition 1995
Reprinted 1995, 1996, 1998, 1999 (twice)

Routledge is an imprint of the Taylor & Francis Group

© 1977, 1986, 1995, 2002 Kenneth Katzner

Typeset in Times by
Florence Production Ltd, Stoodleigh, Devon
Printed by MPG Books Ltd, Bodmin, Cornwall

British Library Cataloguing in Publication Data
A catalogue record for this book is available from the British Library

Library of Congress Cataloging in Publication Data
A catalogue record for this book has been requested

ISBN 0–415–25003–X (hbk)
ISBN 0–415–25004–8 (pbk)

Contents

Contents

Acknowledgments

THE AUTHOR is indebted to the following people who have furnished passages and translations in the language indicated, and also provided valuable assistance and information.

ARTHUR ABRAHAM, Professor of History, Virginia State University, Petersburg, Virginia, U.S.A. (Mende)

DOREEN ACTOM, Embassy of Ghana, Washington, D.C. (Akan)

MINIA AFEWOEKI, Voice of America, Washington, D.C. (Tigrinya)

SAID ALI, Voice of America, Washington, D.C. (Oromo)

JOHN F. BRYDE, University of South Dakota, Vermillion, South Dakota, U.S.A. (Sioux)

ALHAJI FAGGE, Voice of America, Washington, D.C. (Hausa)

PAUL GLAZER, YIVO Institute for Jewish Research, New York, U.S.A. (Yiddish)

RHODA KAYAKJUAK, Ottawa, Canada. (Eskimo)

LELAND D. KEEL, Former Superintendent, Seminole Agency, Hollywood, Florida, U.S.A. Previously Deputy Director, Chickasaw Housing Authority, Ada, Oklahoma. (Chickasaw)

CELINE MATHEW, University of Kerala, Trivandrum, India. (Malayalam)

YESHAYA METAL, YIVO Institute for Jewish Research, New York, U.S.A. (Yiddish)

REV. FRANCIS MIHALIC, Wantok Publications Inc., Wewak, Papua New Guinea. (Tok Pisin)

MYKOLAS MIKALAJUNAS, Vilnius, Lithuania. (Lithuanian)

CINDY SALO, University of Arizona, Tucson, Arizona, U.S.A. (Wolof)

DEAN SAXTON, Sells, Arizona, U.S.A., author, *Papago & Pima–English Dictionary*. (Papago)

GEORGES H. SCHMIDT, Former Chief, Terminology Section, United Nations. (General Linguistics)

GUILLAUME DJIMON ZOUNLOME, Research Assistant, University of Notre Dame, U.S.A. (Fon)

Preface

FOR AS FAR back as we can trace his history, Man has always spoken many different languages. If at one time he spoke a single language, from which all others subsequently descended, linguistic science is unlikely to uncover any firm evidence of such a fact.

In the 19th century a concerted effort was undertaken by scholars to reconstruct what was then thought to be Man's original language. Major contemporary languages were exhaustively analyzed in the hope of discovering some common elements that might point to a single primeval source. Languages of isolated primitive peoples were examined in the hope of finding a revealing "fossil" tongue. But the search was for naught. The trail goes back to the dimmest reaches of history. We are faced with a virtual blank slate about the beginnings of language, and any study of its subsequent development must be confined to the recent historical period. And here we are immediately confronted with a myriad of different languages.

At present the languages of the world number in the thousands. To establish an exact (or even an approximate) number is impossible, for many are scarcely known, and it is often a moot point whether two similar languages are actually separate languages or two dialects of the same language. But the continent of Africa is known to have well over a thousand languages, with 250 in Nigeria alone, 120 in Tanzania, and 100 in Cameroon. The American Indian languages number almost a thousand and the single island of New Guinea contributes some 700 more. India has over 150, Russia about 100, while China has several dozen, as do a number of other countries. Even in the United States more than 50 different Indian languages are spoken.

It is important, however, to view these figures in their proper perspective. A single statistic tells a great deal: among the world's several thousand languages, the top 100 account for over 95 percent of all speakers. Chinese alone accounts for 20 percent, and if we add English, Hindi, Spanish, Arabic, and Bengali, the figure rises to about 45. Russian, Portuguese, Japanese, German, French, and Italian bring it to 60 percent, while the next dozen most important languages raise it to 75. By contrast, the five percent at the bottom include thousands of different languages, the great majority spoken by tiny numbers – a few thousand in some cases, a few hundred in others, many in only a single village, some by only a few families, some even by only one or two people.

At some point the inevitable happens. The members of the rising generation are naturally exposed to more widely-spoken neighboring languages, which they soon begin to speak in addition to, and eventually in place of, their own. The declining language is thus doomed to extinction, its ultimate passing awaiting only the death of the last surviving speaker. This pattern has been occurring in most parts of the world, and has been greatly accelerated in recent decades by the advent of mass communications, which propagate major languages in areas where hitherto only minor languages were spoken. Most of the Indian languages of the United States and Canada are now close to extinction, as are many in Africa, New Guinea, and among the Australian aborigines. In fact, hundreds of tiny languages throughout the world have died out in just the last few decades.

The chart on the following pages lists nearly 600 different languages. The number is arbitrary and could easily have been larger or smaller, but it attempts to cover the entire world without burdening the reader with a multitude of unfamiliar and unimportant names. Each name on the chart also appears in the index, which will direct the reader to information about where it is spoken.

The chart has been arranged to show the major language families of the world. The largest by far is the Indo-European, whose speakers embrace approximately half the world's population. It was the discovery of the existence of this family that led linguists to seek more tenuous links to other families and thus prove the existence of an original common language for all of mankind. But here the effort broke down, and at this stage we must content ourselves with the existence of some 20 important language families and perhaps 50 or more lesser ones.

The chart is followed by a brief description of each of the major language families. The main part of the book contains sample texts and translations for over 200 different languages, followed by certain basic information about that language. The final section contains a country-by-country breakdown.

NOTE: In this book the popular, better known, names of languages and countries are generally given preference over native names, though the latter are also included. Thus Eskimo is used rather than Inuit, Lappish rather than Sami, Persian rather than Farsi, and Hottentot rather than Nama. Myanmar is referred to by its traditional name of Burma, and the English "Ivory Coast" is used in preference to the French "Côte d'Ivoire."

Acknowledgments

Many people assisted in finding the foreign language passages that appear in Part II. Those who contributed passages that are new to this edition, and some that were carried forward, are listed in the "Acknowledgments" section at the end. Special thanks are due my wife, Betty, who made invaluable contributions to the entire manuscript.

Part I
Language families of the world

Language families of the world

Family	Subgroup	Branch	Major languages	Minor languages
Indo-European	Germanic	Western	English, German, Yiddish, Dutch, Flemish, Afrikaans	Frisian, Luxembourgian
		Northern (Scandinavian)	Swedish, Danish, Norwegian, Icelandic	Faroese
	Italic		Latin	
	Romance		Italian, French, Spanish, Portuguese, Romanian	Catalan, Provençal, Rhaeto-Romanic, Sardinian, Moldovan
	Celtic	Brythonic	Welsh, Breton	
		Goidelic	Irish (Gaelic)	Scottish (Gaelic)
	Hellenic		Greek	
			Albanian	
	Slavic	Eastern	Russian, Ukrainian, Belorussian	
		Western	Polish, Czech, Slovak	Sorbian (Lusatian)
		Southern	Bulgarian, Serbo-Croatian, Slovenian, Macedonian	
	Baltic		Lithuanian, Latvian	
			Armenian	
	Indo-Iranian	Iranian	Persian, Pashto, Kurdish, Baluchi, Tajik, Ossetian	Luri, Gilaki, Mazanderani
		Indic (Indo-Aryan)	Sanskrit, Hindi, Urdu, Bengali, Punjabi, Marathi, Gujarati, Oriya, Bhojpuri, Maithili, Magahi, Rajasthani, Assamese, Kashmiri, Nepali, Sindhi, Sinhalese	Bhili, Garhwali, Kumauni, Romany, Maldivian

Family	Subgroup	Branch	Major languages	Minor languages
Uralic	Finno-Ugric	Finnic	Finnish, Estonian, Mordvin, Udmurt, Mari, Komi	Lappish (Sami)
		Ugric	Hungarian	Khanty, Mansi
	Samoyed			Nenets, Selkup, Nganasan, Enets
Altaic	Turkic	Southwestern (Oghuz)	Turkish, Azerbaijani, Turkmen	Gagauz
		Northwestern (Kipchak)	Kazakh, Kyrgyz, Tatar, Bashkir	Kara-Kalpak, Karachai, Balkar, Kumyk, Nogai
		Southeastern (Chagatai)	Uzbek, Uigur	Salar
		Northeastern		Altai, Khakass, Tuvinian
			Chuvash	
				Yakut
	Mongolian		Mongolian	Buryat, Kalmyk
	Tungusic	Northern		Evenki, Even
		Southern		Manchu, Sibo, Nanai (Hezhen)

Family	Subgroup	Major languages	Minor languages
Caucasian	Southern	Georgian	
	Northwestern		Kabardian, Circassian, Adygei, Abkhazian, Abazinian
	North-Central		Chechen, Ingush
	Northeastern (Dagestan)		Avar, Lezgin, Dargwa, Lak, Tabasaran
Independent			Basque
Dravidian		Telugu, Tamil, Kannada (Kanarese), Malayalam	Gondi, Kurukh (Oraon), Kui, Tulu, Brahui
Munda			Santali, Mundari, Ho, Savara (Sora), Korku
Independent			Burushaski
Sino-Tibetan	Sinitic	Chinese	
	Tibeto-Burman	Burmese, Tibetan	Yi (Lolo), Tujia, Bai, Lisu, Lahu, Naxi (Moso), Karen, Kachin (Chingpaw), Chin, Arakanese, Meithei, Bodo, Garo, Lushei, Newari, Jonkha, Lepcha
Tai		Thai, Lao	Chuang (Zhuang), Puyi (Chungchia), Dong (Tung), Dai, Li, Nung, Tho (Tay), Shan
Miao-Yao (Hmong-Mien)			Miao (Hmong), Yao (Mien)
Independent		Japanese	
Independent		Korean	
Mon-Khmer		Vietnamese, Khmer (Cambodian)	Mon, Palaung, Wa (Kawa), Muong, Bahnar, Sedang, Khasi, Nicobarese
Independent			Ainu

Family	Subgroup	Major languages	Minor languages
Austronesian (Malayo-Polynesian)	Western	Indonesian, Malay, Javanese, Sundanese, Madurese, Tagalog, Visayan, Malagasy	Minangkabau, Batak, Aceh (Achinese), Lampung, Rejang, Buginese, Makassar, Balinese, Sasak, Timorese, Tetun, Banjarese, Sea Dayak (Iban), Land Dayak, Ilocano, Bikol, Pampangan, Pangasinan, Maranao, Maguindanao, Tausug, Jarai, Rhade, Cham, Palauan, Chamorro, Yapese
	Micronesian		Marshallese, Gilbertese, Trukese, Ponapean, Kosraean, Nauruan
	Oceanic	Fijian	Motu, Yabim, Tolai
	Polynesian	Maori, Tongan, Samoan, Tahitian	Tuvaluan, Uvean, Futunan, Rarotongan, Tuamotu, Marquesan, Rapanui, Hawaiian
Papuan			Enga, Chimbu, Hagen, Kâte, Kamano, Wahgi, Orokaiva, Toaripi, Dani, Asmat, Ternate
Australian			Aranda (Arrernte), Warlpiri, Pitjantjatjara, Walmajarri, Kala Yagaw Ya
Paleo-Asiatic			Chukchi, Koryak, Itelmen, Nivkh, Ket, Yukagir
Eskimo-Aleut		Eskimo	Aleut

Family	Subgroup	Major languages	Minor languages
Niger-Congo	Mande		Mende, Malinke, Bambara, Dyula, Soninke, Susu, Kpelle, Vai, Loma
	Atlantic		Fulani, Wolof, Serer, Dyola, Temne, Limba, Kissi, Balante
	Gur (Voltaic)		Mossi (Moré), Gurma, Dagomba (Dagbane), Kabre, Senufo, Bariba
	Kwa		Akan, Ewe, Fon, Ga, Adangme, Agni (Anyi), Baule
	Kru		Bete, Grebo, Bassa
	Adamawa-Ubangi	Adamawa	Mbum
		Ubangi	Zande, Sango, Gbaya, Banda
		Ijo (Ijaw)	
	Benue-Congo	Nigerian	Yoruba, Ibo, Efik, Ibibio, Edo, Urhobo, Idoma, Nupe, Tiv
		Bantu	Swahili, Luba, Kongo, Lingala, Mongo, Ngala, Ruanda, Rundi, Kikuyu, Kamba, Sukuma, Nyamwezi, Makonde, Haya, Chagga, Nyakyusa, Ruguru (Luguru), Shambala, Gogo, Ha, Hehe, Yao, Ganda (Luganda), Soga, Nkole (Nyankole), Chiga (Kiga), Gisu, Toro, Luyia, Gusii (Kisii), Meru, Nyoro, Nyanja (Chewa), Tumbuka, Bemba, Tonga, Lozi, Nsenga, Lwena (Luvale), Lunda, Kaonde, Shona, Fang, Bulu, Ewondo (Yaoundé), Duala, Bubi, Mbundu, Chokwe, Ambo, Herero, Makua, Tsonga, Lomwe, Sena, Tswa, Chuabo, Ronga, Nyungwe, Marendje, Sotho, Tswana, Pedi, Swazi, Zulu, Xhosa, Venda, Ndebele

Family	Subgroup	Subbranch	Subbranch	Major languages
Afro-Asiatic	Semitic	North Arabic		Arabic, Maltese
		Canaanitic		Hebrew
		Aramaic		Syriac, Aramaic, Assyrian
		Ethiopic		Amharic, Tigrinya, Tigre, Gurage, Harari, Ge'ez
	Berber			Kabyle, Tachelhit, Tamazight, Riff, Tuareg (Tamashek)
	Cushitic			Somali, Oromo, Sidamo, Hadiyya, Beja, Afar
	Chadic			Hausa
	Omotic			Wolaytta
	Egyptian			Coptic
Chari-Nile	Eastern Sudanic	Nubian		Nubian
		Nilotic	Western	Luo, Dinka, Nuer, Shilluk, Lango, Acholi, Alur
			Eastern	Teso, Karamojong, Masai, Turkana, Bari, Lotuko
			Southern	Kalenjin, Suk (Pokot)
	Central Sudanic			Sara, Mangbetu, Lugbara, Madi
Saharan				Kanuri, Teda (Tibbu)
				Songhai, Djerma
Maban				Maba
				Fur
Khoisan				Hottentot (Nama), Bushman (San), Sandawe, Hatsa (Hadzapi)

North American Indian

Family	Major languages
Algonkian	Cree, Ojibwa (Chippewa), Montagnais, Naskapi, Micmac, Algonquin, Malecite (Maliseet), Blackfoot, Cheyenne, Arapaho, Fox, Delaware, Passamaquoddy
Wakashan	Nootka
Salishan	Flathead, Shuswap, Thompson
Athabaskan	Navajo, Apache, Chipewyan, Carrier, Chilcotin, Dogrib, South Slave, North Slave (Hare), Gwich'in
	Tlingit
	Haida
Siouan	Sioux (Dakota), Crow, Osage, Omaha, Winnebago
Iroquoian	Cherokee, Seneca, Mohawk, Oneida
Penutian	Yakima, Nez Perce, Klamath, Tsimshian, Gitksan, Nishga
Yuman	Yuma, Mohave
Caddoan	Caddo, Pawnee
Muskogean	Choctaw, Chickasaw, Creek, Seminole
Keresan	Keresan
Uto-Aztecan	Papago, Pima, Hopi, Ute, Shoshone, Paiute, Comanche, Kiowa, Nahuatl, Tarahumara, Mayo
Tanoan	Tewa, Tiwa, Towa
Zuñian	Zuñi
Oto-Manguean	Zapotec, Mixtec, Mazatec, Chinantec, Otomi, Mazahua
	Tarasco
Zoquean	Mixe, Zoque
	Totonac
Mayan	Maya (Yucatec), Tzotzil, Tzeltal, Chol, Chontal, Huastec, Quiché, Mam, Cakchiquel, Kekchi

Central and South American Indian

Family	Major languages
Chibchan	Guaymi, Cuna, Bribri, Cabecar, Warao, Paez
Misumalpan	Miskito (Mosquito)
Ge	Kaingang, Chavante
Panoan	Toba, Shipibo
Cariban	Carib
Tupian	Guarani, Cocama, Guajajara
Andean	Quechua, Aymara
	Ticuna
Equatorial	Jivaro (Shuar), Aguaruna, Piaroa
Arawakan	Goajiro, Black Carib, Arawak
Araucanian	Araucanian
	Chiquitano

Artificial

Family	Major languages
	Esperanto, Occidental, Interlingua

Pidgin and Creole

Family	Major languages
	Pidgin English, English creoles, French creoles, Papiamento, Sranan (Taki-Taki), Saramacca, Krio, Crioulo, Kituba, Monokutuba, Fanakalo, Tok Pisin, Hiri Motu, Pijin, Bislama

Indo-European languages

THE INDO-EUROPEAN FAMILY of languages is the world's largest, embracing most of the languages of Europe, America, and much of Asia. It includes the two great classical languages of antiquity, Latin and Greek; the Germanic languages, such as English, German, Dutch, and Swedish; the Romance languages, such as Italian, French, Spanish, and Portuguese; the Celtic languages, such as Gaelic and Welsh; the Slavic languages, such as Russian, Polish, Czech, and Serbo-Croatian; the Baltic languages, Lithuanian and Latvian; the Iranian languages, such as Persian and Pashto; the Indic languages, such as Sanskrit and Hindi; and other miscellaneous languages, such as Albanian and Armenian. In Europe only Basque, Finnish, Estonian, Hungarian, Turkish, and a few languages of Russia are not of this family; the others have apparently all descended from an original parent tongue.

Who were the original Indo-Europeans, and when and where did they live? Since they left no written documents, or artifacts of any kind, our only recourse is to attempt to reconstruct their language. If we assume that a word that is similar in most of the Indo-European languages designates a concept that existed in the original Indo-European society, and that, conversely, a word that varies in most Indo-European languages designates a concept not discovered until later, we may draw certain tentative conclusions. It would appear that the Indo-Europeans lived in a cold northern region; that it was not near the water, but among forests; that they raised such domestic animals as the sheep, the dog, the cow, and the horse; that among wild animals they knew the bear and the wolf; and that among metals they probably knew only copper. Many believe that it was the use of the horse and chariot that enabled them to overrun such an enormous expanse of territory.

The general consensus is that the original Indo-European civilization developed somewhere in eastern Europe about 3000 BC. About 2500 BC it broke up; the people left their homeland and migrated in many different directions. Some moved into Greece, others made their way into Italy, others moved through Central Europe until they ultimately reached the British Isles. Another division headed northward into Russia, while still another branch crossed Iran and Afghanistan and eventually reached India. Wherever they settled, the Indo-Europeans appear to have overcome the existing population and imposed their language upon them. One must conclude that they were a most remarkable people.

The possibility of so many languages having descended from a common ancestor was first suggested in 1786, though the similarity of Sanskrit and Italian was noted as early as the 16th century. By 1818 more than 50 separate languages were established as Indo-European; Albanian was added to the list in 1854 and Armenian in 1875. The total number of Indo-European speakers is about 2¾ billion people, nearly half the earth's total population.

The table below, giving the equivalents of six English words in numerous languages, will serve to illustrate the basic interrelation of the Indo-European languages, as contrasted with the languages of other families.

INDO-EUROPEAN LANGUAGES

English	month	mother	new	night	nose	three
Welsh	mis	mam	newydd	nos	trwyn	tri
Gaelic	mí	máthair	nua	oíche	srón	trí
French	mois	mère	nouveau	nuit	nez	trois
Spanish	mes	madre	nuevo	noche	nariz	tres
Portuguese	mês	mãe	novo	noite	nariz	três
Italian	mese	madre	nuovo	notte	naso	tre
Latin	mensis	mater	novus	nox	nasus	tres
German	Monat	Mutter	neu	Nacht	Nase	drei
Dutch	maand	moeder	nieuw	nacht	neus	drie
Icelandic	mánuður	móðir	nýr	nótt	nef	þrír
Swedish	månad	moder	ny	natt	näsa	tre
Polish	miesiąc	matka	nowy	noc	nos	trzy
Czech	měsic	matka	nový	noc	nos	tři
Romanian	lună	mamă	nou	noapte	nas	trei
Albanian	muaj	nënë	i ri	natë	hundë	tre, tri
Greek	men	meter	neos	nux	rhïs	treis
Russian	mesyats	mat'	novy	noch'	nos	tri
Lithuanian	mėnuo	motina	naujas	naktis	nosis	trys
Armenian	amis	mayr	nor	kisher	kit	yerek
Persian	māh	mādar	nau	shab	bini	se
Sanskrit	mās	matar	nava	nakt	nās	trayas

NON-INDO-EUROPEAN LANGUAGES

	(month)	(mother)	(new)	(night)	(nose)	(three)
Basque	hilabethe	ama	berri	gai	südür	hirur
Finnish	kuukausi	äiti	uusi	yö	nenä	kolme
Hungarian	hónap	anya	új	éjszaka	orr	három
Turkish	ay	anne	yeni	gece	burun	üç

The various branches of the Indo-European family are of sufficient importance to merit a brief discussion in their own right. We shall therefore touch upon the Germanic, Romance, Celtic, Slavic, Baltic, Iranian, and Indic languages.

Germanic languages

The Germanic languages include English, German, Dutch (or Flemish), and the Scandinavian languages: Swedish, Danish, Norwegian, and Icelandic. Yiddish and Luxembourgian are offshoots of German, and Afrikaans is based on Dutch. Frisian, spoken in northern Holland, developed independently, as did Faroese, a Scandinavian language spoken in the Faroe Islands. Native speakers of one or another of the Germanic languages number at least 500 million.

It is generally assumed that by the first century BC Germanic peoples speaking a fairly uniform language were living on both sides of the North and Baltic seas. In time there developed the so-called West, East, and North Germanic dialects. The West Germanic tribes settled in the lands between the Elbe and Oder rivers, and it is here that the German language gradually evolved. The East Germanic tribes settled east of the Oder River, but their languages have long since become extinct. In Scandinavia the North Germanic tribes spoke a language we now call Old Norse, the ancestor of the modern Scandinavian languages. In the 5th century AD three West Germanic tribes, the Angles, Saxons, and Jutes, crossed the North Sea into Britain, bringing with them a language that would later be known as English. And in the 9th century Old Norse was carried by the Vikings far westward to Iceland. The Viking invasions of Britain also introduced many Old Norse words into English.

In the development of any language or language family, certain mutations inevitably occur that set it off from other languages or language families with which it shares a common origin. One such example is the sound shift that gradually occurred in the Germanic languages in the first millennium BC. A number of Indo-European consonants acquired different values in the Germanic languages, as may be shown by a comparison between Latin, which retained the Indo-European consonants, and English, a Germanic language which did not. The Indo-European consonant *d* became *t* in the Germanic languages (e.g., Latin *duo*, English *two*), *k* or *c* became *h* (*collis*/hill), *t* became *th* (*tonitus*/thunder), *p* became *f* (*piscis*/fish), and *g* became *k* or *c* (*ager*/acre). This phenomenon was first described in detail in the 19th century by the German philologist Jacob Grimm (perhaps better known as the author, together with his brother Wilhelm, of *Grimm's Fairy Tales*). Known as Grimm's Law, it was a landmark in the development of modern philology.

Romance languages

The Romance languages are the modern descendants of Latin, the language of the Roman Empire. Of the modern Romance languages, Italian, French, Spanish, Portuguese, Romanian, and Moldovan (a form of Romanian) are each the language of an entire nation, while Catalan, Provençal, Rhaeto-

Romanic, and Sardinian are confined to smaller areas within individual countries. Speakers of the Romance languages number close to 750 million.

As the armies of Rome extended the boundaries of the Empire into much of the continent of Europe, Latin was introduced everywhere as the new language of administration. Spoken Latin remained fairly uniform in the beginning, though it already differed markedly from the Latin of classical literature. But as the Empire began to crumble, and Roman administrators began to disappear, the Latin of each region began to develop in its own individual way. Separated from each other by great distances, and naturally influenced by the speech of surrounding peoples, each developed its own distinctive characteristics, to the point where it became a separate language.

Since we are dealing here with a slow and imperceptible process, it is impossible to say when spoken Latin ends and Romance begins. But the divergence was certainly under way by the 5th century, and by the 8th century we can detect unmistakable differences in the basic vocabulary and grammar of the various Romance dialects. The oldest known text in a Romance language is a poem written in a northern dialect of French and dating from about 880 AD.

The evolution of the Romance languages continued into modern times, continually influenced by new geographic and ethnic factors. Each language has borrowed heavily from various non-Romance languages: French from Germanic and Celtic; Spanish and Portuguese from Arabic; and Romanian from Slavic, Hungarian, Albanian, and Turkish. Many words exhibit remarkable uniformity throughout – e.g., bread: *pane* (Italian), *pain* (French), *pan* (Spanish), *pão* (Portuguese), *pîine* (Romanian) – while others clearly show the effects of isolation and borrowing – e.g., child: *bambino* (Italian), *enfant* (French), *niño* (Spanish), *criança* (Portuguese), and *copil* (Romanian).

Celtic languages

The Celtic languages (the initial *c* may be pronounced as either *s* or *k*) are the indigenous languages of Ireland, Scotland, and Wales. They include Gaelic (known as Irish in Ireland), Welsh, of Wales, and Breton, spoken in northwestern France.

The Celts were once a powerful people who dominated the area of southern Germany and the northern Alps in the first millennium BC. About the beginning of the 5th century BC they began to migrate in all directions, reaching the remotest parts of Europe in a number of successive waves. The date of their arrival in the British Isles is unknown, but we are certain that when the Anglo-Saxons arrived in the 5th century AD they were met by a people speaking a Celtic language. In time the Celts were pushed back by the English into the west and north, leaving only Wales and the Scottish Highlands Celtic-speaking. In the 6th century one large group of Celts emigrated from Cornwall and southern Wales to Brittany, in northwestern France, where today some people still speak the Breton language.

The Celtic languages are, sad to say, the one branch of the Indo-European family whose very survival is seriously endangered. Even in Ireland, Gaelic is spoken by less than half the population, and in Wales and Brittany the percentage of Celtic speakers is even smaller. Cornish, once spoken throughout Cornwall, died out in the 18th century, while the last surviving speaker of Manx, spoken for centuries on the Isle of Man, died in 1974. In Ireland the government mandates the teaching of Irish in the schools, and some efforts are being made to encourage the use of Welsh and Breton. But each is losing ground to the all-pervasive influence of English. As a result, with each passing generation the number of Celtic speakers diminishes.

Slavic languages

The Slavic, or Slavonic, languages, spoken in Russia and most of Eastern Europe, form another major division of Indo-European. The modern Slavic languages number eleven: Russian, Ukrainian, Belorussian, Polish, Czech, Slovak, Bulgarian, Serbo-Croatian, Slovenian, Macedonian, and Sorbian (Lusatian). Speakers of the Slavic languages number about 275 million.

The origin of the Slavic people is unclear. Their homeland appears to have been the area between the Vistula and Dnieper rivers, in present-day Poland and Russia. Perhaps by the 7th century BC they could be identified as a distinct ethnic group. In later centuries they began a slow and steady migration in different directions, eventually dividing into the three distinct groups evident in the Slavic languages of today. The western Slavs (ancestors of the Poles, Czechs, and Slovaks) migrated toward the Elbe and Oder rivers in Germany and Poland, where they eventually adopted the Roman Catholic faith. The southern Slavs moved into the Balkans, where some (the Serbs and the Bulgarians) adopted the Greek Orthodox faith, while others (the Croats and the Slovenes) adopted Roman Catholicism. The eastern Slavs made their way into Russia, where they too, in the 10th century, adopted Greek Orthodoxy.

The first Slavic language used for literary purposes was Old Church Slavonic, written in the Cyrillic alphabet. Cyrillic was named for St. Cyril, a Greek missionary who was thought to have devised it in the 9th century, but it is now generally believed that it was created by someone else a century later. As individual alphabets were later developed for the various Slavic languages, the choice was made entirely by religion. Cyrillic was adopted by the Orthodox Russians, Ukrainians, Belorussians, Bulgarians, Serbs, and Macedonians, while the Latin alphabet was adopted by the Roman Catholic Poles, Czechs, Slovaks, Croats, Slovenes, and Sorbs. Only the use of different alphabets distinguishes Serbian from Croatian, which are otherwise, for all practical purposes, one and the same language: Serbo-Croatian.

Baltic languages

The Baltic languages presently number only two, Lithuanian and Latvian, several others having died out centuries ago. They are the most conservative of the Indo-European languages, retaining a number of archaic features of Indo-European that vanished from the others long before they were committed to writing. The Baltic languages share a number of common features with the Slavic languages, leading some scholars to suggest a Balto-Slavic subgroup within the Indo-European family.

The original Baltic peoples are believed to have moved into western Russia about 2000 BC during the great migrations of the Indo-European tribes. For centuries they occupied a large area extending from the Oka River, near present-day Moscow, westward as far as the Baltic Sea. About the 6th century AD the eastern Balts were forced to move westward by the more numerous Slavs, and soon afterward settled in their present homeland. By the 10th century Lithuanian and Latvian were clearly distinct languages. Today the two are not mutually intelligible, but even a cursory comparison of their vocabulary is sufficient to show their common origin.

Iranian languages

The Iranian languages are dominated by Persian, a major language of antiquity, and today the principal language of Iran. Others include Pashto, spoken in Afghanistan and Pakistan; Kurdish, the language of the Kurds; Tajik, spoken in Tajikistan; Ossetian, spoken in Russia and Georgia; and Baluchi, spoken in Pakistan and Iran. Speakers of Iranian languages number about 125 million.

The Iranian languages and the Indic languages (described below) together form the Indo-Iranian subgroup of the Indo-European family. While the other Indo-European migrations appear to have been toward the west, the Indo-Iranians headed southeast, toward the Caspian Sea and on to Iran and Afghanistan. One branch continued on to India, where the Indic languages eventually developed.

The 7th century BC witnessed the rise of the great religion of Zoroastrianism, whose sacred texts, the *Zend Avesta*, were written in an ancient Iranian language called Avestan. By the following century the might of the Persian Empire had made Persian the dominant language of the ancient world.

Since the conquests of Islam in the 7th century AD the Iranian languages have been written in the Arabic script. Prior to World War II the Soviet government created Cyrillic-based alphabets for Tajik and Ossetian, as well as for Kurdish as spoken in the Soviet Union.

Indic languages

The Indic languages, also known as Indo-Aryan languages, are spoken over a vast area embracing the northern two-thirds of India, as well as most of Pakistan, Bangladesh, Sri Lanka (Ceylon), and Nepal. In India the most important Indic languages are Hindi, Urdu (which closely resembles Hindi),

Bengali, Punjabi, Marathi, Gujarati, Oriya, and Assamese. Urdu and Punjabi, as well as Sindhi, are also spoken in Pakistan, while Bengali is also the language of Bangladesh. Another Indic language, Sinhalese, is the principal language of Sri Lanka, while Nepali is spoken in Nepal, and Kashmiri in Kashmir. Romany, the language of the Gypsies, is also of this family. Speakers of the Indic languages number well over one billion.

The Indic languages were brought to India by Indo-European settlers about 1500 BC. By perhaps 1000 BC the languages of India and Iran were sufficiently different to be considered separate groups. The Indic languages are the modern descendants of Sanskrit, the language of the sacred Hindu scriptures. Sanskrit gradually gave way to the Prakrit, or Middle Indic, languages, and it is out of these that the modern Indic languages evolved. The date of their appearance cannot be fixed precisely, but the first literary documents began to appear about 1200 AD.

Virtually all the Indic languages are written in variations of a script known as Devanagari, which appeared in India about the 7th century AD. The Indic languages of Pakistan (Urdu and Sindhi) are written in the Arabic script.

Uralic languages

OF THE FEW non-Indo-European languages of Europe, most belong to the Uralic family. Of the approximately 20 million speakers of the Uralic languages, virtually all, save for the tiny group of peoples called the Samoyeds, speak one of the Finno-Ugric languages.

The ancestors of the Uralic peoples are believed to have occupied a broad belt of central European Russia about 6,000 years ago. In the 3rd millennium BC they began to migrate in different directions, eventually settling in lands far removed from their original home. Some moved to the northwest as far as Estonia and Finland, others moved due north, while still others migrated north and east into the lands of western Siberia. Their subsequent history is best discussed under their two (unequal) branches: Finno-Ugric and Samoyed.

The Finno-Ugric languages consist of the Finnic branch, of which the most important language is Finnish, and the Ugric, of which the most important is Hungarian. The Finnish tribes probably came to Finland about the beginning of the Christian era. Those that settled south of the Gulf of Finland eventually produced a dialect of Finnish that we now call Estonian. Probably the only people living in Finland at this time were the Lapps, who were driven farther north into the Arctic regions. Since the Lapps are of different racial stock than the other Finno-Ugric peoples, it may be assumed that they once spoke a non-Finno-Ugric language of their own that was completely lost in the wake of the Finnish invasions. But not a single word of that ancient language can be found in modern Lappish.

About 2½ million speakers of Finno-Ugric languages are still to be found in central European Russia. Mordvin, Udmurt, and Mari are spoken over an area approximately coinciding with the original homeland of the Uralic peoples. Apparently these peoples did not participate in the great Uralic migrations, or at least they did not migrate very far. The fourth Finno-Ugric language of Russia, Komi, is spoken farther to the north, probably the result of a migration that paralleled that of the Finnish tribes to the northwest.

The term Ugric is derived from Ugra, an old Russian name for western Siberia. It was to this area that the Ugric peoples migrated in the first centuries of the Christian era. Not long afterward, however, they began a long and slow migration westward, eventually reaching present-day Hungary in the 9th century. Thus we have the rare phenomenon of Hungarian, completely unrelated to any of the languages of nearby countries.

In every migration there are always some that remain behind, and this explains the remote Khanty and Mansi languages of western Siberia. The former is spoken along the Ob River and its tributaries, the latter along the Sosva and Konda rivers, tributaries of the Ob and Irtysh rivers respectively. It is only these languages that bear a noticeable resemblance to Hungarian. To encourage their use, Cyrillic-based alphabets were developed by the Soviet government in the late 1930s.

The other branch of the Uralic family consists of the remote Samoyed languages. They are only four in number, and, of these, two have fewer than 1,000 speakers each. The most important is Nenets, spoken over a vast area of the northern tundra region between the White Sea on the west and the Yenisei River on the east. Selkup is spoken somewhat to the south, on both sides of the Taz River in western Siberia. The other Samoyed languages are Nganasan, of the Taimyr Peninsula (the northernmost area of mainland Russia), and Enets, spoken near the mouth of the Yenisei.

The separation of the Samoyed and Finno-Ugric peoples is believed to have taken place more than 5,000 years ago. The Samoyeds probably headed east and remained for a long time on the taiga of western Siberia. Some time at the beginning of the Christian era they began to migrate northward and westward, eventually to settle over scattered areas of the far north. During the late 16th century, with the first major Russian penetration into Siberia, the Samoyeds came under Russian rule.

The Samoyed languages were never committed to writing in tsarist Russia, but in 1931 the Soviet government introduced a Roman-based alphabet for the Nenets and Selkup languages. Between 1937 and 1940 this was replaced with the Cyrillic. Today textbooks, newspapers, and some native literature are published in Nenets and, to a lesser extent, in Selkup. Both languages are also taught in the schools.

Altaic languages

THE ALTAIC LANGUAGES are spoken over a vast expanse of territory extending from Turkey and the Caucasus on the west, through parts of European Russia, across central Asia, into Siberia, Mongolia, and China, and on to the Pacific Ocean. The name Altaic is derived from the Altai Mountains of western Mongolia, where the languages are believed to have originated. Speakers of the Altaic languages number about 150 million. The family consists of three divisions: Turkic, Mongolian, and Tungusic.

The Turkic languages are a homogeneous group of about 20 languages, which are for the most part mutually intelligible. The most important, of course, is Turkish, which accounts for about 40 percent of all Turkic speakers. To the east of Turkey, in Iran and Azerbaijan, Azerbaijani is spoken. To the north, in the area known as the Caucasus, there are Karachai, of the republic of Karachayevo-Cherkesiya (capital, Cherkessk); Balkar, of Kabardino-Balkariya (capital, Nalchik); Kumyk, of Dagestan (capital, Makhachkala); and Nogai, spoken in a number of different republics. Across the Caspian Sea, in central Asia, there are Turkmen, Uzbek, Kazakh, and Kyrgyz, each spoken in a newly independent nation with a similar name, as well as Kara-Kalpak, of the Kara-Kalpak Republic in Uzbekistan (capital, Nukus). In European Russia, Tatar is spoken in Tatarstan and Chuvash in Chuvashiya. In southern Siberia, in the vicinity of the Altai Mountains, there are Altai, of the Altay Republic (capital, Gorno-Altaisk); Khakass, of Khakasiya (capital, Abakan); and Tuvinian, of the Tuva Republic (capital, Kyzyl-Orda). Far to the northeast, in Yakutiya, Yakut is spoken. In western China the most important Turkic language is Uigur, which also has some speakers in Kazakhstan, Uzbekistan, and Kyrgyzstan.

The Mongolian branch of Altaic consists basically of Mongolian proper, the other languages being little more than dialects of it. Mongolian was the language of the great Mongol Empire established by Genghis Khan in the 13th century. In the 14th and 15th centuries a number of offshoots developed, but even today these are largely intelligible to Mongolian speakers. The two most important Mongolian languages other than Mongolian itself are spoken in Russia. One is Buryat, spoken in the area around Lake Baikal; the other, Kalmyk, is spoken to the west of the Volga River delta. Other dialects of Mongolian are spoken in northwestern China.

The Tungusic languages account for less than one-tenth of one percent of all Altaic speakers. They are spread over a vast area of Siberia and part of China. A northern branch includes Evenki and Even, each spoken in central and eastern Siberia, the former as far east as Sakhalin Island. The southern branch includes Sibo, spoken in northwestern China, and Nanai, or Hezhen, spoken both in China and Russia, near the city of Khabarovsk. Another Tungusic language is Manchu, spoken by the once great Manchu Dynasty. It has all but died out in the 21st century.

It is impossible to point to a single people living in a certain place at a certain time as the progenitor of the modern Altaic speakers. The oldest known Turkic people are the Kyrgyz, of whom documents exist dating as far back as 200 BC. The Turks seem originally to have been a woodland, hunting people in the Altai Mountain region. In the 6th century AD they ruled an empire that extended from the borders of China to the Black Sea. Probably by this time their language had already become distinguishable from Mongolian. In later centuries most of the Turkic peoples fell under the domination of the Mongol Empire. As for the Tungus, virtually nothing is known of their development prior to the 17th century.

The Altaic and the Uralic languages show sufficient similarity in grammar and phonology to lead some linguists to think of them as two branches of a single family: the so-called Ural-Altaic family. A good case can be made for this point of view, for both lack any forms expressing gender, both indicate various grammatical relationships by the addition of numerous suffixes, and both observe a principle known as vowel harmony, in which only front vowels or only back vowels appear in an individual word. But in the crucial matter of vocabulary, almost no correspondences (other than recent borrowings) can be found, and for this reason it is probably best to regard them as separate families. The term Ural-Altaic, therefore, will not be used in this book.

Caucasian languages

THE CAUCASIAN LANGUAGES are spoken in the region known as the Caucasus, lying both north and south of the Caucasus Mountains, between the Black and the Caspian seas. This relatively small area, now mainly in Russia and Georgia, is one of extraordinary linguistic diversity, with languages often varying from town to town and even from village to village. All told, about 50 languages are spoken here, of which about 40 are of the Caucasian family. Speakers of the Caucasian languages number about 6 million.

Of the 40 or so Caucasian languages, only 12 have been committed to writing, and all but one of these only in the 20th century. The remainder are spoken by tiny pockets of people, ranging in number from a few hundred to a few thousand, and some confined to a single village. Only those reduced to writing will be discussed here.

The Caucasian languages are dominated by Georgian, spoken by more people than all the rest put together, and the only one with an ancient literary heritage. Georgian, together with a few minor dialects, constitutes the so-called Southern branch of this family, but it is doubtful whether these languages are actually related to the others. Their inclusion in the Caucasian family stems more from geographic than from linguistic considerations.

The other branches of the Caucasian family are the Northwestern, North-

Central, and Northeastern, or Dagestan. In the Northwestern there is Abkhazian, spoken in Abkhazia (capital, Sukhumi), in the northwestern corner of Georgia facing the Black Sea. Directly to the north, in Russia's republic of Adygeya (capital, Maikop), there is Adygei. To the east, in the republics of Karachayevo-Cherkesiya (capital, Cherkessk) and Kabardino-Balkariya (capital, Nalchik), there is Kabardian. (Karachai and Balkar each refer to a Turkic language also spoken in these republics.) Adygei and Kabardian are closely related and are sometimes referred to collectively as Circassian, a language also spoken in Turkey and Syria. A minor language of the Northwestern branch is Abazinian, also spoken in Karachayevo-Cherkesiya.

The North-Central branch consists of Chechen, spoken mainly in Chechnya (capital, Grozny), and Ingush, spoken in adjacent Ingushetiya (capital, Nazran). Farther east, in the republic of Dagestan (capital, Makhachkala, on the Caspian Sea), no fewer than 30 languages of the Northeastern branch are spoken. Five have been reduced to writing, including Avar, of western Dagestan, and Lezgin, of the southeast in an area that includes the city of Derbent. Between the two lie three lesser languages: Dargwa, Lak, and Tabasaran. Lezgin is also spoken in Azerbaijan.

The Caucasus has had a turbulent history since ancient times and has often served as a refuge for persecuted peoples who fled into the mountain villages to seek protection against invaders. Over the centuries it has been overrun by the Persians, Macedonians, Romans, Arabs, Mongols, and Turks, and it was finally incorporated into the Russian empire about 1865. The great linguistic diversity of the region is not a recent phenomenon, for it was noted by Greek and Roman travelers before the Christian era. Arab geographers later referred to the Caucasus as a "mountain of languages."

Dravidian languages

THE DRAVIDIAN LANGUAGES are found principally in southern India, though there is one in Sri Lanka and one in Pakistan. There are about 30 of these languages in all, but only four of them account for all but 10 million of the approximately 225 million Dravidian speakers.

In southern India the Dravidian languages are dominant. Since the recarving of the country's provincial boundaries along linguistic lines in 1956, each of the four major languages has been spoken in a single state. On the eastern coast Telugu is spoken in Andhra Pradesh (capital, Hyderabad), while Tamil is spoken to the south in Tamil Nadu (capital, Madras). On the west coast Kannada, or Kanarese, is spoken in Karnataka (capital, Bangalore), while Malayalam is spoken to the south in Kerala (capital, Trivandrum). Tamil is also spoken in northeastern Sri Lanka. Tamil and Malayalam are closely related and, along with Kannada, belong to one branch of this family. Telugu, which is quite different from the others, belongs to another branch.

Of the other Dravidian languages, only five need be mentioned here. Three of the five are spoken in central India, where the Indo-European languages are dominant. The most important are Gondi, spoken in Madhya Pradesh and northeastern Maharashtra, and Kui of southern Orissa. Kurukh, or Oraon, is spoken in Bihar, Orissa, and Madhya Pradesh. One other Dravidian language, Tulu, is spoken in the southern state of Karnataka. Finally there is Brahui, spoken in the province of Baluchistan, southwestern Pakistan, and adjacent areas of Iran and Afghanistan.

The Dravidian languages are known to have been spoken in India before the arrival of the Indo-Europeans about 1000 BC. It is considered likely that at one time they were spoken over much of central, and perhaps even northern, India. If this is true, then we may assume that they were driven south by the Indo-Europeans, with only those living in isolated regions remaining behind. The few pockets of Dravidian-speakers in central India would appear to lend weight to this theory.

Munda languages

THE MUNDA LANGUAGES are spoken in scattered sections of northern and central India, mostly in the east, though there is one in the west. Speakers of the Munda languages number only 9 million, about one percent of India's population.

The family comprises about a dozen languages, only five of which will be mentioned here. The most important is Santali, spoken in the states of Bihar, West Bengal, and Orissa, and the only one that has been reduced to writing. To the west of Santali are Mundari and Ho, both spoken in southern Bihar (Mundari to the north of Ho), but a second group of Mundari speakers is located to the south in Orissa. Santali, Mundari, and Ho are closely related and are sometimes grouped under the single name of Kherwari. Another Munda language, Savara, or Sora, is spoken in southernmost Orissa. Finally there is Korku, spoken far to the west, in western Madhya Pradesh and northeastern Maharashtra.

Like the Dravidian languages, the Munda languages are known to predate the Indo-European conquest of India and were at one time undoubtedly spoken over a much larger area than at present. Over the centuries they receded into more remote areas under the impact of peoples with more advanced cultures. One theory links the Munda languages with the Mon-Khmer languages of Southeast Asia; the two are sometimes combined into a broader grouping known as the Austro-Asiatic family.

Sino-Tibetan Languages

THE SINO-TIBETAN FAMILY is presently thought to consist of only two branches. Chinese constitutes one branch (Sinitic) all by itself. The other is the Tibeto-Burman branch, which consists of Burmese, Tibetan, and about 200 lesser languages spoken in China, Burma, India, Nepal, and other countries.

The Tibeto-Burman languages include Yi (Lolo), Tujia, Bai, Lisu, Lahu, and Naxi (Moso), all spoken mainly in China; Karen, Kachin (Chingpaw), Chin, and Arakanese, spoken mainly in Burma; Meithei, Bodo, Garo, and Lushei, spoken in Assam, India; Newari, spoken in Nepal; Jonkha, spoken in Bhutan; and Lepcha, spoken in Sikkim. The total number of speakers is about 60 million.

Another large group of languages, the Tai languages, which include Thai and Lao, was formerly thought to be part of this family, but this connection has now been rejected by most scholars. Other Tai languages are Chuang (Zhuang), Puyi (Chungchia), Dong (Tung), Dai, and Li, spoken in China; Nung, spoken in China and Vietnam; Tho (Tay), spoken in Vietnam; and Shan, an important language of Burma. Speakers of these languages total about 100 million.

Yet another group of languages, Miao-Yao, or Hmong-Mien, was also thought to be part of Sino-Tibetan, but it has now been placed in a separate category whose exact affiliation is unclear.

The many differences of opinion on what constitutes the Sino-Tibetan family only serve to demonstrate the complexity of the problem of classifying languages in general and how much more investigation and comparison remains to be done.

Mon-Khmer languages

THE MON-KHMER LANGUAGES are spoken in Southeast Asia. Their name is derived from two members of the family: Khmer, the national language of Cambodia, and Mon, a minor language today, but at one time one of the most influential in the region. Vietnamese is now also thought to be a Mon-Khmer language, though it is very different from the others, and its inclusion is still questioned by some.

Other members include Palaung, spoken in Burma; Wa, or Kawa, spoken on both sides of the border between Burma and China; Bahnar and Sedang, spoken in Vietnam; and Khasi, spoken in Assam, India. Another, Nicobarese, is spoken on the remote Nicobar Islands in the Bay of Bengal.

The Mons are believed to have lived in Burma since the middle of the first millennium AD. After the Mongol conquest in the 13th century they formed their own kingdom, which for the next 250 years was a great center of Buddhist culture and had wide contacts with the outside world. The Mon alphabet, which had its origin in southern India, was later adopted for writing Burmese. Today the Mons live mainly in Burma, with a minority across the border in Thailand.

The Khmer empire was dominant in Southeast Asia from the 10th through the 14th centuries. The famed ruins of the capital city of Angkor date from this period. Later the Khmers were overcome by the Thais, and toward the end of the 14th century their empire was destroyed.

The Mon-Khmer languages are sometimes combined with the Munda languages of India to form a broader family known as the Austro-Asiatic languages.

Austronesian languages

THE AUSTRONESIAN, or Malayo-Polynesian, family of languages extends from Malaysia and Indonesia to parts of New Guinea, to New Zealand, the Philippines, across the Pacific Ocean, and, westward, to Madagascar off the east coast of Africa. Its speakers number about 325 million, all but one million of whom speak a language of the so-called Western branch. There are three other branches: Micronesian, Oceanic, and Polynesian.

Four members of the Western branch are the official languages of independent countries: Malay in Malaysia, Indonesian in Indonesia, Tagalog in the Philippines, and Malagasy in Madagascar. In Indonesia there are also Javanese and Sundanese (spoken on Java), Madurese (on Java and Madura), Minangkabau, Batak, Aceh, Lampung, and Rejang (on Sumatra), Buginese and Makassar (on Celebes), Banjarese and Dayak (on Borneo), Balinese (on Bali), Sasak (on Lombok), and Timorese (on Timor). In the Philippines there are also Visayan, Ilocano, Bikol, Pampangan, Pangasinan, Maranao, Maguindanao, and Tausug. In Vietnam there are Jarai, Rhade, and Cham, the last-mentioned also spoken in Cambodia. In New Zealand there is Maori, a Polynesian language. And on Taiwan the 300,000 aborigines speak about ten different languages that form a separate division of this family.

Hundreds of Austronesian languages are spoken on the countless islands that dot the Pacific Ocean. North of the Equator, in the Federated States of Micronesia, there are, from west to east, Palauan and Yapese, of the Western branch, and Trukese, Ponapean, and Kosraean, which are Micronesian languages. To the north there is Chamorro, of Guam and Saipan, also of the Western branch. To the east are three other Micronesian languages: Marshallese, of the Marshall Islands; Nauruan, with about 8,000 speakers on the island of Nauru; and Gilbertese, spoken in Kiribati, which straddles the Equator. South of the Equator there are a number of Oceanic languages in Papua New Guinea (though most of the languages here are Papuan), including Yabim and Motu, as well as Tolai, spoken on New Britain. To the east, on the Solomon Islands, some 50 Oceanic languages are spoken, while 100 more are spoken in Vanuatu, and another 25 in New Caledonia to the south. The easternmost of the Oceanic languages is Fijian, of Fiji.

The principal Polynesian languages from west to east are (after Maori): Tuvaluan, of Tuvalu (10,000 speakers); Uvean and Futunan, of the Wallis and Futuna Islands (7,500 speakers each); and Tongan, of Tonga. All lie just west of the International Date Line. East of the Line are Samoan, of Samoa; Rarotongan, of the Cook Islands (5,000 speakers); Tahitian, of Tahiti and the other Society Islands; Tuamotu, of the archipelago of the same name (10,000 speakers); Marquesan, of the Marquesas Islands (5,000); and finally Rapanui, the language of Easter Island (2,000). Far to the north, and by far the easternmost of the Polynesian languages, is Hawaiian. Despite the enormous distances between them, the Polynesian languages show a remarkable degree of uniformity, and in some cases there is even mutual intelligibility.

The background and the details of the great Austronesian migrations are still largely a mystery. The original homeland of the people was no doubt somewhere in Asia, perhaps in India, present-day Malaysia or Indonesia, or even Taiwan. There are signs that the settlement of the islands of the Pacific began as early as 1500 BC, about the same time that some of the Indo-European tribes were settling in their new homelands. One westward migration stands out in sharp contrast to the others: the remarkable journey of the ancestors of the present inhabitants of Madagascar from Indonesia, some 1,500 to 2,000 years ago.

Papuan languages

THE PAPUAN LANGUAGES are spoken principally on the island of New Guinea, though there are a few in Indonesia. The term Papuan is more geographic than linguistic, for the languages exhibit such wide variations among themselves that it seems hardly likely that they belong to a single family. There are more than 1,000 of these languages, but only about 6 million speakers. Few have more than 50,000 speakers, and many have only a few hundred or less.

In the eastern half of New Guinea, now the nation of Papua New Guinea, there are Enga, Chimbu, Hagen, Kâte, Kamano, Wahgi in the north, and Orokaiva and Toaripi in the south. In the western half, now the Indonesian province of Irian Jaya, there are Dani and Asmat. Well to the west, on the Indonesian island of Halmahera, there is Ternate.

The interior of New Guinea is one of the most inaccessible regions on earth, with many of the inhabitants still living in the Stone Age. Adjacent villages separated by a valley or two often speak mutually unintelligible languages. Some of the Papuan languages are virtually unknown, and serious study of them began only after World War II.

Australian languages

THE TERM "AUSTRALIAN LANGUAGES" refers to those spoken by the Australian aborigines. These people number only 50,000, and only about 30,000 of them still speak a native language. The total number of these languages is about 150. They are believed to be all distantly related to each other, but have been broken down into about 15 different families. The vast majority fall into the Pama-Nyungan family, which covers virtually all of the country except for the far north and northwest.

None of the Australian languages has more than 5,000 speakers, and only about ten have more than 1,000. Aranda, or Arrernte, is spoken in and around the town of Alice Springs in the geographic center of the continent. Warlpiri is spoken to the north, in the region of the Tanami Desert. In Western Australia there is a large group of closely related languages called the Western Desert languages, of which the most important is Pitjantjatjara. Also in Western Australia is Walmajarri. Far to the north, in the Torres Strait Islands that lie between Australia and New Guinea, there is Kala Yagaw Ya, which also has some speakers in Townsville, Queensland.

The aborigines are believed to have migrated to Australia from somewhere in Asia (perhaps New Guinea) about 40,000 years ago. A land bridge probably existed at that time, but was subsequently submerged as the waters rose. There was essentially no contact with the outside world until British settlers began arriving near the end of the 18th century. Serious attempts to classify the Australian languages did not begin until the 1960s. A few aborigine words have entered the English language: *boomerang*, *kangaroo*, *wallaby*, and *koala*.

Paleo-Asiatic languages

THE TERM "PALEO-ASIATIC," also known as Paleo-Siberian, is an imprecise designation for a number of minor languages spoken in northern and eastern Siberia. It includes a small group of related languages, plus three additional languages that have no genetic link either with each other or with any linguistic family.

The most important of the Paleo-Asiatic languages is Chukchi, spoken in that part of Siberia nearest Alaska. Related to Chukchi is Koryak, of the Koryak National District, which occupies the upper two-thirds of the Kamchatka Peninsula. Within the Koryak National District there is a third related language, Itelmen. These three form a small family called the Chukchi-Kamchatkan languages.

Three other languages included under Paleo-Asiatic actually defy linguistic classification. Nivkh is spoken along the lower course of the Amur River and also on Sakhalin Island, Ket along the banks of the Yenisei River in central Siberia. Yukagir is spoken in the republic of Yakutiya and in Magadan Oblast.

Some authorities have suggested including the Eskimo and Aleut languages in this family, and even Ainu, which has practically died out in Japan. Since no genetic relationship is involved here, the question of classification seems no more than a matter of personal preference. But it seems best to confine the Paleo-Asiatic family to Russia, placing the languages of other countries elsewhere.

Despite the small numbers of speakers of the Paleo-Asiatic languages, Cyrillic-based alphabets were devised by the Soviet government for Chukchi, Koryak, and Nivkh.

Eskimo-Aleut languages

THE ESKIMO-ALEUT LANGUAGES number exactly two: Eskimo and Aleut. The former is spoken by about 100,000 people in Greenland, Canada, Alaska, and Siberia. The latter is spoken by about 1,000 people in the Aleutian Islands and a few hundred more on the Commander Islands of Russia. Though undoubtedly related to each other, the two languages are vastly different, having diverged from each other several thousand years ago. Attempts have been made to link them with certain Indian languages of Alaska, with the Chukchi language of Siberia, with Ainu of Japan, and even the Uralic and Indo-European languages. Though some similarities have been noted, the Eskimo-Aleut languages are still considered a separate family.

Niger-Congo languages

THE NIGER-CONGO FAMILY of languages is the largest in Africa. It extends from Senegal, in westernmost Africa, across the "hump" to Nigeria, and then down the southern half of the continent as far as South Africa. South of the equator almost all the languages of Africa are of the Bantu group, the largest subdivision of Niger-Congo. There are over a thousand Niger-Congo languages, with as many as 400 million speakers.

Leaving Bantu for last, we may distinguish seven other branches of Niger-Congo. The Mande branch includes Mende, of Sierra Leone; Malinke, of Senegal, Gambia, Guinea, Mali, and Ivory Coast; Bambara, of Mali; and Kpelle, of Liberia. The Atlantic branch includes Fulani, spoken over much of West Africa; Wolof and Serer, of Senegal; and Temne, of Sierra Leone. The Gur, or Voltaic, branch includes Mossi, of Burkina Faso; Gurma, of Ghana, Togo, and Burkina Faso; Dagomba, of Ghana; and Senufo, of Mali and Ivory Coast. The Kwa branch includes Akan, of Ghana; Ewe, of Ghana and Togo; and Fon, of Benin. The Kru branch includes Bete, of Ivory Coast, and Grebo and Bassa, of Liberia. The Adamawa-Ubangi branch includes Zande, of Congo-Kinshasa and the Sudan, and Sango, of the Central African Republic. Ijo, of Nigeria, seems to stand apart from all the others. The seventh branch, Benue-Congo, includes Bantu, but also contains an important group of languages in Nigeria, including Yoruba, Ibo, Efik and Tiv.

Though only a subdivision of Niger-Congo, the Bantu languages in themselves constitute one of the major families of the world. They are spoken south of what is sometimes called the "Bantu line," extending from Cameroon on the west to Kenya on the east. The most important Bantu language by far is Swahili, the most widely spoken African language of East Africa. Other major languages are Luba, Kongo, and Lingala, of Congo-Kinshasa; Kikuyu, of Kenya; Ruanda, of Rwanda; Rundi, of Burundi; Ganda, of Uganda; Nyanja, of Malawi and Zambia; Bemba, of Zambia; Shona, of Zimbabwe; Tswana, of Botswana and South Africa; Sotho, of Lesotho and South Africa; and Zulu and Xhosa, of South Africa. There are more than 300 Bantu languages in all, with as many as 200 million speakers.

Linguistic evidence seems to point to the area of Cameroon, the northwestern corner of Bantu-speaking country, as the original homeland of the Bantu people. They are believed to have migrated into the rain-forest area to the south and east about 2,000 years ago, perhaps because it was better suited to the raising of certain crops. They displaced the indigenous inhabitants of the area almost completely, with the result that only a few isolated pockets of non-Bantu speakers now remain in southern Africa.

Afro-Asiatic languages

THE TERM "AFRO-ASIATIC" is a fairly recent coinage, having replaced the older term Hamito-Semitic. The family embraces six groups of languages spoken by people of vastly different racial, religious, and cultural origins, but it is nonetheless clear that their languages are interrelated. Speakers of the Afro-Asiatic languages number about 350 million, three-fourths of whom are in Africa, the rest in the Middle East.

The six branches of Afro-Asiatic are Semitic, Berber, Cushitic, Egyptian, Chadic, and Omotic. The Semitic languages include Arabic, Hebrew, and Amharic of Ethiopia. The Berber languages are a homogeneous group spoken in Morocco, Algeria, and a number of other countries. The Cushitic languages are spoken principally in Ethiopia and Somalia. The Egyptian branch consisted originally of ancient Egyptian, but is now represented by its sole modern descendant, Coptic. The Chadic branch is dominated by Hausa. The Omotic languages, of which the most important is Wolaytta, are spoken in southern Ethiopia.

27

The terms Hamitic and Semitic are derived from the names of two of the sons of Noah in the Bible, Ham and Shem. The original home of the Hamitic peoples was North Africa, and that of the Semitic peoples the Middle East. The kinship of their languages suggests that at one time they were one people, but that was probably at least 8,000 years ago. Further details on the Semitic, Berber, and Cushitic languages are given under separate headings below.

Semitic languages

In addition to Arabic and Hebrew, the Semitic languages include the Ethiopic languages: Amharic, Tigrinya, Tigre, Gurage, and Harari. Maltese, spoken on Malta, is also Semitic, as is Syriac, now mainly a liturgical language. Arabic dwarfs all the others in number of speakers (about 230 million) and is the official language of more than 15 countries.

The Semitic languages may be traced back some 5,000 years. The oldest of which we have any knowledge is Akkadian, spoken in ancient Mesopotamia about 3000 BC. Two dialects of Akkadian, Assyrian and Babylonian, were widely spoken in the Near East for the next 2,000 years. By the 8th century BC they had given way to Aramaic, which served as the common language of the Near East until well into the Christian era. With the rise of Islam in the 7th century, Arabic, originally a minor language of the Arabian Peninsula, was spread all the way across North Africa to the Atlantic Ocean.

Perhaps as early as 1000 BC Semitic peoples from South Arabia crossed the straits of Africa into Ethiopia. Under the influence of native dialects their language developed into Ge'ez, spoken until the 11th century, and still the classical literary language of Ethiopia. Out of Ge'ez emerged the modern Ethiopic languages that are spoken today.

It was the Semitic peoples who introduced the alphabet to the world. Credit for this landmark in human history goes to the Phoenicians, the date being no later than the 15th century BC. Later Phoenician writing was adopted by the Hebrews and the Arameans. The Greeks borrowed this alphabet about 1000 BC, and it later spread all over the world.

Berber languages

The Berber languages are spoken in North Africa. There are about 12 million speakers in all: 7 million in Morocco, 3 million in Algeria, one million in Niger, 750,000 in Mali, and much smaller numbers in other countries.

In Morocco the most important languages are Tachelhit and Tamazight, the latter spoken by a people called the Beraber. Another Berber language, Riff, is spoken in the north.

In Algeria the principal Berber language is Kabyle, spoken in the mountains east of Algiers. Far to the south, in scattered oases of the Sahara Desert, live the Tuaregs whose language is known as Tamashek. They are concentrated mainly in Niger and Mali, though there are some in Algeria, Libya, and Burkina Faso.

The Berbers have been known since ancient times, and their language at one time was probably spoken over most of North Africa. Their languages are quite similar to each other, so much so that some authorities often speak of a single Berber language. No Berber alphabet exists today, though some transcriptions have been made into Arabic. The Tuaregs have a script of their own called Tifinagh, which dates back to ancient times. It is used mainly for inscriptions, however, and no books or periodicals in it as yet exist.

Cushitic languages

The Cushitic languages are spoken mainly in Ethiopia and Somalia, though they also extend into Eritrea, Sudan, and Kenya. In Ethiopia they are spoken by about half the population, while in Somalia the Somali language is spoken everywhere. The Cushitic languages of Ethiopia include Oromo, Sidamo, and Hadiyya, as well as Somali. Beja is an important language of southern Sudan. Afar is spoken in Ethiopia and Eritrea. There are also some speakers of Somali and Oromo in Kenya. At present Somali and Oromo are the only Cushitic languages with a formal system of writing.

In the Bible Cush was the son of Ham, the son of Noah, and the name became the biblical word for Ethiopia. The Kingdom of Kush was a major rival of Egypt in the 2nd millennium BC. It was located in Nubia, in today's Sudan, but its influence extended well into sub-Saharan Africa. It survived into the 1st millennium BC, when it was finally defeated by the Nubian people. The Nubian language, unrelated to the Cushitic languages, is still spoken in Sudan today.

Chari-Nile languages

THE CHARI-NILE LANGUAGES are spoken mainly in Sudan, Uganda, Kenya, and Chad, and to a lesser extent in Tanzania and Congo-Kinshasa. A rough estimate as to the number of speakers would be 25 million.

Of the two divisions of Chari-Nile, Eastern Sudanic and Central Sudanic, the former is by far the larger. It consists of Nubian, spoken in the Nile Valley of the Sudan, plus the large family of Nilotic languages. A western branch of Nilotic includes Luo, of Kenya; Dinka, Nuer, and Shilluk, of Sudan; and Lango, Acholi, and Alur, of Uganda. An eastern branch includes Teso and Karamojong, of Uganda; Masai, of Kenya and Tanzania; Turkana, of Kenya; and Bari and Lotuko, of Sudan. A southern branch includes Kalenjin and Suk (Pokot), of Kenya. The other division of Chari-Nile, Central Sudanic, includes Sara, of Chad; Mangbetu, of Congo-Kinshasa; and Lugbara and Madi, of Uganda.

The Chari-Nile languages are sometimes grouped with the Saharan languages, which include Kanuri, of Nigeria, as well as with Songhai of Mali, Djerma of Niger, Maba of Chad, Fur of the Sudan, and other languages, to form the larger Nilo-Saharan family.

Khoisan languages

THE FEW NON-BANTU LANGUAGES of southern Africa are of the Khoisan family. The most important is Hottentot, or Nama, of Namibia, which has about 200,000 speakers. Bushman, spoken in Botswana and Namibia, has about 75,000. Two other Khoisan languages are Sandawe and Hatsa (Hadzapi), of Tanzania, the former with about 75,000 speakers, the latter with fewer than 1,000.

The name Khoisan is composed of the word "Khoi," the Hottentot word for Hottentot, and "San," the Hottentot word for Bushman. The most distinctive feature of the Khoisan languages is the presence of the so-called click consonants, made by drawing air into the mouth and clicking the tongue. While a few such sounds are found in other languages such as Xhosa and Sotho, they are known to have been borrowed from the Khoisan peoples who presumably created them. The relationship between the two branches of Khoisan is remote yet fairly certain. But the circumstances of how and when they drifted so far apart are unclear.

American Indian languages

THE AMERICAN INDIAN LANGUAGES number more than a thousand, the vast majority spoken by small tribes of a few thousand people or less. Over one hundred Indian languages are spoken in the United States and Canada, over three hundred in Mexico and Central America, and perhaps a thousand in South America. There are about 20 million Indians in the Western Hemisphere, 90 percent of them in South America.

The enormous task of sorting out these languages began more than a hundred years ago and is still going on. In North America alone there are believed to be some 50 different families. One of the largest is the Algonkian, which includes Cree, Ojibwa (Chippewa), Algonquin, and Blackfoot, spoken mainly in central Canada and the northern American Midwest. The Athabaskan languages, originally spoken in Canada, include Navajo, of the American Southwest, now the most widely spoken Indian language in the United States. The Siouan languages, also spoken mainly in the northern Midwest, include Sioux, or Dakota, as well as Crow, of Montana, and Osage, of Oklahoma. In the Muskogean family there are Choctaw, Chickasaw, and

Creek, all spoken mainly in Oklahoma. The Iroquoian languages include Cherokee, of Oklahoma and North Carolina, and Seneca and Mohawk, of New York. The Uto-Aztecan family includes Papago, Pima, Hopi, Ute, Shoshone, and Comanche, all spoken in the American Southwest.

Mexico, the home of the once great Aztec and Maya civilizations, still has a large Indian population. The Aztec language, known as Nahuatl, is still widely spoken in the states adjacent to Mexico City. It is also of the Uto-Aztecan family. Mayan languages are spoken in both Mexico and Guatemala, while Zapotec, Mixtec, and Otomi, all of the Oto-Manguean family, are spoken in southern Mexico. In South America the most important Indian language by far is Quechua, spoken in Peru, Bolivia, and Ecuador. Next in line come Guarani, of Paraguay, Aymara, of Bolivia and Peru, and Araucanian, of Chile.

It is now agreed that the Indians came to America from Asia, the migration beginning perhaps as long as 25,000 years ago. Small bands of hunters wandered across the land bridge that spanned the Bering Strait and over the centuries their descendants gradually drifted southward. So slowly did these movements take place that probably no single generation was conscious of a migration. These people were not all alike, but differed markedly from each other in physical appearance, customs, and language. Eventually they would inhabit the entire hemisphere from the Arctic to the southernmost tip of South America.

By the time of the arrival of the white man, the Western Hemisphere was already well populated with diverse cultures ranging from rudimentary hunting and gathering economies to the highly developed Aztec, Maya, and Inca civilizations. The Mayas went farthest in the art of writing, their remarkable hieroglyphs having posed a challenge to scholars ever since their discovery by the Spanish in the 16th century. Because of the Indians' Asian origin their languages have been carefully compared with the various languages of Asia, but no significant similarities have been found.

Dozens of modern English words have their origin in one or another Indian language. The Algonkian languages seem to have contributed the most: *moose*, *skunk*, *chipmunk*, *raccoon*, *opossum*, *persimmon*, *squash*, *hominy*, *squaw*, *papoose*, *wigwam*, *powwow*, *moccasin*, *wampum*, and *tomahawk*. *Woodchuck* comes from Cree, *toboggan* from Micmac, *tepee* from Sioux, and *totem* from Ojibwa. From Nahuatl come *tomato*, *chocolate*, *avocado*, *coyote*, and *ocelot*, while *maize*, *potato*, *hammock*, *barbecue*, *canoe*, *cannibal*, and *hurricane* come from various Indian languages of the West Indies. Among South American Indian languages Quechua has contributed *llama*, *puma*, *vicuña*, *quinine*, and *coco*, while from the Tupian languages come *jaguar*, *tapir*, and *petunia*. The word *poncho* comes from Araucanian.

But it is in the geographic place names of the North American continent that the Indian influence is most clearly seen. About half of the 50 United States, including virtually all the Midwestern states, derive their names from an Indian language. Mississippi means "great river" in Ojibwa; Minnesota means "sky-blue waters" in Sioux; Oklahoma means "red people" in Choctaw. Saskatchewan means "swift-flowing" in Cree. Among the many North American cities with Indian names there are Milwaukee, from *Mahn-a-wakee-Seepe* ("gathering place by the river"), Winnipeg ("muddy water"), Tallahassee ("old town"), Tuscaloosa ("black warrior"), Chattanooga ("rock rising to a point"), Kalamazoo ("boiling pot"), Nantucket ("the faraway place"), Pawtucket ("the place by the waterfall"), Woonsocket ("at the very steep hill"), and Walla Walla ("place of many waters").

Artificial languages

THE TERM "ARTIFICIAL LANGUAGES" refers to those that have been artificially constructed, each in the hope that it might eventually become a universal tongue. Although a number of such languages have been created, only one, Esperanto, has achieved a significant measure of international recognition.

The first attempt at an artificial language was Volapük, which appeared about 1880. Though difficult to learn and as a result short-lived, it did inspire others to attempt a better system. In 1887 L. L. Zamenhof introduced Esperanto, with its greatly simplified grammar and logically constructed vocabulary. Esperanto ("one who hopes") soon developed a large following of dedicated speakers, and later a significant body of literature. Many of the world's literary masterpieces have been translated into Esperanto. Numerous attempts to improve or reform it were in the end abandoned, and today it remains basically the same as designed by Zamenhof.

In the 20th century Occidental and Interlingua appeared, but these were designed primarily for scientific and technical use and stress recognizability rather than active speech. The great advantage of artificial languages lies in their simplicity and the absence of irregular grammatical forms. However, they suffer from their lack of native speakers and national prestige, and in recent years interest in them has generally declined. The tremendous increase in the use and study of English since the end of World War II has led many to believe that English, rather than an artificial language, will eventually become mankind's universal means of communication.

Pidgin and creole languages

PIDGINS AND CREOLES are languages that arise to bridge the gap between people who could not otherwise communicate with each other. A pidgin language is one with sharply reduced vocabulary (usually between 700 and 1,500 words) of English, French, Spanish, or Portuguese origin, to which a sprinkling of native words have been added. In some cases, however, it is merely a simplified form of a local language, often with borrowings from another. A pidgin language has no native speakers; i.e., it is always spoken *in addition* to one's mother tongue.

When a pidgin eventually becomes the mother tongue of a group of people it is said to have become "creolized." As such its vocabulary must greatly expand, or re-expand, to accommodate its users' everyday needs. Creoles such as Jamaican English, Haitian Creole (based on French), and Tok Pisin ("Talk Pidgin"), of Papua New Guinea function in a manner not unlike that of any natural language.

English creoles are spoken in many smaller countries of the Western Hemisphere, such as the Bahamas, St. Kitts and Nevis, Barbados, Grenada, Belize, and Guyana. French creoles are spoken in Louisiana (by people known as Cajuns), Guadeloupe, Martinique, St. Lucia, Dominica, and French Guiana. Papiamento, spoken in Curaçao and Aruba in the Caribbean, is based principally on Spanish.

In Suriname (Dutch Guiana), in South America, a language called Sranan, or Taki-Taki ("talkee-talkee"), based on English with numerous Dutch words, has become the lingua franca. Saramacca, a creole based on English but containing several features of African speech, is spoken there by the Bush Negroes, descendants of former African slaves.

Africa too has its share of such languages. A variety of the Pidgin English is widely spoken in Cameroon, as is another in Liberia. Krio, an English creole, is the lingua franca of Sierra Leone. Crioulo, a Portuguese creole, is spoken in Guinea-Bissau, Cape Verde, and São Tomé and Príncipe (all former Portuguese colonies). Kituba, a simplified form of the Kongo language, is spoken in Congo-Kinshasa, while Monokutuba, close to Kituba, is spoken in Congo-Brazzaville. Fanakalo, based largely on Zulu with many English and some Afrikaans words added, is spoken in South Africa among those employed in the mines. Another French creole is spoken on the islands of Mauritius, Réunion, and the Seychelles in the Indian Ocean.

In Papua, in southeastern New Guinea, another pidgin language, Hiri Motu (formerly Police Motu), is spoken in addition to Tok Pisin. It is a simplified form of a language known as Motu, which became the trading language between the Motuans and their customers along the shores of the Gulf of Papua. The curious name of Police Motu stemmed from the fact it was used by the pre-war Papuan native police force, which drew its recruits from all parts of the territory.

On the Solomon Islands, to the east of New Guinea, an English creole known as Pijin is the lingua franca. And in Vanuatu, the former New Hebrides, there is yet another known as Bislama.

Part II
Individual languages

LANGUAGES OF EUROPE

English

OLD ENGLISH

Þanon eft gewiton   eald-gesīðas,
swylce geong manig   of gomen-wāþe,
fram mere mōdge   mēarum rīdan,
beornas on blancum,   Đær wæs Bēowulfes
mærðo mæned;   monig oft gecwæð,
þætto sūð nē norð   be sæm twēonum
ofer eormen-grund   ōþer nænig
under swegles begong   sēlra nære
rond-hæbbendra,   rīces wyrðra.
Nē hīe hūru wine-drihten   wiht ne lōgon,
glædne Hrōðgār,   ac þæt wæs gōd cyning.

Then away they rode, the old retainers
with many a young man following after,
a troop on horseback, in high spirits
on their bay steeds. Beowulf's doings
were praised over and over again.
Nowhere, they said, north or south
between the two seas or under the tall sky
on the broad earth was there anyone better
to raise a shield or to rule a kingdom.
Yet there was no laying of blame on their lord,
the noble Hrothgar; he was a good king.

Beowulf

The spectacular advance of English across the face of the globe is a phenomenon without parallel in the history of mankind. At international
conferences and economic summits, at business meetings and academic
symposiums, over the airwaves and electronic networks, between airline
pilots and traffic controllers, and between captains of ships at sea, English
is overwhelmingly the medium of communication. It is the official language
of dozens of countries in which only a small percentage of the population
actually speaks it. It is the working language of a number of international
organizations (the European Free Trade Association, for one) whose
membership does not include a single English-speaking nation. In many
countries a knowledge of English is helpful – and in some cases essential –
for obtaining a certain job or pursuing a certain career. No one can even
guess the number of people in the world who are currently studying English
as a second language. But a "snowball effect" is clearly taking place; the
more people there are in the world who already speak English, the more the
rest of the world will want to, and is striving to, learn it and join the club.

English is the first language of most of the people in the United States, Canada, the United Kingdom, Ireland, Australia, New Zealand, and dozens of smaller countries and dependent states throughout the world. In the Western Hemisphere these include Bermuda and the Bahamas in the Atlantic Ocean, Jamaica, the Cayman Islands, Virgin Islands, Anguilla, St. Kitts, Nevis, Barbuda, Antigua, Montserrat, St. Vincent, Barbados, Grenada, and Trinidad and Tobago in the Caribbean, Belize in Central America, and Guyana and the Falkland Islands in South America. It is the official language, or at least one of the official languages, of about 15 countries in Africa, and of most of the countless islands that dot the Pacific Ocean. In India it has the title of "associate official language" and is generally used in conversation between people from different parts of the country. In dozens of other countries throughout the world it is the unofficial second language. All told, English is the mother tongue of about 375 million people – far less than Chinese, to be sure, and about the same as Hindi and Spanish. But the number of people who speak English with at least some degree of proficiency is probably twice as large and, unlike the others, it extends in large numbers to every corner of the globe.

In tracing the historical development of the English language, it is customary to divide it into three periods: Old English, which dates from earliest times to 1150; Middle English, 1150–1500; and Modern English, 1500 to the present. The history of the language may be said to have begun with the arrival in Britain of three Germanic tribes about the middle of the 5th century. Angles, Saxons, and Jutes crossed the North Sea from what is present-day Denmark and the coast of northwest Germany. The inhabitants of Britain prior to this invasion spoke a Celtic language which seems to have quickly given way to the new Germanic tongue. The Jutes, who came from Jutland, settled in Kent, the Isle of Wight, and along part of the Hampshire coast. The Saxons, who came from Holstein, settled in the rest of England south of the Thames. The Angles, who came from Schleswig, settled in the area extending northward from the Thames as far as Scotland, and it is from them that the word "English" evolved. They came from the "angle" or corner of land in present-day Schleswig-Holstein. In Old English their name was Engle and their language known as *englisc*.

In the next several centuries four distinct dialects of English emerged. The Humber River divided the northern kingdom of Northumbria, where Northumbrian was spoken, from the kingdom of Mercia, in central England, where Mercian was spoken. South of the Thames the West Saxon dialect developed in the kingdom of Wessex, while Kentish was spoken in Kent. In the 7th and 8th centuries Northumbria enjoyed political and cultural ascendancy in England, but in the 9th century both Northumbria and Mercia were devastated by the invasions of the Vikings. Only Wessex preserved its independence and by the 10th century the West Saxon dialect came to be the official language of the country. Since most surviving Old English works are those written in West Saxon, our knowledge of Old English is derived mainly from this dialect.

The Germanic peoples in early times used a form of writing known as runes. Its letters were made up mainly of straight lines, so as to be suitable for inscriptions carved on wood or stone. With the arrival of Christian missionaries from Ireland and Rome, however, the runes gradually gave way to the Roman alphabet. One runic letter was retained: the þ (called *thorn*), which represented the *th* sound (e.g., *wiþ* – with). A new letter, ð (*eth*), also represented *th* (*bæð* – bath), while the *æ* represented the *a* sound of the word "hat" (*bæc* – back). The sound of *sh* was represented by *sc* (*sceap* – sheep), and the sound of *k* was spelled *c* (*cynn* – kin). The letters *j*, *q*, and *v* were not used, and *f* served for both *f* and *v*.

The Old English vocabulary consisted of a sprinkling of Latin and Scandinavian (Old Norse) words over an Anglo-Saxon base. Latin words included *street, kitchen, kettle, cup, cheese, wine*, and, after the adoption of Christianity, *angel, bishop, abbot, martyr*, and *candle*. The Vikings brought many Old Norse words (*sky, egg, cake, skin, leg, window, husband, fellow, skill, anger, flat, odd, ugly, get, give, take, raise, call, die*), as well as the personal pronouns *they, their*, and *them*. Celtic has left its mark mostly in place names (*Devon, Dover, Kent, Carlisle*), and in the names of most English rivers (*Thames, Avon, Trent, Severn*).

Many Old English words and their Old Norse counterparts competed vigorously with each other for supremacy in the language. Sometimes the Old Norse word won out, sometimes the English, in some cases both words remained in use. For "window" the Norse *vindauga* ("wind-eye") won out over English *eagthyrl* ("eye-hole"), but the English *nosthyrl* ("nose-hole") became the modern "nostril." Norse *anger* now takes precedence over English *wrath*, while English *no* and *from* enjoy supremacy over Norse *nay* and *fro*. But standing side by side in modern English are Norse *raise* and English *rear*, Norse *ill* and English *sick*, as well as other such pairs as *bask/bathe, skill/craft, skin/hide*, and *dike/ditch*. As can be seen, the *sk* sound was most typically Old Norse, and often competed with the English *sh* in the same word. Thus in modern English we have such doublets as *skirt/shirt, scatter/shatter*, and *skip/shift*, which began to diverge in meaning only with the passage of centuries.

The Norman Conquest of 1066 brought the French language to England. For about two centuries after the conquest French was the language of the English nobility. Its impact upon English was tremendous. Thousands of new words were introduced into the language, touching upon the fields of government, religion, law, food, art, literature, medicine, and many others. As with the case of Old Norse, the infusion of French words produced numerous synonyms (English *shut*, French *close*; English *answer*, French *reply*; English *smell*, French *odor*; English *yearly*, French *annual*), as well as many other pairs of words offering subtle distinctions of meaning (*ask/demand, room/chamber, wish/desire, might/power*). It is interesting to note that, while the names of meat-producing animals such as *ox, cow, calf, sheep, swine*, and *deer* are English, the words for the meats derived from them (*beef, veal,*

MIDDLE ENGLISH

Bifel that, in that seson on a day,
In Southwerk, at the Tabard as I lay
Redy to wenden on my pilgrimage
To Caunterbury with ful devout corage,
At night was come into that hostelrye
Wel nyne and twenty in a companye,
Of sondry folk, by aventure y-falle
In felawshipe, and pilgrims were they alle,
That toward Caunterbury wolden ryde;
The chambres and the stables weren wyde,
And wel we weren esed atte beste.
And shortly, whan the sonne was to reste,
So hadde I spoken with hem everichon,
That I was of hir felawshipe anon,
And made forward erly for to ryse,
To take our wey, ther as I yow devyse.

It happened that, in that season on a day,
In Southwark, at the Tabard as I lay
Ready to wend on my pilgrimage
To Canterbury with a fully devout heart,
At night there came into that inn
Full nine and twenty in a company,
Of sundry folk, by chance fallen
Into fellowship, and pilgrims were they all,
That toward Canterbury would ride;
The chambers and the stables were large,
And well we were treated with the best,
And briefly, when the sun had gone to rest,
So had I spoken with them every one,
That I was of their fellowship forthwith,
And made an agreement to rise early,
To take our way, as I shall tell you.

CHAUCER, *The Canterbury Tales*

mutton, pork, bacon, venison) are all French. And to the already existing synonyms, English *wrath* and Old Norse *anger*, the French added a third word: *ire*.

But, despite the great flood of words into English from Latin, Old Norse, French, and later other languages, the heart of the language remained the Old English of Anglo-Saxon times. While fewer than 5,000 Old English words remain unchanged and in common use today, these constitute the basic building blocks of our language. They include the everyday household words, most parts of the body, as well as the numerous pronouns, prepositions, conjunctions, and auxiliary verbs that hold the language together. It was this basic stock, onto which was grafted a wealth of contributions from numerous other sources, that in the end produced what many today believe to be the richest of the world's languages.

In the 14th century English finally came into its own in England. Between 1350 and 1380 it became the medium of instruction in the schools and the language of the courts of law. King Henry IV, who ascended the throne in 1399, was the first English king since the Norman Conquest whose mother tongue was English. By the close of the 14th century, the dialect of London had emerged as the literary standard and Geoffrey Chaucer had written his immortal *Canterbury Tales*.

All great languages have humble beginnings. In the case of English it was the arrival in Britain of a small Germanic tribe from an "angle" of land on the Continent.

Welsh

Pam y caiff bwystfilod rheibus
    Dorri'r egin mân i lawr?
Pam caiff blodau peraidd ifainc
    Fethu gan y sychdwr mawr?
Dere â'r cafodydd hyfryd
    Sy'n cynyddu'r egin grawn,
Cafod hyfryd yn y bore
    Ac un arall y prynhawn.

Gosod babell yng ngwlad Gosen,
    Dere, Arglwydd, yno dy Hun;
Gostwng o'r uchelder golau,
    Gwna dy drigfan gyda dyn;
Trig yn Seion, aros yno,
    Lle mae'r llwythau yn dod ynghyd,
Byth na 'mad oddi wrth dy bobl
    Nes yn ulw yr elo'r byd.

Why are ravenous beasts allowed
    To trample the tender grapes?
Why must sweet flowers
    Fail in the great drought?
Send the healing showers
    To increase the vine shoots,
A healing shower of the first rain
    And another of the latter rain.

Pitch thy tent in the land of Goshen,
    Come thyself, Lord, to abide there;
Descend from the bright heights,
    Make thy dwelling among men.
Abide in Zion, remain there,
    Whither the tribes go up,
Do not ever abandon thy people
    Even to the annihilation of the world.

WILLIAM WILLIAMS PANTYCELYN

Welsh, the language of Wales, is spoken by about 600,000 people, or less than 25 percent of the Welsh population. All, or virtually all, of these people are fluent in English as well. The census of 1981 reported that only about 20,000 could communicate solely in Welsh; this number has declined to nearly zero in the ensuing years. (The question was not even asked in the 1991 census.)

Like Gaelic, spoken in Ireland and parts of Scotland, Welsh is one of the Celtic languages, which constitute one of the many branches of the Indo-European family. Celtic tribes entered Britain sometime after the 5th century BC. The Anglo-Saxon invasions many centuries later drove the Welsh into the west, where they retained their Celtic speech and remained a distinctive people.

The Welsh call their country *Cymru* and their language *Cymraeg*. The alphabet lacks the letters *j*, *k*, *q*, *x*, and *z*, while a number of other consonants are pronounced quite differently from the English. The letter *w* is a vowel, pronounced *u* as in "put," (e.g., *gwr* – man, *bwyd* – food). *Ch* is pronounced as in German (*chwaer* – sister). The letter *f* is pronounced *v* (*nef* – heaven), the *f* sound rendered by *ff* (*ceffyl* – horse). Two special Welsh letters are the *dd*, pronounced as a voiced *th* (*dydd* – day), and *ll*, pronounced approximately *thl*. The latter appears at the beginning of many Welsh city names such as Llandudno, Llangollen, and Llanfyllin. Welsh towns bear some of the most picturesque names of any in the world: Betws-y-Coed, Penrhyndeudraeth, and Pontrhydfendigaid, to name a few.

Gaelic

Ba mhinic do shíl Nóra go mba bhreá an saol
beith ag imeacht roimpi ina seabhac siúil gan
beann aici ar dhuine ar bit—bóithre na hÉireann
roimpi agus a haghaidh orthu; cúl a cinn leis
an mbaile agus le cruatan agus le crostacht a
muintire; í ag siúl ó bhaile go baile agus ó
ghleann go gleann. An bóthar breá réidh roimpi,
glasra ar gach taoibh de, tithe beaga cluthara
ar shleasaibh na gcnocán.

Ba mhinic do shíl Nóra go mba bhreá an saol bheith ag imeacht roimpi
ina seabhac siúil gan beann aici ar dhuine ar bith – bóithre na hÉireann
roimpi agus a haghaidh orthu; cúl a cinn leis an mbaile agus le cruatan
agus le crostacht a muintire; í ag siúl ó bhaile go baile agus ó ghleann
go gleann. An bóthar breá réidh roimpi, glasra ar gach taobh de, tithe
beaga cluthara ar shleasa na gcnocán.

Several times before Nora had thought of what a fine life she would have
as a tramp, independent of everybody! Her face on the roads of Ireland
before her, and her back on home and the hardship and anger of her
family! To walk from village to village and from glen to glen, the fine
level road before her, with green fields on both sides of her and small
well-sheltered houses on the mountain slopes around her!

PADRAIC PEARSE, *The Roads*

Gaelic is spoken both in Ireland and in Scotland, in two distinct varieties that
are generally referred to as Irish Gaelic and Scottish Gaelic. Like Welsh, it
is one of the Celtic languages and thus part of the Indo-European family.

Irish Gaelic, often known simply as Irish, is an official language of the
Republic of Ireland. Although spoken by only 1,250,000 people, or about
one-third of the population, its use has been strongly encouraged by the
government, and it is taught in all Irish schools. In Northern Ireland it is
spoken by some 100,000 people, about 6 percent of the population.
Practically all Gaelic speakers, both in Ireland and in Scotland, speak fluent
English as well.

The traditional Gaelic alphabet, the first of the two samples above, evolved
from the Roman one about the 5th century. It contains only five vowels and
13 consonants; the letters *j*, *k*, *q*, *v*, *w*, *x*, *y*, and *z* are missing. An acute accent
over a vowel indicates that it should be pronounced long, while a single dot
over a consonant indicates that it should be aspirated. Nowadays Gaelic is

generally written in modern English characters. In the new orthography the dot was dropped and the letter *h* placed after the consonant instead (e.g., *ċ* became *ch*).

About the 5th century Gaelic was carried from Ireland to Scotland. With the passage of time the Scottish variety diverged to the point where it was clearly a separate dialect. Unlike Irish Gaelic, however, Scottish Gaelic has no official status and is spoken by only 75,000 people in northwestern Scotland, and in the Inner and Outer Hebrides. Scottish Gaelic frequently uses a grave accent where Irish uses an acute.

English words of Gaelic origin include *bard, glen, bog, slogan, whiskey, blarney, shillelagh, shamrock, colleen, brogue,* and *galore.* Specifically Scottish Gaelic are *clan, loch,* and *ptarmigan.*

French

Au fond de son âme, cependant, elle attendait un événement. Comme les matelots en détresse, elle promenait sur la solitude de sa vie des yeux désespérés, cherchant au loin quelque voile blanche dans les brumes de l'horizon. Elle ne savait pas quel serait ce hasard, le vent qui le pousserait jusqu'à elle, vers quel rivage il la mènerait, s'il était chaloupe ou vaisseau à trois ponts, chargé d'angoisses ou plein de félicités jusqu'aux sabords. Mais, chaque matin, à son réveil, elle l'espérait pour la journée, et elle écoutait tous les bruits, se levait en sursaut, s'étonnait qu'il ne vînt pas; puis, au coucher du soleil, toujours plus triste, désirait être au lendemain.

At the bottom of her heart, however, she was waiting for something to happen. Like shipwrecked sailors, she turned despairing eyes upon the solitude of her life, seeking afar off some white sail in the mists of the horizon. She did not know what this chance would be, what wind would bring it to her, towards what shore it would drive her, if it would be a shallop or a three-decker, laden with anguish or full of bliss to the portholes. But each morning, as she awoke, she hoped it would come that day; she listened to every sound, sprang up with a start, wondered that it did not come; then at sunset, always more saddened, she longed for the morrow.

GUSTAVE FLAUBERT, Madame Bovary

French is one of the world's great languages, rivaled only by English as the language of international society and diplomacy. Besides being spoken in France, it is one of the official languages of Belgium, of Switzerland, and of Canada; it is the official language of Haiti, of more than 15 African countries, and of various French dependencies such as St. Pierre and Miquelon (off the coast of Newfoundland), Guadeloupe and Martinique (in the Caribbean), French Guiana (in South America), Réunion (in the Indian Ocean), and New Caledonia and Tahiti (in the South Pacific). In addition, French is the unofficial second language of a number of countries, including Morocco, Tunisia, Algeria, Lebanon, and Syria. All told, it is the mother tongue of about 75 million people, with millions more familiar with it, to some degree, as a second language.

French is one of the Romance languages, descended from Latin. In French it is *français,* which, when referring to the language, is never capitalized. The appearance of Latin in France (then called Gaul) dates from Caesar's conquest of the region in the period 58–51 BC. Gaul became one of the richest and most important provinces of the Roman Empire, and Latin superseded the various Celtic (Gaulish) tongues as the language of the domain. In the 5th century Gaul was conquered by a Germanic people, the Franks (from whom the name "France" is derived), who eventually abandoned their Germanic tongue in favor of the Romance speech of the population. Although a number of dialects emerged, history favored the north; Paris became the capital of France in the 12th century, and Parisian French gained ascendancy over the others. In the 18th and 19th centuries French was pre-eminent as an international language, though it has been eclipsed by English in the 20th and 21st. French was one of the two official languages of the League of Nations and is now one of the six official languages of the United Nations.

The French alphabet is the same as that of English, though the letter *w* appears only in foreign words. Grave (*è*), acute (*é*), and circumflex (*ô*) accents are used (e.g., *père* – father, *été* – summer, *élève* – pupil, *âme* – soul); the cedilla (*ç*) appears under the letter *c* when preceding *a*, *o*, or *u* to indicate an *s* sound rather than *k* (*leçon* – lesson).

French spelling generally reflects the language as it was spoken four or five centuries ago and is therefore a poor guide to modern pronunciation. Silent letters abound, especially at the ends of words (*hommes* is pronounced *um*; *aiment* pronounced *em*), but a normally silent final consonant is often sounded when it is followed by a word that begins with a vowel. In this process, known as liaison, the consonant becomes part of the first syllable of the following word, so that the sentence *il est assis* (he is seated) is pronounced ē-lĕ-tă-sē. Although French pronunciation is governed by fairly consistent rules, reproducing the actual sounds of the language is difficult for the English speaker, and a good "French accent" is something not easily acquired.

As the two major languages of the Western world, English and French naturally have contributed many words to each other. The enormous impact of Norman French on the English language has already been discussed. More recent French contributions to English – with the French pronunciation retained as closely as possible – include such expressions as *hors d'oeuvre*, *à la carte*, *table d'hôte*, *en route*, *en masse*, *rendezvous*, *carte blanche*, *savoir-faire*, *faux pas*, *fait accompli*, *par excellence*, *bon vivant*, *joie de vivre*, *raison d'être*, *coup d'état*, *nouveau riche*, *esprit de corps*, *laissez faire*, *chargé d'affaires*, *pièce de résistance*, and *R.S.V.P.*

In recent years, however, traffic has been mainly in the opposite direction. To the dismay of purists of the language, to say nothing of the French Academy, French has been virtually inundated with English words of all kinds, such as *le hamburger*, *le drugstore*, *le week-end*, *le strip-tease*, *le pull-over*, *le tee-shirt*, *les blue-jeans*, and *le snack-bar*. The resulting hybrid has been dubbed *franglais* – a combination of *français* (French) and *anglais* (English) – and a campaign has been under way for years to try and reverse the trend.

In some ways it has been successful. In the computer field at least, French appears to be holding its own, more so than other major languages such as German and Russian. The word for "computer" itself, *Computer* in German and *kompyuter* in Russian, in French is *ordinateur*. "Software," which is

Software in German, in French is *logiciel.* For "chip," which is the same in German and Russian as in English, the French is *puce,* the word for "flea." And for "user-friendly" the French have come up with the delightful equivalent *convivial.*

For more general terms, the French word for "commuter" is *navetteur,* from *navette,* or "shuttle." But in many cases the English prevails because of its greater simplicity and brevity. While purists argue for *sac gonflable,* most people would rather say "air bag." And the term "routing slip" has a certain crispness about it that is lacking in the French *fiche de transmission.*

Breton

Treuziñ a rejont "hall" dassonus ar gar. Damc'houllo e oa. Ur beajour warlerc'hiet en devoa lakaet e valizenn war an douar dirak draf an tikedoù hag a glaske eus e wellañ moneiz en e c'hodelloù. En ur c'horn, div blac'h yaouank kazel-ha-kazel, gant o blev a-fuilh war o chouk a selle pizh ouzh taolenn an eurioù. Malo a verzas e oa bet livet a-nevez ar "hall" ront. Marc'hadourez-hioù a oa diskouezet a-drek gwerennoù hag en ur dremen e weljont o skeud dezho o-daou, hi hir ha moan, he daoulagad trist, he dremm skuizh, eñ en e vantell-c'hlav, un tammig joget dre ma oa bet azezet re bell, e vlev o kouezhañ war e dal. En tren, a soñjas, e kavje dour d'o c'hempenn.

They crossed the echoing hall of the station. It was half-lit. A belated traveler had put his suitcase down in front of the ticket barrier and was doing his best to find some money in his pockets. In a corner two young girls, arm in arm with their hair flowing untidily over the backs of their necks, were looking attentively at the timetable. Malo noticed that the round hall had been newly painted. Merchandise was displayed behind windows, and as they passed they saw their two reflections – she tall and slender, sad-eyed, with a tired face, he in his raincoat, a bit creased from having been sat in too long, his hair falling over his brow. On the train, he thought, he would find water to tidy it.

RONAN HUON, *On the Train*

Breton is spoken in Brittany, the peninsula of westernmost France lying between the English Channel and the Bay of Biscay. It is the only Celtic language spoken on the European continent, having been brought from Cornwall and South Wales in the 5th and 6th centuries by Britons fleeing from Saxon invaders.

For centuries the use of Breton was repressed by the French government, and it was forbidden to teach it in the schools. The number of speakers has declined precipitously in recent years: from 500,000 in 1970 to only 200,000 in the year 2000.

A recent effort to reverse this trend has met with some success. A network of schools offering a bilingual curriculum has been established, with over 2,000 students enrolled, while another 3,000 are in other bilingual programs. All told, about 25,000 people are presently studying the language. However, even many of the supporters of this program are not optimistic about the chances of Breton's survival in the long run.

Provençal

Van parti de Lioun à la primo aubo
Li veiturin que règnon sus lou Rose.
Es uno raço d'ome caloussudo,
Galoio e bravo, li Coundriéulen. Sèmpre
Planta sus li radèu e li sapino,
L'uscle dóu jour e lou rebat de l'aigo
Ié dauron lou carage coume un brounze.
Mai d'aquéu tèms encaro mai, vous dise,
Ié vesias d'oumenas à barbo espesso,
Grand, courpourènt, clapu tau que de chaine,
Boulegant un saumié coume uno busco.

From Lyons at the blush of early dawn
The bargemen, masters of the Rhône, depart,
A robust band and brave, the Condrillots.
Upright upon their crafts of planks of fir,
The tan of sun and glint from glassy wave
Their visages have bronzèd as with gold.
And in that day colossuses they were,
Big, corpulent, and strong as living oaks,
And moving beams about as we would straws.

FRÉDÉRIC MISTRAL, *The Song of the Rhône*

Provençal, also known as Occitan, is a Romance language spoken in Provence, the historical region of southeastern France, bordering Italy and facing the Mediterranean Sea. In its broader sense it refers to the many similar dialects spoken throughout southern France. In this sense it is often known as *langue d'oc*, in contrast to *langue d'oïl* of the north, *oc* and *oïl* (modern *oui*) being the respective words for "yes" in the two halves of the country.

No official statistics are available on the number of speakers of Provençal. It is estimated that about 750,000 people speak it regularly and twice that many can understand it.

The high point in the development of Provençal was during the 13th and 14th centuries, when it was the language of the troubadours and the cultured speech of all of southern France. But subsequent encroachments from the north brought this culture to an end, and with it ended troubadour literature and the use of Provençal as the standard idiom of the region. The language split into a number of fragmented dialects, a situation that prevails to this day.

In the 19th century a movement for the revival and standardization of Provençal was spearheaded by the celebrated poet Frédéric Mistral. In attempting to create a new literary standard for the language, he produced a monumental two-volume dictionary of Provençal plus a collection of epic poems that won him the Nobel Prize in 1904. In recent decades the French government has taken a number of steps to promote the teaching and use of the language. Some radio and television programs are broadcast in Provençal and a number of recordings of folk songs have been produced.

Spanish

En efeto, rematado ya su juicio, vino a dar en el más extraño pensamiento
que jamás dió loco en el mundo, y fué que le pareció convenible y nece-
sario, así para el aumento de su honra como para el servicio de su
república, hacerse caballero andante, y irse por todo el mundo con sus
armas y caballo a buscar las aventuras y a ejercitarse en todo aquello
que él había leído que los caballeros andantes se ejercitaban, deshaciendo
todo género de agravio, y poniéndose en ocasiones y peligros donde,
acabándolos, cobrase eterno nombre y fama.

In short, his wits being quite gone, he hit upon the strangest notion that
ever madman in this world hit upon, and that was that he fancied it was
right and requisite, as well for the support of his own honor as for the
service of his country, that he should make a knight-errant of himself,
roaming the world over in full armor and on horseback in quest of adventures, and putting in practice himself all that he had read of as being the
usual practices of knights-errant; righting every kind of wrong, and
exposing himself to peril and danger from which, in the issue, he was
to reap eternal renown and fame.

MIGUEL DE CERVANTES, *Don Quixote*

Spanish is the most widely spoken of the Romance languages, both in terms
of number of speakers and the number of countries in which it is the dominant language. Besides being spoken in Spain, it is the official language of
Mexico, Cuba, the Dominican Republic, and Puerto Rico, of all the Central
American countries except Belize, and of all of the South American countries except Brazil, Guyana, Suriname, and French Guiana. In the United
States there are now more than 25 million speakers of Spanish, living mainly
in California, Arizona, Texas, Florida, and New York, but also in many other
states. Spanish is also spoken in the Balearic and Canary islands (which are
part of Spain), in parts of Morocco, in Western Sahara, and in Equatorial
Guinea. A variety of Spanish known as Ladino is spoken in Turkey and Israel
by descendants of Jews who were expelled from Spain in 1492. All told,
there are about 375 million speakers of Spanish. It is one of the six official
languages of the United Nations.

Pronunciation and usage of Spanish naturally vary between countries, but
regional differences are not so great as to make the language unintelligible
to speakers from different areas. The purest form of Spanish is known as
Castilian, originally one of the dialects that developed from Latin after the
Roman conquest of Hispania in the 3rd century AD. After the disintegration
of the Roman Empire, Spain was overrun by the Visigoths, and in the 8th
century the Arabic-speaking Moors conquered all but the northernmost part
of the peninsula. In the Christian reconquest Castile, an independent

54

kingdom, took the initiative, and by the time of the unification of Spain in the 15th century Castilian had become the dominant dialect. In the years that followed, Castilian – now Spanish – became the language of a vast empire in the New World.

Spanish vocabulary is basically of Latin origin, though many of the words differ markedly from their counterparts in French and Italian. Many words beginning with *f* in the other Romance languages begin with *h* in Spanish (e.g., *hijo* – son, *hilo* – thread). The Moorish influence may be seen in many words beginning with *al-* (*algodón* – cotton, *alfombra* – rug, *almohada* – pillow, *alfiler* – pin). As in British and American English, there are differences in vocabulary on the two sides of the ocean – *patata* (potato) is *papa* in Latin America, while *melocotón* (peach) is *durazno*.

Spanish spelling is based on generally consistent phonetic principles, and reflects better than most languages the way a word is pronounced. The consonants *b* and *v* are pronounced alike, the sound falling somewhere between the two sounds in English (*boca* – mouth, *voz* – voice). The letter *z*, and the letter *c* before *e* and *i*, are pronounced as a voiceless *th* in Castilian, but more like *s* in southern Spain and Latin America (*zapato* – shoe, *ciudad* – city). The letter *j*, and the letter *g* before *e* and *i*, are pronounced like the English *h* (*jardín* – garden, *general* – general), though in Spain it is more guttural than in Latin America. The hard *g* sound is represented by *g* before *a*, *o*, and *u* (*gato* – cat), but *gu* before *e* and *i* (*seguir* – to follow). The *h* is always silent (*hombre* – man), and *rr* is a rolled *r* (*correr* – run).

Ñ, pronounced *ny* as in the English "canyon" (*pequeño* – small), is a separate letter, alphabetized after *n* in Spanish dictionaries. *Ch* is pronounced as in English (*muchacho* – boy). *Ll* is pronounced as in the English "million" in Spain, but as *y* in America (*calle* – street). Traditionally, Spanish dictionaries treated these two digraphs as separate letters of the alphabet, and listed all words beginning with them separately, at the end of *c* and *l* respectively; since the early 1990s, however, the practice has been to alphabetize them conventionally (e.g., listing words beginning with *ch* between *ce* and *ci*).

The stress in Spanish likewise follows a consistent pattern, falling on the next-to-last syllable in words ending in a vowel, *n*, or *s*, and on the final syllable in words ending in other consonants. Exceptions to this rule are indicated by an acute accent (*árbol* – tree, *corazón* – heart).

English words of Spanish origin include *cargo*, *siesta*, *sombrero*, *mesa*, *hacienda*, *patio*, *armada*, *guerrilla*, *junta*, *plaza*, *canyon*, *rodeo*, *pueblo*, *adobe*, *vanilla*, *armadillo*, *tornado*, *embargo*, and *bonanza*.

Catalan

És el mes de gener. L'aire és sereníssim i glacial, i la lluna guaita, plàcidament, a través de l'emmallat de branques d'una arbreda sense fulles, el mas Cotells de Puigcerdà, el qual la rep amablement, esguardant-la amb l'ullet de groga llum d'una de les seves finestres i saludant-la amb el braç de fum blavís que, com de la curta mànega d'un giponet blanc, surt d'una de les seves xemeneies.

It is the month of January. The air is very clear and frosty, and the moon looks down placidly through the mesh of bare branches at the farmhouse of Cotells de Puigcerdà. It receives her tenderly, watching her with the little eye of yellow light from one of its windows, and greeting her with a wisp of bluish smoke that creeps out of one of its chimneys like an arm out of a short sleeve of a white dress.

JOAQUIM RUYRA, *Friar Pancraci*

Catalan is spoken in northeastern Spain, in the Balearic Islands (a province of Spain), in the Principality of Andorra (where it is the official language), and in a small part of France. Historically it was the language of Catalonia, the region that includes Barcelona, but today its speakers extend down the Spanish coast as far as the province of Valencia. In France it is spoken in the province of Pyrénées-Orientales, formerly known as Roussillon, which borders Spain and Andorra.

Almost all of the 7 million speakers of Catalan are in Spain. Those in France number only 250,000, in Andorra 20,000. In Catalonia today it is co-official with Spanish and is taught in all the schools. Catalan is of the Romance family, most closely related to Provençal.

Basque

Antxina, bedar txori abere ta patariak euren berbetea aztu baino lentxoago, eŕege bat bizi zan, gizon zintzo, buruargi, biotz-andi, mendekoak maite ebazan eŕege. Seme bat eukan ta bera alper, buru-eritxi, biotz-gogor, mendekoen ardura bagea. Diru baten auŕea ta atzea baino bére banago ziran aita-seme aren izateak. Aitaren ontasun guztien artean agiriena mendekoak semealabatzat lez eukitea zan. Semearen gaiztakeri ezagunena baŕiz mendekoak aintzat artu ez eze beste gisaren bateko izakitzat eukitea. Eztago zetan esan aita maite maite ebela eŕi atako lagunak, semea uŕetan bére ez.

Long ago, a short time before the plants, the birds, the animals, and all creeping and crawling things forgot their language, there lived a king, a sincere, frank, generous man, a king who loved his subjects. He had a son who was a good-for-nothing, conceited, hard-hearted, and with no compassion for the subjects. The characters of the father and son were as different as the two sides of a coin. The most outstanding of all the father's good qualities was that he treated his subjects as his own children. In contrast, the son's most obvious failing was that he looked on them as creatures of another world. It goes without saying that the people of the realm had great affection for the father but none at all for the son.

Basque stands alone among the languages of Europe. Despite many efforts, no connection between Basque and any other language has ever been proven. Structural similarities with certain languages in Asia have been noted, but as yet it must be considered a completely isolated and independent language.

Basque is spoken on both sides of the Spanish-French border by about 700,000 people. Of these, about 600,000 are in Spain, living mainly in the provinces of Vizcaya, Guipúzcoa, Navarra, and Alava. In France they live in the department of Pyrénées-Atlantiques, in the southwestern corner of the country. Bilbao, the capital of Vizcaya, is the major city of the Basque region. Most Basques are bilingual, speaking Spanish or French (or both) in addition to their own language.

There are a number of widely divergent dialects of Basque. In some the language is known as *Euskara*, in others *Eskuara*. The letter *z* is pronounced *s* (e.g., *zazpi* – seven), while the unusual combination *tx* is pronounced *ch* (*etxe* – house). There is both a soft *r* and a hard *r*, the latter usually spelled *ŕ* (*eŕege* – king). The definite article is merely the suffix *-a* (*gizon* – man, *gizona* – the man), while the plural is formed with the suffix *-k* (*gizonak* – the men).

As the only non-Indo-European language of Western Europe, Basque would appear to be the sole survivor of languages spoken there before the Indo-Europeans arrived. It was probably part of an extended group that included not only Basque but other languages of southern Europe as well. At one time its use extended considerably farther south and west than is the case today.

The name of the game of jai alai comes from Basque. *Jai* means "festival," while *alai* means "joyous."

Portuguese

Foi lá no dia seguinte pela manhã, mas decidiu não subir a perguntar aos actuais ocupantes da casa e aos outros inquilinos do prédio se tinham conhecido a menina do retrato. O mais certo seria responderem-lhe que não a conheciam, que estavam a viver ali há pouco tempo, ou que não se lembravam. Compreende, as pessoas vêm e vão, realmente não recordo nada dessa família, nem vale a pena puxar pela cabeça, e se alguém dissesse que sim, que lhe parecia ter uma vaga ideia, seria com certeza para logo a seguir acrescentar que as suas relações haviam sido apenas as naturais entre pessoas de boa educação.

He went there the following morning, but he decided not to go up and ask the present occupants of the apartment and the building's other tenants if they had known the girl in the photograph. It was more than likely that they would tell him they hadn't, that they had been living there only a short time, or that they didn't remember. You know how it is, people come and go, I really can't remember anything about the family, it's not worth puzzling your head about, and if someone did say yes and did seem to have a vague recollection, they would probably only go on to add that their relationship had been the usual one among the polite classes.

JOSÉ SARAMAGO, All the Names

Portuguese is the national language of both Portugal and Brazil. In the former it is spoken by the entire population of 10 million people, including those in the Azores and on the island of Madeira. In Brazil it is spoken by virtually everyone save the country's few hundred thousand Indians. As Brazil's population continues to soar, so does the number of speakers of Portuguese. The figure for Brazil in the year 2000 was approximately 165 million, up from only 100 million 25 years earlier.

Portuguese is also spoken in countries and territories that were once colonies of Portugal. It is the official language of five countries in Africa: Angola, Mozambique, Guinea-Bissau, Cape Verde, and São Tomé and Príncipe. It is also spoken by small communities in Goa (western India), in East Timor (in Indonesia), and in Macao, which is now part of China.

Portuguese is a Romance language, closely related to, and yet distinctly different from, Spanish. It is softer and less emphatic than Spanish, with a greater variety of vowel sounds, and it contains a number of nasal sounds that do not exist in Spanish. Words beginning with *h* in Spanish frequently begin with *f* in Portuguese (e.g., *hijo/filho* – son), while words ending in *-ción* in Spanish generally end in *-ção* in Portuguese (*nación/nação* – nation). There are a number of words from Arabic in both languages (*algodón/algodão* – cotton) plus a few peculiar to Portuguese (*alfaiate* – tailor). Many words are identical in the two languages (*mesa* – table, *flor* – flower, *lago* – lake), but others are completely different (*perro/cão* – dog, *gracias/obrigado* – thank you).

The Portuguese of Brazil is slower and more measured than that of Portugal, but the Brazilians and Portuguese communicate with each other without the slightest difficulty. As in British and American English there are occasional differences in vocabulary. The word for "boy" is *rapaz* in Portugal but *moço* in Brazil; "girl" is *rapariga* in Portugal and *moça* in Brazil. Some Brazilian words are of Indian origin (e.g., *abacaxi* – pineapple).

The Portuguese nasal vowels are indicated by the letters *ã* and *õ*. The *ç* functions as in French, while the combinations *lh* and *nh* correspond to the Spanish *ll* and *ñ* respectively. The letters *k*, *w*, and *y* are used only in foreign words. The letter *j* is pronounced as in French (not as in Spanish), as is the letter *g* before *e* and *i*. The *h* is always silent. Words ending in *a* (but not *ã*), *e*, *o*, *m*, or *s* generally stress the next-to-last syllable, while those ending in other letters stress the final syllable. Exceptions to this rule are indicated by an acute accent if the vowel has an open sound (*açúcar* – sugar), and by a circumflex if the vowel has a closed sound (*relâmpago* – lightning). The accent marks are also used to distinguish between words that would other-wise have the same spelling, as for example *e*, meaning "and," but *é*, meaning "is," and *por*, meaning "by," but *pôr*, meaning "to put."

José Saramago won the Nobel Prize for Literature in 1998.

Italian

La Pasqua infatti era vicina. Le colline erano tornate a vestirsi di verde, e i fichidindia erano di nuovo in fiore. Le ragazze avevano seminato il basilico alla finestra, e ci venivano a posare le farfalle bianche; fin le povere ginestre della sciara avevano il loro fiorellino pallido. La mattina, sui tetti, fumavano le tegole verdi e gialle, e i passeri vi facevano gazzarra sino al tramonto.

Easter really was near. The hills were clothed in green and the prickly-pear trees were in flower again. The girls had sown basil in the window boxes, and white butterflies came and perched on them. Even the broom on the lava field was covered with poor, pale little flowers. In the morning steam rose from the green and yellow slates on the roofs, where sparrows chattered noisily until sunset.

GIOVANNI VERGA, *The House by the Medlar Tree*

Italian is considered by many to be the most beautiful of the world's languages. As the transmitter of the great culture of the Renaissance, its influence on the other languages of Western Europe has been profound. Besides being spoken in Italy, it is one of the four official languages of Switzerland, and is also widely spoken in the United States, Canada, Argentina, and Brazil. All told, there are about 60 million speakers.

Italian is one of the Romance languages, and has remained closer to the original Latin than any of the others. Its dialects, however, vary tremendously, often to the point where communication becomes a problem. The literary standard came into being in the 14th century, largely through Dante's *Divine Comedy* and the works of Petrarch and Boccaccio. Since these eminent authors chiefly used the dialect of Tuscany (especially Florentine), modern literary Italian is essentially Tuscan. In modern times the dialect of Rome has gained considerable prestige, but it has still failed to eclipse the Florentine standard.

The Italian alphabet consists basically of 21 letters; *j*, *k*, *w*, *x*, and *y* appear only in foreign words. The letter *c* is pronounced *k* before *a*, *o*, and *u*, but *ch* before *e* and *i* (e.g., *carcere* – prison). *Ch* and *cch* are also pronounced *k* (*chiave* – key, *bicchiere* – glass). *G* is pronounced as a hard *g* before *a*, *o*, and *u* (*gamba* – leg), but as *j* before *e* and *i* (*giorno* – day). *Gg* before *e* and *i* is also pronounced *j* (*oggi* – today), *gh* before *e* and *i* is a hard *g* (*lunghezza* – length), *gli* followed by a vowel is pronounced *lli* as in "million" (*biglietto* – ticket), *gn* like the *ny* in "canyon" (*ogni* – every), and *gu* followed by a vowel as *gw* (*guerra* – war). *Z* and *zz* are generally pronounced *ts* (*zio* – uncle, *prezzo* – price), but sometimes as *dz* (*pranzo* – dinner, *mezzo* – middle). *Sc* before *e* and *i* is pronounced *sh* (*pesce* – fish).

The stress in Italian generally falls on the next-to-last or third-from-last syllable. The only written accent is the grave, which is used whenever a word of more than one syllable stresses the final vowel (*città* – city). It is also used on words of a single syllable to distinguish between two words that would otherwise have the same spelling, as for example *e*, meaning "and," but *è*, meaning "is." And it also appears in a few miscellaneous words such as *più* (more) and *già* (already).

English words of Italian origin include *umbrella, spaghetti, macaroni, broccoli, balcony, studio, casino, fresco, gusto, volcano, lava, stucco, gondola, regatta, malaria, bandit, incognito, vendetta, ghetto,* and *inferno*. In the field of music there are *piano, viola, opera, sonata, concerto, oratorio, soprano, aria, solo, trio, quartet, allegro, andante, tempo, libretto, staccato, crescendo, maestro,* and *virtuoso*.

Latin

Quae potest homini esse polito delectatio, cum aut homo imbecillus a valentissima bestia laniatur aut praeclara bestia venabulo transverberatur? quae tamen, si videnda sunt, saepe vidisti; neque nos, qui haec spectamus, quicquam novi vidimus. Extremus elephantorum dies fuit. In quo admiratio magna vulgi atquae turbae, delectatio nulla exstitit; quin etiam misericordia quaedam consecuta est atque opinio eius modi, esse quamdam illi beluae cum genere humano societatem.

What pleasure can it give a cultivated man to watch some poor fellow being torn to pieces by a powerful beast or a superb beast being pierced with a hunting spear? Even were such things worth looking at, you've seen them many times, and we saw nothing new this time. The last day was devoted to the elephants. The vulgar populace was enthusiastic, but there was no pleasure in it; indeed, the show provoked some sort of compassion, a feeling that there is some kinship between this great beast and humankind.

CICERO, *Letters to Friends*

Latin, the language of ancient Rome, is the ancestor of the modern Romance languages. Beginning as a local dialect of a small village on the River Tiber, it spread in the course of history over a large portion of the globe. In the Middle Ages Latin served as the international medium of communications, as well as the language of science, philosophy, and theology. Until comparatively recent times a knowledge of Latin was an essential prerequisite to any liberal education; only in the last century did its study decline, and emphasis shifted to the modern living languages. The Roman Catholic Church has traditionally used Latin as its official and liturgical language.

Latin was brought to the Italian peninsula by a wave of immigrants from the north about 1000 BC. Over the centuries, the city of Rome rose to a position of prominence, and the Latin of Rome became the literary standard of the newly-emerging Roman Empire. Side by side with classical Latin, a spoken vernacular developed, which was carried by the Roman army throughout the empire. It completely displaced the pre-Roman tongues of Italy, Gaul, and Spain and was readily accepted by the barbarians who partitioned the Roman Empire in the 5th century AD. Further divisions led to the eventual emergence of the modern Romance languages: Italian, French, Spanish, Portuguese, and Romanian.

The Latin, or Roman, alphabet was created in the 7th century BC. It was based on the Etruscan alphabet, which in turn was derived from the Greek. The original Latin alphabet was A, B, C (pronounced *k*), D, E, F, G, H, I (which stood for both *i* and *j*), K, L, M, N, O, P, Q, R, S, T, V (which stood for *u*, *v*, and *w*), and X. After the conquest of Greece in the first century BC the letters Y and Z were adopted from the contemporary Greek alphabet and placed at the end. Thus the new Latin alphabet contained 23 letters. It was not until the Middle Ages that the letter J (to distinguish it from I) and the letters U and W (to distinguish them from V) were added.

Latin lacks some of the variety and flexibility of Greek, perhaps reflecting the practical nature of the Roman people, who were more concerned with government and empire than with speculative thought and poetic imagery. Yet the epic poems of Rome's golden age (first century BC), such as Virgil's *Aeneid* and Horace's *Odes,* are among the classics of world literature. In the Middle Ages the writings of the theologians Desiderius Erasmus and John Calvin were in Latin, as were the scientific works of Nicholas Copernicus and later Sir Isaac Newton.

German

Pharao's Anblick war wunderbar. Sein Wagen war pures Gold und nichts andres, — er war golden nach seinen Rädern, seinen Wänden und seiner Deichsel und mit getriebenen Bildern bedeckt, die man aber nicht zu unterscheiden vermochte nach dem, was sie darstellten, denn im Prall der Mittagssonne blendete und blitzte der Wagen so gewaltig, daß die Augen es kaum ertrugen; und da seine Räder, wie auch die Hufe der Rosse davor, dichte Staubwolken aufwirbelten, die die Räder umhüllten, so war es, als ob Pharao in Rauch und Feuersgluten daherkäme, schrecklich und herrlich anzusehen.

Pharao's Anblick war wunderbar. Sein Wagen war pures Gold und nichts andres, – er war golden nach seinen Rädern, seinen Wänden und seiner Deichsel und mit getriebenen Bildern bedeckt, die man aber nicht zu unterscheiden vermochte nach dem, was sie darstellten, denn im Prall der Mittagssonne blendete und blitzte der Wagen so gewaltig, daß die Augen es kaum ertrugen; und da seine Räder, wie auch die Hufe der Rosse davor, dichte Staubwolken aufwirbelten, die die Räder umhüllten, so war es, als ob Pharao in Rauch und Feuersgluten daherkäme, schrecklich und herrlich anzusehen.

Pharaoh was wonderful to behold. His chariot was pure gold, naught else: gold wheels, gold sides, gold axles; and covered with embossed pictures, which, however, one could not see because the whole car flashed and glittered so, as it reflected the midday sun, that the eye could scarcely bear it. The wheels and the hoofs of the steeds whirled up thick enveloping clouds of dust so that it was as if Pharaoh came on in flame and smoke, frightful and glorious to behold.

THOMAS MANN, *Joseph and His Brothers*

German is one of the main cultural languages of the Western world, spoken by approximately 100 million people. It is the national language of both Germany and Austria, and is one of the four official languages of Switzerland. Additionally it is spoken in eastern France, in the region formerly known as Alsace-Lorraine, in the northern Italian region of Alto Adige, and also in eastern Belgium, Luxembourg, and the principality of Liechtenstein.

There are about 1½ million speakers of German in the United States, 500,000 in Canada, and sizable colonies as well in Argentina, Brazil, and such far-flung countries as Namibia and Kazakhstan. In Switzerland High German is used in formal settings, but Swiss German, a distinctly different dialect, is used in everyday speech.

Like the other Germanic languages, German is a member of the Indo-European family. Written German is quite uniform, but spoken dialects vary considerably, sometimes to the point where communication becomes a problem. The dialects fall within two general divisions: High German (*Hochdeutsch*), spoken in the highlands of the south, and Low German (*Plattdeutsch*), spoken in the lowlands of the north. In the Middle Ages Low German was the language of the Hanseatic League and served as a lingua franca over much of northern Europe. An important step in the evolution of a literary standard was Martin Luther's translation of the Bible into East Central German, a dialect that stood roughly midway between those of the north and south.

Today High German is the standard written language, used almost exclusively in books and newspapers, even in the regions where Low German is more commonly spoken. Low German more closely resembles English and Dutch, as may be seen by such words as *Door* (door – High German, *Tür*), and *eten* (to eat – High German, *essen*).

Traditionally German was written in a Gothic style known as *Fraktur*, which dates from the 14th century. In the period following World War II, however, *Fraktur* was largely superseded by the Roman characters used throughout the rest of Western Europe. The Roman script used to contain an additional letter, the *ß* or double *s*, used only in the lower case (e.g., *heiß* – hot), but this was abolished in the spelling reform that took effect in 1998. The letter *j* is pronounced *y* (*ja* – yes), *v* is pronounced *f* (*vier* – four), and *w* is pronounced *v* (*weiss* – white). Diphthongs include *sch*, pronounced *sh* (*Schnee* – snow); *st*, pronounced *sht* (*Strasse* – street); and *sp*, pronounced *shp* (*sprechen* – to speak). The only diacritical mark is the umlaut, which appears over the letters *a*, *o*, and *u* (*Rücken* – back). German is the only language in which all nouns begin with a capital letter.

Since English is a Germanic language, it is not surprising to find a high degree of similarity in the vocabulary of the two languages. *Finger, Hand, Butter, Gold, Ring, Name, warm,* and *blind* are German words meaning exactly what they do in English. Other words that are very similar to their English counterparts are *Vater* (father), *Mutter* (mother), *Freund* (friend), *Gott* (God), *Licht* (light), *Wasser* (water), *Feuer* (fire), *Silber* (silver), *Brot* (bread), *Milch* (milk), *Fisch* (fish), *Apfel* (apple), *Buch* (book), *gut* (good), *alt* (old), *kalt* (cold), and *blau* (blue). More recent German borrowings in English include *schnitzel, sauerkraut, pumpernickel, kindergarten, dachshund, poodle, yodel, lager, ersatz, edelweiss, meerschaum, wanderlust, hinterland,* and *blitzkrieg*. The words *frankfurter* and *hamburger* come from the German cities of Frankfurt and Hamburg respectively.

In the matter of abstract concepts, however, German words often bear little or no resemblance to their English counterparts. In the centuries following the Norman Conquest English adopted thousands of French-based words which were in turn derived from the Latin. A few examples among many of common German words that are completely different from the English are *erhalten* (to receive – French, *recevoir*), *wiederholen* (to repeat – French, *répéter*), *überzeugen* (to convince – French, *convaincre*), and *beschützen* (to protect – French, *protéger*).

The word for German in other languages takes many different forms. In German itself it is *deutsch*, in Spanish *alemán*, in Italian *tedesco*, in the Scandinavian languages *tysk*, and in Russian *nemetsky*.

Dutch

In die nacht wist ik eigenlijk dat ik sterven moest, ik wachtte op de politie, ik was bereid, bereid zoals de soldaten op het slagveld. Ik wou me graag opofferen voor het vaderland, maar nu, nu ik weer gered ben, nu is mijn eerste wens na de oorlog, maak me Nederlander! Ik houd van de Nederlanders, ik houd van ons land, ik houd van de taal, en wil hier werken. En al zou ik aan de Koningin zelf moeten schrijven, ik zal niet wijken vóór mijn doel bereikt is.

During that night I really felt that I had to die, I waited for the police, I was prepared, as the soldier is on the battlefield. I was eager to lay down my life for the country, but now, now I've been saved again, now my first wish after the war is that I may become Dutch! I love the Dutch, I love this country, I love the language and want to work here. And even if I have to write to the Queen myself, I will not give up until I have reached my goal.

ANNE FRANK, *The Diary of a Young Girl*

Dutch is spoken by the 15 million inhabitants of the Netherlands. It is also spoken across the border in northern Belgium, but there it is generally referred to as Flemish. It is the official language of Suriname, in South America, and of the Netherlands Antilles and Aruba in the Caribbean. Afrikaans, spoken in South Africa, evolved directly from the Dutch that was brought there by settlers from the Netherlands in the 17th century.

Dutch, like English, is one of the Germanic languages, and thus part of the Indo-European family. It stands about midway between English and German and is the closest to English of any of the major languages. Dutch is the English name of the language; in Dutch it is called *Nederlands.*

Long a maritime nation, the Dutch have left their imprint on many languages of the world. Many Dutch nautical terms have been adopted into other languages. Dutch idioms and syntax are still evident in present-day Indonesian. English words of Dutch origin include *dock, deck, yacht, easel, freight, furlough, brandy, cookie, cruller, waffle, coleslaw, maelstrom, isinglass*, and *Santa Claus*. Many place names in New York City, such as Brooklyn, Flushing, Harlem, Staten Island, and the Bowery, are reminders of the old Dutch colony of New Amsterdam.

Frisian

It hat eigenskip, dat de Fryske bydrage ta de Amerikaenske literatuer tige biskieden is. Der binne einlik mar trije, fjouwer Fryske nammen, dy 't yn de Amerikaenske literaire wrâld nei foaren komd binne. It binne allegearre nammen fan noch libjende Friezen, in biwiis dat de literaire kunst ûnder de Fryske lânforhuzers har net ier ta bloei set hat. Faeks is it lykwols net sûnder bitsjutting en ûnthjit dat de namme dy 't yn tiidsfolchoarder it lêst komt ek de meast forneamde is.

It stands to reason that the Frisian contribution to American literature is a very modest one. There are really only three or four Frisian names that have come to the fore in the American literary world. They are names of Frisian immigrants who are still living, a proof of the fact that literary art among the Frisian immigrants did not come to early fruition. Perhaps, however, it is not without significance or promise that the name which in point of time comes last is also the most noted.

Frisian is spoken mainly in the Netherlands, in the northernmost province of Friesland (capital, Leeuwarden), which includes the outlying West Frisian Islands. There are about 400,000 speakers here, speaking the dialect known as West Frisian.

About 10,000 speakers of a different dialect, North Frisian, are to be found in Germany. They live on or near the west coast of Schleswig-Holstein, Germany's northernmost province, and on the adjacent North Frisian Islands, including Sylt and Föhr. A third dialect, East Frisian, spoken in a few villages in northwestern Germany, has all but died out.

The Frisians were known as a seafaring and trading people as far back as Roman times. Their language is of the Germanic family, closer to English than Dutch in some respects. Courses in Frisian are offered at a number of Dutch universities.

Flemish

Hij ging buiten, opende duiven- en hoenderkoten en strooide handvollen kempzaad, spaanse terwe, rijst, vitsel, haver en koren. En 't was ineens een geharrewar, gekakel en geslaag van vleugelen. Er waren zwalpers, smieren, hennen, hanen, ganzen, kalkoenen en een overschone pauw. Ze grabbelden met hun rappe bekken gulzig naar het eten, drongen tegen elkander, liepen ondereen en pikten naar de mussen die met grote kladden in den warrelenden hoop neervielen.

He went out of doors, set open the dovecotes and the fowl house, and scattered maize, rice, oats, and corn. There was a flutter, cluttering, cackling, and flapping of wings; all sorts of fowls were there – pouter pigeons and fantails, cocks and hens, geese, turkeys, and a splendid peacock. Greedily they snapped up the food; they pushed and crowded and spread themselves out and pecked at the sparrows that swooped down on the heaving mass in flocks.

FELIX TIMMERMANS, *Pallieter*

Flemish is one of the two languages of Belgium, the other being French. It is spoken in the northern half of the country by about 6 million people, or slightly more than half the population. Flemish is actually the same language as Dutch, spoken in the Netherlands, but cultural and religious distinctions over the centuries have led to the use of separate terms for one and the same language. Historically, Flemish was spoken in the region known as Flanders, whose people are called Flemings and whose name for their language is *Vlaams*.

Luxembourgian

Wo' d'Uelzecht durech d'Wisen ze't,
dûrch d'Fielsen d'Sauer brécht,
wo' d'Rief lânscht d'Musel dofteg ble't,
den Himmel Wein ons mécht;
dât ass onst Land, fir dât mer ge'f
heinidden alles wôn,
onst Hémechtsland, dât mir so' de'f
an onsen Hierzer dron.

O Du douewen, dém séng Hand
dûrch d'Welt d'Natio'ne lét,
behitt Du d'Letzebuerger Land
Vru friemem Joch a Léd!
Du hues ons all als Kanner schon
De freie Géscht jo ginn;
Lôss viru blénken d'Freihétssonn,
de' mir so' lâng gesinn!

Where you see the slow Alzette flow,
the Sura play wild pranks,
where lovely vineyards amply grow
on the Moselle's banks,
there lies the land for which our thanks
are owed to God above,
our own, our native land which ranks
well foremost in our love.

Our Father in Heaven whose powerful hand
makes states or lays them low,
protect Thy Luxembourger Land
from foreign foe or woe.
God's golden liberty bestow
On us now as of yore.
Let Freedom's sun in glory glow
for now and evermore.

Our Homeland (Luxembourg National Anthem)

Luxembourgian, or Luxemburgish, is spoken in the Grand Duchy of Luxembourg. It is basically a dialect of German, but, since Luxembourg is an independent country, its language is generally thought of as a separate language. There are about 350,000 speakers.

Rhaeto-Romanic

A Vella, la veglia capitala da Lumnezia e liug distinguiu da purs e pugnieras, tonscha la splendur dil geraun tochen maneivel dallas cases. El ruaus della dumengia damaun fa ei la pareta che vitg e cultira seigien in esser, ch'igl undegiar dils feins madirs seplonti viavon sur seivs e miraglia, encurend in sinzur davos ils veiders glischonts dellas cases. L'empermischun della stad schai ell'aria cun si'odur pesonta da rosas selvatgas e mèl, mo era cugl aspect penibel da spinas e carduns.

In Vella, ancient capital of the Lumnezia Valley, long the domain of breeders of prized cattle, the splendor of the home fields seems to touch the very houses. In the hush of Sunday morning, one gets the feeling that village and nature are fused into one, that the swaying of the ripening alfalfa seems to stretch beyond the boundaries and walls, almost listening for an echo behind the shining windowpanes of the surrounding homes. The promise of summer is in the very air with the sweet perfume of wild roses and honey, but also with the painful sight of thorns and thistles.

TONI HALTER, *The Herdsman of Greina*

Rhaeto-Romanic is a collective term for three Romance dialects spoken in northeastern Italy and southeastern Switzerland. Of the more than 800,000 speakers of Rhaeto-Romanic, about 90 percent are in Italy, though there the language has no official status. The Swiss dialect on the other hand, known as Romansch, is one of Switzerland's four official languages, despite the fact that it is spoken by only one percent of the population. The passage above is in Romansch.

The two Rhaeto-Romanic dialects of Italy are (1) Friulian, with about 700,000 speakers in the region of Friuli-Venezia-Giulia, near the border with Austria and Slovenia; and (2) Ladin, with about 30,000 speakers in Alto Adige to the west. Romansch is spoken by about 50,000 people in the Swiss canton of Graubünden, bordering Austria and Italy. In ancient times this area was the Roman province of Rhaetia, from which the language derives its name.

Icelandic

Þótt þú langförull legðir
sérhvert land undir fót,
bera hugur og hjarta
samt þins heimalands mót,
frænka eldfjalls og íshafs,
sifji árfoss og hvers,
dóttir langholts og lyngmós,
sonur landvers og skers.

Yfir heim eða himin
hvort sem hugar þín önd,
skreyta fossar og fjallshlíð
öll þín framtiðarlönd.
Fjarst í eilifðar útsæ
vakir eylendan þín:
nóttlaus voraldar veröld,
þar sem viðsýnið skin.

Það er óskaland íslenzkt,
sem að yfir þú býr –
Aðeins blómgróin björgin,
sérhver baldjökull hlýr.
Frænka eldfjalls og íshafs,
sifji árfoss og hvers,
dóttir langholts og lyngmós,
sonur landvers og skers.

Though you wayfaring wander
all the world to explore,
yet your mind has been molded
by your motherland's shore,
kin of ice and volcano,
child of stream and defile,
daught'r of lava and ling-moor,
son of inlet and isle.

Over earth, over heaven,
though your heart may aspire,
yet will cascades and mountains
stud the land you desire.
In the ocean eternal
lies your isle, girt with brine:
nightless world of spring's wonders
where the grand vistas shine.

For the land of your wishes
has an Icelandic form,
but the rocks grow with flowers
and the glaciers are warm,
kin of ice and volcano,
child of stream and defile,
daught'r of lava and ling-moor,
son of inlet and isle.

STEPHAN C. STEPHANSSON,
From a Speech on Icelanders' Day

Icelandic is spoken by the 275,000 inhabitants of Iceland. It is one of the Scandinavian languages, which form a branch of the Germanic languages, in turn a part of the Indo-European family.

Icelandic is remarkably similar to Old Norse, the language of the Vikings, which was brought to Iceland from Norway in the 9th century. Whereas the other Scandinavian languages have been strongly influenced by those of neighboring countries, Icelandic, insular and isolated, has retained its pristine character over the centuries. As a result Icelandic schoolchildren today have little difficulty reading the Eddas and the sagas, the great epics written in Old Norse. Their language is a sort of parent tongue to the other modern Scandinavian languages. As the Viking invasions also brought Old Norse to the British Isles, Icelandic has many features in common with Old English.

Another factor behind the purity of Icelandic is the absence of international words for modern ideas and inventions. Icelanders avoid such words wherever possible, preferring to coin their own purely Icelandic words instead. Thus "telephone" in Icelandic is *sími*, an old Icelandic word for "thread" or "wire." The word for "radio" is *útvarp* ("broadcast"). "Automobile" is *bíll*, but may also be *bifreið* ("moving ride"). "Electricity" is *rafmagn* ("amber power"). For "computer" a special word, *tölva*, was devised.

Icelandic's links with Old English are also reflected in the alphabet, which contains the Old English þ (*thorn*), the unvoiced *th*, and the ð (*eth*), the voiced. It also contains the æ of Danish and Norwegian.

The English words *geyser* and *eider* are of Icelandic origin.

Faroese

Hammershaimb, ættaður úr Sandavági, gav út í 1854 fyrstu føroysku mállælruna og gjørdi ta nýggju rættskrivingina. Tá fór føroyskt at taka danskt mál av ræði. Í fyrstuni vóru nógvir Føroyingar ikki hugaðir fyri tí føroyska málstrevinium, men tjóðskaparhugurin vann sigur, og nú hevur føroyskt fingið somu rættindir sum danskt, og er – formelt – høvuðsmálið. Men nógvir halda at einans føroyskt eigur at verða nýtt í almennum viðurskiftum. Hetta er til dømis støðan hjá loysingarmonnum, t.e. teir, ið vilja hava landið leyst frá Danmark politiskt; soleiðis halda eisini nógv onnur.

It was Hammershaimb, a native of Sandavágur, who in 1854 published the first grammar of Faroese and introduced the modern orthography. From that time on Faroese began to challenge the supremacy of Danish. At first many Faroese were not sympathetic to the Faroese language movement, but the nationally minded won the day and now Faroese has reached a position of equality with Danish and is, formally, the chief language. Many, however, wish Faroese to be the sole official language. This is the standpoint, for example, of the Separatists, i.e., those who wish the country to be politically independent of Denmark, though many others hold it too.

The Faroe Islands are located about 250 miles north of Scotland, midway between Norway and Iceland. They were settled about a thousand years ago by Norwegian Vikings speaking the Old Norse language. Modern Faroese, like Icelandic, strongly resembles Old Norse. It is spoken by most of the islands' 45,000 inhabitants, although the official language is Danish. The alphabet contains the ð (but not the þ) of Icelandic, and the ø of Danish.

Danish

For mange år siden levede en kejser, som holdt så uhyre meget af smukke, nye klæder, at han gav alle sine penge ud for ret at blive pyntet. Han brød sig ikke om sine soldater, brød sig ej om komedie eller om at køre i skoven, uden alene for at vise sine nye klæder. Han havde en kjole for hver time på dagen, og ligesom man siger om en konge, han er i rådet, så sagde man altid her: "Kejseren er i klædeskabet!"

Many years ago there was an Emperor who was so excessively fond of new clothes that he spent all his money on them. He cared nothing about his soldiers, nor for the theater, nor for driving in the woods – except for the sake of showing off his new clothes. He had a costume for every hour of the day. Instead of saying as one does about any other king or emperor, "He is in his council chamber," the people here always said, "The Emperor is in his dressing room."

HANS CHRISTIAN ANDERSEN, The Emperor's New Clothes

Danish is spoken by the 5 million inhabitants of Denmark, where it is the official language, and in Greenland and the Faroe Islands, which are administrative subdivisions of Denmark. It is one of the Scandinavian languages, which constitute a branch of the Germanic languages, in turn a part of the Indo-European family.

Danish is most closely related to Norwegian and Swedish. During the centuries that Norway was part of Denmark (1397–1814), a dialect closer to Danish than Norwegian developed in the Norwegian cities. This is still in use today and is sometimes referred to as Dano-Norwegian.

The Danish alphabet is the same as the Norwegian, consisting of the 26 letters of the English alphabet plus æ, ø, and å at the end. Before 1948 the å was written aa. The spelling reform of that year also abolished the German practice of beginning all nouns with a capital letter.

Norwegian

Påskeøya er verdens ensomste boplass. Nærmeste faste punkt beboerne kan se, er på himmelhvelvet, månen og planetene. De må reise lenger enn noen annen folkegruppe for å få se at det virkelig finnes fastland som ligger nærmere. Derfor lever de stjernene så nær og kan navn på flere av dem enn på byer og land i vår egen verden.

Easter Island is the loneliest inhabited place in the world. The nearest solid land the islanders can see is above, in the firmament, the moon and the planets. They have to travel farther than any other people to see that there really is land yet closer. Therefore, living nearest the stars, they know more names of stars than of towns and countries in our own world.

THOR HEYERDAHL, *Aku-Aku*

Norwegian is the national language of Norway, spoken by virtually all of the country's 4 million inhabitants. It is one of the Scandinavian languages, which are descended from the Old Norse spoken throughout Scandinavia in Viking times. These form a branch of the Germanic languages, in turn a part of the Indo-European family. Norwegian is very similar to Danish and somewhat less similar to Swedish.

Norway and Denmark were one country for four centuries before 1814, and from then until 1905 Norway was under the Swedish crown. During the years of Danish rule a Danish-based "city language" began to develop in Bergen and Oslo, which eventually became the written language of Norway.

In the mid-19th century, however, a movement was begun to develop a new national language for Norway distinct from Danish. Originally known as *landsmål* ("country language"), it is now called *nynorsk* ("New Norse"). Based largely on the dialects of rural Norway, *landsmål* was intended to revive the tradition of Old Norse, interrupted in the 15th century.

The result is that today there are two standard languages in Norway. The Dano-Norwegian variety, originally called *riksmål* ("state language") and now known as *bokmål* ("book language") is still used by most newspapers and on radio and television broadcasts. But *nynorsk* has equal status with *bokmål* in government and also in the schools. Attempts to combine the two into *samnorsk* ("Common Norwegian") have thus far been unsuccessful, but many Norwegians believe that at some point they will merge into one.

Both the Norwegian and Danish alphabets contain the additional letters *æ* and *ø*, which in Swedish are *ä* and *ö*. All three contain the letter *å*.

English words of Norwegian origin include *fjord*, *slalom*, *troll*, *lemming*, *auk*, and *narwhal*.

Swedish

Han stod rak – som en snurra sålänge piskan viner. Han var blygsam –
i kraft av robusta överlägsenhetskänslor. Han var icke anspråksfull: vad
han strävade efter var endast frihet från oro, och andras nederlag gladde
honom mer än egna segrar. Han räddade livet genom att aldrig våga det.
– Och klagade över att han icke var förstådd!

He stood erect – as a peg top does so long as the whip keeps lashing it.
He was modest – thanks to a robust conviction of his own superiority.
He was unambitious – all he wanted was a life free from cares, and he
took more pleasure in the failures of others than in his own successes.
He saved his life by never risking it – and complained that he was mis-
understood.

DAG HAMMARSKJÖLD, *Markings*

Swedish is the most widely spoken of the Scandinavian languages, which
constitute a branch of the Germanic languages, in turn a part of the Indo-
European family. In addition to the 9 million people of Sweden, about
300,000 speakers live on the southwestern and southern coasts of Finland
and on the Åland Islands in the Baltic Sea, which belong to Finland.

Swedish is closely related to Norwegian and Danish. Historically it is
closer to Danish, but the years of Swedish hegemony over Norway
(1814–1905) brought the two languages closer together. A Swedish person
today has more difficulty understanding Danish than Norwegian.

The Swedish alphabet consists of 29 letters, the regular 26 of the English
alphabet, plus å, ä, and ö at the end. The ä and ö distinguish it from
Norwegian and Danish, which use æ and ø.

During the Middle Ages Swedish borrowed many words from German,
while the 18th and 19th centuries witnessed a large infusion of words from
French. In the 20th and 21st centuries English has become by far the largest
source of foreign borrowings.

The English words *smorgasbord* and *tungsten* are of Swedish origin. The
former is a combination of *smörgås* (sandwich) and *bord* (table). The latter
is a combination of *tung* (heavy) and *sten* (stone).

Lappish

Gukken davven Dawgai vuolde
sabma suolgai Same-aednam:
Duoddar laebba duoddar duokken,
jawre saebba jawre lakka,
čokkak čilgin, čorok čaeroin
allanaddik alme vuostai;
šavvik jogak, šuvvik vuowdek,
cakkik caeggo stalle-njargak
maraidaeggje maeraidi.

Far away in the North, under Charles' Wain,
is Lapland faintly to be seen in the distance.
Mountains lie stretched behind mountains;
lakes full to overflowing lie near each other;
summits with ridges, hills with stony slopes rise toward the sky.
Rivers rush, forests sigh,
steep steel-colored promontories jut into roaring seas.

Lapp National Anthem

Lappish is the language of the Lapps, or Laplanders, who live in northern-most Scandinavia, Finland, and a small part of Russia. They number approximately 65,000, of whom only about half still have command of the language. Speakers in Norway number about 20,000, in Sweden 10,000, in Finland 2,000, on the Kola Peninsula of Russia 2,000. Lappish is now gener-ally referred to by its native name of Sami.

Lappish is one of the Finno-Ugric languages, bearing certain similarities to Finnish, but the two languages are actually vastly different. Since the Lapps are of different racial stock from the Finns, it is assumed that about 2,000 years ago they adopted the language of the ancestors of the Finns. Subsequently many words were borrowed from the Scandinavian languages.

Finnish

Sillä minä, Sinuhe, olen ihminen ja ihmisenä olen elänyt jokaisessa ihmisessä, joka on ollut ennen minua, ja ihmisenä elän jokaisessa ihmisessä, joka tulee jälkeeni. Elän ihmisen itkussa ja ilossa, hänen surussaan ja pelossaan elän, hyvyydessään ja pahuudessaan, oikeudessa ja vääryydessä, heikkoudessa ja väkevyydessä. Ihmisenä olen elävä ihmisessä ikuisesti enkä sen tähden kaipaa uhreja hautaani ja kuolemattomuutta nimelleni. Tämän kirjoitti Sinuhe, egyptiläinen, hän, joka eli yksinäisenä kaikki elämänsä päivät.

For I, Sinuhe, am a human being. I have lived in everyone who existed before me and shall live in all who come after me. I shall live in human tears and laughter, in human sorrow and fear, in human goodness and wickedness, in justice and injustice, in weakness and strength. As a human being I shall live eternally in mankind. I desire no offerings at my tomb and no immortality for my name. This was written by Sinuhe, the Egyptian, who lived alone all the days of his life.

MIKA WALTARI, *The Egyptian*

Finnish is the national language of Finland, spoken there by about 5 million people. There are also some 200,000 speakers in northern Sweden and 50,000 in northwestern Russia.

Finnish is one of the few languages of Europe not of the Indo-European family. Like Estonian, spoken across the Gulf of Finland, it is one of the Finno-Ugric languages, which constitute the main branch of the Uralic family.

The Finnish alphabet contains only 21 letters. There are 13 consonants (*d, g, h, j, k, l, m, n, p, r, s, t, v*) and eight vowels (*a, e, i, o, u, y, ä, ö*). There is only one sound for every letter, one letter for every sound, and the stress is always on the first syllable. The language makes no distinction as to gender, and has no articles, either definite or indefinite.

Nonetheless Finnish is an exceedingly difficult language to learn. Aside from foreign borrowings (mostly from the Germanic languages), the long, often compound words bear no similarity whatever to their counterparts in the Indo-European languages. The Finnish word for "question," for example, is *kysymys*, while the word for "twenty" is *kaksikymmentä*. Even the Finnish names of different countries are often hard to recognize: e.g., *Suomi* (Finland), *Ruotsi* (Sweden), *Tanska* (Denmark), *Saksa* (Germany), *Ranska* (France), and *Venäjä* (Russia). The number of case forms for nouns is enormous: whereas German has four cases, Latin five, and Russian six, Finnish has no fewer than 15! In addition to the familiar nominative, genitive, partitive, and ablative, there are also the elative, allative, illative, essive, inessive, adessive, abessive, and several others.

Sorbian

UPPER SORBIAN

Hlej! Mócnje twoju sławił swjatu mi sym rolu.
Twój wobraz tkałe su wšě mysle mi a sony,
wěnc twojich hór a twojich honow horde strony,
a chwalił sobu sym će z horami a z holu!

Plač towarš mój je často był, hdyž dźiwjej bolu
sym z harfy wabił zańdźenosće ćežke stony,
hdyž k njebju wolał sym, su klinčałe kaž zwony
wšě truny. Twój sym z ruku, wutrobu a wołu!

LOWER SORBIAN

Glej! Z mocu som toś twoju swětu rolu sławił.
Twoj wobraz su wše myslenja a sni mě tkali,
wěnk modrych gor' golow śmojtu zeleń w dali,
a chwalił som śi cełu a śi wěnkow nawił!

Gaž zajšłosć spominach, jo cesto płac mě dawił
a martrow śěžke stukanja su tšuny grali,
gaž k njebju wołach, toś su woni zabrincali
mě ako zwony wše, a wšykno som z nich zjawił!

Look! Strongly have I praised your holy fields.
Your image has woven together all my thoughts and dreams,
the string of blue mountains and vast meadows of proud land,
and I have praised you for these mountains and meadows!

Cries were often my companion, when with a sharp pain
I called with my harp the heavy sighs of the past,
when I shouted to heaven all strings sounded like bells.
I am yours with my hand, heart and will!

JAKUB BART-ĆIŠINSKI, *Lusatia*

Sorbian, also known by the names of Wendish and Lusatian, is a Slavic language spoken in Lusatia, an area in easternmost Germany bisected by the River Spree. Although surrounded by German speakers for centuries, the Sorbs have preserved their Slavic speech, and the study and propagation of the language is still encouraged today by the German government.

Despite its small number of speakers (about 50,000), and the small area in which it is spoken, Sorbian has two distinct dialects. Upper Sorbian, centered in the city of Bautzen to the south (the word "upper" refers to the *level* rather than the *location* of the land), is closer to Czech. Lower Sorbian, spoken in the vicinity of Cottbus to the north, more closely resembles Polish. The above poem, by the Sorbs' most famous poet, is shown in each of the two dialects.

Polish

Nadzieja bywa, jeżeli ktoś wierzy,
Że ziemia nie jest snem, lecz żywym ciałem,
I że wzrok, dotyk ani słuch nie kłamie.
A wszystkie rzeczy, które tutaj znałem,
Są niby ogród, kiedy stoisz w bramie.

Wejść tam nie można. Ale jest na pewno.
Gdybyśmy lepiej i mądrzej patrzyli,
Jeszcze kwiat nowy i gwiazdę niejedną
W ogrodzie świata byśmy zobaczyli.

Niektórzy mówią, że nas oko łudzi
I że nic nie ma, tylko się wydaje,
Ale ci właśnie nie mają nadziei.
Myślą, że kiedy człowiek się odwróci,
Cały świat za nim zaraz być przestaje,
Jakby porwały go ręce złodziei.

Hope means that someone believes the earth
Is not a dream, that it is living flesh;
That sight, touch, hearing tell the truth;
And that all the things we have known here
Are like a garden, looked at from the gate.

You can't go in; but you can see it's there.
And if you could see clearly and more wisely
We know we'd find in the world's garden
Some new flower or undiscovered star.

Some people think our eyes deceive us; they say
That there is nothing but a pretty seeming:
And just these are the ones who don't have hope.
They think that when a person turns away
The whole world vanishes behind his back
As if a clever thief had snatched it up.

CZESLAW MILOSZ, *Hope*

Polish is spoken by virtually all of the 40 million inhabitants of Poland, by about 700,000 people in the United States, and by about 250,000 each in Lithuania, Germany, and Canada. It is one of the Slavic languages and thus part of the Indo-European family.

Polish is written in the Roman alphabet, though *q*, *v*, and *x* are used only in foreign words. The letter *j* is pronounced *y*, *w* is pronounced *v*, and *c* is pronounced *ts*. There are numerous diacritical marks, including acute accents, dots, hooks, and, in the case of the *l*, a bar (ł). The letter *ć* is a soft *ch* (e.g., *ćwierć* – quarter), *ś* is a soft *sh* (*śnieg* – snow), *ść* is a soft *shch* (*iść* – to go), *dź* is pronounced like the English *j* (*niedźwiedź* – bear), *ń* is pronounced *ny* as in "canyon" (*jesień* – autumn), *ó* is pronounced *oo* (*góra* – mountain). The letter *ż* is a hard *zh* (*żona* – wife), the letters *ą* and *ę* are nasal vowels (*sąsiad* – neighbor, *pięć* – five), and the barred *ł* is pronounced approximately like a *w* (*głowa* – head). *Ch* is pronounced as in German, but *sz* = *sh* (*szkoła* – school), *cz* = *ch* (*czysty* – clean), *szcz* = *shch* (*szczotka* – brush), and *rz* = *zh* (*grzmot* – thunder). The stress in Polish is always on the next-to-last syllable.

Polish vocabulary naturally resembles that of the other Slavic languages. Such Polish words as *bez* (without), *most* (bridge), *cena* (price), and *zima* (winter) are identical in Russian, Czech, Bulgarian, and Serbo-Croatian. But "peace," which is *mir* in Russian and *mír* in Czech, in Polish is *pokój,* while "island" (*ostrov* in Russian and Czech) in Polish is *wyspa*. The Polish words for "north," "south," "east," and "west" are respectively *połnoc* (which also means "midnight"), *południe* (noon), *wschód* (rising), and *zachód* (setting). Some Polish words seem unpronounceable to one who has never studied the language (e.g., *przemysł* – industry, *sześćdziesiąt* – sixty, *wszechświat* – universe, *szczęśliwy* – happy; lucky). Equally formidable are the names of the Polish cities Szczecin, Bydgoszcz, and Świętochłowice.

Czeslaw Milosz was the winner of the Nobel Prize for Literature in 1980.

Czech

Já vím, ten romantik ve mně, to byla maminka. Maminka zpívala, maminka se někdy zadívala, maminka měla nějaký skrytý, a neznámý život; a jak byla krásná tehdy, když podávala dragounovi pít, tak krásná, že mně kloučkovi se srdce svíralo. Řikali vždycky, že jsem po ní. Tehdy jsem chtěl být po tatínkovi, silný jako on, velký a spolehlivý jako tatínek. Asi jsem se nevydařil. To není po něm, ten básník, ten romantik a kdo ví co ještě.

I know that romantic in me, it was my mother. Mother used to sing, mother lost herself in daydreams, mother had had some secret unknown life; and how beautiful she was when she offered the dragoon a drink, so beautiful that my little childish heart stood still. They always said that I took after her. Then I wanted to be like my father, strong like him, big, and reliable like daddy. Perhaps I haven't turned out well. It isn't after him, that poet, that romantic, and who knows what else.

KAREL ČAPEK, *An Ordinary Life*

Czech is the official language of the Czech Republic, spoken by virtually the entire population of 10 million people. It is closely related to Slovak, spoken in Slovakia, the two languages in fact being mutually intelligible.

Czech is a Slavic language written in the Roman script. The foundations of the alphabet were laid by the great religious reformer Jan Hus, in the early 15th century. The letters *q*, *w*, and *x* are used only in foreign words, while *c* is pronounced *ts* (e.g., *cena* – price), *ch* as in German (*kachna* – duck), and *j* as *y* (*jazyk* – language). Acute accents lengthen the vowels (*kámen* – stone), while a circle over the *u* produces a long *oo* sound (*dům* – house). The chevron over *c*, *s*, and *z* produces *ch*, *sh*, and *zh* respectively (*čislo* – number, *koš* – basket, *život* – life). But *ň* is pronounced *ny* as in "canyon" (*daň* – tax), *ě* is pronounced *ye* (*město* – city), and *ř* is pronounced *rzh*, as in the name Dvořák. The letter *r* serves as a vowel, producing such words as *krk* (neck), *smrt* (death), and *čtvrt* (quarter). The stress is always on the first syllable.

Slovak

Čim menšie je niečo, tým väčšmi kriči. Taký fafrnok, nevie to ešte ani hovoriť, a prekriči celú rodinu, malý úradník urobí viacej štabarcu okolo seba ako desať ministrov, malý vrabec prečviriká svojho starého otca pokojne skáčúceho po chodníku, malý vozík bude rapotať na celú dedinu, kým štyridsať konských síl prebrnkne vedľa teba, že počuješ iba ľahké ssst.

The smaller the fry, the bigger the noise. A small brat that cannot say a single word will outscream the whole family, a minor clerk will make more ado than a dozen ministers, a small sparrow will outtwitter its own grandfather hopping about peacefully on the pavement, and a small farm wagon will disturb the whole village with its rattling and creaking while a forty-horsepower vehicle streaks past and you hear only a slight swish.

JANKO JESENSKÝ, *The Democrats*

Slovak is the language of Slovakia, the eastern third of what was formerly Czechoslovakia. It is spoken by about 4½ million people or 90 percent of the country's population.

Slovak is very similar to Czech, the two estimated to be about 90 percent mutually intelligible. A great number of words are identical in both languages – e.g., *okno* (window), *srdce* (heart), *jazyk* (language), and *zmrzlina* (ice cream), while others, such as *sneh* (snow – Czech, *sníh*) and *vták* (bird – Czech, *pták*) differ by only a letter or two.

The Slovak alphabet is also similar to that of Czech, though it lacks three Czech letters (*ě, ř,* and *ů*) and contains a number of its own. Two are vowels, the *ä*, as in *mäso* (meat), and the *ô*, as in *nôž* (knife), while an apostrophe after the consonants *d, l,* and *t* indicates a soft sound (e.g., *učiteľ* – teacher). The Slovak word for Slovak is *slovenský*, not to be confused with the word for Slovenian, *slovinský*.

Hungarian

A pokoli komédia még egyre tartott börzén. A halálra itélt papírok, a bondavári gyártelep s a bondavári vasút részvényei egyik kézböl a másikba repültek. Most már a komikumig vitték a tragédiát, s kezdett humor vegyülni a szerencsétlenségbe. Ez a szó: "Bondavár" csak arra való volt, hogy derültséget idézzen elő a börzeemberek között. Aki az utolsó részvényén túladhatott nagy veszteséggel, nevetett azon, aki megszerezte azt. Kezdték a részvényeket megfoghatlan becsű tárgyakért cserébe kinálgatni. Ráadásul egy új esernyőre egy ócska esernyőért. Használták előfizetési ekvivalensül olyan lapokért, amiket valakinek a szerkesztő a nyakára köt erővel. Ajándékozgatták jótékony célokra.

The devil's comedy was being played daily on the stock exchange. The Bondavara Company's shares, the Bondavara Railway shares were tossed here and there, from one hand to another. The tragedy had turned to comedy – that is, for some people, who found the game very humorous. The very word Bondavara made the stockbrokers laugh. When it happened that some fool bought a share, no one could help laughing. The shares, in fact, were given in exchange for anything of little value – for instance, as makeweight with an old umbrella for a new one. They were also presented to charitable institutions.

MÓR JÓKAI, Black Diamonds

Hungarian is the national language of Hungary, spoken by virtually all of its 10 million inhabitants. An additional 1½ million speakers live in northwestern Romania, in the area known as Transylvania, which was part of Hungary before World War II. About 500,000 more are to be found in Slovakia to the north, where they constitute about 10 percent of that country's population. Yugoslavia (Serbia) also has some 400,000 speakers, mostly in the northern province of Vojvodina.

Hungarian is one of the Finno-Ugric languages, which include Finnish, Estonian, and a number of languages spoken in Russia. It is thus completely unrelated to any of the languages of Western Europe. Most Finno-Ugric languages, however, belong to the Finnic branch of this group, while Hungarian belongs to the Ugric. The only other existing Ugric languages, and thus the only other languages to which Hungarian is closely related, are the remote Khanty and Mansi languages of Siberia, spoken in an area more than 2,000 miles from Hungary.

As may be gathered from these facts, the original Hungarian people came from Asia, having long lived a nomadic life on the eastern slopes of the Urals. Forced to migrate westward between the 5th and 9th centuries AD, they eventually reached the Danube where they settled in 896. In the ensuing millennium and more the Hungarians have become completely Europeanized, with only their language serving to reveal their Asian origins. While much of Hungary's basic vocabulary is still of Finno-Ugric origin, a large number of loanwords are to be found from the Turkic and Slavic languages, as well as from Latin, Italian, and German.

The Hungarians call their language Magyar. It is difficult for foreigners to learn, with much of its vocabulary from Asia, and its grammar containing a number of complex features not to be found in Western languages. The alphabet, however, is phonetic, with *s* pronounced *sh* (e.g., *sör* – beer), *c* pronounced *ts* (*ceruza* – pencil), *sz* pronounced *s* (*szó* – word), *cs* pronounced *ch* (*csésze* – cup), *zs* pronounced *zh* (*zseb* – pocket), and *gy* pronounced *dy* (*nagy* – big). The many vowel sounds in spoken Hungarian are indicated by acute accents, umlauts, and the unique double acute accent which appears over *o* and *u* (*bőr* – skin, *fű* – grass). The stress is always on the first syllable.

The Hungarian word for a number of nationalities, and countries, is very different from the native name or the name used in other languages. German is *német*, Italian is *olasz*, Polish is *lengyel*, and Russian is *orosz*. Adding the word *ország* (country) to each produces the name of the country: *Németország* (Germany), *Olaszország* (Italy), *Lengyelország* (Poland), and *Oroszország* (Russia). Hungary itself, of course, is *Magyarország*.

The most important English word of Hungarian origin is *coach*, after the village of Kocs (remember *cs* = *ch*), where coaches were invented and first used. Others are *goulash* and *paprika*.

Slovenian

Mračilo se je, s polja so se vračali kmetje in posli. Takrat se je prikazal petelin na Sitarjevi strehi, rdeč in tenak je švignil visoko proti nebu. Nato se je prikazal petelin na skednju, na hlevu, na šupi, na obeh kozolcih; velik je bil plamen, segal je silen od zemlje do nebes. Goreče treske so padale v kolobarju na zoreče polje, kakor da bi jih metala človeška roka. Tako je prižgal Jernej svojo strašno bakljo.

Night was falling; villagers and farmhands were coming home from the fields. On Sitar's roof the red cock suddenly appeared. A tongue-shaped flame shot up skywards; then another was seen on the stables, and yet another on the barn – and then on both sheds. They were leaping up; they seemed to come out of the earth and to reach up to the sky. Burning beams whirled in the air and fell in a circle on the green fields, as if thrown by a mighty human hand. . . . Yerney had set fire to his terrible torch.

IVAN CANKAR, *The Bailiff Yerney and His Rights*

Slovenian is the official language of the new nation of Slovenia, spoken by about 90 percent of the country's 2 million people. There are also about 100,000 speakers in Italy and 20,000 in Austria.

Slovenian is a Slavic language written in the Roman alphabet. The letters *q*, *w*, *x*, and *y* are missing, while *c* is pronounced *ts* (e.g., *cena* – price), *č* is pronounced *ch* (*črn* – black), *š* is pronounced *sh* (*šola* – school), and *ž* is pronounced *zh* (*življenje* – life). The language is most closely related to Serbo-Croatian but the two are not mutually intelligible.

Serbian

То је био афрички слон, још недорастао, млад и бујан; биле су му тек две године. Пре слона стигла је у Травник прича о њему. Све се однекуд сазнавало: како је путовао, како је чуван и негован од пратње, и како је дочекиван, превожен и храњен од народа и власти. И већ су га прозвали «фил», што на турском језику значи слон.

The elephant came from Africa. Young, snappy, and not yet fully grown, he was but two years old. These details, as well as other information, had preceded the elephant into Travnik. Indeed, in Travnik everything was known: how he traveled, how he was looked after by his sizable escort, how he was transported and fed, and how he was received by the authorities along the way. And they referred to him by the Turkish word *fil*, which means elephant.

IVO ANDRIČ, *The Vizier's Elephant*

Serbian is the principal language of Yugoslavia, now reduced to the provinces of Serbia (which includes Kosovo) and Montenegro. In Serbia it is spoken by about 7½ million people, in Montenegro by 650,000. There are also about 1,250,000 Serbs in Bosnia and Herzegovina and 500,000 in Croatia. Serbian is one of the Slavic languages and thus part of the Indo-European family.

Serbian and Croatian, spoken in Croatia, are virtually the same language, often referred to as Serbo-Croatian. The Serbs call the language Serbian, and, being of Eastern Orthodox religious persuasion, write it in a modified form of the Cyrillic alphabet. The Roman Catholic Croats, on the other hand, call their language Croatian and employ the Roman alphabet. But all educated Serbs know the Roman alphabet as well, and many books published in Serbia appear in both.

The Serbian alphabet differs considerably from the Russian. Nine Russian letters are missing from Serbian, but Serbian has six of its own. There is the Roman *j*, pronounced *y*; the џ, pronounced like the English *j*; the љ, pronounced like the *ll* of "million"; the њ, pronounced like the *ny* of "canyon"; the ђ, pronounced *dy* as in "did you"; and the ћ, pronounced *ty* as in "hit you." For each Cyrillic letter in the Serbian alphabet there is a corresponding Roman letter in the Croatian alphabet.

Ivo Andrič was the winner of the Nobel Prize for Literature in 1961.

Croatian

Sjedi tako Filip u sutonu, sluša rodu na susjednom dimnjaku kako klepeće kljunom kao kastanjetom, kako jasno odjekuju pastirski glasovi s potoka gdje se napaja blago, kako lastavice proždrljivo kruže oko dimnjaka kao grabilice, i osjeća u sebi prelijevanje tih životnih odraza, živo i zanosno. Kruže slike oko njega kao ptice i oko njegova pogrebnog raspoloženja i unutarnjih potištenosti, i oko vinograda i oranica, i šumskih parcela što gasnu u teškom, baršunastom zelenilu starinskog damasta i nestaju u smeđim tkaninama daljine.

Thus Philip sat in the twilight and listened to a stork clapping its beak like a castanet on a neighboring chimney, to the shepherds' voices echoing from the stream where they watered their beasts, to the swallows greedily circling around the chimney like birds of prey, and vividly and rapturously he felt flowing into him those multitudinous expressions of life. Images circled round him like birds, round his funereal mood and inner depression and round the vineyard and the plowfields, and the tracts of woodland fading in their heavy, velvety green, like old-fashioned damask, and disappearing in the vague brown tissue of the distance.

MIROSLAV KRLEŽA, The Return of Philip Latinovicz

Croatian is the form of Serbo-Croatian that is written in the Roman alphabet. It is the language of the 5 million Croats, a Roman Catholic people, of whom about 4 million live in the newly independent country of Croatia. There are also about 750,000 in Bosnia and Herzegovina, though there the language is known officially as Bosnian. Some 150,000 Croatian speakers live in Austria, a number that increased about tenfold during the early 1990s.

Croatian and Serbian are essentially the same language, about as different from each other as British and American English. As in English, there are a number of cases in which one word is used in one, and another in the other. For "train" the Serbs generally say *voz* as against Croatian *vlak*, while for "dance" the Serbs prefer *igra* and the Croatians *ples*. For "music" the Serbs say *muzika* as against Croatian *glazba*, while for "theater" there is Serbian *pozorište* and Croatian *kazalište*. In each case, however, both alternatives are understood perfectly well by everyone.

The Croatian alphabet has a Roman letter for each Cyrillic letter of the Serbian alphabet. *Ž, č,* and *š* are pronounced *zh, ch,* and *sh* respectively (e.g., *nož* – knife, *čovjek* – man, *šešir* – hat). *C*, corresponding to the Serbian and Russian ц, is pronounced *ts* (*cipela* – shoe), while *dž*, corresponding to the Serbian џ, is pronounced like the English *j* (*džep* – pocket). *Ć*, corresponding to the Serbian ħ, is pronounced *ty* as in "hit you" (*svijeća* – candle), while *đ*, corresponding to ђ, is pronounced *dy* as in "did you" (*đavo* – devil). The Croatian equivalents of the Serbian љ and њ are *lj* and *nj* respectively.

The Croatian word for Croatian is *hrvatski*, and for Serbian *srpski*. The letter *r* frequently serves as a vowel, as for example in the words *prst* (finger), *vrt* (garden), *krv* (blood), *brz* (fast), *crn* (black), and *trg* (market). The Italian city of Trieste is *Trst* in Croatian.

Romanian

Şi scurt şi cuprinzător, sărut mîna mătuşei, luîndu-mi ziua bună, ca un
băiet de treabă; ies din casă cu chip că mă duc la scăldat, mă şupuresc
pe unde pot şi, cînd colo, mă trezesc în cireşul femeii şi încep a cărăbăni
la cireşe în sîn, crude, coapte, cum se găseau. Şi cum eram îngrijit şi mă
sileam să fac ce oi face mai degrabă, iaca mătuşa Mărioara c-o jordie în
mînă, la tulpina cireşului!

The long and the short of it is that I kissed my aunt's hand and took my
leave like a good boy; I went out of the house as if I were going to bathe;
I crept stealthily as best I could and, all of a sudden, found myself in
my aunt's cherry tree, picking cherries and stuffing them into my shirt
bosom, green ones and ripe ones, just as I found them. And just as I was
most eager and anxious to get the job done as quickly as possible, up
came Aunt Marioara with a stick in her hand, right at the foot of the
cherry tree!

ION CREANGĂ, *Recollections from Childhood*

Romanian, also spelled Rumanian, is the national language of Romania,
spoken by about 90 percent of the country's population, or some 20 million
people. It is also spoken in neighboring Moldova, but there it is referred to
as Moldovan.

As its name suggests, Romanian is one of the Romance languages, the
only one spoken in Eastern Europe. It is descended from the Latin introduced
by the Roman Emperor Trajan when he conquered the region in the 2nd
century AD.

Romania switched from the Cyrillic to the Roman script in 1860. The
present alphabet contains four special letters: the ă, an unstressed vowel (e.g.,
vară – summer); the î, a guttural vowel (*gît* – neck); the ş, pronounced *sh*
(*şase* – six); and the ţ, pronounced *ts* (*preţ* – price). The Romanian definite
article, like that of Bulgarian and the Scandinavian languages, is suffixed to
the noun (*rege* – king, *regele* – the king).

Modern Romanian contains relatively few words from the Latin that was
brought there by the Romans. Over the centuries it has borrowed heavily
from the Slavic languages, from Greek, Turkish, German, and especially
French. It has been estimated that as many as a third of all Romanian words
today are of French origin.

Bulgarian

Сутринта Огнянов се упъти към града. Той измина балканското гърло и излезе при манастира. На поляната пред манастира, под големите орехи се разхождаше игуменът, гологлав. Той се възхищаваше от утринната хубост на тия романтични места и приемаше на големи глътки свежия живителен въздух на планината. Есенната природа имаше ново обаяние с тия позлатени листове на дърветата, с тия пожълтели кадифени гърбове на Балкана и с тая сладостнонежна повяхналост и меланхолия.

In the morning Ognyanov set out for town. He went through the gorge which led him out to the monastery. Under the great walnut trees in the meadow in front of the monastery the abbot was walking bareheaded to and fro. He was enjoying the beauty of this romantic spot and drinking in the fresh, bracing air of the mountain. The autumn landscape had a new charm with the golden leaves of the trees, the yellowed velvety hills of the Balkan range, and the atmosphere of sweetly tender decay and melancholy.

IVAN VAZOV, *Under the Yoke*

Bulgarian is spoken by about 90 percent of the population of Bulgaria, or some 7 million people. It is one of the Slavic languages and, in fact, played an important role in the historical development of this family. When the first alphabet for the Slavic languages was devised in the 9th century, it was a dialect of Bulgarian that served as the base. Old Bulgarian, or Old Church Slavonic as it came to be called, long served as the literary vehicle of all the Slavic languages. During the Middle Ages it was one of the three major literary languages of Europe.

The modern Bulgarian alphabet is virtually the same as the Russian, except that the ъ, the little used "hard sign" in Russian, in Bulgarian serves as a vowel. It is pronounced something like the *u* in the English word "fur" and is, in fact, the second letter in the word Bulgaria. Bulgarian also differs from the other Slavic languages in that it makes use of articles, both definite and indefinite, the former being suffixed to the noun. The verb has no infinitive form; like the English infinitive, which is formed by placing the word "to" in front of the verb, the Bulgarian infinitive is formed with the word *da*.

Macedonian

За нас, како за народ што успеа да го оформи својот литературен јазик дури во последниве децении, ќе биде многу поучно да знаеме какви биле општо основните карактеристики на развојот на литературните јазици во словенскиот свет. Ќе биде поучно особено поради тоа што ќе најдеме во тој развој ред аналогии со тоа што се случувало кај нас и што ќе можеме да забележиме извесни закономерности таму каде што инаку може да ни се чини дека некоја појава произлегува само од нашата посебна ситуација.

For us, a nation which has succeeded in formulating its literary language in the course of the last few decades, it would be very instructive to know the nature of the fundamental characteristics of the development of literary languages in the Slavic world. It would be particularly instructive in that we would find in that development a number of analogies to what has happened in our own case, and we would be able to note certain correspondences, whereas otherwise it might appear that certain phenomena arise solely out of our own particular situation.

Macedonian is the principal language of the new nation of Macedonia, wedged between Yugoslavia, Bulgaria, Greece, and Albania. It is spoken by about two-thirds of the population, or close to 1½ million people. There are also some speakers in Greece.

Macedonian is closely related to Bulgarian, and is considered by some (especially the Bulgarians) to be merely a dialect of that language. It is written in the Cyrillic alphabet with the additional letters ѓ and ќ, not to be found in any other language. It also contains the *j* of Serbian.

Albanian

Maletë me gurë,	Mountains and stones,
fusha me bar shumë,	Lush meadows unshorn,
aratë me grurë,	A river beyond,
më tutje një lumë.	Fields full of corn.
Fshati përkarshi.	Out yonder, the village,
me kish' e me varre,	Its church and its graves,
rotul ca shtëpi	Cottages here and there,
të vogëla fare.	Low under their eaves.
Ujëtë të ftotë,	Chill water springs.
era punemadhe,	A keen wind blows.
bilbili ia thotë	The nightingale sings.
gratë si zorkadhe.	And the women . . . they're like does!
Burrat nënë hie	Idlers in the shade,
lozën, kuvëndojnë; –	Kept by their wives;
pika që s'u bie.	A plague on them all
se nga gratë rrojnë!	For wasting their lives!

ANTON ZAKO ÇAJUPI, *My Village*

Albanian is spoken by the entire population of Albania (about 3 million people), by another 1½ million in the Yugoslav province of Kosovo, and about 500,000 in Macedonia. There are also Albanian-speaking communities in Italy and Greece.

The Albanians call their language *shqip* and their country *Shqipëria*. There are two distinct dialects: Tosk, spoken in the south, and Gheg, spoken in the north. Standard Albanian is based on Tosk.

Albanian is an Indo-European language, constituting a separate and independent branch of this family. Its origin is uncertain and it was not until 1854 that it was conclusively proven to be Indo-European. The vocabulary contains many words not to be found in any other Indo-European language, though there has been considerable borrowing from Latin, Greek, Turkish, and the Slavic languages. Albanian adopted the Roman alphabet in 1908.

Greek

CLASSICAL GREEK

φίλοι, κακῶν μὲν ὅστις ἔμπειρος κυρεῖ,
ἐπίσταται βροτοῖσιν ὡς ὅταν κλύδων
κακῶν ἐπέλθῃ πάντα δειμαίνειν φιλεῖ·
ὅταν δ' ὁ δαίμων εὐροῇ, πεποιθέναι
τὸν αὐτὸν αἰεὶ δαίμον' οὐριεῖν τύχην.
ἐμοὶ γὰρ ἤδη πάντα μὲν φόβου πλέα
ἐν ὄμμασιν τἀνταῖα φαίνεται θεῶν,
βοᾷ δ' ἐν ὠσὶ κέλαδος οὐ παιώνιος·
τοῖα κακῶν ἔκπληξις ἐκφοβεῖ φρένας.

> My friends, whoever's wise in ways of evil
> Knows how, when a flood of evil comes,
> Everything we grow to fear; but when
> A god our voyage gladdens, we believe
> Always that fortune's never-changing wind
> Will blow. As my eyes behold all things
> As fearful visitations of the gods,
> So my ears already ring with cureless songs:
> Thus consternation terrifies my sense.
>
> AESCHYLUS, *The Persians*

Greek, the first great language of Western civilization, is considered by many to be the most effective and admirable means of communication ever devised. Its lucidity of structure and concept, together with its seemingly infinite variety of modes of expression, render it equally suitable to the needs of the rigorous thinker and the inspired poet. We can only surmise how classical Greek must have sounded to the ear, but the spoken word was probably no less beautiful than the written.

MODERN GREEK

Κι ὁ νοῦς του ἀγκάλιασε πονετικὰ τὴν Κρήτη. Τὴν ἀγαποῦσε
σὰν ἕνα πράμα ζωντανό, ζεστό, ποὺ 'χε στόμα καὶ φώναζε, καὶ μά-
τια κι ἔκλαιγε, καὶ δὲν ἦταν καμωμένη ἀπὸ πέτρες καὶ χώματα κι
ἀπὸ ρίζες δεντρῶν, παρὰ ἀπὸ χιλιάδες χιλιάδες παππούδες καὶ μάνες, ποὺ δὲν πεθαίνουν ποτέ τους, παρὰ ζοῦν καὶ μαζεύουνται κάθε
Κυριακὴ στὶς ἐκκλησιὲς κι ἀγριεύουν κάθε τόσο, ξετυλίγουν μέσα
ἀπὸ τὰ μνήματα μιὰ θεόρατη σημαία καὶ πιάνουν τὰ βουνά. Κι
ἀπάνω στὴ σημαία ἐτούτη, χρόνια σκυμμένες οἱ ἀθάνατες μάνες,
ἔχουν κεντήσει μὲ τὰ κορακάτα καὶ γκρίζα καὶ κάτασπρα μαλλιά
τους τὰ τρία ἀθάνατα λόγια: ΕΛΕΥΤΕΡΙΑ 'Η ΘΑΝΑΤΟΣ.

Full of pity, his spirit embraced Crete. Crete was to him a living, warm
creature with a speaking mouth and weeping eyes; a Crete that consisted
not of rocks and clods and roots, but of thousands of forefathers who
never died and who gathered, every Sunday, in the churches. Again and
again they were filled with wrath, and in their graves they unfolded a
proud banner and rushed with it into the mountains. And on the banner
the undying Mother, bowed over it for years, had embroidered with
their black and gray and snow-white hair the three undying words:
FREEDOM OR DEATH.

NIKOS KAZANTZAKIS, *Freedom or Death*

Greek-speaking people moved into the Greek Peninsula and adjacent areas
from the Balkan Peninsula in the 2nd millennium BC. In time, four distinct
dialects evolved: Aeolic, Ionic, Arcado-Cyprian, and Doric. It was in the
Ionic dialect that the epic poems of Homer, the *Iliad* and the *Odyssey*,
appeared, perhaps in the 9th century BC. With the rise of Athens in
succeeding centuries, Attic, the dialect of Athens and an offshoot of Ionic,
began to produce the great literature of the classical period. Attic became the
dominant form of the language and the basis of the *Koine*, or common
language, whose use passed far beyond the borders of present-day Greece.
The conquests of Alexander the Great carried it as far east as India. It was
the second language of the Roman Empire, and later the ruling language of
the Byzantine Empire. The New Testament was written in the *Koine*, and it
is used by the Eastern Orthodox Church to the present day.

The Greek alphabet, an adaptation of the Phoenician, dates from about
1000 BC. It was the first alphabet in which letters stood for vowels as well
as for consonants, in contrast to the Semitic alphabets, which had only consonants. Like the Semitic alphabets, it was at first written from right to left,
but then shifted to a style in which lines alternated from right to left and left
to right, and then shifted again to the present left-to-right direction. An earlier
form of Greek writing, known as Linear B, was discovered on clay tablets

in Crete and Peloponnesus. Deciphered in 1952, it came into use about 1500 BC but was largely abandoned by 1200.

Greek was the official language of the Byzantine Empire from the 4th to the 15th century and thereafter continued to be spoken by Greeks under Turkish rule. Modern Greek began to take shape about the 9th century, and became the official language of the kingdom of Greece when independence was achieved in 1829. Today Greek is spoken by about 10 million people, including some 500,000 on the island of Cyprus. In addition to the common speech, known as Demotic, an imitation of classical Greek, known as Pure, has been revived for literary purposes.

The impact of Greek upon the vocabulary of all languages, including English, has been enormous. Such prefixes as *poly-* (much, many), *micro-* (small), *anti-* (against), *auto-* (self), *hemi-* (half), *hetero-* (different), *chrono-* (time), *tele-* (distance), *geo-* (earth), *physio-* (nature), *photo-* (light), *hydro-* (water), *litho-* (stone), *phono-* (sound), *anthropo-* (man), *psycho-* (mind), and *philo-* (love), each generate dozens of vital words in scientific, technical, and other fields. Equally important Greek suffixes are *-meter* (measure), *-gram* (letter), *-graph* (write), *-scope* (see), *-phone* (sound), and *-phobia* (fear). The names of the Greek letters (e.g., alpha, beta, gamma, delta, iota, pi, omega) are used for many purposes in all Western languages.

Romany

So me tumenge 'kana rospxenava, ada živd'ape varikicy Romenge. Me somas išče tykny čxajori berša efta – oxto. Ame samas terde kakesa Pxuroronkosa ade smolensko veš. Tele b'el'v'el bolype azurestar sa butydyr i butydyr kerd'ape molyvitko. Syge lyja tetamas'ol i syr kontrast sa pašidyr i pašidyr jek jekxeste jagune zygzagi p'erečšingirde bolype. Pe bax, ame čxavore, zalyžijam kašta xoc' pe kurko, pxenesas, variso žakiri.

What I am going to tell you now has been experienced by many Gypsies. I was only a little girl of seven or eight. We camped with our uncle Pxuroronko in the forest of Smolensk. Towards evening the blue sky gradually assumed a lead color. Soon it grew dark and as a contrast the zigzags of fire cut across the sky close to each other. Fortunately, we children had gathered such a heap of firewood that it would have been sufficient for a whole week – maybe we had a presentiment.

The Ghosts

Romany is the language of the Gypsies, or the Roma. The origin of the Gypsies was long a matter of speculation. The English word "Gypsy" stems from an early belief that they came from Egypt. This has now been disproved.

The question was resolved by the science of linguistics. Detailed study of the Romany language has shown that the Gypsies originally came from India. The common features it shares with Sanskrit and later Indian languages can lead to no other conclusion.

The Gypsies are believed to have begun their migration westward about 1000 AD. Loanwords in their language from Persian, Armenian, and Greek provide some indication of the general course of their travels. Today Gypsies are to be found in many countries, but the heaviest concentration is in Eastern Europe, particularly in Romania, Slovakia, Hungary, the Czech Republic, and Poland. A rough estimate of their numbers would be in the neighborhood of 5–6 million.

The name Romany is derived from the Gypsy word *rom*, which means "man." Dialects vary considerably, each strongly influenced by the language of the country in which it is spoken. The English word "pal" is of Gypsy origin, coming from the Romany word *phral*, which means "brother."

Yiddish

איך בין געשטאַנען אויפֿ'ן באַלקאָן אין אַן אַטלאַסענער זשופּיצע, אין
אַ סאַמעטן היטל, מיט רויטע פּאות, און נעקוקט. ווי גרויס איז די דאָזיקע
וועלט, ווי רײַך אין מענשן, טראָפֿן אויסטערלישקייטן ? און ווי הויך
גרייכט דער הימל איבער די דעכער ? און ווי טיף איז די ערד אונטער
די שטיינער ? און פֿאַרוואָס האָבן בחורים און מיידלעך זיך אַזוי ליב ?
און וואו איז דער גאָט, וואָס וועגן אים רעדט מען שטענדיק אין אונזער
שטוב ? איך בין געווען דערשטוינט, אַנטציקט, פֿאַרגאַפֿט. איך האָב
געהאַט דאָס געפֿיל, אַז איך מוז באַשיידן דאָס דאָזיגע רעטעניש, איך
אַליין, מיט מײַן אייגענעם קאָפּ...

I stood on the balcony in my satin gabardine and my velvet hat, and
gazed about me. How vast was this world, and how rich in all kinds of
people and strange happenings! And how high was the sky above the
rooftops! And how deep the earth beneath the flagstones! And why did
men and women love each other! And where was God, who was
constantly spoken of in our house? I was amazed, delighted, entranced.
I felt that I must solve this riddle, I alone, with my own understanding.

ISAAC BASHEVIS SINGER, *The Purim Gift*

Yiddish until recent times was the language spoken by the majority of the
Jews of the world. Prior to World War II more than 10 million people, about
two-thirds of world Jewry, spoke or at least understood Yiddish.

Yiddish originated nearly a thousand years ago among Jewish emigrants
from northern France who settled in a number of cities along the Rhine and
adopted the German dialects of the area. Their speech, however, was strongly
influenced by Hebrew, which remained for Jews everywhere the language of
religion and scholarship. In the 14th and 15th centuries Yiddish was carried
eastward into Poland, Lithuania, and Russia, where it absorbed elements from
the various Slavic languages. Thus it is the result of the fusion of a number
of linguistic elements, to which it added many unique characteristics of its
own. A rich body of literature exists in Yiddish, highlighted by such names
as Sholom Aleichim, Isaac Loeb Peretz, and, more recently, Isaac Bashevis
Singer.

Yiddish is written in Hebrew characters with the important difference that
it uses letters for vowels. German is the dominant element in the language,
accounting for about 80 percent of the vocabulary as against ten percent each
for Hebrew and the Slavic languages. Yiddish is exceptionally idiomatic,
with many words and expressions that are virtually untranslatable. Many
Yiddish words have entered the English language and are now to be found
in standard English dictionaries. A few of the best known are *chutzpah*

102

(effrontery), *schlemiel* (dolt), *schmaltz* (sentimentality), and the expression *mazel tov* (good luck).

The mass exodus of Jews from eastern Europe between 1880 and 1920 carried Yiddish to many parts of the world. The largest communities were in the eastern United States, the largest of all being in New York City. But many settled in Western Europe, Canada, South America (particularly Argentina), and even Australia. In the years before and after World War II many Yiddish-speaking Jews made their way to Israel.

The destruction of European Jewry in World War II reduced the number of Yiddish speakers by half. And the remaining number has declined precipitously as Jews now everywhere speak the language of their homeland. But efforts are being made in many countries to encourage its study and thus extend its life for at least a few more generations.

Isaac Bashevis Singer won the Nobel Prize for Literature in 1978.

Estonian

Oma kõvad käed mu pihku anna,
hoian sind, mu vaprat sõjameest.
Pea mul omad jälle risti panna
sinu ja su relvavende eest.

Nõnda mehine on nüüd su pale –
kui sa läksid, olid alles poiss . . .
Tule, tule aga lähemale –
tõsinend sa metsades ja sois.

Lapsesilmad! . . . aga nagu teaksid
nad nii mõndagi, mis ränk ja võik;
teaksid vahest rohkem kui nad peaksid,
nagu teaksid–nagu teaksid kõik.

Ära seisa nõnda kaua tummalt!
Mis su pilgu taga – koormab suud . . .
Kahelt suurelt–Elult, Surmalt–kummalt
oled, ainumane, märgitud?

Let me hold your hands in resignation,
Soldier, whom this mortal strife must take.
Soon my hands will fold in supplication
For your own and all your comrades' sake.

Now your changing face is even dearer.
I recall you as a schoolboy when
You first left me. Come, dear child, come nearer!
You have grown mature in wood and fen.

Yet your vivid eyes are still ingenuous,
Though they must have witnessed what is vile –
Things that men will do when life is strenuous
And resorts to cruelty and guile.

Do not stand there rigid and unspeaking;
In your glance are things that cry for breath.
Which of those two lords of man is seeking
To command your valor, Life or Death?

MARIE UNDER, *Soldier's Mother*

Estonian is the native language of Estonia, where it is spoken by about one million people, or two-thirds of the total population. It is one of the Finno-Ugric languages, the main branch of the Uralic family. Its closest relative is Finnish, spoken across the Gulf of Finland. The two languages are sufficiently similar to be mutually intelligible, at least for those Estonians who speak the dialect of the north. Estonian is not in any way related to its nearest geographic neighbors, Latvian and Lithuanian.

Estonian's similarity to Finnish can easily be seen by comparing the vocabulary of the two languages. The Estonian words *pää* (head), *puu* (tree), *kuu* (moon), *suu* (mouth), *muna* (egg), *käsi* (hand), *tuli* (fire), *liha* (meat), *tasku* (pocket), and *raha* (money) are exactly the same in Finnish. Others such as *öö* (night – Finnish, *yö*) and *ida* (east – Finnish, *itä*) differ by only a letter or two. Some, however, are completely different – "train" is *rong* in Estonian but *juna* in Finnish, "pen" (*sulepää*) is *kynä*, "flower" (*lill*) is *kukka*, and "year" (*aasta*) is *vuosi*. Others reflect borrowings from different languages – "cup" is *tass* as in German *Tasse*, but *kuppi* in Finnish as in Swedish *koppen*. "Doctor" is *arst* in Estonian as in German *Arzt*, but *lääkäri* in Finnish as in Swedish *lä karen*.

Like Latvian and Lithuanian, Estonian is written in the Roman alphabet. It lacks the letters *c*, *q*, *w*, *x*, *y*, *z*, but contains the letter *õ*, found in no other language of eastern Europe. Umlauts may appear over the letters *a*, *o*, and *u*.

Lithuanian

Keistas, nesuprantamas disonansas tarp šios vargų ir tamsumo jūros atrodė nauja brangi bažnyčia. Aišku buvo, kad ji, tokia daili ir didelė, pakliuvo čion kažin kaip, kažkokiu fatališku žmonių nesusipratimu, padariusi jiems didelę nuoskaudą, iščiulpusi jų visas sultis, palikusi jiems tik skurdą – bent šimtmečiui. Žiūrėdamas į ją, jauti, kad ji pati gėdinasi savo puikybės, gėdinasi žmonių tamsumo, jų neturto ir, rodos, turėtų kojas, tuoj pabėgtų iš to miestelio.

The elaborate new church seemed a strange and incomprehensible anomaly amidst this sea of misery and ignorance. It was clear that the church, so elegant and grand, had turned up here in some way by some fatal misunderstanding of the people and had brought great offense to them. It had drained their last ounce of strength and left them only poverty – for a century at least. Looking at it, one senses that it is ashamed of its splendor, ashamed of human ignorance and poverty, and that, if it had legs, it would quickly flee this town.

ANTANAS VIENUOLIS, *The Last Place*

Lithuanian is the native language of Lithuania, where it is spoken by over 3 million people, or about 80 percent of the total population. It is one of the two Baltic languages (the other being Latvian), which form a branch of the Indo-European family.

Lithuanian is perhaps the oldest of all the modern Indo-European languages. It has been said that the speech of a Lithuanian peasant is the closest thing existing today to the speech of the original Indo-Europeans. Lithuanian also bears certain remarkable similarities to Sanskrit, the progenitor of the modern Indic languages. The Lithuanian words *sūnus* (son) and *avis* (sheep) are identical to the Sanskrit, while many others such as *dūmas* (smoke, Sanskrit – *dhūmas*), *vilkas* (wolf, Sanskrit – *vrkas*), and *antras* (second, Sanskrit – *antaras*) differ only by a letter or two. Some Lithuanian words are thought to be even older than their Sanskrit counterparts: i.e., they may have disappeared from Sanskrit before the latter was committed to writing.

The Lithuanian alphabet contains 32 letters with a number of diacritical marks to indicate special sounds. The letters *č*, *š*, and *ž* are pronounced *ch*, *sh*, and *zh* respectively (e.g., *čia* – here, *širdis* – heart, *žmogus* – man), while vowels include *ą*, *ę*, *į*, *ų*, *ė*, and *ū* (*į* – to, *abėcėlė* – alphabet, and *jūra* – sea).

Latvian

Reiz, sensenos laikos, aiz trejdeviņām jūram un trejdeviņiem kalniem dzīvoja kāds tēvs, kam bija trīs dēli – divi gudri un tas trešais es. Bet kaimiņos dzīvoja divi briesmīgi sumpurņi – katrs savā pusē tai zemītei. Viņi nemitīgi kāvās savā starpā, bet visvairāk cieta cilvēki, kas dzīvoja vidū. Tad reiz tēvs sasauca savus dēlus kopā un teica: "Ejiet pasaulē un mācieties, kā sumpurņus pievārēt. Tad nāciet atpakaļ un rādiet, ko protat. Kurš būs tēvu zemes cienīgs, tam tā paliks."

Once upon a time, in a faraway land, beyond many seas and mountains, there lived a man who had three sons. The first two were smart, the third was – I. But on each side of my father's land there were two monsters who constantly fought each other, and the innocent people in the middle always suffered. One day my father called his sons to him and said: "Go into the world and learn how to slay the monsters. Then come back and show me what you have learned. The one who is worthy of his father's land will inherit it."

MARTINS ZIVERTS, *Kurrpurru*

Latvian, also known as Lettish, is the native language of Latvia, the middle of the three Baltic republics. It is spoken by about 1,350,000 people, or just over half the population. It is closely related to Lithuanian, spoken just to the south, but the two are not mutually intelligible.

Latvian is written in the Roman alphabet with a number of diacritical marks to indicate special sounds. A macron (horizontal line above) indicates a long vowel (e.g., *māte* – mother, *tēvs* – father), while *č*, *š*, and *ž* are pronounced *ch*, *sh*, and *zh* respectively (*četri* – four, *seši* – six). A cedilla under certain consonants adds a *y* sound (*nedēļa* – week). The stress is always on the first syllable.

The relationship of Latvian to Lithuanian may be seen in such words as *galva* (head), *siena* (wall), *alus* (beer), and *sala* (island), which are the same in both languages. But in basic vocabulary the differences outweigh the similarities – "blood" is *asins* in Latvian but *kraujas* in Lithuanian, and Latvian *kurpe* (shoe) in Lithuanian is *batas*.

LANGUAGES OF
THE FORMER SOVIET UNION

Russian

Вот весенний вечер на дворе. Воздух весь размечен звуками. Голоса играющих детей разбросаны в местах разной дальности, как бы в знак того, что пространство всё насквозь живое. И эта даль – Россия, его несравненная, за морями нашумевшая, знаменитая родительница, мученица, упрямица, сумасбродка, шалая, боготворимая, с вечно величественными и гибельными выходками, которых никогда нельзя предвидеть! О, как сладко существовать! Как сладко жить на свете и любить жизнь! О, как всегда тянет сказать спасибо самой жизни, самому существованию, сказать это им самим в лицо!

A spring evening. The air punctuated with scattered sounds. The voices of children playing in the streets coming from varying distances as if to show that the whole expanse is alive. And this expanse is Russia, his incomparable mother; famed far and wide, martyred, stubborn, extravagant, crazy, irresponsible, adored, Russia with her eternally splendid, and disastrous, and unpredictable adventures. Oh, how sweet to be alive! How good to be alive and to love life! Oh, the ever-present longing to thank life, thank existence itself, to thank them as one being to another being.

BORIS PASTERNAK, *Dr. Zhivago*

Russian is spoken across the vast expanse of Russia: still, after the breakup of the Soviet Union, the largest country in the world. Spanning eleven time zones, it extends from Kaliningrad, facing the Baltic Sea, to easternmost Siberia, facing the Pacific Ocean and the Bering Strait.

Of the country's 145 million people, about 120 million are native Russians, with many of the rest speaking the language with varying degrees of fluency. Between 25 and 30 million Russians also live in the newly independent states that were once part of the Soviet Union, the numbers by country as follows:

Ukraine	15 million	Estonia	300,000
Kazakhstan	5 million	Lithuania	300,000
Belarus	3½ million	Turkmenistan	250,000
Uzbekistan	1 million	Georgia	150,000
Latvia	750,000	Azerbaijan	150,000
Kyrgyzstan	600,000	Tajikistan	100,000
Moldova	500,000		

There are also now about 500,000 Russian speakers in Israel, 250,000 in the United States, and 40,000 in Canada.

Russian is the most important of the Slavic languages, a branch of the Indo-European family. It is written in the Cyrillic alphabet, which is based largely on the Greek, and named after a Greek scholar and missionary named Cyril who lived in the 9th century. While tradition holds that he and his brother Methodius were its inventors, it is now generally believed that they actually invented a different alphabet called Glagolitic, which is older but no longer in use. Cyrillic was probably invented by someone else at a later date.

Though appearing formidable to one who has never studied it, the Russian alphabet is not difficult to learn. A number of letters are written and pronounced approximately as in English (*A, K, M, O, T*), while others, though written as in English, are pronounced differently (B = V, E = YE, Ë = YO, H = N, P = R, C = S, X = Kh). The Greek influence may be seen in the Г (*G*), Д (*D*), Л (*L*), П (*P*), and Ф (*F*). Other letters are Б (*B*), З (*Z*), У (*U*), Ж (*ZH*), И (*I*), Ц (*Ts*), Ч (*Ch*), Ш (*Sh*), Щ (*Shch*), Э (*E*), Ю (*Yu*), and Я (*Ya*). The Ы is a vowel pronounced something like the *i* in "bit," the Й is used in forming diphthongs, and the Ъ and the Ь are the so-called hard and soft signs respectively.

But Russian is not an easy language to master, though many do. Its grammar is complex and it is notorious for its long words (e.g., *zdravstvuyte* – hello, *chuvstvovat'* – to feel, *upotreblyat'* – to use, *dostoprimechatel'nosti* – sights, *zhenonenavistnichestvo* – misogyny), long personal and place names (Nepomnyashchiy, Dnepropetrovsk), and for its unusual consonant clusters (*vzvod* – platoon, *tknut'* – to poke, *vstrecha* – meeting). Nouns, pronouns, adjectives, and numbers are declined in six cases: nominative, genitive, dative, accusative, instrumental, and prepositional or locative. The Russian verb has two aspects, each represented by a separate infinitive: the imperfective to indicate a continuing action, and the perfective to indicate an action already completed or to be completed. The genders number three (masculine, feminine, and neuter), with a different declensional pattern for each (though the neuter is similar to the masculine), and a fourth one for the plural. The stress is impossible to predict in an unfamiliar word, and frequently shifts in the course of declensions or conjugations.

English words of Russian origin include *vodka, tsar, samovar, ruble, pogrom, troika, steppe*, and *tundra*. The word *sputnik* entered the language in 1957, while the 1980s produced *glasnost* and *perestroyka*. The post-Soviet period has seen a huge influx of foreign, mostly English, words into Russian from the fields of business, politics, and computers, as well as from everyday life. A few among many are *konsalting* (consulting), *defolt* (default), *konsensus* (consensus), *khaker* (hacker), and *killer* (pronounced *keeler*). Legislation has been proposed to mandate the use of Russian words instead of their foreign counterparts but, as is the case in other countries, it is not likely to get very far.

Boris Pasternak won the Nobel Prize for Literature in 1958.

Belorussian

Партызаны падхапіліся, як па камандзе, калі маці падышла. Пастарэлая, ссутуленая, у чорнай хустцы – помню, бачу яе і цяпер – Марына падоўгу стаяла каля кожнай труны, узіраючыся ў твары забітых. Не, яна не плакала. Зрэдку варушыліся засмяглыя вусны. Што яна казала? Чытала малітву? Ці слала праклёны забойцам? Я баяўся; ці не памутнеў ад гора яе розум?

The partisans jumped aside, as if by command, when the mother approached. Aged, bent over, in a black kerchief – I remember, I can see her even now – Marina stood for a long time beside each grave, staring into the faces of the dead. No, she did not cry. Now and then her parched lips moved. What was she saying? Was she reciting a prayer? Or cursing the killers? I was worried: had her mind become clouded from grief?

IVAN SHAMYAKIN, *Snowy Winters*

Belorussian is the language of the new nation of Belarus, where it is spoken by about two-thirds of the population, or 6½ million people. When Belarus became independent in 1991, Belorussian was proclaimed the country's sole official language.

In practice, however, Russian remains dominant. Most Belorussians also speak Russian and tend to use it everyday life. In the cities, with the exception of Grodno near the Polish border, one hears little else.

In 1995 Russian was restored as an official language in Belarus along with Belorussian. The likelihood is that the use of Belorussian will decline, rather than increase, in the decades to come.

Belorussian is written in the Cyrillic alphabet with two letters not found in Russian, the *i* and *ў*.

Moldovan

A fost odată ca-n poveşti,
A fost ca niciodată,
Din rude mari împărăteşti,
O prea frumoasă fată.

Once on a time, as poets sing
High tales with fancy laden,
Born of a very noble king
There lived a wondrous maiden.

Şi era una la părinţi
Şi mândră-n toate cele,
Cum e Fecioara între sfinţi
Şi luna între stele.

An only child, her kinsfolk boon,
So fair, imagination faints;
As though amidst the stars the moon,
Or Mary amidst the saints.

Din umbra falnicelor bolţi
Ea pasul şi-l îndreaptă
Lăngă fereastră unde-n-colţ
Luceafărul aşteaptă.

From 'neath the castle's dark retreat,
Her silent way she wended
Each evening to the window seat
Where Lucifer attended.

Privea în zare cum pe mâri
Răsare si străluce,
Pe mişcătoarele cărări
Corăbii negre duce.

And secretly, with never fail,
She watched his gracious pace,
Where vessels drew their pathless trail
Across the ocean's face.

MIHAI EMINESCU, *Lucifer*

Moldovan is the language of the new nation of Moldova, wedged between Romania and Ukraine. It is spoken by about 3 million people, or two-thirds of the country's population.

Moldovan is actually the same language as Romanian, which since 1860 has been written in the Roman alphabet. Between the two world wars, this area, historically known as Bessarabia, was part of Romania. In 1940, however, it was incorporated into the Soviet Union. The Roman alphabet was replaced with the Cyrillic and the language was called (in English) Moldavian.

Cyrillic lasted for fifty years. In 1989, even before the breakup of the Soviet Union, the country's parliament passed a law naming Moldovan as the sole official language and stipulating that it would be written in the Roman alphabet. Since most Moldovans were familiar with the Roman alphabet in one way or another, the changeover was accomplished rather easily in just a few years.

Тече вода в синє море,
Та не витікає;
Шука козак свою долю,
А долі немає.
Пішов козак світ за очі;
Грає синє море,
Грає серце козацькеє,
А думка говорить:
«Куди ти йдеш, не спитавшись?
На кого покинув
Батька, неньку старенькую,
Молоду дівчину?
На чужині не ті люде, –
Тяжко з ними жити!
Ні з ким буде поплакати,
Ні поговорити».

Сидить козак на тім боці, –
Грає синє море.
Думав, доля зустрінеться, –
Спіткалося горе.
А журавлі летять собі
Додому ключами.
Плаче козак – шляхи биті
Заросли тернами.

The river to the blue sea flows
But flows not back again.
The Cossack seeks his fortune too,
But all his search is vain.
Wide in the world the Cossack goes,
And there the blue sea roars,
The Cossack's heart is boisterous too,
This question it explores:
"Where have you gone without farewell?
To whom has all been left
Of father and old mother now
And of your maid bereft?
These alien folk have alien hearts;
It's hard with them to live!
No one is here to share one's tears
Or gentle words to give."

The Cossack haunts the farther coast, –
And still the blue seas roar.
He hoped to find his fortune there,
But met with sorrow sore.
And while the cranes in coveys seek
The ocean's farther bournes,
The Cossack weeps – the beaten paths
Are overgrown with thorns.

TARAS SHEVCHENKO, *Kobzar*

Ukrainian is the national language of Ukraine. It is spoken by the country's Ukrainian population of 35 million people, but many Ukrainians consider Russian to be their first language and prefer to use it in daily life. This is also largely true of the more than one million Ukrainians living in Russia. Other former Soviet republics with large Ukrainian populations are Kazakhstan (750,000) and Moldova (250,000). There are also many Ukrainian speakers in Belarus and Poland, as well as in Canada (mainly Alberta and Saskatchewan) and the United States.

The use of Ukrainian was severely repressed in Soviet times from 1930 onward, but at independence in 1990 it was made the country's sole official language. Since then the government has aggressively encouraged, and even required, its use in official circles and in the schools. But this is meeting resistance from Russian speakers, who are content to have no more than a working knowledge of the language.

Like Russian, Ukrainian is a Slavic language and thus part of the Indo-European family. The dialects of the western part of the country contain many Polish words; those of the east, Russian. It is written in the Cyrillic alphabet, with three additional letters not found in Russian: the ϵ, pronounced *ye* as in "yet," the *i*, pronounced *ee* as in "meet," and the *ï*, pronounced *ye* as in "year."

Azerbaijani

Мејдана јығылан чамаат көзүнү даш булагдан чыхан нова зилләмишди.

Бирдән су сәсләнди, шән бир курулту илә ахмаға башлады. Узун илләр су һәсрәтиндә олан әһали һәјәчанла бахыр, сусурду. Сүкуту сујун шаграг сәси позурду. Инсанлар гурумуш сәһрада илкин су көрмүш јолчулар ками мәфтунлугла бахыр, динмир, санки сујун сәраба чеврилəчəјиндән горхурдулар. Лакин көрдүкләри һәгигәт иди. Шаирә Натәван доғма елинә Шушаја булаг чəкдирмишди. Бирден һамы чошду, су һәсрәтилə јанан синәләр галхыб енди:

– Јашасын Натәван.

– Вар олсун Хан гызы.

Meydana yığılan camaat gözünü daş bulaqdan çıxan nova zilləmişdi.

Birdən su səsləndi, şən bir gurultu ilə axmağa başladı. Uzun illər su həsrətində olan əhali həyəcanla baxır, susurdu. Sükutu suyun şaqraq səsi pozurdu. İnsanlar qurumuş səhrada ilkin su görmüş yolçular kimi məftunluqla baxır, dinmir, sanki suyun səraba çevriləcəyindən qorxurdular. Lakin gördükləri həqiqət idi. Şairə Natəvan doğma elinə Şuşaya bulaq çəkdirmişdi. Birdən hamı coşdu, su həsrətilə yanan sinələr qalxıb endi:

– Yaşasın Natəvan.

– Var olsun Xan qızı.

The crowd that had gathered in the square gazed at the stone fount.

Suddenly a great noise was heard and the water burst forth with a happy sound. The people, having dreamed of water for many a year, watched in anxious silence. Only the gay murmur of the stream could be heard. Like travelers in the desert coming upon water for the first time, the people watched with delight, but remained silent, as if afraid the water would suddenly disappear like a mirage. But what they were seeing was real. The poetess Natavan had laid a pipe into her native land of Shushu. Suddenly everyone cried out, their chests heaving with the oppressive thirst:

"Long live Natavan!"

"Glory to Khan Gyzy!"

AZIZA JAFARZADE, *Tales of Natavan*

Azerbaijani, also known as Azeri, is spoken both in Azerbaijan and Iran, on the west bank of the Caspian Sea. In the former it is spoken by about 7 million people and is the official language of the country. In Iran it is spoken by another 10 million people in the northwesternmost part of the country, an area also known as Azerbaijan. There are about 250,000 speakers in Iraq.

Azerbaijani is a Turkic language, and thus part of the Altaic family. Traditionally it was written in the Arabic script, but in 1924 the Soviet government introduced the Roman alphabet, and in 1940 the Cyrillic. There are eight characters not found in Russian: ғ, ә, j, ҝ, ө, ү, h, and ҹ.

Following independence in 1991 the government announced that it would reintroduce the Roman alphabet and it is now being phased in. In the new orthography г became *q*, ғ became *ğ*, j became *y*, ҝ became *g*, ө became *ö*, ү became *ü*, ш became *ş*, ҹ became *ç*, ч became *c*, and ы became *ı* (the Turkish undotted *i*).

Georgian

„დმერთისა შეშვედრე, ნუთუ კვლა დამხსნას სოფლისა შრომასა,
ცეცხლსა, წყალსა და მიწასა, ჰაერთა თანა შრომასა;
მომცნეს ფრთენი და აღვფრინდე, მივჰხვდე მას ჩემსა ნდომასა,
დღისით და ღამით ვჰხედვიდე მზისა ელვათა კრთომასა.

„მზე უშენოდ ვერ იქმნების, რათგან მზე ხარ მისი წილი,
განაღამცა მას ეხვევ მისი ეტლი, არ თუ წბილი!
მუნა გნახო, მადვე გსახო, განმინათლო გული ჩრდილი,
თუ სიცოცხლე მწარე მქონდა, სიკვდილიმცა მქონდა ტკბილი!

Entreat God for me; it may be He will deliver me from the travail of the
world and from union with fire, water, earth and air. Let Him give me
wings and I shall fly up, I shall attain my desire – day and night I shall
gaze on the sun's rays flashing in splendor.

The sun cannot be without thee, for thou art an atom of it; of a surety
thou shalt adhere to it as its zodiac, and not as one rejected. There shall
I seek thee; I shall liken thee to it, thou shalt enlighten my darkened
heart. If my life was bitter, let my death be sweet!

SHOTA RUSTAVELI, The Knight in the Tiger's Skin

Georgian is the native language of Georgia, an ancient country located in
Transcaucasia on the southeastern corner of the Black Sea. It is spoken by
about 4 million there, or 80 percent of the total population.

Georgian belongs to the Caucasian family of languages, which are not all
genetically related to each other. It is the most widely spoken of these
languages, and the only one with an ancient literary tradition.

The earliest Georgian alphabet, known as Khutsuri ("church writing"),
dates from the 5th century AD. The present script, called Mkhedruli ("secular
writing"), was introduced in the 11th century. It is written from left to right.
There are 33 letters, with no upper or lower case, and with one letter for each
sound, and one sound for each letter.

The Georgians call themselves *Kartvelebi* and their land *Sakartvelo*. The
language contains some unusual consonant clusters, as may be seen in the
names of such Georgian cities as Tbilisi, Mtskheta, Tkvarcheli, and
Tskhinvali. Many Georgian surnames end in *-idze*, *-adze*, *-dali*, and *-shvili*
(Joseph Stalin's original Georgian name was Dzhugashvili).

The Knight in the Tiger's Skin, the great epic of Georgian literature, was composed about the year 1200. It consists of more than 1,600 four-line stanzas, two of which are shown above. Little is known of the author other than his name.

Armenian

Անցնեի իմ լավ ուղին լավաբար,
Կյանքս չտայի կասկածի մեգին...
Այնպես կուզեի մեկն ինձ հավատար,
Այնպես կուզեի հավատալ մեկին:

Ճահեի կրիվն այս անհավապար,
Սիրո՛վ շահեի փոքրին ու մեծին..
Այնպես կուզեի մեկն ինձ հավատար,
Այնպես կուզեի հավատալ մեկին:

Թող լռությունը անՀեղ որոտար,
Եվ լռեր հավետ աղմուկն անմեկին...
Այնպես կուզեի մեկն ինձ հավատար,
Այնպես կուզեի հավատալ մեկին:

Oh to walk my way with kindness,
And not betray my life to a cloud of suspicions . . .
How I wish that someone would believe me,
How I wish that I could believe someone.

To triumph in an unequal battle,
To embrace with love both small and big,
How I wish that someone would believe me,
How I wish that I could believe someone.

Let the silence burst forth with fury,
And the eternal noise die down for good . . .
How I wish that someone would believe me,
How I wish that I could believe someone.

HAMO SAHYAN

Armenian is the native language of Armenia, the landlocked country in Transcaucasia bordering Turkey and Iran. It is spoken by virtually the entire population, or close to 3½ million people. There are also about 400,000 speakers in neighboring Georgia and sizable communities in Azerbaijan, Iran, Lebanon, Syria, Iraq, Turkey, and the United States.

Armenian constitutes a separate and independent branch of the Indo-European family. The Armenians are an ancient people whose history dates back about 2,500 years. The alphabet was invented by Mesrop Mashtots, a missionary, about the year 400 AD. Originally it consisted of 36 letters (30 consonants and six vowels) to which two were added in the 12th century. There is only one sound for each letter, and one letter for each sound. Most Armenian surnames end in -*yan* (-*ian*), as in Mikoyan and Khachaturian.

The Armenians call their country *Hayastan* and their language *Hayaren*. During many centuries of Persian domination so many Iranian words entered the language that even in the 19th century many linguists thought it a dialect of Persian. It was not until 1875 that it was established as an independent language. Much of the Armenian vocabulary is not to be found in any other Indo-European language. Undoubtedly many words were derived from languages that are now extinct.

Ossetian

Фæззæг

Æхсæлы ызгъæлы,
Лæджирттæг фæбур . . .
Мигъ бады цæгаты,
Нæ йæ тавы хур . . .

Æркарстам, æрластам
Нæ хортæ, нæ хос . . .
Чи кусы йæ мусы,
Чи'лвыны йæ фос . . .

Хор бирæ, фос бирæ
Хуыцауы фæрцы . . .
Нæ хæхбæсты бæркад,
Цы диссаг дæ цы!

Зымæг

Хъызт зымæг, тыхст зымæг,
Нæ катай, нæ мæт!
Йæ бонтæ – фыдбонтæ,
Йæ бахсæв – мæлæт.

Нæ хъæутæ – лæгæттæ,
Нæ фезмæлд – зæйуат.
Фыдæлтæй нын баззад
Зæйы сæфтæн рад.

Нæ мæгуыр, нæ сидзæр,
Æнæ хай куыстæй,
Хуыцаумæ дзыназынц
Ыстонгæй, сыдæй . . .

Autumn

The juniper sheds its foliage,
The buckwheat has turned yellow . . .
The fog has settled on the northern slope,
Which is not warmed by the sun . . .

We have mown and carted away
Our grain, our hay . . .
Some work at threshing,
While others shear their sheep . . .

122

There is much grain and cattle
With the help of God . . .
The abundance of our mountain land,
What a wonder you are!

Winter
Cruel winter, oppressive winter,
Our despair, our sorrow!
Its days are bitter,
Its nights like death.

Our villages are caves,
Our homes are scenes of avalanches.
Our ancestors have ordained that we
Perish in turn under an avalanche.

Our poor ones, our orphans,
Without a drop of work,
To God cry out
Hungry, frozen . . .

KOSTA KHETAGUROV

Ossetian is spoken on the slopes of the Caucasus Mountains, which divide Russia from Georgia. The area in Russia is known as the North Ossetian Republic (capital, Vladikavkaz), while the area in Georgia is called the South Ossetian Autonomous Region (capital, Tskhinvali). Ossetian speakers number about 500,000, two-thirds of whom live in North Ossetia.

Ossetian is an Iranian language: the only one of any consequence spoken in the Caucasus. The Ossetians are believed to be descended from an ancient people called the Alani or Alans. Separated from other Iranian-speaking peoples for nearly 2,000 years, their language has been strongly influenced by the nearby Slavic and Caucasian languages.

There are two important dialects of Ossetian, Iron and Digor, the former (shown above) being the more widely spoken. Written Ossetian may be immediately recognized by its use of the *æ*, a letter to be found in no other language using the Cyrillic alphabet.

Kabardian

ДамэшхуитӀыр ишэщӀарэ зэзэмызэ ар игъэхъейуэ бгъэшхуэ гуэри уафэгум щесырт, мэкъупӀэр къиуфэрэзыхьу. Хуэмурэ хьэуам ар щесырт, къищэкӀун гуэрхэр къилъыхъуэу. Зыхуейр и нэм къыщыпэщӀэмыхуэм, дамэшхуитӀыр зыплӀытхурэ иудыныщӀри, мэщ хьэсэбгъум зритауэ, бгъэр елъэтэкӀырт. Мыхъейуэ икӀи дахэ дыдэу ар зэресыр хьэлэмэт щыхъуат Бэрокъуэми, и нэр тенауэ абы кӀэлъыплъыррт. Зы напӀэзыпӀэ закъуэкӀэ бгъэр къызэтеувыӀэ хуэдэ хъуащ, итӀанэ и дамитӀ шещӀар зришэлӀэжщ, и щхьэр егъэзыхауэ зыкъуритӀупщхьэхри, мэшым зыхидзащ. Дакъикъэ ныкъуи дэмыкӀауэ, бгъэжьым зыкъуиӀэтыжащ, дамэшхуитӀыр хьэлъэу иудыныщӀэурэ. Лъэбжьанэ жанхэмкӀэ тхьэкӀумэкӀыхьыр бгъэм зэщӀиубыдауэ и лъэныкъомкӀэ къихьу щилъагъум, Бэрокъуэм и плӀэм илъ фочыр къипхъуэтащ.

Spreading its two tremendous wings and occasionally flapping them, a great eagle soared through the sky, circling over the meadow. It glided slowly through the air, seeking some prey. Not spotting what it was looking for, it flapped its great wings about five times and, coming to a millet patch, began to circle the perimeter. Baroko was delighted that the bird glided gracefully without flapping its wings and kept his eyes riveted on it. In an instant the bird seemed to stop, then, folding its wings, swept down headfirst and dove into the millet. Not a half-minute later it flew up again, violently flapping its wings. Seeing that the eagle's sharp claws were clutching a hare and that it was flying directly toward him, Baroko grabbed the gun on his shoulder.

KHACHÍM TEUNOV, *The Shadzhamokov Family*

Kabardian is spoken in the Caucasus region of Russia, principally in the republics of Kabardino-Balkariya (capital, Nalchik) and Karachayevo-Cherkesiya (capital, Cherkessk). It is spoken by two peoples: the Kabardians, who number about 325,000, and the Circassians (Russian, *cherkesy*), who number about 50,000. The language is thus sometimes referred to as Kabardin-Cherkess.

The Kabardians, Circassians, and a third people (the Adygeis, who speak the closely related Adygei language) are sometimes referred to collectively as Circassians. Historically, the Circassians date back to ancient times, and until the middle of the 19th century occupied almost the entire region between the Caucasus Mountains, the Kuban River, and the Black Sea. Following the annexation of the region by Russia in 1864, several hundred thousand Circassians migrated south, and some are still to be found today in Turkey and Syria.

Kabardian belongs to the Northwestern branch of the Caucasian family of languages. It is written in the Cyrillic alphabet with only one additional letter, the I, which is common to many of the Caucasian languages.

Chechen

Ламанах духдуьйлу шал шийла шовданаш
Шиэн бекъачу кийрана Іаббалца ца молуш,
Іин кІоргиэ буьйлуш, мела муж муьйлуш,
Варшан йистиэ йолу маргІал сийна буц
Шиэн оьздачу зоьрхана буззалца ца юуш,
Орцал лахабуьйлуш, сема ладуьйгІуш,
Иччархочун тоьпуо лацарна, кхоьруш,
Дехачу диэгІана буткъа мотт хьоькхуш,
Мокхазан бердах куьран га хьоькхуш,
Попан орамах торгІала тІа детташ,
Лергаш дуьхьал туьйсуш, кур аркъал туьйсуш,
Гу лекха буьйлуш, гІелашка ва гІергІаш,
Масаниэ сай лиэла гІелашца ва боцуш!
Вай биэн дац, ва кІентий, аьллар ца хуьлуш?

From the depths of the mountains gush the ice-cold springs,
But he doesn't fill his lean stomach there.
Rather he descends to the depths of the ravine and drinks from a
 warm puddle.
The wooded slope is bordered by rising fresh blue grass,
But he doesn't fill his noble belly there.
Coming out below the wooded hills, he listens carefully,
Anxious to avoid the dreaded hunter's gun.
Licking his long body with his slender tongue,
Sharpening his branched antlers on the flinty shore,
Striking his spotted hind leg on the plane tree's root,
Pointing his ears forward, tossing his antlers onto his back,
Climbing high on the hill, bellowing to the does,
How many stags walk without their mates?
And are there not many lads besides us of whom the same is true?

The Stag (Chechen folk song)

Chechen is spoken in Russia's republic of Chechnya (in Russian pronounced *chech-NYA*), located in the Caucasus with its capital at Grozny. Together with the closely related Ingush language (the two are for the most part mutually intelligible), it constitutes the North-Central branch of the Caucasian family of languages. There are about one million speakers. As in Kabardian and other Caucasian languages, the alphabet contains the additional letter I.

126

Avar

Зодоса цIер гIадин гулла балелъул
Гуллий кьураб керен кьуризабичIо.
Кьвагьулаго чабхъен тIаде кIанцIидал
Кодоб бирданги ккун тIаде вахъана.
ЦохIо кьвагьун аралъ кIиго вегана,
КIиго кьвагьаралъги лъабго лъукъана.
Вакка-ваккаравго ккезе гьавуна.
Боял тIуризарун, тIаде гулла бан
ТIаде чи виччачIо цохIо гIадамцин.

The bullets fly like hail from the sky.
But he doesn't turn his breast away from them.
And when they set upon him with guns ablaze
He stood up tall with rifle in hand.
One shot and two men fell,
A second shot wounded three more.
Whoever appeared met his death.
He scattered the army with a hail of bullets,
Not a single soul could get near.

Zelimkhan (Avar song of heroism)

Avar is spoken in Russia's republic of Dagestan (capital, Makhachkala), situated in the Caucasus on the west bank of the Caspian Sea. In this single republic, smaller than Scotland, some 30 different languages are spoken, most of them falling within a single subdivision of the Caucasian family known as the Dagestan languages. Avar, spoken in the southwestern part, ranks first in number of speakers with about 600,000. Like the other Caucasian languages, it contains the special letter I. The Avars of today (Russian, *avartsy*) bear no relationship to the ancient Avars (Russian, *avary*), a powerful Turkic-speaking people of the 6th and 7th centuries.

Tatar

Өстенə искерə төшкəн язгы пальто, аягына тула оек белəн резина галош кигəн Газинур, Миңнурыйның ике белəгеннəн тотып, соңгы мəртəбə аның кадерле күзлəренə текəлеп карады. Миңнурый гаҗəеп зур түземлелек күрсəтə иде. Йокысыз үткəн төн аның матур йөзенə тирəн кайгы эзен салса да, анда: «Син киткəч, ике кечкенə бала белəн мин берүзем нишлəрмен, көнемне ничек үткəрермен?» – дип аптырап, өметсезлеккə төшү дə, тетрəү дə юк иде. Ул бер генə тапкыр да еламады. Тик менə хəзер, китəр минутта, Газинур аның ике белəгеннəн тотып, күзлəренə текəлгəч кенə, аның озын керфеклəре дерелдəп китте.

Wearing a shabby spring coat, country-style overshoes, and woolen stockings, Gazinur held Minnuri's hand in his, and looked into her dear eyes for the last time. Although the sleepless agonizing night had left a trace of sadness on her pretty face, she showed no signs of despair or confusion. In her loving look there was no suggestion of the usual question in such situations: "What will I do without you, alone, with two small children? How will I live?" Only now, at the moment of saying goodbye, when Gazinur took Minnuri in his arms, did her long eyelashes begin to quiver.

ABDURAKHMAN ABSALYAMOV, *Gazinur*

Tatar, also spelled Tartar, is spoken principally in European Russia, though there are also speakers in Siberia, the Crimea, Central Asia, and other countries. The Tatars are divided into a number of branches, the most important being the 5 million Volga Tatars, who inhabit the lands drained by the Volga River and its tributaries. The greatest concentrations of Volga Tatars are in the republic of Tatarstan (capital, Kazan), where they number about 3 million, and in the neighboring republic of Bashkortostan, where they number about 2 million. Another one million Tatar speakers are scattered throughout parts of European Russia.

A second branch of the Tatars, known as the Siberian Tatars, live in western Siberia, mainly along the Irtysh River. They number about 100,000. A third branch, the Crimean Tatars, were deported from the Crimean Peninsula to Central Asia in 1944. Today they number about 400,000 in Uzbekistan and 300,000 in Kazakhstan. Some 250,000 others returned to the Crimea in the 1990s.

Tatar is a Turkic language belonging to the Altaic family. The Tatars first appeared in Russian history in the 13th century when, as the Mongols, they overran most of the country and settled down to rule. The new state was known as the Golden Horde, with its capital at Sarai, near the modern city of Astrakhan. Over the course of the next two centuries they absorbed the

Turkic language of the area and much of Turkic culture as well. When the Horde began to crumble in the 15th century, a number of new Tatar khanates were formed: Kazan, Astrakhan, Siberian, and Crimean. Kazan and Astrakhan, the largest of the four, were overrun and conquered by Russia a century later.

Originally written in the Arabic script, Tatar switched to the Roman alphabet in 1928. In 1938 the Soviet government introduced the Cyrillic alphabet with six additional letters: ә, ө, γ, җ, ң, and h. In the year 2000 the government of Tatarstan announced that it will gradually replace the Cyrillic alphabet with the Roman. The process is scheduled for completion in 2011. This will be the first use of the Roman alphabet in the post-Soviet Russian Federation.

Bashkir

Ятаҡхана тып-тын булып ҡала. Көндөң күп өлөшөндә гөрләп торған ятаҡханаға бындай тынлыҡ килешмәй. Мәктәптә уҡыусы «художниктәр» тарафынан стенаға күмер, карандаш кәләмдәр менән эшләнгән рәсемдәр зә ятаҡхана өҫтөнә моңайып карап ҡалған һымаҡ була.

Уның урынына был минутта ашханала көслө шау-шыу, йәнлелек башлана. Уҡыусылар ҡыҙарып янған тоноҡ нурлы электрик лампаһы яҡтыһында, кухнялаге киң төплө бәләкәй тәҙрәнән ҡалай һауыттарға һалдырып аш алалар.

All is quiet in the dormitory. For a place usually bustling with activity all day, such quiet is unusual. Even the charcoal and pencil drawings on the walls done by the school "artists" look down somehow dejectedly.

At that moment there is a commotion in the mess hall. In the dim reddish light of an electric lamp the students are served tin bowls of soup through a small window.

SAGIT AGISH, The Foundation

Bashkir is spoken principally in Russia's republic of Bashkortostan (capital, Ufa), which lies to the west of the southern slopes of the Ural Mountains. It is another of the many Turkic languages of Russia, and has about one million speakers. It is very similar to Tatar, also widely spoken in Bashkortostan. The Bashkir alphabet is based on the Cyrillic, with the additional letters ғ, ҙ, ҡ, ң, ө, ҫ, ү, һ, and ә.

Chuvash

Çулçă сарса тикĕсленнĕ йывăçсем пархатарлă сывлăмпа çăвăннă хыççăн çăмăллăн вăшлатса иртекен çилпе шăлăнса тасалнă та йăлтăркка ешĕл курăнаççĕ. Темле йывăç та ÿсет çĕр çинче, пурин валли те вырăн çитет, темелле: хăшĕ пахчара саркаланса савăнать, хăшĕ çурт умĕнче юри тăратнă хурал пек ларать, ял урлă каçакан тарăн çырмара та йăмрасем таçта çÿле кармашаççĕ. Çырма варринче çеç, лутра карлăклă кĕпер тĕлĕнче, иртен-çÿрен валли ятарласа çавра хапха касса хăварнă пек, уçлăх юлнă. Çав патвар йăмрасем çырмана пĕтĕмпе хупăрласа илнĕ, хĕвел çути аяла кăнтăр варринче те хĕсĕнсе кăна сăрхăнать.

The leafy trees, bathed in pure morning dew and dried in the soft wind, make a beautiful scene. They catch your eye wherever you look. The trees are everywhere. All sorts grow on the earth, there is plenty of room here for every kind of plant. You can see some in the orchards where they enjoy the grassy fertile soil. Others you can see lined up in front of the houses like guards. Even the ravine dividing the village is crowded with tall willow trees. Only down at the bottom a tiny bridge with low railings makes a gate in the wall of them. The trees and bushes seem to have conquered the whole ravine. Even at noon the rays of the sun struggle fiercely to get through the thick branches to the shaded roots.

NIKOLAI ILBEKOV, *Brown Bread*

Chuvash is spoken in Russia's middle Volga region, especially in the republic of Chuvashiya whose capital is Cheboksary. Though it is one of the Turkic languages, it differs markedly from the others, and the question of its affiliation was long a subject of debate. There are about 1½ million speakers. Chuvash is written in the Cyrillic alphabet with four non-Russian letters: ă, ĕ, ç, and ÿ.

Kalmyk

Бахта ил нәр болад, күргн үзгдәд хуурв. Гиичин улс мөрләд, нәәрин нөөрмү улс тарлһнла, Булһн гертән тесҗ сууҗ ядад, Киштә талан гүүһәд күрәд ирв. – Нүднчн хавдад же болад бәәжч, мә эн киитн усар уһаҗ ав, – гиҗ келәд Киштә бор ааһар, бутхачсн, шаврта ус утхҗ авад Булһнд өгв. – Нә болв. Хавдрнь бийнь хәрх. – Шулун кел, ямаран бәәдлтә, кениг дурасн юмн бәәж? – гиҗ сурад, Булһн, торад ямаран хәрү өкән медҗ ядҗ бәәсн Киштән өвдг түшәд суув.

The noisy party was over, at last the bridegroom had appeared. When the groom's family had left and the last sleepy guests had gone their way, Bulgan could not sit home and raced to see her girlfriend Kishtya. "Your eyes are awfully swollen, wash your face with some cold water," said Kishtya, taking a cup of cloudy water and handing it to her. "It's all right. The swelling will subside on its own. I'd rather you tell me what you think of my fiancé, whom he reminds you of," asked Bulgan, resting her elbows on Kishtya's knees. Kishtya sat silently, not knowing how to answer her questions.

BAATAR BASANGOV, *The Truth of the Past*

Kalmyk, or Kalmuck, is spoken in Russia's republic of Kalmykia (capital, Elista), located just to the west of the Volga River delta, northwest of the Caspian Sea. Its speakers, the Kalmyks, a Buddhist people numbering about 150,000, are the descendants of Mongol nomads who migrated to this region from central Asia in the 17th century. The language is thus most closely related to modern Mongolian, as well as to Buryat, of southern Siberia, the three belonging to the Mongolian branch of the Altaic family. The Kalmyk alphabet is based on the Cyrillic, with the non-Russian letters ә, h, җ, ң, ө, and ү.

Mordvin

Теде мейле Чурьканов эсензэ ёжос сась а ёвтавикс якшамодо. Пеензэ калцкаевсть вейс, рунгованзо прок ульнесть сялгонезь кельме эень салмукскеть. Сорнось рунгозо, эзть кунсоло кедтне ды пильгтне. Сон панжинзе сельмензэ ды несь кодамо-бути тусто сув ёнов молиця валдо, кона совась решоткасо пирязь сэрей вальматнева. Куватьс эзь чарькодеве капитанонтень, косо сон ашти.

Later Churkanov regained consciousness from the indescribable cold. His teeth were chattering, his body felt as if it were being pricked with needles of cold ice. His body shivered, his hands and feet were numb. He opened his eyes and glimpsed a sort of hazy light coming in through the high grated windows. For a long time the captain had no idea where he was.

A. SHCHEGLOV, *Happiness*

Mordvin is spoken over a broad area of European Russia, lying generally in the middle Volga region and extending as far as the Ural Mountains. There are about one million speakers, one-third of whom live in the republic of Mordovia with its capital at Saransk.

Mordvin belongs to the Finnic branch of the Finno-Ugric languages, the main division of the Uralic family. There are two dialects, Erzya and Moksha, which are sufficiently different that communication can sometimes be a problem. The word "no" for example is *aras'* in Erzya, but *ash* in Moksha. The passage above is in Erzya.

Within the republic of Mordovia Erzya is generally spoken in the east, while Moksha is spoken in the west. Speakers of the former outnumber those of the latter by about two to one. The Mordvin alphabet contains exactly the same letters as the Russian.

Udmurt

Дёми армие мынонзэ уно уйёсты изьылытэк витиз. Таманлы умме усьылыкуз но пӧртэм вӧтъёсын курадӟылйз. Тушмонъёсын ожмаськылйз.

Гожтэт басьтэм бераз Дёми кык нунал ӵоже военкоматысь ӧз кошкылы ни. Туннэ солы военкомат ивортйз:

– Ну, Демян Платонович, дасяськы! Армие мыныны туннэ ик быгатйськод.

– Мон дась! – шумпотыса, мултэс квараен черектйз Дёми.

Dyoma had not slept for several nights awaiting his induction into the army. And when he did doze off for a bit he had all kinds of dreams. He was fighting the enemy.

After receiving his orders Dyoma did not leave the induction center for two days. Today the induction center told him:

"Well, Demyan Platonovich, get ready! Today is the day you may enter the army."

"I am ready!" cried Dyoma in a loud voice.

PYOTR BLINOV, *I Want to Live*

Udmurt is spoken mainly in Russia's republic of Udmurtiya, which lies just to the north of Tatarstan, and whose capital is Izhevsk. Another of the Finno-Ugric languages, it is most closely related to Komi, the two forming the so-called Permian branch of this family. There are about 600,000 speakers. It is written in the Cyrillic alphabet, but with frequent use of the dieresis, which appears over six different letters: ё, ö, й, ж, ӟ, and ӵ. The last four of these are not to be found in any other language.

Mari

Марий элысе моло йогын вӱд дене таҥастарымаште Элнетыште
шолым волташат, пырням покташат йӧсӧ. Элнет пеш талын йога.
Йогышыжла, осал янлыкла сержым пурын каткала. Серыште
кокшӱдӧ ияш пӱнчӧ шога гынат, тудымат вожге вӱдышкӧ
шуҥгалтара. Элнет ик сержым пуреш, вес веланже ошмам шава,
тӱрлӧ-тӱрлӧ тӱрлем дене сылнештараш тӧча. Тиде ок сите гын,
Элнет южо вере ожнысыла кадырген каяш ӧркана да, гоч
пӱчкын, корныжым угыч виктарен, ӧрдыжкӧ каен колта, а
тошто корнешыже икса лийын кодеш. Южгунам тыгай икса
ятырак кугу, келге лиеш да тыгай иксаште кол пеш чот тӱла.

Floating logs and rolling timber is more difficult on the Ilet than on other
rivers of the Mari region. The Ilet is very turbulent. As it flows along,
like a ferocious animal, it gnaws and eats away its own shores. If a two-
hundred-year-old pine tree should be standing on the shore, the river
pushes it – roots and all – into the water. The Ilet gnaws at one shore,
but on the other it deposits sand as if trying to decorate it with various
designs. And as if this were not enough, if the river is too lazy to flow
as before – wriggling along, then cutting straight across, correcting its
bed – it strikes out in another direction, while bays are formed over the
old bed. Sometimes such a bay is rather large and deep, and various
fishes spawn there.

SERGEI CHAVAIN, *The Ilet*

Mari is spoken principally in Russia's republic of Mari-El (capital, Ioshkar-
Ola), located in central European Russia directly north of Chuvashiya
and Tatarstan. About 300,000 speakers live here, with 100,000 others in
Bashkortostan to the east, and another 100,000 in neighboring regions.

Mari is one of the Finno-Ugnic languages. There are two main dialects,
Meadow and Hill, the former spoken by about 80 percent of the total. The
Mari alphabet contains the non-Russian letters *ä*, *ҥ*, *ö*, *ÿ*, and *ӹ*.

Komi

Оліс-выліс Öньö-макö. Сылöн вöлі вит монь: сёй монь, сюмöд-тупыль-монь, турун-кöрöб-монь, рос монь да гадь монь. Öньö-макö ачыс век педзö. Сёй моньöс вала ыстас. Зэрмас дай сёй монь нильзяс. Сюмöд-тупыль-моньöс ыстас пывсян ломтыны. Сійö истöг тувсö öзтас, а биыс бöжас кутчысяс, дай сотчас. Турун-кöрöб-моньöс ыстас мöслы турун сетны. Тöв пöльыштас да турун-кöрöб-моньöс мöслы вомас нуас. Мöс сійöс сёяс. Рос моньöс ыстас сарай чышкыны да джодж плака костö сибдас. Гадь монь сералас, сералас дай потö. А Öньö-макö век педзö.

Once upon a time there lived a man named Önyö-makö. He had five daughters-in-law: one made of clay, another of birch bark, another of hay, another who was a broom, another a bubble. Önyö-makö himself just stood around. The daughter-in-law of clay he sent to fetch water. It began to rain and she was washed away. The daughter-in-law of birch bark he sent to light the fire in the bath. She struck a match, her tail caught fire, and she burned up. The daughter-in-law of hay he sent to feed hay to the cow. The wind began to blow and swept her into the mouth of the cow. The cow ate her up. The daughter-in-law who was a broom he sent to sweep the shed but she got caught between the floor-boards. The daughter-in-law who was a bubble laughed and laughed until she burst. And Önyö-makö just stood around.

Komi is another of the Finno-Ugric languages spoken in northeastern European Russia. It is closely related to Udmurt, spoken to the south, the two constituting the Permian branch of this family.

There are two dialects of Komi. Traditionally they were known as Zyrian and Permyak, but in the Soviet era the former was designated Komi-Zyrian or simply Komi, the latter Komi-Permyak. Komi-Zyrian is spoken by about 275,000 people in what is now the Komi Republic (capital, Syktyvkar), which extends over a large area (the size of California) eastward to the North Ural Mountains and north past the Arctic Circle. Komi-Permyak is spoken by about 125,000 people in the much smaller Komi-Permyak National District (capital, Kudymkar), bordering the Komi Republic on the south.

Komi is written in the Cyrillic alphabet with two additional letters, the *i* and *ö*.

Turkmen

Түркменистан Меркези Азияда ерлешйәр, онуң гадымы тарыхы бар. Гечмишде бизиң юрдумызда хас улы цивилизациялар дөрәпдир. Олар Парфия патышалыгыдыр, әгирт улы Селжуклар, Үргенч империяларыдыр. Шонуң үчин-де бизиң топрагымызда хер 50 километрден тарыхы ядыгәрликлериң бардыгы төтәнден дәлдир. Олар гечмишде ажайып десгаларың бина эдилендигине, бизиң себитимизиң гүлләп өсендигине шаятлык эдйәр. Хава, тарых Гүнбатар билен Гүндогарың арасындакы гадымы чакны-шыклар хакында шаятнамалардан долупдыр. Булар Рим легионерлериниң чозушларыдыр ве Чингиз ханың бизиң себитимизе гандөкүшликли йөришидир. Эмма урушлардан башга-да тарых бизиң гүнлеримизе хызматдашлыгың гымматлы ыкдысады нусгаларыны хем етирди. Бу болса геосыясы чатрыкда Түркменистаның ичинден гечйән Бейик Йүпек ёлуна өврүлди.

Türkmenistan Merkezi Aziýada ýerleşýär, onuň gadymy taryhy bar. Geçmişde biziň ýurdumyzda has uly ciwilizaciýalar döräpdir. Olar Parfiýa patyşalygydyr, ägirt uly Seljuklar, Ürgenç imperiýalarydyr. Şonuň uçin-de biziň topragymyzda her 50 kilometrden taryhy ýadygärlikleriň bardygy tötänden däldir. Olar geşmişde ajaýyp desgalaryň bina edilendigine, biziň sebitimiziň gülläp ösendigine şaýatlyk edýär. Hawa, taryh Günbatar bilen Gündogaryň arasyndaky gadymy çaknyşyklar hakynda şaýatnamalardan dolupdyr. Bular Rim legionerleriniň çozuşlarydyr we Çingiz hanyň biziň sebitimize gandöküşlikli ýörişidir. Emma uruşlardan başga-da taryh biziň günler-imize hyzmatdaşlygyň gymmatly ykdysady nusgalaryny hem ýetirdi. Bu bolsa geosyýasy çatrykda Türkmeninstanyň içinden geçýän Beýik Ýüpek ýoluna öwrüldi.

Turkmenistan, a country of Central Asia, has an ancient history. Great civilizations of the past flourished on our territory. There were the Parthian kingdom, the great Seljuk Empire, and the Urgench empire. It is no accident that in our country every fifty kilometers or so you will see an historic monument attesting to the great events of the past, from the time when our region was flourishing. Yes, history is full of evidence of ancient wars between East and West. There were the invasion of our region by the Roman legionnaires, and the bloody campaigns of Genghis Khan. But aside from wars, this history provided a valuable basis for economic development. Lying at a geopolitical crossroads, it gave rise to the great Silk Route which passed through the territory of Turkmenistan.

Turkmen, also known as Turkoman, is spoken in the new nation of Turkmenistan, lying on the eastern shore of the Caspian Sea and bordering Iran and Afghanistan. It is spoken there by about 3½ million people, or 70 percent of the population. There are also about one million speakers in Iran and 500,000 in Afghanistan.

Closely related to Turkish, Turkmen is a member of the Turkic branch of the Altaic family of languages. Traditionally it was written in the Arabic script, but in 1927 the Soviet government introduced the Roman alphabet, and in 1940 the Cyrillic. Following independence in 1991 the new government decreed a gradual transition back to the Roman alphabet. The Russian letter *в* was replaced by *w*, *x* by *h*, *ж* by *ž*, *ы* by *y*, *й* by *ý*, initial *e* by *ýe*, *э* by *e*, *ё* by *ýo*, *ю* by *ýu*, *я* by *ýa*, *ч* by *ç*, and *ш* by *ş*. For the non-Russian letters, *ә* became *ä*, *ө* became *ö*, *ү* became *ü*, *ң* became *ň*, and *җ* became *j*.

Uzbek

– Хайр, биз бу дағдағаларни ўртадан кўтаришга ҳаракат қилурмиз, – деди Навоий қатъий оҳанг билан. – Гарчи бу мазҳабларнинг бирини ўзгасидан афзал кўрмасак ҳам, улуснинг бирлигини эътиборга олурмиз. Иним, дунёда китоб ўқимоқдан, тафаккурдан, шеър айтмоқдан ўзга завқбахш машғулот йўқдир. Табиатим кўпроқ бу томонга мойил эди. Сокин бир масканда яшаб, бу завқ дарёсида сузмоқчи эдим. Лекин, менга, маълумингиз, давлатда вазифа бердилар ... Ёлғиз эл ва улус манфаатини назарга олиб, мансабни қабул этдим. Бу муборак юртда қилинадиган ишлар бениҳоят кўпдир. Бу ишларнинг ҳар бирига элимиз асрлардан бери ташнадир.

– Xayr, biz bu dag'dag'alarni o'rtadan ko'tarishga harakat qilurmiz, – dedi Navoiy qat'iy ohang bilan. – Garchi bu mazhablarning birini o'zgasidan afzal ko'rmasak ham, ulusning birligini e'tiborga olurmiz. Inim, dunyoda kitob o'qitmoqdan, tafakkurdan, she'r aytmoqdan o'zga zavqbaxsh mashg'ulot yo'qdir. Tabiatim ko'proq bu tomonga moyil edi. Sokin bir maskanda yashab, bu zavq daryosida suzmoqchi edim. Lekin, menga, ma'lumingiz, davlatda vazifa berdilar ... Yolg'iz el va ulus manfaatini nazarga olib, mansabni qabul etdim. Bu muborak yurtda qilinadigan ishlar benihoyat ko'pdir. Bu ishlarning har biriga elimiz asrlardan beri tashnadir.

"Then let us try to prevent such dissension," said Navoi firmly. "We must not show preference for any one religious doctrine. Brother, there is no pleasanter occupation in this world than just reading books, contemplating and writing verses. By nature I am cut out for just such a life. I should like to live in some quiet place and float lazily on the sea of enjoyment but, as you know, I have been given a court appointment. I accepted it for the sake of the people and the country. There is an endless number of things to be done in this land and the people have awaited each one of them for centuries."

AIBEK, *Navoi*

Uzbek is spoken in Uzbekistan, the most populous of the newly independent states of central Asia. There are about 20 million speakers here, or 80 percent of the total population. Another 5 million speakers are to be found in neighboring countries: 2 million in Afghanistan, one million in Tajikistan, 650,000 in Kyrgyzstan, 400,000 in Turkmenistan, and 350,000 in Kazakhstan.

Uzbek is another of the Turkic languages, part of the Altaic family. Much of its vocabulary, however, is Persian, rather than Turkish, as Tajik (Persian) speakers have long been prominent in the Uzbek cities of Samarkand and Bukhara.

At the time of the Russian Revolution Uzbek was written in the Arabic script, but this was replaced by the Roman alphabet in 1927 and the Cyrillic in 1940. In 1993 the new government announced that the country would gradually revert back to the Roman alphabet, the target date being 2005. The four Uzbek letters not in the Russian alphabet were changed as follows: ÿ became *o*', г became *g*', қ became *q*, and х became *h*.

Aibek is the pseudonym of Musa Tashmukhamedov, whose historical novel *Navoi* was published in 1945. Its title is the name of a famous Uzbek poet and statesman of the 15th century.

Kazakh

Бойдақ жылқының бәрі жайылысты тастап, сонау биік
адырдың басына шығып ап үздеп тур. Өрістен қайтқан
қоралы қой да су маңына шубырып, баурын сызға төсеп,
бүйірін соғып жатыр. Жайылысты ойлар емес. Қумаса су
қасынан турар емес. Сиыр атаулы Бақанас суынан бөлінген
қара су, шалшық суларға кіріп, көлбей-көлбей жатып апты.
Бірен-саран оқшау шыққан тайынша, қунажын болса,
сәйгелдің қуғынына ушырап, қутырғандай жосып жүр.
Қуйрығын шаншып алып, қос танауы делдиіп, екі көзі дәл
бір сойғалы жатқандай аларып, ежірейіп ап, жынданғандай
жүйткиді.

The flocks had left the pastures and were herded together on the bleak
crest of a distant hill, whence they had been driven by the tireless and
vicious gadflies. The sheep returning from the meadows wallowed limply
in the mud at the side of the river. The cows had waded into the water
and stood dozing, only their heads showing above the water. The few
calves left on the bank were rushing frantically to and fro, trying to shake
off the gadflies. With lashing tails, distended nostrils, and bulging eyes,
they dashed about, as if to escape slaughter.

MUKHTAR AUEZOV, *Abai*

Kazakh is the native language of Kazakhstan, which stretches from the
Caspian Sea to the Chinese border. It is spoken by about 8 million people
there, or slightly more than half the population. There are also about one
million speakers in Uzbekistan, one million in China, and 100,000 in
Mongolia.

Kazakh is one of the Turkic languages which form a branch of the Altaic
family. It was originally written in the Arabic script, but in 1926 the Soviet
government introduced the Roman alphabet, and then in 1940 replaced it
with one based on Cyrillic. It contains a number of special characters,
including *ә, ғ, қ, ң, ө, ұ, ү, h,* and *i.* There are tentative plans to revert back
to the Roman alphabet some time in the future.

Tajik

Аз Тирезаҳои фарохи троллейбус иморатҳои зебои се-чор ошьёна, дарахтони баланд-баланди хиёбон ва гурӯҳ-гурӯҳ одамон, лентаи кино барин, як-як аз мадди назар мегузаштанд. Қодирҷон ба берун нигоҳ карда ҳайрон мешуд, ки Душанбеи дилкушо чи қадар тез ободу васеъ шуда истодааст. Дирӯзакак дар ҷои ана он бинои сербари Унвермаги Марказӣ қатор-қатор дӯкончаҳои молфурӯшии тахтагӣ меистоданд. Вай аз дил гузаронд, ки шаш моҳ боз дар ҳамин шаҳр таҳсили илм мекунаду аммо ҳанӯз на ҳамаи растаю хиёбонҳои онро дидааст.

Through the wide windows of the trolleybus there flashed by, as if in a motion picture, the attractive three- and four-storey buildings, the immensely tall trees, the avenues, and the endless stream of people. Kadirzhan looked out and marveled at how fast Dushanbe was being built up. On the spot where there now stood the tall building of the Central Department Store it seemed that only yesterday there were rows of wooden trading benches. He reflected that although he had been studying in the city for six months, he had still not gotten around to seeing all the avenues and squares.

ABDUMALIK BAKHORI, *A Window Without Light*

Tajik is the principal language of Tajikistan, which borders Afghanistan and China. It is spoken by about 5 million people there, or more than 80 percent of the country's population. Tajik is actually the same language as Persian, though since 1940 it has been written in the Cyrillic alphabet. An Iranian language and thus of the Indo-European family, it stands apart from the other major languages of former Soviet Central Asia, which are all Turkic.

The Tajik alphabet contains six letters not in the Russian alphabet – four (ғ, қ, х, and ч) that appear in other former Soviet languages, and two (ӣ and ӯ) that are unique to Tajik. There are tentative plans to switch to the Arabic (not the Roman) alphabet at some point in the future.

Kyrgyz

Сүрөттүн тээ ички тереңинде – күзгү асмандын ала-бүркөк чет жакасы. Шамал бирин-серин булуттарды бир жакка бет алдырып, алыста кылтайган чокуларга жандатып, кыялата айдап бара жатат. Андан берки көрүнүштө – бозоргон сары талаа, кең өзөн. Чет-четтен чийлер ыкташып, жаан-чачындан кийин топурагы борпоң тоборсуп карайган жолдо, катарлаш баскан эки жолоочунун изи тигинден бери чубайт. Жолоочулар улам жакындаган сайын алардын издери жерге даана түшүп, өздөрү азыр дагы бир-эки кадам шилтешсе, рамканын сыртына аттап, ушундан ары кетип калчудай сезилет.

The background of the picture is a patch of bleak autumn sky with the wind chasing scattered clouds along the highest mountain tops in sight. A broad valley with a steppe of golden bronze color and two wayfarers walking side by side on the road black and damp from recent rains, with waving clusters of needle grass on both its sides, form its foreground. In the course of coming to the fore the footprints gradually become clearer and it seems that they will disappear behind the frame if they take one step more.

CHINGIS AITMATOV, *Jamila*

Kyrgyz is spoken in the new nation of Kyrgyzstan by more than 3 million people out of a total population of 5 million. Like Turkmen, Uzbek, and Kazakh, it is one of the Turkic languages, which form a branch of the Altaic family.

Kyrgyz was written in the Arabic script until 1928, when the Roman alphabet was introduced, which in turn was replaced by the Cyrillic in 1940. It contains three additional letters, the ү, ө, and ң. A transition to the Roman alphabet is planned for the future.

Chingis Aitmatov, born in 1928, is Kyrgyzstan's most renowned writer.

Nenets

Тецьда нгэрм' нянгы яха'на ханярина варк' тамна нгокаць. Харевдавэй' сармикэця' нись пин' Арктика' латдувна сарвырнгаць, пыдо' сынггоси' Северной Ледовитой океан' нгохо'на илець. Вадмбои' варк' Сибирь еси' ня'авха'на нгадиберцеты'. Салабаха'на варк' Берингов ямд ереберцеты', сян по' тяхана нгани' ханена' Охотской ямгана сэр' варкм хадаць.

In the northern polar countries there were bears everywhere. The fearless animals bravely roamed the great expanses of the Arctic or lived placidly on the islands of the Arctic Ocean. Occasionally bears were discovered at the mouths of the Siberian rivers. By floating on ice floes they reached the Bering Sea, and a few years ago trappers caught a white bear in the Sea of Okhotsk.

Nenets is spoken in northernmost Russia, in an area extending from the White Sea (in Europe) on the west to the Yenisei River (in Asia) on the east, a distance of about 1,500 miles. Its speakers, the Nenets (Russian, *nentsy*), number about 35,000. Most of them live in the Nenets National District, with its capital at Naryan Mar; about 3,500 live in the Yamal-Nenets National District to the east, whose capital is Salekhard. Nenets is the most widely spoken of the Samoyed languages, which forms the smaller of the two branches of the Uralic family.

145

Khanty

Этәр, ватлəг котəл вəлгал. Мәрәм пајдывтәт чымəл н'өгагасәт. Т'и котəлнə мä т'әкäјəглäмнä ула мәнгäлəм. Мәӈ рытна мәнгäлөг.

Воронтнə јəм вəлгал. Мәӈ пӱт'кäл'и лулпəнытə тəгы колəнтəгалөг.

Т'и алнə воронтнə äрки ул вəлгал.

Кунтəнə киллөг ула ван'галөг тəлəп, мәӈəн лəгə əддə југ канӈа амəгалөг. Мəӈтөг ул литä äр пəдəкпä нөрəгтəгäлөг. Мäпөӈкäмөг вäл'онтог көт'əрки нуг-лөккäл.

It was a bright and calm day. Only the leaves of the birch tree rustled softly. That day I went with my younger sisters to pluck berries. We went by boat.

It was good in the forest. We listened to the singing of the little birds. In that year there were a lot of berries in the forest.

When we had plucked our pots full, we put them beside a big tree. We ran far and wide to eat berries. Before me, out of the bushes leaped a streaked squirrel.

Khanty is spoken in western Siberia, along the banks of the Ob River and its numerous tributaries. Khanty and Mansi, spoken just to the west, are known as the Ob-Ugric languages, which, together with Hungarian, constitute the Ugric branch of the Finno-Ugric languages. The area in which Khanty and Mansi are spoken is known as the Khanty-Mansi National District. Its capital, Khanty-Mansiisk, stands near the confluence of the Ob and Irtysh rivers. Speakers of Khanty number about 15,000. There are several dialects and subdialects.

Buryat

Доржо утаатай бүрүүлхэн гэрээ һанана. Эгээ түрүүнээ эхээ энхэрүү дулаанаар үгылбэ. Дэлхэй дээрэхи эгээл һайн һайхан, эгээл сэсэн эхэ хадаа Доржын өөрынь эхэ гээшэл! Мүнөө баһал унтангүй хэбтэжэ болоо. Уургайгаа орхижо ниидэһэн дальбараагаа үгылжэл һууна хаш даа. Юугээ хэжэ, юугээ оёжо һууна хаб? Эхэнь мүнөө үнеэгээ һаажа байгаа бэзэ. үбэл болохоһоо урид Доржодоо эльгээхэээ дулаахан оймһо оёжо һүүна гу? Аханарайнь самсада халааһа табихаяа зүү һабагшалхаяа байжа болоо. Инагхан Доржынь шарай эхэдэнь тэрэ зүүнэйнь һүбэ соогуур харагдан байжашье болоо юм аалам?

Dorzho missed his smoky, dimly lit yurt. For the first time he felt a tender nagging loneliness for his mother. She was the loveliest, smartest mother in the world, Dorzho's mother! Perhaps she too was lying awake at this moment. She probably missed her little bird who had left his nest. What was she doing and what was she sewing? At that moment she was probably milking a cow. Or perhaps knitting warm stockings to send to Dorzho before winter? Perhaps she was making the payments for her brother's shirts. And perhaps through the eye of the needle she seemed to see the face of her dear Dorzho?

CHIMIT TSYDENDAMBAYEV, *Dorzho, Son of Banzar*

Buryat is spoken in southern Siberia, in the area surrounding Lake Baikal. The great majority of its speakers live in Russia's republic of Buryatiya (capital, Ulan-Ude), while others are to be found in the nearby Aginsk Buryat and Ust-Ordynsk Buryat national districts. There are about 375,000 speakers.

Buryat is one of the Mongolian languages, which form a branch of the Altaic family. It is closely related to Mongolian proper, spoken across the border in Mongolia. It is written in the Cyrillic alphabet, with the additional letters *ө*, *γ*, and *h*.

While the Mongolian languages are vastly different from the Turkic languages (the major branch of Altaic), they do adhere strictly to the "vowel harmony" principle of all the Altaic languages. In the passage above notice how many of the words contain only one vowel – *a*, *o*, or *э* – used again and again.

Yakut

Кыра, «антон» дэнэр самолетунан көтөн кэлэн, үоһэттэн көрдөххө, – хотугу өрүс хаҥас биэрэгэр баар Суокурдаах боһүөлэк маҥан таба тириитигэр уонча хас испиискэни мээнэ бырахпыт кэриэтэ. Дьиэлэр ол курдук ойом-сойом тураллар, олбуор, уулусса энгин диэн суох.

Мин Суокурдаахха үс хоннум. Өрүс уҥуор хараалга – таба турар сиригэр, элбэх табаны өлөрдүлэр, ону ыйаан туттараллар – ити табаһыттар үлэлэрин биир түмүгэ. Мин бастыҥ табаһыттары кытта кэпсэттим, уочарка суруйаары «матыры-йаал» хомуйдум. Үһүс күммэр – субуота этэ. Суокурдаахха кэлэн, били «антон» почта аҕаларын күүтэбин – ол самоле-тунан төннүһээри.

If you fly on an AN-2, or "Anton" as they call the plane out here, and view from on high the village of Suokurdaakh on the left bank of the northern river, it seems to resemble ten small matchsticks tossed onto a white reindeer skin. The houses stand every which way – there are neither yards nor streets.

I spent three nights in Suokurdaakh. On the far side of the river, in the corral, many reindeer had been slaughtered. The carcasses were hung up – a way of measuring the work of the herders. I talked with the leading herders and collected some "material" for an article. On the third day of my stay in Suokurdaakh – it was a Saturday – I waited for the same "Anton," which was scheduled to arrive with the mail and on which I was to return home.

NIKOLAI GABYSHEV

Yakut, now often referred to by its native name of Sakha, is spoken in Russia's republic of Yakutiya (capital, Yakutsk). Now also known as Sakha, it is a vast expanse of 1.2 million square miles in northeastern Siberia bisected by the Lena River.

A Turkic language, Yakut represents the easternmost extension of this group, having been brought here by settlers from Central Asia some 500–800 years ago. Today there are about 300,000 speakers. It is written in the Cyrillic alphabet with the additional letters *ө*, *ү*, *ҕ*, *ҥ*, and *h*.

Evenki

Энӣм хуюкэ̄ндӯв бӯчэ̄н. Амӣндӯй 1933 анӈанӣлā инчэ̄в. Тадук
учичилчāв байкитскайдӯ школадӯ. Учитчачāв 1935 анӈанӣлā.
Маначāв тар школадӯ дыгинмэ классил. Тадук Турулэ̄ суручэ̄в.
Хавалилчāв Турудӯ типографиядӯ. Типография эвэдывэ газе-
тава ювдеӈкин. Тар газета гэрбӣн «Ō̄макта Ин.» Хавалчāв
тадӯ иланма анӈанӣл. Тадук Илимпийскай Райком комсомол
минэ Игаркалā алагувдāв уӈчэ̄н.

My mother died when I was small. Until 1933 I lived with my father.
Then I began studying at the Baikit school. I studied until 1935. I finished
the fourth grade in that school. Then I went to Tura. I began working at
a printing plant in Tura. The printing plant put out an Evenki newspaper.
The name of the newspaper was *New Life*. I worked there for three years.
Then the Ilimpea regional committee of the Komsomol sent me to study
in Igarka.

Evenki is spoken over a vast expanse of territory, extending from Central
Siberia, into a small part of China, and on to the Pacific Ocean. Its speakers
number only about 30,000, half of whom live in Russia, half in China.

In Russia the Evenki National District of some 286,000 square miles
(larger than Texas) stands astride the Lower Tunguska and Stony Tunguska
rivers in central Siberia. But, despite its huge size, only a few thousand of
the country's Evenkis live there. The rest are to be found in scattered settlements to the east, a few even as far as Sakhalin Island. In China they live
mainly in a small border area between Inner Mongolia and Manchuria.

The Evenki are a nomadic people who live by hunting, fishing, and reindeer herding. Their language belongs to the Tungusic branch of the Altaic
family of languages. In Russia it is written in the Cyrillic alphabet with the
additional letter ӈ.

Chukchi

Игыр вай ӈэлвыл пъоӈгэлеркын. Ӈотқэн йъилгын рэплыткугъэ=ым, ӈэлвыл ратаӈпаагъа пъоӈгэлек.

Ы'етык ӈэлвыл наранлеӈӈоӈын алялқэты, чама=ым чинит ӈэнри ратагъяӈыӈогъа. Амватапванвэты наранлеӈӈоӈын, лыгэн=ым тэӈыскыгйит. Прикатира рэгитэркынин ватапъян, ынкыри лыгэн нэрэнлеркын. Ынӈин ымльаляӈэт.

Гырокы=ым нэрэльуркын алялқыян, рыратылқыян, нивқинэт: «Ӈутку тымгылқык ныгръоркын ӈэлвыл.» Ынкы лыгэн ныгръоқэн ӈэлвыл. Гыръольыт рэквытти чаакаеты нытақэнат, каляйӈатыльыт нынватқэнат.

At the present time the herd is searching for mushrooms. When the month is over the herd will stop searching for mushrooms.

When the snow begins to fall the herd will be driven to places where there is no longer any snow, or it may head there on its own. They will be driven to places with an abundance of Iceland moss, in general to nice places. The leader will find places with Iceland moss and will drive them there. Thus it shall be all winter.

In the spring they will seek places free from snow, flat country, saying, "Here, where there is no wind, the herd can bear their young." It is here that they bear their young. Those who give birth are kept in one place, those who run away are brought back.

Chukchi is spoken in northeasternmost Siberia, principally in the Chukchi National District, whose capital is Anadyr. With only 12,000 speakers, it is nonetheless the most important member of the Paleo-Asiatic family of languages.

Chukchi is written in the Cyrillic alphabet with the additional letters қ and ӈ. A curious feature of the language is that the letter *k* is pronounced *k* by men but *ts* by women, while the combination *rk* is pronounced *rk* by men but *tsts* by women. Thus the Chukchi word for "walrus" is pronounced *kyrky* by men but *tsytstsy* by women.

LANGUAGES OF
THE MIDDLE EAST

Yeryüzü kendi kendine bir toprak.
Yurt bir toprak üstünde var olduğumuz.
Ta dev atalardan beri, ta dev çocuklara dek,
Ekmek, tuz.

Peki nasıl ayak basmıştır onlar,
Yurda, benim at koşturduğum yere?
Kavak uykusunda, yer türküsüñde kocaman
Süt üzre büyüdüğüm köylere.

Peki nasıl ayak basmıştır onlar,
Yurda, benim bayrak diktiğim yere?
Bu ekin serinliğine gündüzün,
Geceleyin bu çınar gölgelere.

Yeryüzü kendi kendine bir toprak.
Yurt bir toprak üstünde yaşadığımız
Yurt ormanlarıyla yeşil, yurt dağbaşlarıyla mavi
Ölsek bile içimizde kalan hız.

The world is just the soil by itself.
Homeland is the ground which our lives exalt.
From giant forefathers to giant children,
Bread and salt.

How then did they ever set foot,
Where my horses gallop, on my homeland?
Or on the villages where I grew up on milk
In the poplar's sleep, in the soil's song, grand?

How then did they ever set foot,
Where I raised my flag, in my country?
By day, on the coolness of the crops . . .
By night, on the shades of the sycamore tree . . .

The world is just the soil by itself.
Homeland is the ground which our lives exalt.
Green with our land's forests, blue with her hills,
Even if we die its speed never comes to a halt.

FAZIL HÜSNÜ DAĞLARCA Homeland

Turkish is the national language of Turkey, spoken by about 60 million people, or 90 percent of the country's population. There are also some 750,000 speakers in Bulgaria, 150,000 in Cyprus, and 100,000 in Greece. In recent decades a large Turkish-speaking community has formed in Germany, numbering over 2 million people, and smaller ones exist in France, Austria, the Netherlands, Belgium, and other European countries.

Turkish was originally written in the Arabic script, which had been in use since the conversion of the Turks to Islam in the 10th century. But the Arabic script is poorly suited to Turkish, and in 1928 President Mustafa Kemal Atatürk introduced a slightly modified version of the Roman alphabet, consisting of 21 consonants and eight vowels. In Turkish the letters *q*, *w*, and *x* are absent, while the letter *c* is pronounced like the English *j* (e.g., *cep* – pocket), *j* like the French *j* (*jale* – dew), *ç* is pronounced *ch* (*çiçek* – flower), and *ş* is pronounced *sh* (*şişe* – bottle). The letter *ğ* merely serves to lengthen slightly the preceding vowel (*dağ* – mountain).

The Turkish vowels are divided into the so-called front vowels, *e*, *i*, *ö*, *ü*, and the back vowels *a*, *ı* (undotted *i*), *o*, *u*. The dotted *i* retains the dot even when capitalized, as in İstanbul. As in all the Altaic languages, most Turkish words adhere to the principle of vowel harmony: that is, all the vowels in a given word belong to the same class (front or back), and any suffixes added generally contain vowels of the same class. Thus the plural of a noun with a front vowel or vowels is formed with the suffix *-ler* (e.g., *ev* – house, *evler* – houses), while the plural of a noun with a back vowel or vowels is formed with the suffix *-lar* (*at* – horse, *atlar* – horses). In the accompanying poem, notice the word *uykusunda* ("in its sleep"), with the vowel *u* appearing throughout, as against *türküsünde* ("in its song"), *büyüdüğüm* ("where I grew up"), and *gündüzün* ("by day"), with the vowel *ü* throughout. As an agglutinative language, Turkish frequently adds on suffix after suffix, thus producing words that may be the equivalent of a whole phrase or sentence in English.

The English words *caviar*, *yogurt*, and *shish kebab* are of Turkish origin. The word *tulip* comes from a Turkish word for "turban", because its flower was thought to resemble a turban. The word *meander* comes, via the Greek, from the ancient name of the Menderes River of western Turkey which was noted for its winding course.

Arabic

بِسْمِ اللَّهِ الرَّحْمَنِ الرَّحِيمِ ۝

الْحَمْدُ لِلَّهِ رَبِّ الْعَالَمِينَ ۝ الرَّحْمَنِ الرَّحِيمِ ۝

مَالِكِ يَوْمِ الدِّينِ ۝ إِيَّاكَ نَعْبُدُ وَإِيَّاكَ

نَسْتَعِينُ ۝ اهْدِنَا الصِّرَاطَ الْمُسْتَقِيمَ ۝

صِرَاطَ الَّذِينَ أَنْعَمْتَ عَلَيْهِمْ غَيْرِ الْمَغْضُوبِ

عَلَيْهِمْ وَلَا الضَّالِّينَ ۝

1. In the name of Allah, the Beneficent, the Merciful.
2. Praise be to Allah, the Lord of the Worlds.
3. The Beneficent, the Merciful.
4. Master of the Day of Judgment.
5. Thee (alone) do we worship, and Thee (alone) we ask for help.
6. Show us the straight path.
7. The path of those whom Thou hast favored; not (the path) of those who earn Thy anger nor of those who go astray.

Opening *sura* (chapter) of the Koran

Arabic is one of the world's major languages, spoken in a broad belt extending from the Arabian Peninsula north to the Fertile Crescent and then west to the Atlantic Ocean. It is the official language of Saudi Arabia, Yemen, United Arab Emirates, Oman, Kuwait, Bahrain, Qatar, Iraq, Syria, Jordan, Lebanon, Egypt, Sudan, Libya, Tunisia, Algeria, Morocco, and Mauritania, making it the mother tongue of about 230 million people. In addition many millions of Moslems in other countries have some knowledge of Arabic, it being the language of the Moslem religion and of the sacred Koran. In 1974 Arabic was made the sixth official language of the United Nations.

Great languages spring from great empires, and Arabic is no exception. A Semitic language closely related to Hebrew, its use was confined to northwestern and central Arabia until the 7th century AD. But the spectacular Islamic conquests of that century carried the language far beyond its original borders, and it supplanted almost all the previous languages of Iraq, Syria, Egypt, and North Africa. After further conquest in succeeding centuries Arabic was spoken as far east as Afghanistan and as far west as Spain.

The Arabic alphabet dates from about 500 AD. It was based on the alphabet of an ancient people called the Nabateans, who in turn borrowed it from Aramaic. By the early Mohammedan period two scripts were in use: the Naskhi, the ordinary cursive form used in books and correspondence, and the Kufic, an angular script used mainly for decorative purposes. The present alphabet of 28 letters consists basically of consonants, the vowel signs being indicated by marks above or below the letters. While these marks are generally omitted, they do appear in elementary school books and in all editions of the Koran. Like the other Semitic languages, Arabic is written from right to left. (In the text above the numbers appear at the end, rather than the beginning, of each verse.) The script is employed in many other languages whose speakers are Moslems: e.g., Persian, Pashto, Urdu, and Sindhi.

Spoken Arabic naturally varies from country to country, but classical Arabic, the language of the Koran, has remained largely unchanged since the 7th century. It has served as a great unifying force in the development and standardization of the language. When educated Arabs from different countries meet, they generally converse in classical Arabic. On the southern coast of the Arabian Peninsula the people speak a number of dialects known collectively as South Arabic, but these differ so greatly from the Arabic of the north that South Arabic is often considered a separate language.

Arabic has contributed many words to the English language, many of them beginning with the Arabic definite article *al-*. These include *algebra, alcohol, alchemy, alkali, alcove, alfalfa*, and *albatross*. Others are *mosque, minaret, sultan, elixir, harem, giraffe, gazelle, cotton, amber, sofa, mattress, tariff, magazine, arsenal, syrup*, and *artichoke. Coffee* is also an Arabic word, which entered English by way of Turkish and Italian. The word *assassin* comes from a similar Arabic word meaning "hashish addicts."

Hebrew

וְהָיָה ׀ בְּאַחֲרִית הַיָּמִים נָכוֹן יִהְיֶה הַר בֵּית־יְהוָה בְּרֹאשׁ
הֶהָרִים וְנִשָּׂא מִגְּבָעוֹת וְנָהֲרוּ אֵלָיו כָּל־הַגּוֹיִם: וְהָלְכוּ
עַמִּים רַבִּים וְאָמְרוּ לְכוּ ׀ וְנַעֲלֶה אֶל־הַר־יְהוָה אֶל־בֵּית
אֱלֹהֵי יַעֲקֹב וְיֹרֵנוּ מִדְּרָכָיו וְנֵלְכָה בְּאֹרְחֹתָיו כִּי מִצִּיּוֹן
תֵּצֵא תוֹרָה וּדְבַר־יְהוָה מִירוּשָׁלָ͏ִם: וְשָׁפַט בֵּין הַגּוֹיִם
וְהוֹכִיחַ לְעַמִּים רַבִּים וְכִתְּתוּ חַרְבוֹתָם לְאִתִּים וַחֲנִיתוֹתֵיהֶם
לְמַזְמֵרוֹת לֹא־יִשָּׂא גוֹי אֶל־גּוֹי חֶרֶב וְלֹא־יִלְמְדוּ עוֹד
מִלְחָמָה:

And it shall come to pass in the end of days, that the mountain of the Lord's house shall be established as the top of the mountains, and shall be exalted above the hills; and all nations shall flow unto it. And many peoples shall go and say: "Come ye, and let us go up to the mountain of the Lord, to the house of the God of Jacob; and He will teach us of His ways, and we will walk in His paths." For out of Zion shall go forth the law, and the word of God from Jerusalem. And he shall judge between the nations, and shall decide for many peoples; and they shall beat their swords into plowshares, and their spears into pruning hooks; nation shall not lift up sword against nation; neither shall they learn war any more.

Isaiah ii 2–4

Hebrew is one of the world's oldest languages, spoken and written today in much the same way as it was more than two thousand years ago. After ceasing to exist as a spoken language about 250 BC, it was reborn as a modern language in the 19th century, and today it is the principal language of the state of Israel. Books, newspapers, and magazines published in Israel today are written in a Hebrew that is much the same as the language of the Bible.

For over three millennia Hebrew has been the religious, and often the literary and secular, language of the Jewish people. A Semitic tongue, it was spoken during the period of the migration of the Patriarchs into Palestine and remained the language of the Jews throughout the Old Testament period. In the post-biblical period Hebrew gradually gave way to Aramaic as the spoken language, but continued throughout the centuries to serve as the language of ritual and prayer.

156

The renaissance of Hebrew as a spoken language in the 19th century may be ascribed almost entirely to the efforts of one man: Eliezer ben Yehudah, who devoted his life to the revival of the language, and at the same time adapted it for modern use through the introduction of thousands of modern terms. Hebrew gradually came into use among the Jewish settlers in Palestine and became the official language of the state of Israel when that nation was created in 1948. Today about 4 million people speak Hebrew either as their maternal, adopted, or religious tongue.

The earliest Hebrew alphabet, based on the Phoenician, dates from about 1000 BC. During the 5th century BC it gave way to an Aramaic script, which over time evolved into the one used in Israel today and in synagogues throughout the world. It consists of 22 letters (all consonants, with no capitals), five of which have a different form when they appear at the end of a word. The names of the letters are based on Hebrew words: e.g., *aleph, beth, gimel, daleth* are from the words for "ox", "house", "camel", and "door" respectively. These were later adopted by the Greeks as *alpha, beta, gamma,* and *delta.*

The alphabet is written from right to left without vowels. Thus the word *kelev* (dog) appears as the Hebrew equivalents of, from right to left, *k, l,* and *v.* It is therefore impossible for one not familiar with the language to know how to pronounce a word from the way it is written. About the 8th century a system developed for indicating vowels through the use of small dots and dashes placed above and below the consonants. These signs are still in use today, but they are confined to school books, prayer books, and textbooks for foreigners, and are not to be seen in newspapers, magazines, or books of general use. The text above contains the vowel signs as well as a series of marks called the trope, which indicates the notes to be used when the passage is chanted in the synagogue.

English words of Hebrew origin include *amen, hallelujah, sabbath, rabbi, cherub, seraph, Satan, kosher, manna, shibboleth,* and *behemoth.* There are also the names of the Jewish holidays (*Rosh Hashanah, Yom Kippur, Chanukah,* and *Purim*), as well as such as terms as *Torah, bar mitzvah, haggadah,* and *megilah.* More recent contributions are *kibbutz* and *sabra.*

Coptic

ⲁⲓϭⲱϣⲧ ⲉⲭⲙ̄ ⲡⲕⲁϩ ·
ⲁⲩⲱ ⲉⲓⲥϩⲏⲏⲧⲉ ⲙⲙⲛ
ⲗⲁⲁⲩ ⲉϩⲣⲁⲓ̈ ⲉⲧⲡⲉ · ⲁⲩⲱ
ⲛⲉⲩϣⲟⲟⲡ ⲁⲛ̄ ⲛ̄ϭⲓ ⲛⲉⲥ
ⲟⲩⲟⲉⲓⲛ · ⲁⲓ̈ⲛⲁⲩ ⲉⲛⲧⲟⲩⲉⲓ̄ⲏ
ⲁⲩⲱ ⲛⲉⲩⲥⲧⲱⲧ ⲡⲉ
ⲁⲩⲱ ⲛⲧⲁⲗ ⲧⲏⲣⲟⲩ ⲛⲉⲩ
ϣⲧⲣⲧⲱⲣ · ⲁⲓ̈ϭⲱϣⲧ
ⲁⲩⲱ ⲉⲓ̈ⲥϩⲏⲏⲧⲉ ⲛⲉ ⲙⲛ̄ ⲣⲱ
ⲙⲉ ⲡⲉ · ⲁⲩⲱ ⲛϩⲁⲗⲁⲁ
ⲧⲉ ⲧⲏⲣⲟⲩ ⲛⲧⲡⲉ ⲛⲉⲩϩⲓ̈
ⲛⲉⲩⲉⲣⲏⲩ ⲡⲉ · ⲁⲓ̈ⲛⲁⲩ
ⲁⲩⲱ ⲉⲓ̈ⲥ ⲡⲕⲁⲣⲙⲏⲗⲟⲥ ⲁϥ
ⲣ̄ϫⲁⲉⲓ̈ⲉ · ⲁⲩⲱ ⲙⲡⲟⲗⲓ̈ⲥ
ⲧⲏⲣⲟⲩ ⲁⲩⲣⲟⲕϩⲟⲩ ⲙ
ⲡⲉⲙⲧⲟ ⲉⲃⲟⲗ ⲙⲡⲭⲟⲉⲓ̈ⲥ
ⲁⲩⲱ ⲁⲩⲧⲁⲕⲟ̄ ⲙⲡⲉⲙⲧⲟ̄ ⲉ
ⲃⲟⲗ ⲛⲧⲟⲣⲅⲏ ⲙⲡⲉϥϭⲱⲛⲧ ·

I beheld the earth, and, lo, it was without form and void; and the heavens,
and they had no light. I beheld the mountains, and lo, they trembled, and
all the hills are moved. I beheld, and, lo, there was no man, and all the
birds of the heavens were fled. I beheld and, lo, the fruitful place was a
wilderness, and all the cities thereof were broken down at the presence
of the Lord, and by his fierce anger.

Jeremiah iv 23–26

Coptic is the modern descendant of the ancient Egyptian language. As such
it belongs to a separate branch of the Afro-Asiatic family. The word "Copt"
is derived from the Greek, and later the Arabic, word for "Egyptian."

The hieroglyphic writing of ancient Egypt dates as far back as 3000 BC.
In addition to the thousands of ideographs, it contained a set of 24 special
signs representing consonants only. About the 7th century BC an alternate
simplified writing system known as Demotic was introduced, which simi-

larly had no vowels. (With reference to Greek, Demotic denotes the everyday speech of modern Greece.)

Following the conquest of Egypt by Alexander the Great in 333 BC Greek became the language of government and of the upper classes, and a large number of Greek words entered the language. The introduction of Christianity in the first century AD led to the translation of the Bible into what was now Coptic. A new alphabet was devised consisting of 24 Greek letters (17 consonants and seven vowels), as well as seven from Egyptian Demotic to represent sounds that did not exist in Greek. Thus the Coptic alphabet, having vowels, provides a better indication than Demotic of the pronunciation of many ancient Egyptian words.

In the year 451 a schism occurred in the Christian Church over the nature of Christ. The Egyptians adhered to the "monophysite" view, which soon led to the establishment of Egypt's Coptic Church. After the Moslem conquest of Egypt in 642 Coptic began to give way slowly to Arabic, but it was another thousand years before it died out completely as a spoken language. To this day it remains the liturgical language of the Coptic Church, whose present membership is about 6 million.

Syriac

ܡܪܝܐ ܗܝ ܐܪܥܐ ܒܡܠܐܗ. ܬܒܝܠ ܘܟܠܗܘܢ ܥܡܘܪܝܗ. ܡܛܠ ܕܗܘ ܒܝܡܡܐ
ܣܡ ܫܬܐܣܝܗ. ܘܥܠ ܢܗܪܘܬܐ ܐܬܩܢܗ. ܡܢܘ ܕܢܣܩ ܠܛܘܪܗ ܕܡܪܝܐ.
ܘܡܢܘ ܕܢܩܘܡ ܒܐܬܪ ܩܘܕܫܗ. ܐܝܢܐ ܕܕܟܝܢ ܐܝܕܘܗܝ ܘܒܪܝܪ ܠܒܗ. ܗܘ
ܕܠܐ ܝܡܐ ܒܢܟܠܐ ܠܚܒܪܗ ܘܠܐ ܝܡܐ ܒܕܓܠܘܬܐ. ܗܢܐ ܢܣܒ ܒܘܪܟܬܐ
ܡܢ ܡܪܝܐ. ܘܙܕܝܩܘܬܐ ܡܢ ܐܠܗܐ ܦܪܘܩܗ. ܗܢܘ ܕܪܐ ܕܒܥܝܢ ܠܗ.
ܘܕܒܥܝܢ ܐܦܘܗܝ ܕܝܥܩܘܒ. ܐܪܝܡܘ ܬܪܥܐ ܪܝܫܝܟܘܢ. ܘܐܬܬܪܝܡܘ ܬܪܥܐ ܕܡܢ
ܥܠܡ. ܘܢܥܘܠ ܡܠܟܐ ܕܐܝܩܪܐ. ܡܢܘ ܗܢܐ ܡܠܟܐ ܕܐܝܩܪܐ. ܡܪܝܐ ܥܫܝܢܐ ܘܓܢܒܪܐ.
ܡܪܝܐ ܓܢܒܪܐ ܒܩܪܒܐ. ܐܪܝܡܘ ܬܪܥܐ ܪܝܫܝܟܘܢ. ܘܐܬܬܪܝܡܘ ܬܪܥܐ ܕܡܢ
ܥܠܡ. ܘܢܥܘܠ ܡܠܟܐ ܕܐܝܩܪܐ. ܡܢܘ ܗܢܐ ܡܠܟܐ ܕܐܝܩܪܐ. ܡܪܝܐ ܚܝܠܬܢܐ.
ܗܘܝܘ ܡܠܟܐ ܕܐܝܩܪܐ.

The earth is the Lord's, and the fullness thereof; the world, and
they that dwell therein.

For he hath founded it upon the seas, and established it upon the
floods.

Who shall ascend unto the mountain of the Lord? And who shall
stand in His holy place?

He that hath clean hands, and a pure heart; who hath not lifted up
his soul unto vanity, nor sworn deceitfully.

He shall receive the blessing from the Lord, and righteousness
from the God of his salvation.

This is the generation of them that seek Him, that seek thy face, O
Jacob.

Lift up your heads, O ye gates; and be ye lifted up, ye everlasting
doors; that the King of glory may enter.

Who then is the King of glory? The Lord strong and mighty, the
Lord mighty in battle.

Lift up your heads, O ye gates; yea, lift them up, ye everlasting
doors; that the King of glory may enter.

Who then is the King of glory? The Lord of hosts, He is the king
of glory.

Twenty-fourth Psalm

Syriac is a dialect of Aramaic, the dominant language of the Near East from
about the 6th century BC through the 6th century AD. Aramaic (though not
the Syriac dialect) was the language spoken by Jesus of Nazareth. Two books

160

of the Old Testament, Ezra and Daniel, are partly in Aramaic, as are sections of the Babylonian Talmud, the Midrash (Jewish commentaries on the Bible), and the Dead Sea Scrolls. The Aramaic script eventually became the basis of the modern Hebrew alphabet, of the Arabic (via the Nabateans), and possibly of the Brahmi script that gave rise to all the alphabets of modern India.

The Syriac dialect developed around the city of Edessa (now Urfa, in southeastern Turkey), the leading center of Christianity after about 200 AD. It eventually became the most important of the Aramaic dialects and, after Greek, the most important language in the eastern Roman Empire. Syriac (or Aramaic) continued to be spoken until the rise of Islam, when it quickly gave way to the dominant influence of Arabic. By the 8th century the language remained in use mainly for liturgical purposes.

In modern usage the term Syriac generally refers to the liturgical language of the Maronite Catholic Church, the Syrian Catholic Church, the Syrian Jacobite Church, the Nestorian (or sometimes Assyrian) Church, and a number of others. The term Aramaic refers to the language as it is still spoken in small communities in Syria (in and around the village of Malula, north of Damascus) and in Turkey (near the town of Mardin, east of Urfa). Another form of Aramaic, generally referred to as Assyrian, is spoken by about 150,000 people in Iraq, 100,000 in Iran, and smaller numbers in Lebanon, Syria, and Russia.

Aramaic was first written in the Phoenician alphabet but by the 8th century BC a distinctive Aramaic script had evolved. The first Syriac alphabet developed from a later form of Aramaic used at Palmyra in Syria. This gradually evolved into the script known as Estrangelo, which was used almost exclusively until the 5th century. At that time the Eastern Church split into a number of factions, with each producing a modified version of its own. Three scripts are in use today: Estrangelo, Jacobite (or Serto), and Nestorian. The text above is in Nestorian.

Persian

چیزی می‌گویم و چیزی می‌شنوی. در آن زمان عاشق‌شدن یک دختر
پانزده ساله خود معصیتی بود که می‌توانست خون برپا کند. چه رسد به نامه
نوشتن. چه رسد به رد کردن خواستگار. عاشق‌شدن؟ آن هم عاشق شاگرد
نجّار سر گذر شدن؟ این که دیگر واویلا بود. آن هم برای دختر بصیرالدوله.
فکر آن هم قلب را از حرکت می‌انداخت. خون را سرد می‌کرد. انگار که آب
سربالا برود. انگار که از آسمان به‌جای باران خون ببارد. با شاخ غول درافتادن
بود که من درافتادم و نوشتم. آرزویی را که بر دلم سنگینی می‌کرد، عاقبت
نوشتم. آنچه را به‌محض خواندن نامهٔ او و به عنوان پاسخ به ذهنم رسیده بود
و دلم می‌خواست به صدای بلند برایش بخوانم، نوشتم.

حال دل با تو گفتنم هوس است
خبر دل شنفتنم هوس است
طمع خام بین که قصّهٔ فاش
از رقیبان نهفتنم هوس است

I say something and you hear something. At that time it was a sin for a
fifteen-year-old girl to fall in love. It could cause bloodshed. Let alone
writing a love letter or rejecting a suitor for marriage. To fall in love?
It was a scandal for the daughter of an aristocrat named Basiraldoleh to
fall in love with a carpenter's helper in the marketplace. Even thinking
of love was like heart failure, frozen blood going against the stream, or
raining blood from the sky. What I did was like challenging a horned
monster. Finally, I wrote down all the desires and wishes of my heart. I
wrote down what I had in mind in response to his letter. I wished to read
to him loudly and clearly whatever I put down in that letter.

I am longing to tell you the state of my heart.
I am longing to know the state of your heart.
I am longing to hide from my peers the story of my love.

FATANAH HADJ-SEYED JAVADI (PARVIN),
The Morning of the Hangover

Persian is also one of the world's oldest languages, dating back to the great Persian Empire of the 6th century BC. Today it is spoken by about 40 million people in Iran and another 8 million in Afghanistan. It is the most important of the Iranian languages, a branch of the Indo-European family.

Persian originated in southern Iran, an area known as Parsa, now still called Fars. The Greeks called it Persis, thus giving rise to the name Persia. In Iran today the language is known as Farsi. (In Afghanistan it is known as Dari.)

The Persian Empire was founded by Cyrus the Great in 550 BC. Its language, known as Old Persian, was written in cuneiform, the wedge-shaped characters used throughout much of the ancient world. It can be seen today on monuments such as the great Behistun Rock, in western Iran, containing a trilingual cuneiform inscription in Persian, Elamite, and Babylonian. The religion of the empire was Zoroastrianism, whose sacred texts were written in a dialect of Old Persian called Avestan. The empire came to an end in 330 BC when it was conquered by Alexander the Great.

Middle Persian developed during the Sassanid dynasty, which came to power in 226 AD. Also known as Pahlavi, it was written in an alphabet of Aramaic origin. In 651 Persia was overrun and conquered by the Arabs, who brought with them the religion of Islam and ruled the region for the next four centuries. While the Pahlavi script was replaced by a modified version of the Arabic which remains in use today, Persia generally retained its separate identity and Persian continued to be spoken.

Next to rule Persia were the Seljuks, a Turkic people who came to power in the 11th century. The Seljuks converted to Islam, and adopted the language of their Persian instructors and advisers. Persian was also the official language of the Mogul Empire, the Moslem dynasty that ruled India for three centuries until 1857. A variety of Persian called Tajik is spoken in Tajikistan, but there it is written in the Cyrillic alphabet.

English words of Persian origin include *shawl*, *pajama*, *taffeta*, *khaki*, *kiosk*, *divan*, *lilac*, *jasmine*, *julep*, *jackal*, *caravan*, *bazaar*, *checkmate*, *dervish*, and *satrap*.

Pashto

در ریزی و کړه خپل یار ته   دواړه شونډے کړه په بیار ته

زړهٔ مے نه کیږی ګلزار ته   زهٔ چه ستا و مخ ته کورم

چه نظر کا ستا رخسار ته   ګل له شرمه خولے پربریدی

منتظر یم و خپل وار ته   که مے وار درباندے جوړ شی

چه خپیر خپیر کورے و خار ته   کلله دا در باندے بنائی

که دے مینه شی بهار ته   آئینے و ته نظر کړه

زار و چا ته کړے خوشحاله

چه دے نه کوری خوک زار ته

When her petall'd lips are parting,
Whitest pearls do lose their lustre;
When her glance to me is darting.
Fades the fairest flower cluster;
Roses shamed, forget to blossom
Brighter radiance to discover
In the budding of a bosom
Flaunting as to bee the clover;
She the rose, her grace bestowing
On the thorn that waits her pleasure,
I the fountain, faintly glowing,
Mirror of a garden's treasure,
Lover, loved, together knowing
Rapture passing dream or measure.

KHUSHHAL KHAN KHATAK, *Love in a Garden*

Pashto, also known as Pushtu, is one of the two major languages of Afghanistan, the other being Persian. It is spoken by about 15 million people there (about 60 percent of the population), mostly in the eastern and southern parts of the country. Another 20 million speakers live across the border in Pakistan, in the North-West Frontier Province whose capital is Peshawar.

Pashto is the language of the Pashtuns, the indigenous inhabitants of Afghanistan. Like Persian, it is one of the Iranian languages, and thus part of the Indo-European family. It is written in the Perso-Arabic script, but the alphabet contains a number of letters not to be found in either Persian or Arabic.

The term "Pashto" actually refers to the more important of the two dialects: the so-called "soft" dialect of Afghanistan which preserves the ancient *sh* and *zh* sounds. In Pakistan, where the "hard" *kh* and *gh* are preferred, the language is generally referred to as Pakhto. But with the large number of Afghanis now living in Pakistan, this distinction has begun to blur.

ئەگەر جوانی نەمامێکی سەوزی پاراو بێ ، چاو جووتێ
گوڵی گەشە بە تەوقەسەرەکەیەوە ،

چاو جووتێک شائەمستێرمیە بە بەرزایی ی ئاسمانەوە
چرییسکەچرییسك ئەد رەوشێتەوە ، جووتێک گەوهەری
پرشنگدارە تاجی عەشقو جوانی ئەرازێنێتەوە ،

جووتێک پەنجەرەی رووناکە ئەنواررێ بە سەر باخچەی
رۆحا ،

چاو د وو پەررمیە لە کتێبێکی مقد س، پررە لە ئایەتی
حسن إ حقیقەتەکانی رۆح ، سررەکانی د ڵ ، رازەکانی
د ەروونی بە حەرفی نوور تیا نووسراوە إ

ئاخۆ لە چاو بەلیخ تر، لە چاو پرر معناتر، لە چاو
سحراوبی تر چیی ئەشەرێکی رۆحی ، چیی کتێبێکی
ئاسمانیی هەیە ؟

یەکێک لە معجزەکانی چاو ئەوەیە، وەك بەرد ی بە
قییمەت بە هەموو رەنگێکەوە مەقبوولە : هەند ێ چاو
وەك شەوە رەشن ، هەند ێکییش چەشنی پییروزه شیینن ،
هەند ێ چاوی تریش هەن ئەلێی چاوی هەلۆن ،
چەشنی یاقووت ئاگریان لۆ ئەبێتەوە .

لا ی من وایە چاوی رەش بە جلوەی حزن و د لۆیی
فرمێسکەوە قەرراراییچەی هەموو چاوەکانە ، ئەوەند ه
شیيریین ، ئەوەند ه بۆ وێنەیە إ

If beauty is a tender succulent plant, then eyes are two bright flowers crowning it. Eyes are a pair of kingly stars glittering through the deep heavens; two precious stones that adorn the crown of love and beauty; two bright windows overlooking the garden of the soul.

Eyes are two pages from a sacred book, full of words of excellence, and written into them with words of light are the realities of life, the secret of the heart, and the inner mysteries of the conscience.

I wonder what other vestiges of the soul, what other heavenly books there are, which are more expressive, more beautiful, and more enchanting than eyes.

One of eyes' wonders is that, like gems, they go with every color. Some are black like jet; some blue like turquoise; others resemble the eyes of an eagle shining like rubies.

ABDULLAH GORAN, *Eyes*

There are nearly 20 million speakers of Kurdish, scattered over a number of countries. About 8 million are in Turkey, 5 million in Iran, 4 million in Iraq, and one million in Syria. Some are also in Armenia, and there is now a sizable Kurdish community living in Germany. Kurdish belongs to the Iranian branch of the Indo-European family of languages.

An ancient people with a strong sense of cultural identity, the Kurds have never had a land of their own. The general area in which they live is often referred to as Kurdistan. Their language is generally written in the Arabic script with a number of diacritical marks and dots to represent consonants and vowels not found in Arabic. The Soviet government developed a Cyrillic-based alphabet for use in the Transcaucasian republics. In the 1930s two Roman alphabets were developed in Iraq and Syria, but these are no longer in use.

Maltese

L-Arċipelagu Malti huwa magħmul mill-Gżejjer ta' Malta, Għawdex, Kemmuna u żewġ gżejjer oħra, Kemmunett u Filfla li mhumiex abitati. Il-Maltin jitkellmu lingwa antika ħafna li hi ta' nteress kbir għalling-wisti. Bażikament Semetika, maż-żmien assimilat għadd kbir ta' kliem rumanz, sakemm illum hi tirrapreżenta l-għaqda ta' żewġ friegħi ling-wistiċi. Dan il-fatt jirrifletti l-qagħda ta' Malta fil-Baħar Mediterran, nofs triq bejn l-Ewropa t'Isfel u l-Afrika ta' Fuq.

The Maltese Archipelago consists of the islands of Malta, Gozo, and Comino and two other uninhabited islands, Cominotto and Filfla. The Maltese speak a very ancient language which is of great interest to linguists. Basically Semitic, it assimilated a large number of Romance words over the years, with the result that today it represents the fusion of two linguistic branches. This fact reflects the position of Malta in the Mediterranean Sea, halfway between southern Europe and North Africa.

Maltese is spoken on the island of Malta, in the Mediterranean Sea. Its basis is Arabic, which was brought to the island by Moslem conquerors in the 9th century. In the year 1090 the Arabs were driven out by Normans from Sicily, who introduced a large number of Romance words into the vocabulary.

The Maltese alphabet contains the additional letters *ħ*, pronounced like the English *h* but comparatively stronger, and the *għ*, which, like the *h* (without a bar), serves only to lengthen the preceding or succeeding vowel. Other letters are *ċ*, pronounced *ch*; *ġ*, pronounced like the English *j*; and *ż*, pronounced like the English *z* (the letter *z*, without the dot, is pronounced *ts*). *J* is pronounced *y*, *x* as *sh*, and the letter *q* is a glottal stop. There are about 400,000 speakers of Maltese.

LANGUAGES OF ASIA

अस्ति हस्तिनापुरे कर्पूरविलासो नाम रजकः । तस्य गर्द-
भो ऽतिभारवाहनादुर्बलो मुमूर्षुरिवाभवत् । ततस्तेन रज-
केनासौ व्याघ्रचर्मणा प्रच्छाद्यारण्यसमीपे सस्यक्षेत्रे मोचितः ।
ततो दूरादवलोक्य व्याघ्रबुद्ध्या क्षेत्रपतयः सत्वरं पलायन्ते । स
च सुखेन सस्यं चरति । अथैकदा केनापि सस्यरक्षकेण धूसर-
कम्बलकृततनुत्राणेन धनुष्कार्ण्डं सज्जीकृत्यावनतकायेनैकान्ते
स्थितम् । तं च दूरे दृष्ट्वा गर्दभः पुष्टाङ्गो गर्दभीयमिति मत्वा
शब्दं कुर्वाणस्तदभिमुखं धावितः । ततस्तेन सस्यरक्षकेण गर्द-
भोऽयमिति ज्ञात्वा लीलयैव व्यापादितः ।

In Hastinapura there was a washerman named Vilasa. His donkey was near death, having become weak from carrying excessive burdens. So the washerman covered him with a tiger-skin and turned him loose in a cornfield near a forest. The owners of the field, seeing him from a distance, fled away in haste, under the notion that he was a tiger. Then a certain corn guard, having covered his body with a gray blanket, and having made ready his bow and arrows, crouched down in a secluded spot. Then the donkey, having grown plump from eating, spied him at a distance, and supposing him to be a she-donkey, trotted up to him braying. The corn guard, discovering him to be only a donkey, killed him with ease.

The Donkey in the Tiger-Skin, from the *Hitopadeśa*

Sanskrit is the ancient literary and classical language of India, the sacred language of the Hindu religion. Brought to India from the northwest in the 2nd millennium BC, Sanskrit (which means "refined," "perfected," or "elaborated") eventually gave rise to the Prakrit ("natural" or "common") languages. These in turn gave rise to the modern Indian languages, such as Hindi, Punjabi, Gujarati, Marathi, and Bengali, as well as Nepali, spoken in Nepal, and Sinhalese, spoken in Sri Lanka.

Sanskrit is an Indo-European language, whose entry into the Indian subcontinent marked a new advance for this far-flung family. Its Indo-European origin was, of course, unknown to the ancient and even the medieval world. It was only in the 18th century that the striking similarity of Sanskrit to Latin and Greek was first noted in detail. In 1786 a British linguist and jurist, Sir William Jones, delivered a famous speech in Calcutta stating that the two languages bore "a stronger affinity to Sanskrit than could have been produced by accident," and therefore all three must "have sprung from some common source." This in time led to the discovery of the inter-relationship of all the Indo-European languages, which in turn laid the foundation of the science of modern comparative and historical linguistics.

The oldest form of Sanskrit is known as Vedic Sanskrit, after the Vedas, the ancient hymns of the sacred Hindu scriptures. The oldest of the Vedas, the Rig-Veda, dates from about 1500 BC. The 1st millennium marked the rise of Classical Sanskrit, which was codified by the eminent grammarian Panini about 500 BC. But Sanskrit gradually lost ground as a spoken language (it is doubtful whether it was even Panini's mother tongue), and its use became limited to ritual and learning. It continued, however, to flourish as the language of scholarship in India, and the output of literary works continued without diminution until well into the 19th century. Although the competition of English as the language of government and science, coupled with the rising influence of the modern Indian languages, have undercut much of Sanskrit's former pre-eminence, it is still widely studied and even spoken to a small extent in India today. Remarkably, several thousand people still claim it as their mother tongue.

Sanskrit is written in an alphabet known as Devanagari. To trace its origin is to trace the development of writing in India. The source of all the indigenous alphabets of India is an ancient script known as Brahmi, which dates at least as far back as the 3rd century BC. In the opinion of most scholars it was of Semitic origin, probably Aramaic. One of its many offshoots was the Gupta script, used throughout the powerful Gupta empire in the 4th–6th centuries AD. The Devanagari characters developed from a variety of Gupta, the earliest inscriptions appearing in the 7th century. The alphabet, which is written from left to right, consists of 48 signs, of which 34 are consonants and 14 are vowels or diphthongs. It is considered one of the most perfect systems of writing ever devised.

The English words *Brahmin, mantra,* and *karma* are of Sanskrit origin.

गोबर ने और कुछ न कहा। लाठी कन्धे पर रखी और चल दिया। होरी उसे जाते देखता हुआ अपना कलेजा ठंढा करता रहा । अब लड़के की सगाई में देर न करनी चाहिए। सत्रहवाँ लग गया; मगर करें कैसे ? कहीं पैसे के भी दरसन हों। जब से तीनों भाइयों में अलगौझा हो गया, घर की साख जाती रही । महतो लड़का देखने आते हैं, पर घर की दशा देखकर मुँह फीका करके चले जाते हैं। दो-एक राजी भी हुए, तो रुपए माँगते हैं। दो-तीन सौ लड़की का दाम चुकाये और इतना ही ऊपर से खर्च करे, तब जाकर व्याह हो। कहाँ से आवें इतने रुपए। रास खलिहान में तुल जाती है। खाने-भर को भी नहीं बचता। व्याह कहाँ से हो ? और अब तो सोना ब्याहने योग्य हो गयी । लड़के का व्याह न हुआ, न सही । लड़की का व्याह न हुआ, तो सारी बिरादरी में हँसी होगी ।

Gobar said nothing more. He put his staff on his shoulder and walked away. Hori looked with pride at the receding figure of his son. He was growing into a fine young man. Time he married. But Hori had no money for the marriage. With the division in the family they had fallen on evil days. People did come to see Gobar and approved of him. But when they saw the family down and out, they washed their hands of the idea. Those who agreed pitched the demand for bride money so high that Hori was helpless. He had to marry off Sona too. It was bad enough if a son did not marry, but for a grown-up girl to remain unmarried was sacrilege. How could he look his friends in the face with an unmarried girl in the house?

PREMCHAND, *Godan*

Hindi is the most widely spoken language of India, centered principally in the states of Uttar Pradesh and Madhya Pradesh in the north-central part of the country. Its 400 million speakers rank it as one of the leading languages of the world, though it is understood by less than half the country's population.

Speakers of Hindi are also to be found in such far-flung places as Mauritius, in the Indian Ocean, and Fiji, in the Pacific, where in each case they constitute about one-third of the population. There are also many speakers in South Africa, Kenya, Trinidad, Guyana, and Suriname. All this was the result of large-scale Indian immigration into these countries: farm workers in the 19th century, shopkeepers and small business owners in the 20th.

Like most of the languages of northern India, Hindi is descended from Sanskrit and thus belongs to the Indic group of the Indo-European family of languages. Hindi and Urdu, the official language of Pakistan and spoken largely by Moslems, are virtually the same language, though the former is written in the Devanagari alphabet and the latter in the Perso-Arabic script. Pure Hindi derives most of its vocabulary from Sanskrit, while Urdu contains many words from Persian and Arabic.

Prior to independence in 1947, Hindi and Urdu, taken together, were referred to as Hindustani, which served as the lingua franca of much of India for more than four centuries. Its development into a national language had its beginnings in the colonial period, when the British began to cultivate it as a standard among government officials. At independence, which created the state of Pakistan for most of the country's Moslems, Hindi was chosen as India's national language. However, its failure to win acceptance among speakers of other languages has forced it to share the title of official language with English. Conversations between people from different parts of the country, especially between those of the north and south, are most often conducted in English.

English words of Hindi origin include *cot, loot, thug, chintz, bandanna, dungaree, rajah, pundit, coolie, chutney, tom-tom*, and *juggernaut*.

Urdu

ستاروں سے آگے جہاں اور بھی ہیں   ابھی عشق کے امتحاں اور بھی ہیں

تہی زندگی سے نہیں یہ فضائیں   یہاں سینکڑوں کارواں اور بھی ہیں

قناعت نہ کر عالم رنگ و بُو پر   چمن اور بھی آشیاں اور بھی ہیں

اگر کھو گیا اک نشیمن تو کیا غم   مقاماتِ آہ و فغاں اور بھی ہیں

تُو شاہیں ہے پرواز ہے کام تیرا   ترے سامنے آسماں اور بھی ہیں

اسی روز و شب میں اُلجھ کر نہ رہ جا   کہ تیرے زمان و مکاں اور بھی ہیں

Beyond the stars there are still other worlds;
There are other fields to test man's indomitable spirit.

Not devoid of life are those open spaces of heaven;
There are hundreds of other caravans in them as well.

Do not remain contented with this sensible world;
Beyond it there are other gardens and nests as well.

If thou hast lost one nest, what then?
There are other places for sighing and wailing as well.

Thou art an eagle; thy business is to soar in the empyrean;
Thou hast other skies in which thou canst range as well.

Be not entangled in this world of days and nights;
Thou hast another time and space as well.

MUHAMMAD IQBAL, *Bal-e-Jibril*

Urdu is the official language of Pakistan and is also widely spoken in India. In Pakistan it is the mother tongue of about 10 million people but is spoken fluently there as a second language by perhaps 100 million more. In India, where it is spoken by some 50 million Moslems, it is one of the official languages recognized by the constitution.

174

Urdu was originally the variety of Hindi spoken for centuries in the neighborhood of Delhi. In the 16th century, when India fell under Moslem domination, a large number of Persian, Arabic, and Turkish words entered the language via the military camps and the marketplaces of Delhi. Eventually a separate dialect evolved called Urdu ("camp language"), written in Arabic characters with extra letters added for sounds peculiar to Indian and Persian words. This is the most important difference today between Urdu and Hindi, as the latter is written in the Devanagari characters.

After the partition of India in 1947, Hindi became the principal language of India, and Urdu of West Pakistan (now Pakistan). The older term Hindustani, embracing both languages, has fallen into disuse since partition.

ਜੈ ਘਰਿ ਕੀਰਤਿ ਆਖੀਐ ਕਰਤੇ ਕਾ ਹੋਇ ਬੀਚਾਰੋ ॥ ਤਿਤੁ ਘਰਿ ਗਾਵਹੁ ਸੋਹਿਲਾ ਸਿਵਰਿਹੁ ਸਿਰਜਨਹਾਰੋ ॥੧॥ ਤੁਮ ਗਾਵਹੁ ਮੇਰੇ ਨਿਰਭਉ ਕਾ ਸੋਹਿਲਾ ॥ ਹਉਵਾਰੀ ਜਿਤੁ ਸੋਹਿਲੇ ਸਦਾ ਸੁਖੁ ਹੋਇ ॥੧॥ ਰਹਾਉ ॥ਨਿਤ ਨਿਤ ਜੀਅੜੇ ਸਮਾ- ਲੀਅਨਿ ਦੇਖੇਗਾ ਦੇਵਣਹਾਰੁ ॥ ਤੇਰੇ ਦਾਨੇ ਕੀਮਤਿ ਨਾ ਪਵੈ ਤਿਸੁ ਦਾਤੇ ਕਵਣੁ ਸੁਮਾਰੁ ॥੨॥ਸੰਬਤਿ ਸਾਹਾ ਲਿਖਿਆ ਮਿਲਿ ਕਰਿ ਪਾਵਹੁ ਤੇਲ ॥ ਦੇਹੁ ਸਜਣ ਅਸੀਸੜੀਆ ਜਿਉ ਹੋਵੈ ਸਾਹਿਬ ਸਿਉ ਮੇਲੁ ॥੩॥ ਘਰਿ ਘਰਿ ਏਹੋ ਪਾਹੁਚਾ ਸਦੜੇ ਨਿਤ ਪਵੰਨਿ ॥ ਸਦਣਹਾਰਾ ਸਿਮਰੀਐ ਨਾਨਕ ਸੇ ਦਿਹ ਆਵੰਨਿ ॥੪॥੧॥

Sing ye, my comrades, now my wedding song!
In the Temple House where saints sing His Name, where saintly
      hearts glow all day and night with His Love,
Sing ye, my comrades, now the song of His Praise!
Sing the song of my Creator!
I fain would be a sacrifice for the harmony divine that giveth
      everlasting peace!
My Lord careth for the smallest life,
The Bounteous Giver meets the needs of each,
No arithmetic can count His gifts,
Naught is it that we can render unto Him.
The Auspicious Day has dawned!
The Hour is fixed for my wedding with my Lord!
Come, comrades! Assemble and make rejoicings,
Anoint the Bride with oil and pour on her your blessings!
Comrades! Pray, the Bride may meet her Lord!
This message to every human being!
This call is for all.
O Man! Remember Him who calls!

Adi Granth (Holy Book of Sikhism)

Punjabi, often spelled Panjabi, is spoken in the Punjab, the historic region now divided between India and Pakistan. In Pakistan it is the daily language of about half the population, or 75 million people, though Urdu is the official language of the country. People in the northern half of Pakistan speak a separate dialect known as Lahnda, or Western Punjabi; those of the south speak Eastern Punjabi, the variety spoken in India.

In India Punjabi is the official language of Punjab state, and is also spoken in the neighboring states of Haryana and Himachal Pradesh. In addition, about 25 percent of the people living in the New Delhi metropolitan area speak Punjabi in everyday life. All told, there are about 25 million speakers in India.

Like Hindi and the other languages of northern India, Punjabi belongs to the Indic branch of the Indo-European family of languages. It is closely associated with the Sikh religion and its alphabet, known as Gurmukhi, was the vehicle for recording the teachings of the Sikh Gurus. It was invented by the second of the Sikh Gurus in the 16th century. Gurmukhi means "proceeding from the mouth of the Guru."

In Pakistan Punjabi, like Urdu, is written in the Perso-Arabic script. However, most official correspondence in Pakistan is done in Urdu.

Sindhi

مونکي اکڙين . وڏا نُورا لاٰئيا   پَ تَرِ بِٽ پِسن ، کُٽان جي کر سامهون .

اکڙيون پِرين ري . جي سي پيوسَن   پَ تَدکِدي کي ڪانگن . نِيرالا نِيٽ ٿيان .

نِن نيٽ ڪي نِيران . جِن ساجرِ سيٽ سايِينا پَ جي . جسي پِ جان . کر حضوري جَچ ڪيو .

ڏِسَن ڏهاڙي . نوءِ نَرِسَن اوڏهين پَ آيا سيجايٰ . نيٽ ٿاري پِرينءَ کي .

اکين کي آهين . عجب جهڙيون عادتون پَ سوري پرائي سات جا وجيو وهائين .

اُتي لِئو لا ئين . جِت حاجَت ناه هٿيار جي .

These paltry eyes of mine
Have brought me favor's grace.
If evil but before them be,
They see Love in its place.
If paltry eyes of mine
Did aught but Love disclose
I'd pluck them out to cast
As morsels for the crows.
Mine eyes have made a feast
Where kin and friends engage.
It is as if life, body, soul
Had gone on pilgrimage.
All day they look and yet
They halt out there to see.
They saw and recognized Love
And have returned to me.
Strange habits have mine eyes
To trade with others' pain.
Love's conquest they have made
Where weapon brings no gain.

SHAH ABDUL LATIF BHITAI, *Risalo*

Sindhi is spoken in Pakistan and is also one of the constitutional languages of India. It is spoken by about 15 million people in the province of Sind, in southern Pakistan, and by about 2½ million more across the border in India. The largest Sindhi-speaking city is Hyderabad, Pakistan.

Sindhi is an Indo-European language, related to Urdu and the languages of northern India. In Pakistan it is written in the Arabic script with several additional letters to accommodate special sounds.

राधा राधा राधा राधा कृष्ण जी । ... ॥
रास-मंडलिम च्यन प्रेनुक मम ।
सास-वज मनु गांमनु नन्नम ॥
अक-अकिस अश्-वास लब्रधान आस नादा । राधा ॥

तुन आमन्य तंत्य मंत्य भांमत्य ।
न्याय अंजुरित पागम ऍमेसुन्य ॥
नारुद सुदाम शुक्रदेव ध्रुव तु प्रह्लादा । ... ॥

कुल्य कल तु क्रज्ञि मुज्ञि मुचुशाचित ।
सीन मंज मागुवद् पीर भांविन ॥
गोकलक्य मुक्क गांमत्य दादा पदादा । ... ॥

अकुय तु कृष्ण जुव सारिनय सूत्य ।
ज्ञीव-पण कतु ज्ञानु तत्ति आंस्य कृत्य ॥
कृष्णय अवाधि-मान तम-रंस्त सांरय वाधा । .... ॥

परमानंदु चेति लज्जिनय अंद ।
पूशिनय युथुय प्रेम अंदय-वंद ॥
राधा-सारखतिधि करुनन प्रसादा । ५

In the rasa circle, drunk with the wine of love, thousands of Gopis were absorbed in dancing. Holding one another's hand they shouted (repeating, Radha-Krishna! Radha-Krishna!)

Bhaktas like Narada, Sudama, Shuka, Dhruva, and Prahlada were there, mad with joy – their doubts dissolved, their minds having found the truth.

Trees, plants, stones opened their eyes and revealed the secrets of their innermost hearts. All in Gokal felt liberated (from bondage of earthly existence) with their grandfathers and great-grandfathers.

One Krishna was with each and every soul. The species of souls present there were so many that I cannot tell their number. Among them all Krishna alone is eternal, all else is subject to disappearance (to be eliminated as not true and real).

May you too, Paramananda, attain the goal! May such love continue to bless you all along! (Rejoice that) Radha as Sarasvati (Goddess of Poetry and Eloquence) has bestowed on you her grace.

PARMANAND, *The Dance of the Gopis*

Kashmiri is the principal language of the state of Kashmir, long disputed between India and Pakistan. In India it is one of the official languages recognized by the constitution. Although part of the Indic branch of the Indo-European family of languages, it actually belongs to a small subdivision called the Dardic languages. Latest figures show about 4 million speakers.

Kashmiri is written in both the Devanagari (Hindi) and the Arabic script, each with additional diacritical marks to represent special sounds in the language. The former is generally used by Hindus, the latter by Moslems. Moslem speakers of Kashmiri also tend to use many words of Persian and Arabic origin.

Pʰʌqir Ali sɛnʌs hin hirʌnɛ ćʌγa ɛćʌm.

Iˑnɛ iˑɛn bʌm, iˑik Dərbɛˑśo bilom. Siśpərɛ teˑrɛ horuˑtʌm b̥ʌm. Hʌn guntsʌnolo huyɛˑs Hʌnumʌn Muˑn yʌkʌlʌtɛ uyərćər tsuˑmi. Huyɛˑs ruˑŋolo fʌt no gućʌmi. Gućaiyʌsər eˑyɛnomtsɛ qau mʌnimi: "Dərbɛˑśo ! Dərbɛˑśo !" nosɛn. Diˑtʌlimi. Diˑtʌl bərɛˑmi kɛ hin buˑt paˑkiˑza dʌsiˑnʌn ɛˑśkitsər dumobo.

Iˑnɛ sɛnomo : "Mi bʌb'a goˑr qau ɛćai" ɛsomo. Sɛnʌsər iˑnɛ dʌsin motsi noltʌn iˑsɛ Hʌnumʌn Muˑn yaˑrər niˑmi. Niˑʌsər iˑsɛ ȼiȿɛ hʌn hiŋʌn sɪka manimi. Ulo nići kɛ hin γɛniśɛ sʌlʌtʌŋɛ hirʌn horuˑtom bai; buˑt mariŋ mariŋ tʌlo gośiŋʌnts sitaˑriŋ noka horućʌm baˑn. Dərbɛˑśo niˑn sʌlaˑm ɛtimi. Inɛ hiˑrɛ sʌlamɛ juwaˑb duˑmərimi. Duməriˑn yuguśʌntser oˑsimi: "Dərbɛˑśu.ər hʌn həriˑpʌn sitaˑrɛtɛ 'ɛˑγərin." Uˑɛ tʌloˑwɛ sitaˑriŋ noka buˑt uyʌm ućəreka həriˑpʌn 'ɛˑγərumʌn.

I shall tell the story of a man called Faqir Ali.

He had a son, his name was Derbesho. He was staying at the Shishper grazing ground. One day he took the goats off to graze in the direction of Hunumun Mun. Leaving the goats in the pasture, he laid himself down. When he had lain down and had gone to sleep, a call came: "Derbesho! Derbesho!" He woke up. On waking up he saw that a beautiful maiden had come up to his head.

She said to him: "My father is calling you." When she said this he followed the girl and came to the foot of Hunumun Mun. On approaching it, a door opened in the mountain. When he went in a man with a golden mustache was sitting there, and seven beautiful women were sitting there with sitars. Derbesho entered and salaamed. The man responded to his salaam. Having done so he said to his daughters: "Play a tune for Derbesho on the sitar." The seven took their sitars and while singing with sweet voices played a tune.

Burushaski is spoken by a mere 40,000 people in the Karakoram Mountains of northwestern Kashmir. It is of special interest to philologists, in that it appears to be completely unrelated to any other language of the area, or for that matter to any other language of the world. It is probably a remnant of some prehistoric language community, all but obliterated by successive Dravidian and Indo-European invasions. Burushaski has not been committed to writing. The text above is merely a phonetic transcription of the spoken language.

Gujarati

માનવીનું હૈયું

માનવીના હૈયાને નંદવામાં વાર શી ?
અધઓલ્યા   ઓલડે,
થોડે   અબોલડે,
પોચાશા હૈયાને પીંજવામાં વાર શી ?

સ્મિતની જ્યાં વીજળી,
જરીશી ફરી વળી,
એના એ હૈયાને રંજવામાં વાર શી ?
એવા તે હૈયાને નંદવામાં વાર શી ?

માનવીના હૈયાને રંજવામાં વાર શી ?
એના એ હૈયાને નંદવામાં વાર શી ?

How little it takes to break the human heart!
A word half spoken;
A word unspoken;
How little it takes to bleed the heart!

The lightning flash of a teeny smile;
How little it takes to please that heart!
And how little it takes to break it!

How little it takes to please the human heart!
And how little it takes to break it!

UMASHANKAR JOSHI
The human heart

Gujarati is spoken principally in the state of Gujarat, westernmost India, bordering Pakistan and the Arabian Sea. Like the other languages of the northern two-thirds of India, it is descended from Sanskrit, and is thus a member of the Indo-European family. Gujarati is written in an alphabet similar to that of Sanskrit and Hindi, but without the "headstroke," or horizontal line, at the top. With about 50 million speakers, it is one of the official provincial languages recognized by the Indian constitution.

Marathi

मला उगीच ग्रंधुक ग्रंधुक ग्रशा गोष्टी ग्राठवतात. परंतु त्या जशा ग्राठवतात तशाच खरोखर झाल्या, कीं, त्यांच्या-संबंधीं ग्राठवणींत माझ्या चपल कल्पनेनें त्यांत ग्रापलें चापल्य बरें-च योजिलें ग्राहे, तें कांहीं सांगतां येत नाही.तरी पण ग्रातां ग्रधिक चर्पटपंजरी न लावतां जी म्हणून ग्रगदीं जुनी ग्राठवण मला होते ग्राहे तिथून मी ग्रापलें चरित्र सांगण्यास प्रारंभ करतों ग्राणि ग्रशा तन्हेनें माझ्या ग्राठवगीरासून प्रारंभ करून मग ग्राधोंच्या गोष्टी जसजशा मला। कळल्या (ग्रर्थातच लोकांच्या तोंडून) तसतशा सांगेन.

I have a sort of hazy recollection of certain events, but I am unable to state for a certainty whether they really happened as I remember them, or whether these memories are greatly embellished by my fertile imagination. However, enough of these tiresome reflections. Let us begin the story of my life with the earliest recollection that comes to mind. Having thus begun, I shall recount later on what I know of earlier events (as told, of course, by those around me).

HARINARAYAN APTE, I

Marathi is spoken in the Indian state of Maharashtra, located on the west coast and facing the Arabian Sea. It includes the city of Bombay, but Poona, the capital of the powerful Maratha kingdom of the 17th century, has always been the center of Marathi culture. In southwesternmost Maharashtra a separate and distinct dialect known as Konkani is spoken; this dialect also extends into the small adjacent state of Goa.

Like Hindi, Marathi is one of the Indic languages and thus part of the Indo-European family. Its alphabet is essentially the same as the one used in Hindi. With about 75 million speakers, it ranks as one of the major languages of India.

কত অজানারে জানাইলে তুমি,
 কত ঘরে দিলে ঠাঁই---
দূরকে করিলে নিকট বন্ধু,
 পরকে করিলে ভাই।
   পুরানো আবাস ছেড়ে যাই যবে
   মনে ভেবে মরি কী জানি কী হবে,
   নূতনের মাঝে তুমি পুরাতন
      সে কথা যে ভুলে যাই
   দূরকে করিলে নিকট বন্ধু,
      পরকে করিলে ভাই

জীবনে মরণে নিখিল ভুবনে
 যখনি যেখানে লবে,
চিরজনমের পরিচিত ওহে,
 তুমিই চিনাবে সবে।
   তোমারে জানিলে নাহি কেহ পর,
   নাহি কোনো মানা, নাহি কোনো ডর
   সবারে মিলায়ে তুমি জাগিতেছ,
      দেখা যেন সদা পাই
   দূরকে করিলে নিকট বন্ধু,
      পরকে করিলে ভাই

Thou hast made me known to friends whom I knew not. Thou hast given me seats in homes not my own. Thou hast brought the distant near and made a brother of the stranger.

I am uneasy at heart when I have to leave my accustomed shelter; I forget that there abides the old in the new, and that there also thou abideth.

Through birth and death, in this world or in others, wherever thou leadest me it is thou, the same, the one companion of my endless life who ever linkest my heart with bonds of joy to the unfamiliar.

When one knows thee, then alien there is none, then no door is shut. Oh, grant me my prayer that I may never lose the bliss of the touch of the one in the play of the many.

RABINDRANATH TAGORE, Gitanjali

Bengali is spoken in the region historically known as Bengal, now lying in both India and Bangladesh. In the latter it is spoken by virtually the entire population of 125 million; in India it is spoken by about 80 million people in the state of West Bengal. With its more than 200 million speakers, Bengali ranks sixth among all the languages of the world; only Chinese, English, Hindi, Spanish, and Arabic have more.

Bengali is one of the Indic languages, a part of the Indo-European family. It is most closely related to Assamese and Oriya, particularly the former. The alphabet is based on, but is distinctly different from, the Devanagari of Sanskrit.

The largest Bengali-speaking city is Calcutta, the capital of West Bengal. The dialect spoken there is considered the standard; the one spoken in Bangladesh is somewhat different. The word Bangladesh is a combination of the words for "Bengali" and "country."

Bengali literature is dominated by the great writer and poet Rabindranath Tagore (1861–1941), who won the Nobel Prize for Literature in 1913.

Oriya

ଦକ୍ଷିଣ ଦେଶରେ ସିନ୍ଧୁ ନାମକ ଏକ ଗଜ୍ୟ ଥୁଲ୍ଲା। ସେଠାରେ ଶରବାହୁ ବୋଲ୍ ଜଣେ ଗଜା ଥଲେ। ତାଙ୍କର ଦୁଇଟି ଗଣୀ ଥାନ୍ତ୍ରୀ। ବଡ଼ଗଣୀର ନାମ ପ୍ରେମଶୀଲା, ସାନ ଗଣୀର ନାମ କନକମଞ୍ଜରୀ। ସାନ ଗଣୀଟି ବଡ଼ ସୁନ୍ଦର। ତାହାରେ ଗଜା ବଡ଼ ସ୍ନେହ କରୁଥାନ୍ତ୍ରୀ। ବଡ଼ ଗଣୀଟିକୁ ଦେଖି ପାରନ୍ତି ନାହିଁ। କେତେ ଧନ ଗଲ୍ପରେ ଦୈବଯୋଗେ ବଡ଼ ଗଣୀର ଗୋଟିଏ ପୁଅ ଜନ୍ମ ହେଲା। ବଡ଼ ଗଣୀର ପୁଅ ହେବା ଦେଖି ସାନଗଣୀ ମନେ ମନେ ଚନ୍ତାକର ଦାରୁଥିଲା, ତାର ତ ପୁଅ ହେଲ୍ଣି ସେ ଗଜ୍ୟ ପାଇବ, ଭଲ ମନ୍ଦ ହେଲେ ଗଜା ମୋତେ କାଣ୍ଟୁ ଗଜ୍ୟରୁ ତଡ଼ଦେବେ। ମୁଁ ଏବେ କ ଉପାୟ କରୁଛି ?

In the southern regions there was a kingdom called Sindhu. Its ruler was a rajah named Birobahu. He had two queens. The older queen was called Premosila, the younger Konokomonjori. The younger queen was very beautiful and the rajah doted upon her, but the older queen he didn't care for at all. It happened that after a while the older queen gave birth to a son. Learning of this, the younger queen thought to herself, "She has borne a son who will rule someday. The first chance the rajah gets he will probably banish me from the kingdom. What am I going to do now?"

MAHESVARA MISRA, *Tales of Abolakara*

Oriya is spoken in eastern India, principally in the state of Orissa, which faces the Bay of Bengal. It belongs to the Indic branch of the Indo-European family of languages. There are about 35 million speakers.

The distinctive Oriya alphabet, though of the same origin as the other languages of India, is markedly different in appearance. Instead of the horizontal line along the top, most Oriya letters contain a large semicircle. This stems from the fact that the script was originally designed for writing on palm leaves using a stylus. A continuous horizontal line would have caused the long slender leaves to split, so rounded characters were used instead.

Assamese

অসমীয়া ভাষা অতি প্ৰাচীন আৰু ঐতিহ্যপূৰ্ণ। খৃষ্টীয় সপ্তম শতিকাতে বিখ্যাত চীনা পৰিব্ৰাজকাচাৰ্য্য হিউৱেন চাঙে ইয়াৰ বৈশিষ্ট্যৰ কথা প্ৰকাৰান্তৰে উল্লেখ কৰি গৈছে। হিউৱেন চাঙে লিখিছিল, "কামৰূপৰ ভাষা মধ্য ভাৰতৰ ভাষাৰ পৰা কিছু পৃথক।" অৰ্থাৎ সেই সুদূৰ অতীততে, হয়তো বা তাৰো বহু কালৰ পূৰ্বেই আৰ্য্য সম্ভূত অসমীয়া ভাষাই স্থানীয় আৰ্য্যেতৰ বিভিন্ন ভাষাৰ প্ৰভাৱত পৰি স্বকীয়া ৰূপ গ্ৰহণ কৰিছিল।

Assamese is a very ancient language with a long tradition behind it. Hieun-Ts'ang, the great Chinese traveler of the 7th century AD, made mention of its distinctiveness in an indirect way. He wrote, "The language of Kamarupa," i.e., modern Assam, "differs a little from that of mid-India." This means that Assamese, which is derived from the Old Indo-Aryan language, acquired its distinctive shape and form in that distant past, maybe even long before that time, through the influence of the local non-Aryan languages surrounding it.

Assamese is spoken in easternmost India, in the state of Assam which borders Burma and China and is bisected by the Brahmaputra River. Most of its speakers live in a 50-mile-wide swath on either side of the river.

Though spoken by only 15 million people (less than 2 percent of India's population), Assamese is one of the constitutionally recognized languages of the country. It is another of the Indic languages, a part of the Indo-European family. Its alphabet is virtually the same as that of Bengali, to which it is closely related.

अम्बरे वदन झपावह गोरि

राज सुनइछि चान्दक चोरि ॥

घरे घरे पहरी गेल अछ जोहि

अबही दूपण लागत तोहि ॥

सुन सुन सुन्दरि हित-उपदेश

सपनेहु जनु हो विपद-कलेश ॥

हास-सुधारस न कर उजोर

घनिके वनिके धन बोलब मोर ॥

अधर-समीप दसन कर जोति

सिंदुर-सीम वैसाउलि मोति ॥

O bright girl, please cover your face with a piece of cloth: they report the theft of the moon in the kingdom.

The watchman has carried out a house-to-house search and then he has gone away: now you will be accused of the offense.

Hear, O beautiful girl, this wholesome advice in order that you may not, even in dream, have any misfortune or trouble.

You should not let the nectar of your smile shine forth outside, or a wealthy trader will claim your face as his property.

On the skirts of your lips, the teeth are shining; they look like pearls set in vermilion.

A Song of Vidyapati

Maithili is spoken in eastern India, principally in the northern half of the state of Bihar, by about 10 million people. There are also some 3 million speakers in neighboring Nepal.

Another of the Indic languages, Maithili is closely related to Bhojpuri and Magahi, also of Bihar, the three often combined under the single term Bihari. Bhojpuri is spoken by about 25 million people in western Bihar, with another 1½ million in Nepal, and 200,000 on the island of Mauritius. Magahi speakers number about 10 million in an area to the south of where Maithili is spoken.

Although a rich body of poetry exists from the 15th century onward, Bihari ceased to be cultivated as a written language in the 19th century. It was therefore not designated as one of the constitutional languages of India. In this century a movement was begun to revive written Maithili and have it declared a separate language. While some success has been achieved in this direction, Hindi is the language used in Bihar for official correspondence and instruction in the schools.

చెవులు గోరును మంచి జిలిబిలి పాటల,
తియ్యని మాటల తెనగు వినగ
చర్ంబు గోరును సరవి తోడుత శీత
మృదుల సంస్పర్శ సంపదల నె పుడు
కన్నులు గోరును కమనీయ వర్ణంబు
లై' నట్టి రూపంబుల నువ్వు తోడ
నాలుక గోరును, నయము తోడుత, తిపి,
యొగరు, కారము, చేదు' ప్ప, పులుసు,
ముక్కు_ గోరును సద్గంధములను జెలగి,
చెవులు చర్ంబు కన్నులు, జిహ్వా ముక్కు_,
నిన్ని యును గూడినటువంటి యిల్లు రోసి,
తన్న గనుగొని సుఖియింప దగును వేమ.

The ears delight in gentle harmonious songs and sweet words well ordered; the skin in like manner is gratified by coolness and soft touches; the eyes desire forms adorned with lovely hues and delicately proportioned; the tongue naturally is pleased with tastes astringent, pungent, bitter, salt, and acid; and the nose takes pleasure in grateful scents. But let us abhor the corporeal mansion that renders us subject to the five feelings perceived by the ears, skin, eyes, tongue, and nose. See that thou art a being distinct from these earthly ties; and thus shalt thou be happy, O Vema!

The Verses of Vemana

Telugu is spoken principally in the state of Andhra Pradesh, southeastern India, whose capital is Hyderabad. With about 75 million speakers, it is the most widely spoken of the Dravidian languages of southern India, completely unrelated to those of the north. The Telugu alphabet developed out of the ancient Brahmi script that gave rise to virtually all of the alphabets of India. It closely resembles that of Kannada.

Kannada

ರಾಮ ಐತಾಳರು ನದಿಯನ್ನು ದಾಟ ಕಣ್ಮರೆಯಾಗುವ ತನಕ ಅವರ ತಂಗಿ ಸರಸೋತಮ್ಮ ನೋಡುತ್ತ ನಿಂತಿದ್ದಳು. ಅನಂತರ ಬೇಸರವೆಂದು ಮನೆಯ ಕಡೆಗೆ ಹೊರಟಳು. ಆದರೆ ಪಾರೋತಿಯು, ಅವಳು ಕರೆದರೂ ಹೋಗಲಿಲ್ಲ. ಇನ್ನೂ ಅಲ್ಲಿಯೇ ನಿಂತಿದ್ದಾಳೆ. ಈಗ ಆಕೆ ಯನ್ನು ಗಂಡನ ಮರಳಿ ಬರುವ ಚಿಂತೆ ಕಾಡುತ್ತಿಲ್ಲ. ಬೇಸಾಯದ ಚಿಂತೆ ಕಾಡುತ್ತಿತ್ತು. 'ನೆರೆ ನೀರು ಇನ್ನು ನಾಲ್ಕು ದಿವಸ ಇದೇ ರೀತಿ ನಿಂತುಬಿಟ್ಟರೆ, ಮುಂದಿನ ವರ್ಷ ಉಣ್ಣುವುದು ದೇನನ್ನು ?' ಎಂಬ ಚಿಂತೆ. ಹಾಗೆ ಕೇಳಿದೋದರೆ ರಾಮ ಐತಾಳರ ಸಂಸಾರದಲ್ಲಿ — ಚಿಂತೆಯ ಭಾರವನ್ನು ಈ ಇಬ್ಬರು ಹೆಂಗಸರು ಹೊತ್ತಂತೆ ಯಜಮಾನರಾದ ಐತಾಳರೇ ಹೊರುವಂತಿಲ್ಲ. ಅವರಮ ಇದ್ದುದರಲ್ಲೇ ಲಘುಜೀವನ. ಪೌರೋಹಿತ್ಯದ ದೆಸೆಯಿಂದಾಗಿ ಅವರು ಸಾಗು ವಳೆಯ ಕಡೆಗೆ ಸಮನಾಗಿ ಮನಸ್ಸು ಕೊಡುವುದೂ ಕಡಿಮೆ.

As Rama Aytala crossed the river and disappeared from view, his sister Sarasotamma stood there watching him. Then she felt tired and started out for home. But Paroti did not move, though she called to her. She still stood there. She was not troubled now by the thought of her husband's return. Only the thought of tilling the land bothered her. She thought, "If the floodwaters remain at their present level for many more days, what will we eat next year?" Such things mattered little to the master Rama Aytala, who could not bear the burden of thoughts and worries as these two women did. His life was easy, all things considered. Owing to his priestly duties, he gave little thought to matters of sowing and tilling.

K. S. KARANTA, *Back to the Soil*

Kannada, also known as Kanarese, is spoken in southwestern India, principally in the state of Karnataka (formerly Mysore) whose capital is Bangalore. A member of the Dravidian family of languages, it is spoken by about 40 million people. The Kannada alphabet is very similar to that used in Telugu, but the language itself is more closely related to Tamil and Malayalam.

கொந்தவிழ் மலர்ச்சோலை நன்னீழல் வைகினுங்
குளிர்தீம் புனற் கையள்ளிக்
கொள்ளுகினுமந்நீ ரிடைத்திளைத்தாடினுங்
குளிர்சந்தவாடை மடவார்
வந்துலவுகின்றதென முன்றிலிடை யுலவவே
வசதிபெறுபோதும் வெள்ளூ
வட்ட மதிப்பட்டப் பகற் போலநிலவுதர
மகிழ்போதும் வேலையமுதம்
விந்தைபெறவாறுசுவையில் வந்ததெனவமுதுண்ணும்
வேளையிலுமாகலங்தம்
வெள்ளளிலைய டைக்காய் விரும்பிவேன் டியவண்ணம்
விளையாடி விழிது யிலினுஞ்
சந்ததமு நின்னருளை மறவாவரந்தந்து
தமியேனை ரக்ஷ புரிவாய்
சர்வபரிபூரண வகண்டதத்துவமான
சச்சிதானந்த சிவமே.

Whether in grateful shade I dwell of groves
Rich in clustered blooms, or cool sweet draughts
I quaft from limpid stream,
Or in its waters bathe and sport,
Or, fanned by fragrant breezes fresh.
That like maidens in the courtyard play,
I revel in the full moon's day-like splendor.
Or in dainties I feast where in ocean's ambrosia
Haply hath wondrous entered, or in garlands,
Perfumes, betel I joy, or rest in sleep,
Thy grace may I never forget! This boon
To me grant and from the world guard me,
O Sivam, all pervading, infinite, true,
Thou art the one Reality, Knowledge, Pure and Bliss!

SAINT THAYUMANAVAR, *God and the World*

Tamil is spoken principally in the Indian state of Tamil Nadu (formerly Madras), located on the southeastern (Coromandel) coast and extending down to the southernmost tip of the subcontinent. There are about 65 million Tamil speakers in India. It is also spoken by about 5 million people in northeastern Sri Lanka, about one million in Malaysia, and in smaller communities in Singapore, Mauritius, Trinidad, Guyana, and parts of East Africa.

Tamil is the oldest and most richly developed of the Dravidian languages. The alphabet, like all the indigenous alphabets of India, is derived ultimately from the ancient Brahmi script. *Curry* and *mulligatawny* are two Tamil words that have entered the English language. The latter is a combination of the Tamil words for "pepper" and "water."

Malayalam

കളത്തിലെ കെട്ടുപിണഞ്ഞ നാഗങ്ങളെയും അവയിൽ
കണ്ണനട്ടിരിക്കുന്ന, ആ നിലവിളക്കിലെ നാളംപോലെ തിള
ങ്ങുന്ന, പെൺകിടാവിനെയും അവൻ മാറിമാറി നോക്കി.
അവളുടെ കഴുത്തിൽ കുടുക്കിക്കെട്ടി കല്ലുപതിച്ച ആഭരണം
വെട്ടിതിളങ്ങുന്ന. ദീപനാളങ്ങൾ മറച്ചിട്ടില്ലാത്ത മാറിൽ
പുളഞ്ഞുമറിയുന്നു.......... പതുക്കെപ്പതുക്കെ അവന്റെ കണ്ണിൽ
നിന്നു പന്തലും മറ്റവും ആളുകളും ഒഴിഞ്ഞുപോയി. ഇപ്പോൾ
കൊടുംകാട്ടിലാണ്. ഉയരത്തിൽ, മാനംമുട്ടിനില്ക്കുന്ന ഒരു
വൃക്ഷത്തിന്റെ കവുളിയിൽ രാജകുമാരൻ ഇരിക്കുന്നു.

Appunni looked now at the interlocked snakes in the "square," now at
the girl sitting amidst the lamps with her eyes fixed on the snakes, herself
golden like the flame of the lamps. A jewel set with stones flashed and
gleamed in the hollow of her neck. The flames turned and twisted like
snakes on her bare breasts. Slowly, very slowly, the pandal and the
people and the courtyard vanished from his sight. He was now in a thick
forest. The prince was sitting on a tall tree whose top touched the
heavens.

M. T. VASUDEVAN NAIR, Nalukettu

Malayalam, with the stress on the third syllable, is spoken in southernmost
India, in the state of Kerala (capital, Trivandrum) on the western (Malabar)
coast. There are about 35 million speakers.

Malayalam is another of the Dravidian languages, closely related to Tamil.
It actually developed about a thousand years ago out of the western dialects
of Tamil. Though its distinctive alphabet is ultimately derived from the
ancient Brahmi script, its present form dates from the 17th century. The
English words *teak*, *copra*, and *atoll* come from Malayalam.

Sinhalese

මල් රැසකින් ෙබාෙහෝ මල් දම් ගොතන්නේ
යම් ෙසේ ද, එෙසේ ම, උපන් මිනිසා විසින් ෙබාෙහෝ කුසල්
කටයුතු ය.

සාමාන්‍ය මල් සුවඳක් හෝ සඳුන්, තුවරලා
ඉද්ද වැනි මල්වල සුවඳක් හෝ උඩු සුළඟට ෙනා යයි.
එෙහත් සත්පුරුෂයන්ෙග (සිල්) සුවඳ උඩු සුළඟට ද යයි.
සත්පුරුෂයා සියලු දිශාවල ම සිල් සුවඳ පතුරුවයි.

සඳුන්, තුවරලා, මහෙනල්, දෑසමන් යන සියලු
මල් ජාතීන්ෙග සුවඳට වඩා සිල් සුවඳ උසස් ය.

As many kinds of garlands can be made from a heap of flowers, so many good works should be achieved by a mortal when once he is born.

The scent of flowers does not travel against the wind, nor that of sandalwood, of tagara, or jasmine. But the fragrance of good people travels even against the wind. A good man pervades every quarter.

Sandalwood, tagara, a lotus flower, jasmine – among these kinds of perfumes the perfume of virtue is unsurpassed
The Dhammapada (ancient Buddhist scriptures)

Sinhalese, or Sinhala, is the principal language of Sri Lanka, the other being Tamil. It is spoken by about 15 million people, or three-fourths of the total population, living mainly in the southern and western two-thirds of the island. An Indic language descended from Sanskrit, it was brought to the island by settlers from northern India in the 5th or 6th century BC. The alphabet, however, with its generally rounded letters, more closely resembles those of the Dravidian languages of southern India.

The English words *tourmaline* and *beriberi* are of Sinhalese origin. The word *serendipity* comes from Serendib, an old name of Sri Lanka.

Nepali

एक दिन एउंटा कुकुर मासुको पसलबाट मामुको चोक्टो चोरेर बस्तीतिर भाग्यो । बाटामा ठूलो खोलो पथ्यर्यो । त्यस खोलामाथि सांघु थियो । सांघुमा हिंड्दा त्यस कुकुरले तल खोलामा ब्राफ्नो छाया देख्यो । यो ता ब्रर्को कुकुर पो मुखमा मासु च्यापेर जांदो रहेछ भनी ठानेर त्यो मासु खोस्नलाइ झंट्यो । ड्याङ गर्दा ता ब्रापुनैं मुखको मासु पो पानीमा खस्यो । छायाका कुकुरको मुखको मासु नदेख्ता त्यसका मनमा ब्राफूले च्यापेका मासुको समझ्ना भयो । तर पानीमा खसेको मासुको चोक्टो त्यस कुकुरले केही गरेर पनि पाएन ।

One day a dog who had taken a piece of meat from a butcher shop set off for home. On the way he came to a large river. Over the river there was a bridge. While running across the bridge the dog looked down and saw his reflection in the river. Thinking that this was another dog with a piece of meat in its mouth, he set out to take it for himself. When he barked the meat fell from his mouth into the water. Not seeing the meat in the mouth of the dog reflected in the water, he remembered the meat which he himself had been holding. But no matter what he did, he could not find the piece of meat that had fallen into the water.

Nepali is the national language of Nepal. It is the mother tongue of about 15 million people there and is spoken fluently as a second language by about 2 million others. Additionally it is spoken by about 2½ million people in India, mainly in northernmost West Bengal (in and around the city of Darjeeling) and in the state of Sikkim. It is also the principal language of southwestern Bhutan.

Like the major languages of northern India, Nepali is one of the Indic languages and thus of the Indo-European family. The alphabet is the same as that used for Sanskrit and Hindi.

Tibetan

གསུང་དང་བླ་མ་རྣམས་ལ་ཕྱག་འཚལ་ལོ། །

རྗེ་འགྲོ་བ་མགོན་པོ་དེ་ཞབས་ལ་འདུད། །

བླ་མ་མི་འགྱུར་ཚེ་ཀྱི་དང་ལ་བཞུགས། །

སྤྱན་རས་གཟིགས་གྱུང་ཚེ་ཀྱི་དང་ལ་བཞུར། །

ཐུག་རྗེ་ཆེན་པོ་ཚེ་ཀྱི་དང་ལ་བཞུགས། །

ཐང་སྟོང་རྒྱལ་པོ་ཚེ་ཀྱི་དང་ལ་བཞུགས། །

པོ་ཆེན་གོང་མ་ཚེ་ཀྱི་དང་ལ་བཞུགས། །

རྒྱུ་སྤྲི་ཁྱིམ་པ་ཡིག་དྲུག་མ་ཉི་རྡོངས། །

ༀ་མ་ཎི་པདྨེ་ཧཱུྂ།

Let us salute the Teachers!
Bow to the feet of the Venerable Lord of Living Beings!
Abide in the spiritual essence of the Eternal Teacher!
Abide in the spiritual essence of Avalokiteçvara!
Abide in the spiritual essence of the All-Merciful One!
Abide in the spiritual essence of Thaṅ-stoṅ rgyal-po!
Abide in the spiritual essence of the sublime Paṇḍita!
You, country-folk, recite the six-lettered māṇi!
    Oṁ māṇi padme hūṅ!

                    The Ceremony of Breaking the Stone

Tibetan is spoken by about 2 million people in what was formerly Tibet, now the Tibet Autonomous Region of China. Another 3 million speakers live in the Chinese provinces of Szechwan (Sichuan), Tsinghai (Qinghai), and Kansu (Gansu). Additionally about one million people in Nepal speak Tibetan as a second language. A dialect of Tibetan called Jonkha is the principal language of Bhutan.

Tibetan and Burmese are the two most important languages of the Tibeto-Burman branch of the Sino-Tibetan family. They are, however, only distantly related and actually belong to different subdivisions of this branch. The Tibetan alphabet dates from the 7th century AD. It is based on the Sanskrit, having been adapted by a Tibetan minister sent to study in Kashmir.

Uigur

كەچ مەز گەلى ئۇرۇمچى كوچىلىرىنى تاماشا قىلماقتىسمەن.
كوچىنىڭ نېرىلى دوخمۇشىدىن بىمركەشى كوزىنى مىنىڭددىن ئۇزمەى
قاراپ كېلىۋاتىمدۇ. مەن ئوزەمنىڭ تۇرقۇمدىن لور ئۇنۇپ چاپانلىرىمنى
تىلمىشتۇرۇپ، ئۇلاقچامنى تۇزەئۇرەك كىيىپىمۇ ئالدىم. قىزىردىپ
كەتتىم ئىتىممالىم، پۇتۇن بەدەنلىمردەم ئوت ئىلىپ بىنىدۇققانلىدەك
بولدى. «نىمانچە قاراپدىغانئىدۇ، بۇ ئادەم»

قامەلۇم كەشى ماڭا بىلىينلمشمىپ كېلىۋاتىمدۇ. تېغىنچە
مىنىڭددىن كوزىنى ئالغىنى يوق. ئۇنىڭ چىمرايىمدا بىلمەن
كەلگەنسىيرى قىزىردىپ كۇلۇمسىرەش ئالامەتى پەيدا بولدى. مانا
ئۇ ئەلدى يېنىمىدا. ئۇ ماڭا قول ئۇزۇۋئۇپ: «سىز مېنى ياخشى
ئونالمايۇاتىسىز ھە؛» ـ دېيدى

It is evening. I am walking along the streets of Urumchi. On the other side of the street, not taking his eyes off me, stands a man. Concerned about my appearance, I straighten my clothes and adjust my hat. Apparently I even blushed. Suddenly I felt hot. "I wonder why that man is watching me."

The stranger comes closer and closer without ever taking his eyes off me. The closer he comes, the broader the smile on his face. Finally he walks right up to me and, extending his hand, says, "It seems you do not recognize me, correct?"

Uigur is spoken over a large area of western China called the Sinkiang (Xinjiang) Uigur Autonomous Region, whose capital is Urumchi. There are about 8 million speakers here, plus another 150,000 across the border in Kazakhstan.

Uigur is a Turkic language and thus of the Altaic family. The Uigurs are an ancient people whose history can be traced back to the early centuries of the Christian era. About the middle of the 8th century they established a large and powerful state in eastern Turkestan. When this was overrun a hundred years later, they established a new kingdom in western China that survived until the Mongol invasion of the 13th century.

The ancient Uigurs developed a script of their own, which was written vertically from left to right. Though not completely original (having been adapted from an earlier script called Sogdian), it had considerable influence upon writing in Asia even after the dissolution of the Uigur kingdom. In the 13th century the Mongols adopted the Uigur script for writing their own language, and in turn passed it on to the Manchus, who were to rule China for over 250 years.

Meanwhile the Uigurs had long since adopted Islam, and with it the Arabic script that they still use today. A new Roman-based alphabet was introduced in China in the 1960s but it failed to take hold.

ᠨᠡᠷ᠎ᠡ ᠶᠢᠨ ᠪᠢᠴᠢᠭᠲᠡᠨ᠎ᠠᠴᠠ ᠪᠢᠴᠢᠭᠲᠡᠨ᠎ᠡ

1240 онд Хэрлен мөрний хөдөө аралд Огөөдэй хааны ордонд их хуралдаан хуралдах үед Монголын Нууц товчоог төгсгөн зохиожээ. Монгол хэлэн дээр хятад үсгээр бичсэн Нууц товчооны эх нь Бээжингийн номын сангаас олдсон юм. Үүнийг Хятадын эрдэмтэн нар судлаж хэдэн удаа хэвлүүлснээс гадна Оросын эрдэмтэн Кафаров, Кучин, Германы Хайниш, Францын Пеллио зэргийн хүн судлаж орос, герман, францаар орчуулж хэвлүүлсэн юм. Одоогийн монгол хэлээр хийсэн орчууллага 1947 онд Улаанбаатарт хэвлэгдсэн болно.

In 1240, when the great Khuraltai (Assembly) was held in the Palace of Ogodai Khan in the valley of the Kerulen River, the writing of the Secret History of Mongolia was completed. The original of the Secret History, printed in Mongolian using Chinese letters, was found in the Peking Library. It has been studied and published several times by Chinese scholars, while the Russian scholars Kafarov and Kuchin, Haenisch of Germany, and Pelliot of France have studied and published it in Russian, German, and French. In 1947 a translation in the modern Mongolian language was published in Ulan Bator.

Mongolian is spoken in both Mongolia and China. In Mongolia proper (traditionally known as Outer Mongolia) there are about 2½ million speakers, while in the Inner Mongolian Autonomous Region of China (traditionally known as Inner Mongolia) there are about 5 million. Another 200,000 speakers live in northwest China, and about 50,000 in Manchuria.

Standard Mongolian is often referred to as Khalkha, to distinguish it from a number of related languages and dialects. These include Buryat and Kalmyk, spoken in Russia. All of these belong to the Mongolian branch of the Altaic family of languages.

The original Mongolian alphabet was adapted from that of the Uigurs in the 13th century. It is written vertically, perhaps under Chinese influence, but, unlike most vertical scripts, it begins at the left. It was used in Outer Mongolia until 1941, and is still used among Mongolian speakers in China, though in a somewhat modified form.

In 1941 the Mongolian People's Republic replaced the old alphabet with a new one based on the Cyrillic. It was the first appearance of Cyrillic in Asia outside the Soviet Union. The alphabet is the same as the Russian, but contains two additional vowels, the ө and γ.

Chinese

In the North it is already late autumn but the summer heat hasn't completely subsided. Before sunset, it is still quite hot in the sun and sweat starts running down your back. You leave the station to have a look around. There's nothing nearby except for the little inn across the road. It's an old-style two-storey building with a wooden shopfront. Upstairs the floorboards creak badly but worse still is the grime on the pillow and sleeping mat. If you wanted to have a wash, you'd have to wait till it was dark to strip off and pour water over yourself in the damp and narrow courtyard. This is a stopover for village peddlers and craftsmen.

GAO XINGJIAN,
Soul Mountain

北方，這季節，已經是深秋。這裡，暑熱卻並未退盡。太陽在落山之前，依然很有熱力，照在身上，脊背也有些冒汗。你走出車站，環顧了一下，對面只有一家小客棧，那是種老式的帶一層樓的木板舖面，在樓上走動樓板便格吱直響，更要命的是那烏黑油亮的枕蓆。再說，洗澡也只能等到天黑，在那窄小潮濕的天井裡，拉開褲襠，用臉盆往身上倒水。那是農村裡出來跑買賣做手藝的落腳的地方。

Chinese is spoken by more people than any other language in the world. All but about 100 million of China's 1¼ billion people, or 1,150,000,000, speak one or another of its dialects. There are another 20 million speakers on Taiwan, 7 million in Thailand, 5 million in Malaysia, 2½ million in Singapore, one million in Vietnam, and lesser numbers in other countries including the United States and Canada. Thus Chinese has more than twice the number of speakers of English, though of course it lacks the universality of English and is spoken by few people not of Chinese origin. Chinese has been an official language of the United Nations since the founding of the organization in 1945.

China constitutes a separate branch of the Sino-Tibetan family of languages. Though it has many dialects, Mandarin (based on the pronunciation of Beijing) is considered the standard and is spoken by nearly three-fourths of all Chinese-speakers in China, or about 900 million people. The Mandarin-speaking area covers more than three-fourths of all of China: the entire north but also the southern provinces of Kweichow (Guizhou) and Szechwan (Sichuan). All the other dialects are confined to the southeastern corner of the country, between the lower course of the Yangtze River and the South China Sea.

The non-Mandarin dialects are:

(1) Wu, spoken by about 80 million people in Shanghai and the surrounding areas;
(2) Cantonese, spoken by about 50 million people in the extreme southern provinces of Kwangtung (Guangdong) and Kwangsi (Guangxi) and also in Hong Kong;
(3) Min, spoken by about 40 million people in Fukien (Fujian) Province and generally subdivided into Northern Min, or Fuzhou, and southern Min, or Amoy. Amoy is also the principal dialect of Taiwan.
(4) Hsiang, with 40 million speakers in Hunan Province;
(5) Hakka, with 30 million speakers in Szechwan, Kwangtung, Kwangsi, Fukien, and also on Taiwan.

In addition, the Min dialects are widely spoken in Malaysia and Singapore, while Cantonese is also spoken in Thailand, Vietnam, and Cambodia. Most Chinese in the United States speak Cantonese.

Chinese, like the other languages of the Sino-Tibetan family, is a tonal language, meaning that different tones, or intonations, distinguish words that otherwise are pronounced identically. The four Chinese tones are (1) high level; (2) high rising; (3) low rising; (4) high falling to low. It is not unusual for a syllable to be pronounced in each of the four tones, each yielding a word with a completely different meaning. For example, the word *ma* in tone one means "mother," while *ma*² means "hemp," *ma*³ means "horse," and *ma*⁴ means "to curse." In fact each tone usually offers a large number of homonyms. *Yi* in tone one can mean, among other things, "one," "clothes," "doctor," and "to cure"; yi^2 "aunt," "doubt," "suitable," and "to shift"; yi^3 "already," "because of," and "by"; yi^4 "easy," "strange," "benefit," and the number "100 million."

Chinese is written with thousands of distinctive characters called ideographs, which have no relation to the sound of a word. A large dictionary will contain as many as 40,000 to 50,000 of them. Chinese children learn about 2,000 by the time they are ten, but one must know two or three times that number to be able to read a newspaper or a novel. One kind of Chinese typewriter has 5,400. The number of strokes required to draw a single character can be as high as 33.

The earliest Chinese characters were pictographs, such as a crescent for the moon, or a circle with a dot in the center to represent the sun. Gradually these gave way to nonpictorial ideographs, which, in addition to standing for tangible objects, also represented abstract concepts. Today two characters (sometimes the same, sometimes different) often stand side by side to form a third. Thus two "tree" characters mean "forest," while "sun" + "moon" = "bright," and "woman" + "child" = "good." Sometimes the two characters are superimposed upon each other, their relative position giving a clue as to the meaning of the newly formed character. When the character for "sun" is placed above the character for "tree" the new character means "high" or "bright," but when it is placed below, the new character means "hidden" or "dark." No matter how many single characters are combined into one, the resulting character always has the same square appearance and is the same size as any other character.

The majority of Chinese characters, however, consist of two elements: a signific, which indicates the meaning of a word, and a phonetic, which indicates the sound. The significs, or radicals, number 214, and indicate the class of objects to which the word belongs. For example, all words relating to wood, such as "tree" and "table," contain the "wood" radical. The phonetic consists of the character for a word whose meaning is totally unrelated to the word in question, but whose pronunciation happens to be the same. Thus the character for "ocean" consists of the signific "water" plus the phonetic "sheep," because the word for "sheep" is pronounced the same as the word for "ocean." In some cases the phonetic stands alone, as in the case of the character for "dustpan," which also stands for the Chinese possessive pronoun, since the word for the pronoun is the same as the word for "dustpan."

Despite their complexity, the Chinese characters do have the advantage of making written communication possible between people speaking mutually unintelligible dialects and languages. A given word may be quite different in Mandarin and Cantonese, but it would be written identically in the two dialects. Since the Chinese characters are also used in Japanese, each language, when written, is partially understandable to a speaker of the other, despite the fact that the two languages are totally unrelated.

Numerous attempts have been made over the years to simplify the Chinese system of writing. In 1955 the Chinese People's Republic initiated a plan to simplify more than 1,700 characters, this number to be increased gradually so that over half of the most commonly used symbols would eventually be simplified. But the ultimate hope for easy readability of Chinese would appear to be an alphabetic script. In 1958 a new Chinese alphabet based on the Roman was introduced, but thus far it appears to have made little headway.

English words of Chinese origin include *tea, typhoon, sampan, kaolin, kumquat, kowtow,* and *shanghai.*

Chuang

Daᴆsam bəima le, ceзŋeiᴆ couᴆ sieŋз banᴆfap haiᴆ de, ₦ᴏnz ᴣeu, de heuᴆ Daᴆsam ma ranz guᴆcəmz, couᴆ gaŋз:" Nueŋҷ ha! Mᴡŋz nəuz mᴡŋz youƨ laз ƨaŋƨ, rəmҷ daŋƨ mᴡŋz ciҷ gieŋᴆ, mᴡŋz ƨəᴡƨ rᴏŋz laз ƨaŋƨ bəi, gou əu rəmҷ dəuз daŋƨ, yəᴡз mᴡŋz gieŋᴆ Бouз gieŋᴆ?" Daᴆsam Бouз roҷ Daᴆŋeiᴆ sieŋз haiᴆ de, ciҷ rᴏŋz laз ƨaŋƨ bəi ninz. Daᴆŋeiᴆ əu rəmҷgᴏnз ma daŋƨ, Daᴆsam couᴆ dai lo.

After Dasam's return, her middle sister began to think of how she could do away with her. Once she invited Dasam to her house for a chat and said, "Sister! You used to say that if you sat in a big tub and were splashed with water, you would instantly become beautiful. Why don't you climb into the tub and let me splash water on you to see if you become beautiful?" Dasam did not suspect that Daney was planning to kill her and slid down to the bottom of the tub. Daney then took some boiling water and poured it all over her. Dasam died instantly.

The Chuang, or Zhuang, are the largest ethnic minority in China. Numbering about 15 million, they live chiefly in the Kwangsi Chuang (Guangxi Zhuang) Autonomous Region which borders Vietnam. There are also some in adjacent provinces to the north and east. Most Chuang speakers are fluent in Chinese.

Of the major languages of Asia, Chuang is most closely related to Thai. The alphabet, developed in the 1950s, is based largely on the Roman.

Miao

1. ꓭ\[no]Ꞓꓛꙋꓷ_ꓬꞁꓔ。ᏟꚉꞒꓔꙋꓵꓥꟙꚉ.

2. ꓔ'ꓐꙋꓛꚉꓬꞁ。ꓷ_ꓯꓩꓨ‾Ꮯꓔ。ꓩꞁ。ꓚ‾Ꮯꙋꓔ‾Ꮯ''ꓔ₈.

3. ꓷ_ꓯꙋꓩꓨ‾ꓔ=ꓮ'Ꞅ=。ꞁꓚꓔꓔꞀ‾ꓔ。ꓚꞁ\[L]ꞁ꒳\[o]ꓕꓩꚉꙋꓔꞁ.

4. Ꞁꚉꓛ\[o]ꓔꙋꞀ\[o]ꓣ‾。ꓬꞁꓩ。ꓛꓷ_\[L]꒳。ꓚꓕ'‾ꓩ‾Ꞁꞁꓔ₈.

1. Hearken: Behold, the sower went forth to sow.

2. And it came to pass, as he sowed, some seed fell by the wayside, and the birds came and devoured it.

3. And other fell on the rocky ground, where it had not much earth; and straightaway it sprang up, because it had no deepness of earth.

4. And when the sun was risen, it was scorched; and because it had no root it withered away.

From Luke viii 5–6

Miao, also known as Hmong, is spoken over a large area of southern China, principally in the province of Kweichow (Guizhou), but also in Yunnan, Hunan, Kwangtung (Guangdong), and as far north as Hupei (Hubei). In all there are about 8 million speakers in China. Together with another language known as Yao it constitutes a separate family whose affiliation is uncertain.

Another 500,000 Miao (Hmong) live in Vietnam, about 200,000 in Laos, and 50,000 in Thailand. At the end of the Vietnam war about 200,000 Hmong from Vietnam and Laos were resettled in the United States. About half are now in California, but many others live in Minnesota, Wisconsin, and other states.

Miao was first written in an ideographic script, but in 1904 a missionary, Samuel Pollard, developed the so-called Pollard script shown above. The simple, purely geometric symbols each stand for a syllable rather than a word. Although it enjoyed considerable success in China for many years, it is now giving way to a new Roman-based alphabet. In Vietnam and Laos the language was not reduced to writing. English-Hmong dictionaries have recently been compiled in the United States based on phonetic transcription.

Yi

1. 万 艮 四 和 支 田 劝
2. 勹 口 狗 丫 艹
3. 匚 口 匀 秃 忺
4. 三 口 吕 凵 勹
5. 甹 口 尒 中 毗
6. 乃 口 屮 孖 缽
7. 玊 口 回 弖 雩
8. 讯 口 力 弱 七
9. 乃 口 力 澬 兓
10. 九 口 力 匊 亡

1. In ancient times there were differences between man and animal.
2. January likes the autumn rain.
3. February likes the leaves of the grasses.
4. March likes the frog.
5. April is the four-legged snake.
6. May is the house lizard.
7. June assumes the form of man.
8. July has mother's transformation.
9. August unites mother's spirit.
10. September is in mother's bosom.

Passage describing the growth of a child during its
mother's pregnancy

Yi, also known as Lolo, is spoken by about 7 million people in southern China, in the provinces of Szechwan (Sichuan), Kweichow (Guizhou), and Yunnan. It is a member of the Tibeto-Burman subgroup of the Sino-Tibetan family of languages. The Yi are fierce tribesmen who resisted outside incursions for centuries.

The Yi script is probably a thousand years old. Its origin is unclear. It was used traditionally by priests and practitioners of various forms of magic. The characters, which generally represent syllables, number in the thousands:

remarkable, since the language, even including its many dialects, contains only a fraction of that many syllables. In the 1970s the Chinese government selected 819 of them to be used in a standardized written form of the language. Some of them were devised solely to transcribe loanwords from Chinese. Recent reports indicate that this has not caught on.

Sibo

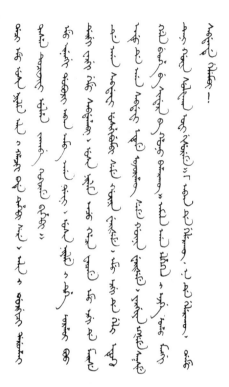

Once upon a time there was a farmer living in the vicinity of the mountains. In the mountains there always appeared tigers which caused harm to animals. One rainy night the farmer's house was leaking everywhere. The farmer was very angry. He did not know what to do. Later when the rain let up he wanted to take a rest. Then he said, "I'm not afraid of the sky and I'm not afraid of the earth, but I am afraid of the leaking!"

Sibo is spoken by a mere 40,000 people in western China. The largest concentration of Sibos is in the Sinkiang (Xinjiang) Uigur Autonomous Region in an area near the border with Kazakhstan.

An offshoot of the now extinct Manchu language, Sibo is a member of the Tungusic branch of the Altaic family of languages. Its vertical script is similar to that of Manchu, which in turn was adapted from the Uigur script in the 13th century.

Naxi

Box 1:   The yak he dances there it is the custom
Box 2:   on La-ts'ü-höddü gko
Box 3:   the stag said he would like to dance there.
Box 4:   For the stag
Box 5:   to dance is not the custom,
Box 6:   the elkskin shoes with the white front
Box 7:   the sons of bitterness wear;
Box 8:   the stag he dances there it is the custom.
Box 9:   Where the pines are the young deer wanted to dance,
Box 10:   the cloven-hoofed they sway in rhythm,
Box 11:   they sway and dance as is the custom.
Box 12:   All the people of the village.

Excerpt from *Mun Ndzer Ä Lä Dzhu*, or Song of
the Dead, Relating the Origin of Bitterness

Naxi, pronounced *nah-shee*, and also known as Moso, is spoken in Yunnan Province, southern China, in and around the town of Lijiang in a bend of the Yangtze River. It is a member of the Tibeto-Burman branch of the Sino-Tibetan family of languages. There are about 280,000 speakers.

The Naxi script is one of the few pictographic systems still extant in the 21st century. The system is not used for communication or record-keeping, but rather to record ancient stories which are read aloud by *dongba*, or priests. The few *dongba* still alive are currently compiling a 100-volume collection of Naxi stories, together with translations into Chinese.

213

夜明けまえの暗闇に眼ざめながら、熱い「期待」の感覚をもとめて、辛い夢の気分の残っている意識を手さぐりする。内臓を燃えあがらせて嚥下されるウイスキーの存在感のように、熱い「期待」の感覚が確実に躰の内奥に回復してきているのを、おちつかぬ気持で望んでいる手さぐりは、いつまでもむなしいままだ。力をうしなった指を閉じる。そして、躰のあらゆる場所で、肉と骨のそれぞれの重みが区別して自覚され、しかもその自覚が鈍い痛みにかわってゆくのを、明るみにむかっていやいやながらあとずさりに進んでゆく意識が認める。そのような、躰の各部分において鈍く痛み、連続性の感じられない重い肉体を、僕自身があきらめの感情において再び引きうける。それがいったいどのようなものの、どのようなときの姿勢であるか思いだすことを、あきらかに自分の望まない、そういう姿勢で、手足をねじまげて僕は眠っていたのである。

Awakening in the predawn darkness, I grope among the anguished remnants of dreams that linger in my consciousness, in search of some ardent sense of expectation. Seeking in the tremulous hope of finding eager expectancy reviving in the innermost recesses of my being – unequivocally, with the impact of whisky setting one's guts afire as it goes down – still I find an endless nothing. I close fingers that have lost their power. And everywhere, in each part of my body, the several weights of flesh and bone are experienced independently, as sensations that resolve into a dull pain in my consciousness as it backs reluctantly into the light. With a sense of resignation, I take upon me once more the heavy flesh, dully aching in every part and disintegrated though it is. I've been sleeping with arms and legs askew, in the posture of a man reluctant to be reminded either of his nature or of the situation in which he finds himself.

KENZABURO OE,
The Silent Cry

Japanese is spoken by virtually the entire population of Japan, now about 125 million.

No definite link has been established between Japanese and any other language, living or dead. Though it adopted the Chinese pictographic characters in the 3rd century AD, Japanese is not in any way related to Chinese. It does resemble Korean in grammatical structure, and some have argued that they are distantly related. But this remains to be proven.

The Japanese ideographs, known as *kanji*, number in the thousands. An educated person can read as many as 5,000 of them; school children are expected to know close to 1,000 by the time they complete elementary school. After World War II the government published a list of 1,850 that it considered basic; this was expanded to 1,945 in 1981.

The *kanji* designate the chief meaningful words of the language: nouns, verbs, and adjectives. They are supplemented, however, by the *kana*, or syllabic characters, which are used chiefly to designate suffixes, particles, conjunctions, and other grammatical forms. There are two types of *kana*, each consisting of 50 characters: the *hiragana*, which is cursive in shape and in general use, and the *katakana*, which is angular in shape and is used mainly in imperial proclamations and in the transcription of foreign words. Each *kana* character stands for a single syllable rather than for a whole word. Theoretically any Japanese word can be written exclusively in the *kana* (children's primers are written entirely in *katakana*) but the large number of homonyms in the language makes this impractical. Modern Japanese, therefore, is written with a mixture of *kanji* and *kana* characters. (As can be seen in the passage above, the *kana* are easily distinguishable from the *kanji* by their greater simplicity of design). The Roman alphabet, called *Romaji* in Japan, has also begun to come into use, but it is confined mainly to the spelling of foreign names (especially brand names) and in international acronyms.

English words of Japanese origin include *kimono, geisha, sukiyaki, sushi, hibachi, jujitsu, karate, samurai, hara-kiri*, and *kamikaze*.

Kenzaburo Oe was the winner of the Nobel Prize for Literature in 1994.

Korean

진달래꽃

나 보기가 역겨워.
가실 때에는
말없이 고히 보내 드리우리다.

영변(寧邊)에 약산(藥山)
진달래꽃
아름따다 가실 길에 뿌리우리다.

가시는 걸음걸음
놓인 그 꽃을
사뿐히 즈려 밟고 가시옵소서。

나 보기가 역겨워
가실 때에는
죽어도 아니 눈물 흘리우리다

When you take your leave,
Tired of seeing me,
Gently and silently I'll bid you go.

From Mount Yag of Yongbyon
An armful of azaleas I shall pick,
And strew them in your path.

Go now I pray, with short steps!
Let each footstep gently tread
The flowers which I have spread for you.

When you take your leave,
Tired of seeing me,
Though I should die, I shall not weep.

KIM SO-WOL, *The Azalea*

Korean is spoken in South and North Korea by about 70 million people. There are another 2 million speakers in China, 700,000 in Japan, and smaller numbers in Russia, Kazakhstan and Uzbekistan. About 600,000 Koreans live in the United States.

Korean, like Japanese, is not known to be related to any other language, though its grammatical structure is somewhat similar to Japanese, and more than half of its vocabulary has been borrowed from the Chinese. Korean used the Chinese characters for writing long before the invention of the Korean alphabet, and continued, even after its invention, to use the two together. (In the fourth line of the poem above the proper nouns *Yongbyon* and *Yag San* appear with the Chinese characters following in parentheses). This practice was abolished in North Korea after World War II, but in the South the Chinese characters continue to be used. Students in South Korean secondary schools today are required to learn 1,800 Chinese characters.

The Korean alphabet, known as Hangul, is the only true alphabet native to the Far East. It was invented in the years 1443–44 by the King of Korea, Sejong. Each of the 40 letters represents a single or double consonant or vowel – not a syllable as in Japanese, or a concept as in Chinese. Korean writing differs from that of most other languages in that the letters of each syllable are grouped together into clusters – as if the English word "seldom" were written

```
S D              S  E  D  O
E O    or
L M              L     M
```

The third word of the last line of the poem above, for example, consists of two clusters, each containing three letters arranged vertically. The first contains the letters *n*, *u*, and *n*, the second *m*, *u*, and *l*. *Nun* is the Korean word for "eye," *mul* the word for "water." Together they form the word *nunmul*, which means "tear" or "tears."

Burmese

မဲဇာချောင် တောင်ခြေက လွမ်းပါရ
ပွဲခါညောင် ရေစင်သွန်းချိန်မို့
သဲသာသောင်မြေကျွန်းရယ်က ခွေပတ်လည်။

ရေဂ်လှိုသာ ရမ်းပါရ
တမ်းတကာ တဖွိုဖွိုနှင့်
ပြည်ရွှေဘို အောင်ဠာနဆီသို့
မြတ်ဘိုးတော် စေတီယတို့ကို
ဦးချစ်တ်ရည်။

လေပြည်လာ တုန်ကာအေးတာမို့
နေခြည်ဖြာ ချုလှာနှင့်ထွေးပါရ
ဆွေးသပ ဖြေမတည်
ရေကြည်ကြည်ကျ သွင်သွင်မစဲ။

ဆီးနှင်းငယ်ထန်
မိုးလောက်ပင် ပုံသဏ္ဍာန်မို့
မွန်ပြာလှုံ တောင်ယံထဲမှာ
မှိုင်းရီလို့မ။ ။

From Mèza Mountain's melancholy shade my heart turns
    homeward.
There Bo tree roots now run with water poured by festive hands.
Here gray sands lie about me, desolate.

Thoughts span the wastes that lie between.
Pulsing, throbbing, longing
Toward Shwébo, seat of victory where
Great Bo Daw sits enthroned among the myriad shrines.
Deep in obeisance I incline.

Sun rays fold me round about when cold winds
Whining, mourning, thrusting,
Search and chill. No shield I find

When sad, disconsolate remembrances come crowding.
Here pure, clear waters sound unceasingly.

Dews fall and fill the skies as thick as rain
Gathering, darkening, glooming,
The far off mountain summits breasting,
The whole of heaven's vault to mists of blue is changing.

> AWAY-YAUK-MIN ("The Exiled Noble"),
> *Mèza-gyaung*

Burmese is spoken by two-thirds of the population of Burma (now officially called Myanmar), or about 35 million people. It is one of the Tibeto-Burman languages, a branch of the Sino-Tibetan family.

The Burmese alphabet was adapted from that of the Mons, despite the fact that the two peoples fought each other for centuries and their languages are unrelated. The Mon alphabet was derived from Grantha, an offshoot of the Brahmi script that originated in ancient India. As in the Oriya language of India, the Burmese alphabet consists almost entirely of circles or portions of circles used in various combinations. It was intended for writing on palm leaves, the letters traced by means of a stylus. There are 45 letters in all: 33 consonants and 12 vowels.

Thai

นาคีมีพิษเพี้ยเพียง   สุริโย
เลื้อยบ่ห้าเคโช   แฝมฃา
พิษมันอยยิ่งโยโส   แมลงป่อง
ฝูแต่หางเฅงฅา   อวดอ้างฤทธี

ผลมะเฅือเมื่อสุกไซร้   มีพรรณ
ภายนอกฅูแดงนาน   ชาดบ้าย
ภายในแมลงวัน   หนอนบ่อน
เฅกเฅ่นชนชาติร้าย   นอกนั้นฅูงาม

Great indeed is the power of the dragon as the sun,
Yet humbly and slowly it meanders its way shy,
Minuscule indeed is the power of the tiny scorpion,
Yet it swaggers its tail and boasts to the sky.

Ripened figs are pretty and pleasing to the eyes,
Their colors seduce both the sight and palate,
Alas, the cores rot with maggots inside,
For evils are but false fronts and gilded waste.

Old Thai Verses

Thai is spoken by about 35 million people in Thailand, about 60 percent of the country's population. It belongs to a group of languages called the Tai languages, which includes Lao, of Laos, and the Shan language of northern Burma. These languages were once thought to be a branch of the Sino-Tibetan family and thus related to Chinese, but this relationship has now been rejected by most linguists.

The Thai alphabet dates from the 13th century. It was created by the King of Thailand, who took the alphabet then in use by the Khmers (which had its ultimate origin in India). To it he added a number of new symbols, as Thai and Khmer have very different sound patterns. The vowels are not represented by an individual letter but by a mark written above, below, before, or after the consonant with which it is pronounced.

Thai, like Chinese, is a tonal language, meaning that different tones, or intonations, distinguish words that would otherwise be homonyms. Of the five tones, four are indicated by signs over the consonants, the absence of a sign indicating that the fifth tone is to be used. Words are not separated from each other, and the letters generally flow uninterruptedly until the idea changes.

Malay

Maka ada-lah kira-kira sa-puloh minit lama-nya, maka meletup-lah ubat bedil itu saperti bunyi petir; maka terbongkar-lah batu kota itu sa-besar-besar rumah, dan ada yang sa-besar gajah, beterbangan ka-dalam laut; maka ada batu yang terbang sampai ka-saberang dan mengenaï rumah-rumah. Maka terkejut-lah orang semua-nya sebab menengar bunyi-nya itu, serta dengan besar-besar hairan, sebab sa-umor hidup mereka itu belum pernah menengar bunyi yang demikian, dan sebab melihatkan bagaimana besar kuasa ubat bedil itu, sampai boleh ia mengang-katkan batu sa-besar-besar saperti rumah.

In about ten minutes' time the gunpowder exploded, with a noise like a clap of thunder. The masonry of the fort went up, in great masses the size of houses. Some pieces, as big as elephants, were hurled into the sea, others flew across the river and struck some houses on the other side. Everybody was thunderstruck by the noise, and amazed, because in all their lives they had never heard anything like it, and because they saw how great was the power of gunpowder, that it could lift rocks as big as houses.

ABDULLAH BIN ABDULKADIR,
Hikayat Abdullah (autobiography)

Malay is spoken in Malaysia and in a number of adjacent countries. In Malaysia it is the mother tongue of about 10 million people, or half the total population. There are also about 2 million speakers in the southernmost provinces of Thailand, as well as 500,000 in Singapore and 250,000 in Brunei.

For centuries Malay was also spoken along the eastern coast of Sumatra, and on the western, southern, and eastern coasts of Borneo (Kalimantan), which are now part of Indonesia. As this area lay on the great trade routes in colonial times, Malay became the lingua franca of much of present-day Indonesia. When the Republic of Indonesia was established in 1949, Malay was chosen over others as that country's official language, though it was called Indonesian. There are some differences in vocabulary between the two countries, but their languages are essentially one and the same.

Malay is a member of the Austronesian family of languages. Beginning in the 14th century, with the conversion of many Malays to Islam, an adaptation of the Arabic script was used for writing. In the 19th century the British developed a Roman-based alphabet that is in general use today. It differed somewhat from the one developed by the Dutch for Indonesian, but in 1972 the two systems were made the same.

Prefixes and suffixes as we use them are virtually absent in Malay. Many grammatical functions are accomplished by adding an extra word. The plural of a noun is most commonly indicated by simply saying it twice, as in *rumah-rumah* in the above passage, which means "houses." After numbers, however, the noun reverts to the singular and an additional word is added, which serves as a "classifier" of the noun that follows. There are essentially three classifiers: *orang* ("person") is used with people, *ekor* ("tail") with animals and other living creatures, and *buah* ("fruit") with inanimate objects. Thus "two children" in Malay is *dua orang budak*, and "two cats" is *dua ekor kucing.*

The centuries of colonial rule brought many Portuguese, Dutch, and English words into Malay, such as *buku* (book), *pensel* (pencil), *siling* (ceiling), and *sekolah* (school). English words of Malay origin include *gingham, sarong, bamboo, rattan, kapok, cockatoo, paddy,* and *amok. Orangutan* is a combination of the Malay words *orang* (person) and *hutan* (forest). *Compound,* in the meaning "enclosed area," comes from the Malay *kampong,* which means "village."

Lao

ໂອ້ດອກຈຳປາ ເວລາຊົມບ້ອງ ນຶກເຖິງພັນຊຸ່ອງ
ນອງເຖິງຫົວໃຈ ເຮົານຶກຂຶ້ນໄດ້ ໃນກິ່ນເຈົ້າຫອມ
ເຖິງສວນດອກໄມ້ ບິດາປຸກໄວ້ ຕັ້ງແຕ່ນານມາ
ເວລາງ່ວມເຫງົາ ເຈົ້າຊ່ວຍບັນເທົາ ເຮົາຫາຍໂສກາ
ເຈົ້າດອກຈຳປາ ຄູ່ຄຽງເຮົ້າມາ ແຕ່ນານນ້ອຍເອີຍ

ກິ່ນເຈົ້າສຳຄັນ ຕິດພັນຫົວໃຈ ເປັນຫນ້າຮັກໄຄ່
ແພງໄວ້ເຊີຍຊົມ ນານເຫງົາເຮົາດົມ ໃຫ້ຈຳປາຫອມ
ເມື່ອດົມກິ່ນເຈົ້າ ປານພັບຜູ້ເກົ່າ ທີ່ພາກຈາກໄປ
ເຈົ້າເປັນດອກໄມ້ ທີ່ງາມວິໄລ ຕັ້ງແຕ່ໄດນາ
ເຈົ້າດອກຈຳປາ ມາລາອັນຮັກ ຂອງຮຽນນີ້ເອີຍ.

Oh Champa! When I sense your fragrance, a thousand memories
  stir in my heart.
Your sweet scent reminds me of the garden of my father.
And I recall all my dreams, all my melancholy, and all my
  childhood joys.
Champa, you are for me the flower of my childhood.

Your perfume awakens in me delightful memories.
When I inhale your fragrance I seem to recall in my heart
My beloved whom I have lost.
Champa, the most beautiful flower of Laos, you are for me the
  flower of my love.

Champa, Flower of Laos

Lao is the national language of Laos. It is spoken by about 4 million people
there, or 80 percent of the population. Lao is closely related to Thai, spoken
in neighboring Thailand, the two belonging to the Tai family of languages.
There are actually far more speakers of Lao in Thailand than in Laos: about
15 million. In Thailand it is sometimes referred to as Northeastern Thai.

The Lao script is believed to have been adapted from that of the Mons,
the people who ruled Burma for many centuries. Its ultimate source was the
Brahmi script of ancient India.

Khmer

ជព្ជូរយើងនៅចំស្រុកសម្បូណិ៌
អស់ញញាក្សៃថ្ងូរថាឃ្លានចារអត់
ពេលបានជួបគ្នានឹកគ្រាកំសត់
នឹកការជួរចត់ប្រិចគេធ្វើបាប ។

ឆ្នាំចិតសិបប្រាំរំដោះភ្នំពេញ
រាស្ត្រប្រិចគេដេញរត់ចេញខ្នាត់ខ្នាយ
បងខ្លះបែកបូនកូនខ្លះបែកម្តាយ
ខ្លះដប់ឆ្នាំប្ញាយពុំទាន់ជួបគ្នា ។

ដើរផងរត់ផងភ្នែកមើលឆ្នាឆ្នាប់
ត្រចៀកផ្ទៀងស្តាប់ក្រែងឮមាត់ហៅ
អ្នកក្រុងរាប់សែនប្រិចគេណ្ដេចេញក្រៅ
យាយខ្លះបែកចៅយំពួហ្ញីរៗ ។

Now we're in the land of plenty.
We no longer hear the moans of
   hunger and loss.
But when we meet we remember the
   hardships
And horrible crimes that were
   committed.

In 1975 Phnom Penh was "liberated."
The people were evacuated helter-
   skelter.
Children were separated from their
   brothers and mothers.
After ten years some have yet to find
   each other.

Running and walking, looking
   everywhere at once,
They strained to hear a familiar voice
   that might be calling.
Thousands of people leaving the city at
   the same time.
A grandmother, separated from her
   family, hears her child's cry.

TRUNG HUY KIM,
The Spirits are Crying

Khmer is the national language of Cambodia, spoken there by over 10 million
people. There are also about one million speakers in Vietnam and 750,000
in Thailand. It is a member of the Mon-Khmer family of languages.

Khmer was the language of the great Khmer empire which ruled Southeast
Asia from the 10th to the 14th centuries. The Khmer script evolved out of
an ancient script called Pallava which was ultimately derived from the
Brahmi script of India. It later served as the basis of the Thai alphabet, which
was invented in the 13th century.

Có nhà viên-ngoại họ Vương,
gia-tư nghĩ cũng thường-thường bậc trung
Một trai con thứ rốt lòng,
Vương Quan là chữ nối dòng nho-gia.
Đầu lòng hai ả tố-nga,
Thúy Kiều là chị em là Thúy Vân.
Mai cốt-cách tuyết tinh-thần,
mỗi người một vẻ mười phân vẹn mười.
Vân xem trang-trọng khác vời:
khuôn trăng đầy-đặn nét ngài nở-nang;
hoa cười ngọc thốt đoan-trang,
mây thua nước tóc tuyết nhường màu da.
Kiều càng sắc-sảo mặn-mà,
so bề tài sắc lại là phần hơn.
Làn thu-thủy nét xuân-sơn,
hoa ghen thua thắm liễu hờn kém xanh.
Một hai nghiêng nước nghiêng thành,
sắc đành đòi một tài đành họa hai.
Thông-minh vốn sẵn tư trời,
pha nghề thi họa đủ mùi ca ngâm.

There was a burgher in the clan of Vuong,
  a man of modest wealth and middle rank.
He had a last-born son, Vuong Quan – his hope
  to carry on a line of learned folk.
Two daughters, beauties both, had come before:
  Thúy Kiêu was oldest, younger was Thúy Vân.
Bodies like slim plum branches, snow-pure souls:
  each her own self, each perfect in her way.
In quiet grace Vân was beyond compare:
  her face a moon, her eyebrows two full curves;
her smile a flower, her voice the song of jade;
  her hair the sheen of clouds, her skin white snow.
Yet Kiêu possessed a keener, deeper charm,
  surpassing Vân in talents and in looks.
Her eyes were autumn streams, her brows spring hills.
  Flowers grudged her glamour, willows her fresh hue.
A glance or two from her, and kingdoms rocked!
  Supreme in looks, she had few peers in gifts.
By Heaven blessed with wit, she knew all skills:
  she could write verse and paint, could sing and chant.

The Tale of Kieu

Vietnamese is spoken in Vietnam by about 70 million people. Its linguistic affiliation has long been a matter of debate. It is now thought by most to belong to the Mon-Khmer family of languages which includes Khmer (Cambodian), but this is not entirely certain. The only language closely related to Vietnamese is Muong, spoken in northern Vietnam.

Vietnam was ruled by China until the middle of the 10th century. So many Chinese words entered the language that Vietnamese was long thought to be related to Chinese. It was written using the Chinese characters until the 17th century, when Catholic missionaries devised a Roman-based orthography. It contains a complex system of diacritical marks, some distinguishing certain vowel sounds, others indicating tone. As can be seen in some of the lines above, a letter may often contain two diacritical marks.

The Tale of Kieu, the Vietnamese national poem, was written by Nguyen Du in the early 19th century. It is 3,254 lines in length; educated Vietnamese know most of them by heart.

227

Setiap kita bertemu, gadis kecil berkaleng kecil
Senyummu terlalu kekal untuk kenal duka
Tengadah padaku, pada bulan merah jambu
Tapi kotaku jadi hilang, tanpa jiwa

Ingin aku ikut, gadis kecil berkaleng kecil
Pulang kebawah he jembatan yang melulur sosok
Hidup dari kehidupan angan-angan yang gemerlapan
Gembira dari kemayaan riang

Duniamu yang lebih tinggi dari menara katedral
Melintas-linta diatas air kotor, tapi yang begitu kauhafal
Jiwa begitu murni, terlalu murni
Untuk bisa membagi dukaku

Kalau kau mati, gadis kecil berkaleng kecil
Bulan diatas itu, tak ada yang punya
Dan kotaku, ah kotaku
Hidupnya tak lagi punya tanda.

Every time we meet, little girl with your begging bowl,
Your smile is too eternal to know sorrow,
You look up at me, at the light red moon,
But my city has disappeared, soulless.

I want to go with you, little girl with your begging bowl
To your home, under the bridge, which expunges every shape,
To live from the life of radiant fantasies,
To be gay in the illusion of happiness.

Your world that is higher than the cathedral spire
Flashes past on the dirty water, but you know it by heart,
Your soul is so pure – far too pure
To share my sorrow.

If you die, little girl with the begging bowl,
Then the moon up there will no longer have an owner,
And my city, ah, my city
Will live on without a beacon.

TOTO SUDARTO BACHTIAR, *The Beggar Girl*

Indonesian is the national language of Indonesia. When independence was declared in 1945, *bahasa Indonesia* ("Indonesian language") was decreed as the country's official language. It is actually the same language as Malay, spoken in Malaysia. Although Indonesian is the mother tongue of only about 25 million people out of a population of 225 million, it is estimated that as much as three-fourths of the population now understands it.

At independence the spelling systems of the two countries differed somewhat, as the Malay system was developed by the British, and the Indonesian by the Dutch. In 1972 the two were unified, with the Malay variant adopted in most cases. Indonesian *j* gave way to Malay *y* (*kayu* – wood), and *dj* to Malay *j* (*gajah* – elephant). The *ch* sound, which was *ch* in Malay but *tj* in Indonesian, is now rendered by the letter *c* (*kucing* – cat), while the *sh* sound, *sh* in Malay but *sj* in Indonesian, is now *sy* (*syarat* – condition).

A number of Indonesian words, however, have been adopted from Javanese, the country's most widely spoken language, in preference to the Malay. For "city" Malay *bandar* is *kota* in Indonesian, "room" is *bilik* in Malay but *kamar* in Indonesian, and "shop" is *kedai* in Malay but *toko* in Indonesian. The Indonesian plural, like the Malay, is formed by merely repeating the word, as in *angan-angan* in the poem above, which means "fantasies."

Javanese

Kulamun durung lugu
Aja pisan dadi ngaku-aku
Antuk siku kang mangkono iku kaki
Kena uga wenang muluk
Kalamun wus pada melok

If you do not understand all these teachings perfectly, do not presume to boast of possessing the knowledge they contain. He who does shall incur wrath, my friend. For only he who has first mastered them completely has the right to consider them his own.

Javanese is spoken in the central and eastern parts of Java, the most populous island of Indonesia. A member of the Austronesian family, it has about 80 million speakers.

At independence in 1945, Indonesian (essentially Malay) was chosen as the nation's official language. Most Javanese now speak it as a second language. But Javanese remains the language of everyday use in central and eastern Java, and also of most radio and television programs.

The traditional Javanese script is derived from an ancient script known as Kavi, which in turn was based on the Brahmi script of southern India. After about 1400 the Arabic script was also widely used. The passage above appears first in the Javanese, then in the Roman alphabet, which is now in general use.

Sundanese

Dumadakan aja angin ribut katjida di laut, nepi ka ombak-ombak ngarungkup kana parahuo. Tidinja murid-murid njalampeurkeun, seug Andjeunna digugahkeun, bari undjukan: Aduh Gusti, mugi tulungan, abdi tiwas! Dawuhana Na ka maranèhna: Naha maranèh sarieum, èh nu leutik kapertjajaan? Geus kitu tuluj gugah, sarta njeuseul ka èta angin djeung kana laut, djep djèmpe-rèhè pisan Ari èta djelema pada hèraneun, sarta ngaromong kieu: Na ieu tèh djelema naon, nepi ka angin djeung laut gè narurut ka Andjeunna!

And, behold, there arose a great tempest in the sea, insomuch that the ship was covered with the waves: but he was asleep. And his disciples came to him, and awoke him, saying, Lord save us: we perish. And then he saith unto them, Why are ye fearful, O ye of little faith? Then he arose and rebuked the winds and the sea; and there was a great calm. But the men marvelled, saying, What manner of man is this, that even the winds and the sea obey him!

Matthew viii 24–27

Sundanese is one of the major languages of Indonesia, spoken in western Java where the capital, Jakarta, is located. There are about 30 million speakers, many of whom speak Indonesian as well. Sundanese is a member of the Austronesian family of languages. It is written in both the Javanese script and the Roman alphabet shown above.

Madurese

E dimma bhai bada bengko se elebbhoenana dhibiqna, ngotjaq dhilloe
barija: pada salamet sabhala bengko areja. Lamon e dissa bada anaq
salamet, tanto katebhanan salamma dhibiqna, nangeng lamon tadag,
salamma dhibiqna abalija pole ka dhibiqna. Mondhoek e bengko
djaroewa, ngakan ban ngenom sabharang apa se esoghoewaghi biq oreng
djaroewa, karana oreng se alako patot olle opa, addjhaq le-ngalle
pamondhoeghan.

When you enter a house, say first: "Peace be on this house." And if a
peaceful person is present there, your peace shall rest upon him; but if
not, it shall return to you. Remain in the same house, eating and drinking
whatever is given to you, do not go from house to house.

Madurese is spoken on, and named after, the small island of Madura, lying
off the northern coast of eastern Java. But more than half of its 10 million
speakers live on Java itself, on the part of the island that is closest to Bali.

Like Sundanese, Madurese was traditionally written in the Javanese script
but now the Roman alphabet has come into use. Madurese is another of the
Austronesian languages.

Buginese

[Buginese script text]

When the sun is shining the Creator, holder of Man's destiny, asks the escort, "Why, oh people, have Rukkelengpoba and his family for three days and three nights left the top of the sky?" Before the escort can answer, Rukkelengpoba, Sangiang padju, Rumamakkompo, Balassariú, immediately appear. The Creator is not pleased when he sees Rukkelengpoba and his family. In an angry voice the Creator asks, "Where hast thou been, oh Rumamakkompo and thy family? For three nights already thou hast been absent from the top of the sky."

Galigo (Buginese mythology)

Buginese is spoken on the island of Celebes (Sulawesi), Indonesia. There are about 4 million speakers, living mainly on the southern peninsula. The Buginese alphabet is believed to be derived from the Kavi script used in writing Javanese. Like the other languages of Indonesia, Buginese belongs to the Austronesian family.

Batak

ᯖᯖᯉᯖᯖᯖᯖᯖᯖᯖᯖᯖᯖᯖᯖᯖᯖ

(Batak script text — 14 lines)

When they got back to their village Adji Panurat stole away to the jungle; he is afraid to see his younger brother. Adji Pamasa told his balbal [spirit that can beat up people or other things] to head him off. "When you meet him drive him home. If he doesn't want to, hit him over the head but don't kill him, so be it," said Adji Pamasa. The balbal went to head (Adji Panurat) off. He met Adji Panurat. He led him (toward the house). He refused. Therefore he hit him over the head. Adji Panurat saw stars in front of him. Therefore he consented to go home.

Batak is spoken on Sumatra, the westernmost of the major islands of Indonesia. There are about 4 million speakers, living mainly in the northern half of the island. The distinctive Batak alphabet, also based on the Kavi script, consists of 16 basic characters, each of which may be modified by the use of certain marks. It is rapidly disappearing in favor of the Roman alphabet, and relatively few people remain today who are able to read it. Batak belongs to the Austronesian family of languages.

Tok Pisin

Long Muglim klostu long Mount Hagen planti man i belhat tru. As bilong trabel em i man Kei na Ruri na Maga Nugints – tripela i bin trikim moa olsem 1000 man. Ol i tok ol man hia i mas tromoim $10 inap long $100 bilong baim sampela retpela kes. Samting olsem 300 retpela kes ol i bin haitim insait long wanpela haus. Ol i makim de bilong opim sampela kes na soim ol man ol kes hia i mas pulap long mani. Ol i opim sampela bek na 5-pela bokis hia na ol ston tasol na sampela nil i kapsait i kam daun. Ol man i lukim, ol sampela i lap na narapela gen i belhat.

At Muglim near Mt. Hagen there are many very angry people. The reason for this is that three men – Kei, Ruri, and Maga Nugints – tricked more than 1,000 people. They told the people they had to buy red wooden suitcases, which cost from $10 to $100 apiece. They then hid approximately 300 such boxes inside a house. They set a date when they would publicly open the boxes and show the people that they were now full of money. They did open five sacks and five of the boxes but only some stones and nails fell to the ground. Some of those who saw this laughed and others got very angry.

Tok Pisin ("Talk Pidgin") is a variety of Pidgin English spoken in Papua New Guinea. It is now the mother tongue of about 100,000 people but it has become the indispensable lingua franca for most of the country. As many as 3 million people, or 60 percent of the population, are able to converse in it.

The basic vocabulary consists of only about 1,500 words. But there are also curious compounds, such as *haus kuk* ("house cook"), for "kitchen"; *haus sik* ("house sick"), for "hospital"; and *haus pepa* ("house paper"), for "office." The common word *bilong* (from "belong"), which simply means "of," appears in *glas bilong lukluk* ("glass belong look-look," for "mirror"); *lait bilong klaut* ("light belong cloud", for "lightning"); and *man bilong longwe ples* ("man belong long-way place," for "foreigner"). The ubiquitous suffix *-pela* (from "fellow") appears in the plural of personal pronouns (e.g., *mi* – I, *mipela* – we), in numerals up to 12 (*wanpela* – one, *tupela* – two), in one-syllable adjectives (*bikpela* – big, *gutpela* – good), and in some other common words (*dispela* – this, *sampela* – some).

Aranda

Yapalpe pmere rrirtne nhanhe ikwerenge, Yapalpe nteme rrirtne nhanhe ire. Imankenge kwete nteme apme kwerlaye ire nhanhele nerlaneme.

Relhe nhakwe irlenge ware petyemale intetyarte, pmere ikwerenge irlenge kertne nteme intetyarte apme kwerlaye ire. Itenyele apme kwerlaye ire kwenhe alknge pange neke. Irlenge ware relhe mape intetyarte nhakwe iliwele.

Petyemale, intemale, itne pmere-werne alpeke. Itne itenyele intemenge werenye kngerrtyele warneke. Pmere lanhe ikwerele intemale itne kemirremale ihetyarte.

Kethe nhenge irlenge nhakwele itne interyarte. Pmere mwekenhe nhanhe nekale. Kele thwenge peke apme kwerlaye itnenhe kwatyele peke kngeke. Thwenga apme kwerlaye ire kwatye kwane intemenge.

Long, long ago, in the waterhole of Glen Helen, there lived a rainbow serpent.

People used to come and camp there, making their camp a good distance away from the waterhole where the rainbow serpent lived. They didn't want to camp anywhere near that rainbow serpent with its blind eyes. Instead they camped some distance away on the high flat ground.

They came and camped there for a while and then went back to their own place. If they camped too close to that waterhole a big wind would blow. Then they would have to get up and move away from that place.

They would make their camp far away in the open country. The waterhole was a sacred place. The rainbow serpent might take them into the water and drown them. Perhaps the rainbow is still lying there today, deep under the water.

The Rainbow Serpent Story

Aranda, also known as Arrernte, is one of the many languages spoken by the Australian aborigines. Its 3,000 or so speakers are located in and around Alice Springs, the largest town in Australia's Outback, in the geographic center of the continent. A bilingual school there teaches aboriginal children to read and write both English and their own language.

Tagalog

Hagurin ng tanaw ang ating palibot:
taniman, gawaan, lansangan, bantayog,
lupa, dagat, langit ay pawang sinakop,
at kamay ng tao ang nagpapakilos.

Ang mga kamay ko'y binihasang sadya
sa kakaharaping gawai't dalita;
pangit ang daliring humabi ng sutla,
tumuklas ng ginto'y kamay ng paggawa.

Habang ang kamay mo o aking Pagibig,
kambal na bulaklak – mabango, malinis;
kung may sakit ako o nasa panganib,
dantay ng kamay mo ay isa nang langit.

Nguni't tingnan yaong kamay ng Orasan,
may itinuturo't waring nagsasaysay:
"Tao, kayong lahat ay may katapusan
na itatadhana nitong aking kamay!"

Observe carefully our world:
fields, factories, streets, statues,
earth, sea, sky have been dominated
by the hand of men, which can move mountains.

I too trained my hands for expert work,
to prepare for the hard days ahead;
how ugly my words woven in silk,
compared to the hands of the worker mining gold.

My hands, oh dearest love, were
like flowers, clean and fragrant;
and when I am ill or in danger,
the touch of your hand is healing balm.

And all the while the hands of the clock,
point to the prophetic mouth:
"Man, all of you will meet the end
decreed by this – time's hand."

AMADO V. HERNANDEZ, The Hand

Tagalog, with the stress on the second syllable, is the national language of the Philippines. As far back as 1937 Tagalog, originally confined to southern Luzon, was made the country's official language and given the new name of Pilipino. Its study has been strongly encouraged by the government, and it is now the language of instruction in most Philippine schools. As a result more than three-fourths of the country's population of 75 million is now able to speak it, despite the fact that it is the mother tongue of only about 20 million.

Tagalog is a member of the Austronesian family of languages. The three centuries of Spanish rule in the Philippines left a strong imprint on the vocabulary. *Mesa* (table), *tenedor* (fork), *papel* (paper), and *asero* (steel) are only a few of hundreds of Spanish words in Tagalog. The English word *boondocks* comes from the Tagalog word for "mountain," *bundok*.

Visayan

May usa ka magtiayon dugay nang katuigan nga nangagi nga may usa ka anak nga lalaki nga ilang ginganlan si Juan. Sa nagatubo si Juan, nalipay usab ang iyang mga ginikanan uban ang pagtuo nga aduna na silay ikatabang sa panimalay. Labi na ang amahan nalipay gayud pag-ayo tungod kay duna na man siyay ikatabang sa pagpangahoy nga maoy iyang pangita alang sa panginabuhi sa matag adlaw.

Many years ago there was a couple who had a son whom they named John. As John grew up, his parents were happy, believing that now they would have help in the household. The father especially was very happy because now he would have help in gathering firewood which was the means by which he earned his living from day to day.

Visayan, with the stress on the second syllable, is a collective term for three closely related yet distinctly different languages spoken mainly on the middle islands of the Philippine archipelago. The languages are:

(1) Cebuano, spoken by about 15 million people on Cebu, Bohol, eastern Negros, western Leyte, and northern Mindanao;
(2) Hiligaynon, spoken by 6 million people on Panay and western Negros;
(3) Waray-Waray, or Samaran, spoken by 3 million people on Samar and eastern Leyte.

The above passage is in Cebuano. Like Tagalog, the Visayan languages are of the Austronesian family.

LANGUAGES OF OCEANIA

Maori

Me he manu rere ahau e,
Kua rere ki to moenga,
Ki te awhi i to tinana,
E te tau tahuri mai.

Kei te moe te tinana,
Kei te wake te wairua,
Kei te hotu te manawa,
E te tau tahuri mai.

Haere, haere ra e hine,
Whakangaro i konei
Waiho ahau i muri nei,
Tangi hotu hotu ai.

Thro' the stillness of the night, love,
To a heart that's longing for you;
Swiftly as a bird in flight, love,
Fly, my darling, fly to me.

Oft' when twilight shades are falling,
I can sense your presence near me;
And your sweet voice softly calling,
Calling to me tenderly.

When my eager arms enfold you,
Never more to let you fly away;
Dear, forever I will hold you,
To my heart, Eternally.

Manu Rere (Maori love song)

The Maoris are the native inhabitants of New Zealand. Today they live mostly on North Island. Although they number about 350,000, a recent survey showed that only 70,000 were fluent in the language and another 50,000 could understand it. The government of New Zealand has taken steps to encourage its use and Maori-language kindergartens have been established in many schools. In 1987 it was made co-official with English.

Historically the Maoris are a Polynesian people whose original home was Tahiti. Their migration halfway across the Pacific Ocean is believed to have occurred in successive waves, the last and greatest taking place in the middle of the 14th century. The Polynesian languages, which extend as far as Hawaii, form a branch of the Austronesian family.

Chamorro

Manhanao mameska ham gi painge yän si Kimio yän si Juan.
Manmangone' ham mas de dos sientos libras na guihän. Pues, anai
manmunhayan ham mameska gi oran a las dos, nu mandeskansa ham.
Despues nai manana guenao gi oran a las siete, humanao ham yän si
Kimio para in bende i guihän gi äs Bernado. Despues nai munhayan ma
fahan i sisienta libras, humanao ham para Sinajana yä lumiliko' ham
manbende sina buente kuarenta libras na guihän.

Kimio, Juan (and I), we went fishing last night. We caught more than
two hundred pounds of fish. Then, when we finished fishing at two
o'clock, we rested. Then in the morning at six o'clock, Kimio and I went
to sell the fish at Bernardo's. Then we finished, they bought sixty pounds,
we went to Sinajana and went around selling maybe forty pounds of fish.

Chamorro is spoken on the island of Guam in the Western Pacific Ocean as
well as on the Northern Mariana Islands which lie just to the north. Latest
figures show approximately 50,000 speakers on Guam (out of a total population of 150,000) and 15,000 more on the Marianas, most of them on the
island of Saipan. Chamorro belongs to the Western branch of the
Austronesian family. Numerous Spanish words in the vocabulary reflect the
three centuries of Spanish rule in Guam.

Marshallese

Maȟjeł yej tijtiryik yew r&yhar-tahtah yilew Tiraj Teyr&yt&wr&y. Majr&w yej yijew j&yban kiyen yew han Maȟjeł yim yeleg harm&j jan kajj&wj&w hay&l&g kew yilikin rej j&q&y yi'y&y. Yepjay, yilew hay&l&g yin Kiwajleyen yej jikin yew k&yin kariwew han kiyen yilew hay&l&g yin Maȟjeł. Harm&j r&yin yewen Yepjay rej jerbal yilew Kiwajleyen, jikin kekkeylaq miyjeł han rittariṅahyey yin Hamedkah. Pikinniy yim Yan&yweytak rej yijekew Hamedkah yehar teyej bahaṁ yi'y&y.

The Marshalls District is the easternmost of the Trust Territory of the Pacific Islands. Majuro is the capital, and many people from the outer islands live there. Ebeye on Kwajalein Atoll is the subcapital of the Marshalls. The people on Ebeye work at Kwajalein, the missile testing range of the American military. Bikini and Eniwetok are the atolls where America tested bombs.

Marshallese is spoken in the Marshall Islands, which lie north of the equator and just west of the International Date Line. It is spoken by virtually all of the islands' 65,000 inhabitants.

Marshallese is one of the Micronesian languages, which form a branch of the Austronesian family. The alphabet includes an ampersand (&), which represents a vowel sound somewhere between *e* and *i*, as well as a number of special diacritical marks.

Fijian

Na gauna e dau qolivi kina na kanace e na mataka lailai sara, ni sā bera ni cadra na mata ni siga. E na gauna oqō era moce tū kina. Ni ra sā moce tū, era qeleni sara vakalewelevu, ia na gauna sā katakata mai kina na mata ni siga era sā dui veilakoyaki. E na gauna sā via yakavi kina na vanua era sota tale ki na vanua era via lakova, me ra laki moce kina.

The time to catch mullet is in the very early morning before the sun appears. At that time the fish are asleep. While they are asleep they lie close together in large numbers, but when the sun becomes hot they disperse. When the evening draws in, they assemble again in the spot they visit, to go to sleep there.

Fijian is the indigenous language of the island of Fiji in the central Pacific Ocean. It is spoken by about 400,000 people, or half the country's population. Fijian is the most important of the Oceanic languages, a branch of the Austronesian family. The alphabet lacks the letters *h*, *x*, and *z* while the letters *f*, *j*, and *p* appear only in foreign words. The letter *b* is pronounced *mb*, *d* is pronounced *nd*, *g* is *ng* as in "sing," and *q* is pronounced *ng* as in "finger." A line over a vowel lengthens its sound.

Samoan

E i ai le fale o le tagata Samoa i totonu o le nu'u, ae peita'i o ana
fa'ato'aga e masani ona i ai i le maila po'o le sili atu i uta. Na te tōtō i
ana fa'ato'aga ana mea'ei, taro, fa'i, ma 'ulu; ne te tōtō fo'i niu mo popo,
ma koko. O nei mea na te fa'atau atu i le fai'oloa i totonu o le nu'u po'o
i Apia. Mai tupe ua maua na te fa'atau ai pisupo ma apa i'a, ma 'ie mo
ona lavalava atoa ma lavalava o lona aiga.

A Samoan has his house in the village, but his plantations are often a
mile or more inland. On his plantation he grows his foodstuffs, taro,
bananas, and breadfruit; he also grows coconuts for copra, and cocoa.
These things he sells to the merchants in the village or in Apia. With
the money received he buys tinned meat and tinned fish, and materials
for clothes for himself and his family.

Samoan is spoken by about 200,000 people in Samoa (formerly Western
Samoa), an independent island state, and by 40,000 in American Samoa
(a U.S. territory) in the South Pacific Ocean. It is a member of the Polynesian
branch of the Austronesian family of languages. The Samoan alphabet
contains only 14 letters: the five vowels plus the consonants *f*, *g*, *l*, *m*, *n*, *p*,
s, *t*, and *v*. The letters *h*, *k*, and *r* appear only in words of foreign origin,
while *b*, *c*, *d*, *j*, *q*, *w*, *x*, *y*, and *z* are missing entirely. The sign ' represents a
break or hesitation between two vowels (e.g., *la'au* – tree, *fa'i* – banana).

Many Samoan words are simple compounds. *Fale* (building) + *oloa*
(goods) = *faleoloa* (store), while *vai* (water) + *tafe* (to flow) = *vaitafe* (river).
English has contributed innumerable new words such as *taimi* (time), *apu*
(apple), *aisa* (ice), *loia* (lawyer), *kolisi* (college), and *niusipepa* (newspaper).

Tahitian

Teie te ravea no to te feia Tahiti taioraa i te mau "mahana" i tahito ra, mai te tahi aahiata te taioraa e tae noa'tu i te tahi. Te taio ra hoi ratou i te mau pô o tei ohie hoi i te faataa no te mea ua huru ê te marama i te tahi arui i to te tahi, e to'na vairaa i nia i te ra'i, e mea ê atoa ïa. Te mau mahana râ, ua huru â te huru, aore hoi te râ e huru ê, e aore hoi to'na vairaa ê i nia i te ra'i tera mahana e tera mahana, (e mea ê rii roa'e, eiaha i te rahi). No reira, te haapao ra te maohi i te pô ei faataaraa taime; ua topa hoi ratou i te i'oa i nia i te pô hoe ra. E 28 (piti ahuru ma vau) "auri" ta te ava'e hoe i taua anotau ra, e te mairihia ra te i'oa o taua maororaa taime ra: e marama.

This is how the ancient Tahitians counted the "days" from one daybreak to the next. They counted the nights instead, which were easy to distinguish from each other, the moon never being the same shape or in the same place two nights in a row. The days were all alike, with the sun always the same shape and in the same place (approximately). That is why the natives arranged their life by the nights to which they had given names. The month had 28 "nights," the period being called a "moon."

Tahitian is the indigenous language of Tahiti and the other Society Islands (such as Moorea), which form a part of French Polynesia. It is another of the Polynesian languages and has about 150,000 speakers. The alphabet contains only 13 letters: the five vowels plus the consonants *f*, *h*, *m*, *n*, *p*, *r*, *t*, and *v*. The English word *tattoo* is of Tahitian origin.

Tongan

Ko te taupoou ko Hina, pea na feongoaki mo te manaia ko Sinilau, pea faifai tena feongoaki kua ka la kei manofo ia Hina kua tokanga kia Sinilau. Pea hau leva i te aho e taha o too mai tona kiefau o vala, pea too mai leva mo tona kafakula o fau; pea alu atu leva mo te vaa-akau o hopo ki tai, o kaukau; o tau leva ki te fenua o Sinilau.

There was a virgin named Hina, and she and the handsome man Sinilau heard reports of one another, and as time went on and they continually heard one another's praises, Hina could rest no longer, because of her thoughts of Sinilau. So one day she clothed herself with her fine mat, and took her necklace and put it on, and she went with a pole and leaped into the sea, and swam, and came to the land of Sinilau.

Tongan is spoken in the Kingdom of Tonga, an island nation in the Pacific Ocean just east of Fiji. Another of the Polynesian languages, it has about 100,000 speakers. The English word *taboo* is of Tongan origin.

LANGUAGES OF
THE WESTERN HEMISPHERE

Hawaiian

Ke aloha o ke Akua — Love that is of God
'A'ole ho'i e ho'ohiehie, — Is not full of vanity,
'A'ole he hikiwawe ka huhū, — Is not quick to anger,
'A'ole no'ono'o 'ino. — Nor thinketh evil to any man.

O ke aloha o ke Akua — Love that is of God
'A'ole pāonioni ke aloha, — Is love without strife
'A'ole ha'anui aku ke aloha, — Is love that vaunteth not itself,
'A'ole he ha'akei. — Is humble and not puffed up.

O ke aloha o ke Akua — Love that is of God
'A'ole ia he ho'opunipuni, — Is without deceptions,
'A'ole 'imi i kona mea iho, — Seeketh not its own,
'A'ole he kua'aku'ai. — Giveth not to receive.

Ke mau nei keia mau mea, — These things still abide,
Ka mana'o'i'o, ka mana'olana, — Faith and hope and the love
A me ke aloha o ke Akua, — That is of God and of these
Ke aloha na'e ka i 'oi. — Love is the greatest.

The Love of God

Hawaiian is the indigenous language of the Hawaiian Islands. A member of the Polynesian family, it was brought to Hawaii from the Society Islands, 2,500 miles to the south, between the 5th and the 8th centuries.

Until well into the 19th century Hawaiian was still the everyday language of most of the islands' natives. But the steadily increasing American influence led to a wholesale shift to English within only a couple of generations. Laws adopted in 1893 and 1905 forbade the use of Hawaiian in the schools. By the beginning of World War I there was hardly a Hawaiian child who could speak the language any more. Only on the isolated island of Ni'ihau did people continue to speak, read, and write the language.

In the 1970s an effort was begun to revive the study and speaking of Hawaiian. At the state's Constitutional Convention in 1978 a provision was passed granting Hawaiian the same official status as English. In 1987 indigenous language immersion classes were offered in a number of elementary schools: the only such schools in the United States. In 1997 a Hawaiian language college was established as part of the University of Hawaii at Hilo. It is the first college in the United States to be conducted entirely, and to offer a graduate degree, in a Native American language.

Hawaiian is considered one of the most musical languages in the world, containing only the five vowels and seven consonants: *h, k, l, m, n, p,* and *w*. The paucity of consonants, plus the fact that every Hawaiian syllable and word ends in a vowel, produces curious renditions of certain English expressions, such as the Hawaiian equivalent of "Merry Christmas," *Mele Kelikimaka*. Perhaps the best known Hawaiian word is *aloha*, meaning "love" or "affection," but also used both for "hello" and "goodbye." *Ukulele* is also a Hawaiian word, as are *hula*, *lei*, *luau*, and *poi*.

Eskimo

ᑕᐃᒪᒐᓂᑦ ᐸᐃᐸᓕᒃᒥ ᐃᓄᒃᓱᒃᒍᐊᓕᓚᐅᖅᑕᒥ ᐱᒋᐊᖅᓂᖃᖅᓱᓂ. ᓯᓚᖅᔪᐅᑉ ᐃᓄᒋᑦ ᐃᑳᖅᕆᐅᕈᓇᖅᓯᖅᓯᒪᓕᖅᐳᑦ ᑐᑭᓯᐊᑐᕋᐅᑎᔪᒪᓂᖅᒧᑦ ᐅᖃᐅᓯᖃᖃᑎᒌᖏᑐᓐᓂᒃ ᐊᒥᓱᓂᒃ ᓯᓚᖅᔪᐊᖅᒥ. ᑭᓯᐊᓂᓕ ᖁᕕᐊᓇᖅᑑᕗᖅ ᓯᓚᖅᔪᐊᖅᒥ ᖃᐅᔨᒪᑉᓗᓂ ᐃᓄᐃᑦ ᐃᓚᖏᑦ ᐃᖃᖅᓴᒃᑲᐅᓐᓂᖅᒪᑕ ᑕᐃᒃᑯᐊ ᑕᕿᐅᖅᔪᐅᑉ ᐊᑮᐊᓂ ᐄᐅᕐᑉᒥᐅᑦ ᑎᑭᓚᐅᖅᓯᒪᔪᑦ ᐊᒃᓱᕈᖅᖢᑎᒃ ᐱᓕᕆᕙᓚᐅᖅᓂᖅᒪᑦᑕ ᐃᓄᖅᕈᑎᑎᓂᑦ ᐊᑐᖅᑕᐅᔪᓐᓇᖅᑐᓐᓂᒃ ᑎᑎᕋᐅᓯᓕᐅᓚᐅᖅᓂᖅᒪᑕ. ᓴᐃᓚᐱᒃᔅ-ᔅᑎᑐᑦ ᑎᑎᕋᐅᓯᖅ, ᐱᓕᐊᖅᖢᒍ, ᑎᑎᕋᐅᓯᑦᓯᐊᒪᕆᐅᕗᖅ, ᐊᑐᖅᑕᐅᓕᖅᑐᖅ ᐃᓄᒃᓂᑦ ᐊᒥᓱᓐᓂᑦ ᑲᓇᑕᒥᐅᑕᐅᔪᓐᓂᑦ.

Taimmaganit, paipalikmik Inukshukgualilauqtami pigiaqniqaqshuni. Silaqjuup inugit ikaaqriurunaqsiqsimaliqput tukisiaturautijumaniqmut uqausiqaqatigiingitunnik ammisunik silaqjuaqmi. Kisianili quvianaqtuuvuq silaqjuaqmi qauyimabluni Inuit ilangit iqaqsakkaunniqmata taipkua taqiuqjuup akiani Europmiut tikilauqsimayut aksuruqllutik pilirivalauqniqmatta inuqrutitinit atuqtauyunnaqtunnik titirausiliulauqniqmata. Syllabics-stitut titirausiq, piliaqllugu, titirausitsiamariuvuq, atuqtauliqtuq Inuknit amisunnit Canadamiutauyunnit.

Ever since the building of the great Tower of Babel, humanity has been trying to bridge communication gaps among the many languages of the world. It is therefore satisfying to learn about the inventiveness of certain individuals, such as those early Europeans who labored among our people to come up with a workable written language. Syllabics in partic- ular has become a unique writing system for many Canadian Inuit.

Eskimo is spoken over a vast expanse of territory extending from Greenland in the east, across Canada and Alaska, and ultimately into easternmost Siberia. Speakers in Greenland number 50,000, in Canada 25,000, in Alaska 20,000, in Siberia 1,000. Most of Canada's Eskimos live in the huge new territory (created in 1999) of Nunavut, the eastern two-thirds of the Northwest Territories. There they comprise about 85 percent of the population.

The word Eskimo is rapidly falling into disuse. It was derived from the Cree language, spoken to the south in the area of Hudson Bay, and means "eaters of raw flesh." The preferred term today is Inuit, the word for "people" in their language.

There are many dialects of Eskimo but it is remarkable, considering its enormous range, that they fall into only two major groups. Inuit, which accounts for over 95 percent of the total number of speakers, is spoken in Greenland, Canada, and northern Alaska. (In Greenland it is known as Greenlandic, in Canada as Inuktitut, in Alaska as Inupiaq.) The other dialect, Yupik, is spoken in southern Alaska, including St. Lawrence Island, and also in Siberia. The line dividing the two extends across central Alaska, reaching Norton Sound on the west coast between the towns of Unalakleet, where Inuit is spoken, and St. Michael, which is Yupik-speaking.

The only language related to Eskimo is the Aleut language of the Aleutian Islands. The two are not mutually intelligible, but there are sufficient similarities to indicate that they were a single language several thousand years ago.

The writing of Eskimo dates as far back as 1721 when Protestant missionaries brought the Roman alphabet to Greenland. In Canada a syllabic system was introduced in 1876, the same one that had been developed earlier for the Cree Indians and is still used by them. (The passage on the opposite page, which is in Inuit, is shown in both the Cree syllabics and the Roman alphabet).

No writing system existed for the Eskimos of Siberia until the early 1930s, when the Soviet government introduced a Roman-based alphabet. This, however, was replaced by the Cyrillic alphabet as early as 1937.

Igloo and *kayak* are two Eskimo words that have entered the English language. In Eskimo they simply mean "house" and "boat."

Aleut

Agánan, agánan, tánan akúya, akúya,
Wákun qayáxtalkinín aganágan
Cuqígan tamadágin, tamadágin
Ayágagilik taĭyágugilik;
Agánan, agánan, tánan akúya, akúya,
Wákun ayagángin, wákun taĭyágungin
Ásik kukiming álulik aladaqalidáqing
Tága axtagalíkumán,
Tutaqangúluk tutálik wángun sagálik ulálik ulalíting.

These countries are created, created.
There are hills on them.
There are little hills on each of them, each of them.
There are women, there are men.
These countries are created, created.
On them are women, on them are men.
With me they laughed and joked.
And so when we separated [they did the same]
I have not heard [such things] as if in a sleep
I heard or felt pleasure.

Aleut is spoken by about 1,000 people in the Aleutian Islands and by a few hundred more on the Commander Islands, which belong to Russia. It is related to Eskimo but only distantly, the two languages being in no way mutually intelligible. The first alphabet for the Aleut language was developed by a Russian missionary about 1825 and was based on the Cyrillic alphabet. Although the Aleutian Islands passed with Alaska to the United States in 1867, the Roman alphabet was not introduced until the 20th century.

Tlingit

Athapaskan tóo-nux uyúh kawsi.àh hah Lingít koostèeyee. Lingít tlàgoo tóo-x' uyúh yéi kudoonéek, yúh hah shugóon súkw, àn gulukóo yéigah, àgah uwéh dak-x' hus woolilàh. Yáh yeedút dlèit kách Arctic Circle yéi yuságoo yei-x' uwéh hus woolilàh. Dlèit káh koonujéeyee, hús uwéh yéi's kawjixít, hah shugóon súkw nakée, t'éex' kàh-nux, yáh-nux yun hus oowu.át. Yúh sh-kulnèek ko.àh tléil uwooyàh. Doo toondutánee koodzi-teeyee káh tléil yúh áh koosu.at'ee yéi-dei doo yútx'ee tèen googu.àt, kuh yun dugawútx'ee tèen, ch'uh yúh t'éex' kàh-nux yun hus gwa.àdit. Tléil tsoo hus uh wooskóh t'éex' áh yéi tèeyee. Koosu.át'ee yéh uyóo yóo nakée; tléil dah súh áh koo.éix; tsoo ut woo.àdee útx'ee sánee tsóo tléil áh yéi ootíh. Tléil tsoo áh yéi kootée. Tákw-x' tlukw kookooshgitch. Wooch goowunádei kah utxàyee tsóo tléil áh yéi ootíh Tléil uh t'éi-t uh yuxdoowuhanee út koostíh. Yát'ah tléil yéi x'awdután uyúh, tléil àdei út koowoogagoowoo yéh. Adei ko.àh shukdéi koogooxlus'ées. Yéi ut kuwoo.àkw àdei uh n'gu.àdee, yut'ix'ee út-x kah jèe-x' gooxsutée.

The Tlingit tribe is one of the Athabaskan tribes. It is told in some of the Tlingit legends that during Noah's flood the Athabaskan tribe, as the waters subsided, landed in the area of the Arctic Circle. The theory of many writers is that the Athabaskans came across the Bering Ice Bridge. This doesn't stand to reason. Why should a family or group of people – men, woman, children, and older people – go up North? Just to cross an Ice Bridge that they did not know existed? It was a cold, desolate, unin-habited place, dark during part of the year, without much variety of food and with no protection. This is not to say that a group of people could not land at such a place by accident. But to go there willfully, at great discomfort to the whole group, is not reasonable.

The Tlingit Indians live in the Alaskan Panhandle, in and around the cities of Juneau, Sitka, and Ketchikan, as well as on a number of islands in the Alexander Archipelago. Their language shows a number of similarities with those of the Athabaskan family, but its exact linguistic classification remains uncertain. There are about 1,000 speakers.

Cree

ᓀᐦᐃᔭᐍᐏᐣ ᐁᑿ ᐁᐘᑯ, ᓇᒨᔭ ᐱᑯ ᐆᒪ ᑭᔮᓇᐤ ᐆᒪ ᑳ ᐃᓯ ᓀᐦᐃᔭᐍᔮᕽ, ᓇᒨᔭ ᐱᑯ ᐁᐘᑯ, ᓇᓈᑐᕽ ᐆᑭ ᐍᒌᐿᔮᓂᐘᐠ ᓇᐦᑲᐏᔨᓂᐘᐠ ᑈᑕᐠ, ᐅᐢᑳᔭᐠ ᐆᑭ ᒥᐢᑕᐦᐃ ᐁ ᐘᓂᐦᑖᒋᐠ ᐲᑭᐢᑵᐏᐣ, ᐁᑿ ᐆᑭ ᐁ ᐃᑘᒋᐠ ᓇᐦᑲᐏᔨᓂᐘᐠ ᐑᐢᑕᐚᐤ, ᒥᐦᒉᐟ ᐊᓂᑭ ᐅᐢᑳᔭᐠ ᓇᒨᔭ ᐁ ᐋᐸᒋᐦᑖᒋᐠ ᐊᓂᒪ ᓇᐦᑲᐍᐏᐣ, ᐑᐢᑕᐚᐤ ᐅᑎᓯ ᐲᑭᐢᑵᐏᓂᐚᐤ, ᐁᑯᓯ ᐁᑿ ᐊᓂᑭ ᑫᐦᑌ ᐊᔭᐠ ᓂᑕᐍᔨᐦᑕᒷᐠ ᐑᐢᑕᐚᐤ ᐅᑑᐢᑳᔨᒥᐚᐘ ᑕ ᐋᐸᒋᐦᑖᔨᐟ ᐊᓂᒪ ᐅᓇᐦᑲᐍᐏᓂᐚᐤ, ᓇᒨᔭ ᐑ ᐋᐸᒋᐦᑖᐘᐠ ᐁᐘᑯ ᐊᓂᒪ ᐅᐲᑭᐢᑵᐏᓂᐚᐤ ᐆᑭ ᐅᐢᑳᔭᐠ, ᐃᔮᔭᐤ ᐆᒪ ᐋᑲᔮᓰᒧᐏᐣ, ᐁᐘᑯ ᒥᐢᑕᐦᐃ, ᓇᒨᔭ ᑲᑫᑎᕽ ᐊᔨᐚᐠ ᐋᐸᒋᐦᑖᐘᐠ.

nêhiyawêwin êkwa êwako, namôya piko ôma kiyânaw ôma kâ-isi-nêhiyawêyahk, namôya piko êwako, nanâtohk ôki wêcîpwayâniwak nahkawiyiniwak pwâtak, osk-âyak ôki mistahi ê-wanihtâcik pîkiskwêwin; êkwa ôki ê-itwêcik nahkawiyiniwak wîstawâw, mihcêt aniki osk-âyak namôya ê-âpacihtâcik anima nahkawêwin, wîstawâw otisi-pîkiskwêwiniwâw, êkosi êkwa aniki kêhtê-ayak nitawêyihtamwak wîstawâw otôsk-âyimiwâwa ta-âpacihtâyit anima onahkawêwiniwâw; namôya wî-âpacihtâwak êwako anima opîkiskwêwiniwâw ôki osk-âyak, iyâyaw ôma âkayâsîmowin, êwako mistahi, namôya kakêtihk ayiwâk âpacihtâwak.

It is true not only for the Cree language, the language we speak, not for that language alone but for the various tribes, the Chipewyans and the Saulteaux and the Dakotas, that the young people have lost much of their language; and the Saulteaux say the same, that many of the young people do not use Saulteaux, their own language, and therefore these elders, too, want their young people to use their Saulteaux language; but the young people will not use their own language but, rather, English, they use a lot of that, they use English a great deal more.

Cree is the most important of the Indian languages of Canada, with a total of 75,000 speakers. About one-third live in Manitoba, another third in Saskatchewan, the rest in Alberta (15,000) and Quebec (10,000). One dialect of Cree known as Attikamek, spoken by about 4,000 people along the St. Maurice River in Quebec, is different enough from standard Cree to be considered by some as a separate language.

Cree to this day is written in a system of syllabic symbols introduced by a Protestant missionary in the year 1840. The same system is used for writing the Inuktitut (Eskimo) language in Canada. Cree belongs to the Algonkian family of languages.

Ojibwa

eppi· ko me·no·kkemikin kecci-mo·ške?an iw si·pi·we˜ e·nta·ya·n.
mi· tašš kwa ema· ekote ?owa·t ekiw keno·še·k keye· kwa ekiw ešikume·-
kok. nentatto·n tašš kwa iw pi·wa·pekko·ns menka·we·penakwa·
wi·-pwa·-ša·pekkošuwa·t ekiw keno·še·k keye· ešikume·kok. pi·cin
tašš ekwa nentawa-ena·p ema· si·pi·we·n?ink e·ya·mekakk iw nentasso·-
na·kan. nuwa·penta·n kwa kuma·ppi·cc iw mema·sekka·k iw pi·-
wa·pekko·ns. mi· a·ši ki·-tekoššink aw ki·ko˜. mi· tašš eša·ya·n
keye· kwa mi· nena·?etta·ppenama·n iw nentanitt. mi· tašš pecipuwak
aw ki·ko˜. na·nenkotenonk ni·š nente·-pecipuwa·k ci·pwa·-kekkina-
-kencipe?iwe·wa·t.

In springtime the creek near my house runs very deep. Then the pike
and dogfish swim upstream there. Then I put wire netting there to keep
the pike and dogfish from swimming through. At frequent intervals I go
and look there in the creek where my trap is placed. In time I see the
wire moving. That is when the fish have arrived. Then I go and tie fast
my fish spear. Then I spear those fish. Sometimes I manage to spear two
of them before they all get away.

Ojibwa or Ojibway, also known as Chippewa, is spoken both in Canada and
the United States. In Canada there are about 25,000 speakers, evenly divided
between Ontario and Manitoba, with another 1,500 in Saskatchewan. In the
United States there are about 5,000 in Michigan, Wisconsin, Minnesota, and
North Dakota. Ojibwa belongs to the Algonkian family of languages.

Micmac

Lnoi gtjisagmaoag maopeltoôg, etli Sagmaois Migmagig tan tetotgig. Oetjategemg gespeg misôgo elsetgog gisna teoapsgig. Maopeltoôg nata-matnageoinoag ag nata-gesgmaplgigoateget. Oenotjgig pegisitolgopeneg alasotmeoinoeg 1600eg netna negem gtjisagmaoag amsgoeseoeg sigentasis, Nige ola ganataoagig, nipnigos-24 tesogonitag-1610eg. Apogonemoasniga oenotjgig tan-oigoltitag Togo saseoltitis angoôoei, ag tan gôgoel menoegetis. Maopeltoôg negm-nepgis-oigeoigos-11 tesogonitag 1611eg. Lôg metj gesalaseniga oenotjga ag togoamoatj, tan-pegoatolgos metj pemiag gis-sist gasgimtlnaganipongeg tjel eloigneg tesisgegipongeg tjel-nan.

The headman or Grand Chief of a large band of Micmac Indians living along the south shore of the Bay of Fundy, Membertou, was also a great warrior and renowned shaman. When the French arrived in the early 1600s he converted to Christianity, and on June 24, 1610 became the first native chieftain to be baptized in what is now Canada. He helped the French establish a settlement in this area and traded furs with them for European goods. Membertou died on September 18, 1611, but the Micmac-French alliance which he began lasted for more than a century.

The Micmac Indians live primarily in Nova Scotia. There they number about 7,000, while others are to be found in New Brunswick and on the southern coast of Newfoundland. One small group, speaking a somewhat different dialect, lives near the town of Restigouche, on the southern Gaspé Peninsula. The Micmac language is of the Algonkian family. The English word *toboggan* is of Micmac origin.

Navajo

Naakidi neeznádiin dóó ba'ąą hastą́diin dóó ba'ąą náhást'éí nááhaiídąą' Naabeehó Yootó dóó kinteel bita' Dinétah hoolyéegi kéédahat'íí ńt'éé', dóó índa shádi'ááh dóó e'e'aahjigo dadeezná jiní. Ła' t'éiyá Tséyi'jigo adahaazná jiní; náánáła' t'éiyá Mą'ii Deeshgiizh dóó Soodził bine'jį' adahaazná jiní, dóó náánáła' éí Tóntsaajį' adahaazná jiní. Táadi neeznádiin dóó ba'ánigo nááhaiídą́ą́' Naabeehó dibé dóó łį́į' bee dahazlį́į' dóó díí naaldooshii shódayoost'e'go nikidadiibaa' jiní. Naakaii ádaaníigo t'éiyá 165 nááhaiídą́ą́' Naabeehó 3500 yilt'eego kéédahat'íí ńt'éé' – dííshjį́į́góó 150,000 yilt'é jiní.

Until about 268 years ago the Navajo lived in an area between Santa Fe and Aztec called *Dinetah*, and after that time they began to move southward and westward. Some moved toward the Canyon de Chelly; others migrated toward Jemez and to Mount Taylor, and still others to Tunicha. More than 300 years ago the Navajo acquired sheep and horses and began to raid the settlements. According to Spanish accounts 165 years ago the Navajo population was about 3,500; today there are about 150,000.

The Navajo are the largest Indian tribe in the United States. They number about 150,000, the majority living on large reservations in New Mexico, Arizona, and Utah. They are an offshoot of the Apache, who are believed to have migrated from Canada to the American Southwest about a thousand years ago. The Navajo language, like the Apache, is of the Athabaskan family. The Navajo call themselves Diné, "The People."

ᏓᎦᏏ ᏃᎴ ᎠᏫ ᏕᎾᏓᏁᎸᏔᏁᎢ ᎦᏔᏉᎩᏁᎢ ᏧᎤᏓᏒ ᏭᏂᎷᎯᏍᏗ. ᏓᎦᏏ
ᎱᏓᏁᎸᏔᏁᎢ ᏧᏓᎩᏍᏗᎯ. ᎠᏎᏃ ᎱᏓᎷᎸ ᎤᎾᏙᎩᏍᏗ ᏧᏓᎾᏛᎴ
ᏓᎦᏏ. ᎦᏔᏉᎩᏁ ᏧᎤᏓᏒ ᏗᏓᎴᏂᏍᎬ ᏥᏕᎤᏍᏓᏁ ᏓᎦᏏ. ᏕᎤᏍᏓᎾ
ᏕᏁᏤᎴᎢ ᏂᎦᎷᎬᎾᏉ ᎠᏫ ᎤᎾᏙᎯᏍᏗ ᎨᏎᎢ. ᎠᏫ ᎱᏓᏒᏍᏓᎾ
ᏓᎦᏏ ᏊᎾᏉ ᎤᏬᏉᎶᎩ ᏥᏭᎸᏰᎴ. ᏊᏓᏒᏍᏗᏍᎬ Ꮏ ᎤᏬᏓᏒ
ᏥᎾᏂᎦᎷᎬᎾᏉ ᏗᎠᏙᎯᏍᎨ ᎸᏓᎴ ᏓᎦᏏ. ᎠᎬᏜᏃ ᎤᏓᏁᎸᏔᏬ
ᎤᏉᎶᎪ ᏭᎸᏰᎸ ᎨᏎᎢ. ᏓᏥᎩᏰᎢ ᎠᏫ ᎠᏓᏂᏔᏗ ᎬᏗ.

The turtle and the deer challenged each other to see which one would reach the seventh mountain first. The turtle claimed he would win. But before the race the turtle planned a ruse. He posted another turtle on each of the seven mountains. He told them to yell before the deer got there. When the race began the deer quickly ran past the turtle, who then crawled into the leaves. As the deer approached each mountain another turtle would yell. Back at the starting point the challenger was still lying under the leaves. The deer was defeated by deception.

Cherokee is spoke by upwards of 10,000 people, the great majority living near the town of Tahlequah in northeastern Oklahoma. About 1,000 speakers live in western North Carolina, on a reservation near the town of Cherokee. The Cherokee language is of the Iroquoian family, most closely related to Seneca, Mohawk, and Oneida.

Cherokee writing, pictured above, is the creation of Sequoyah, one of the great names in the history of the American Indian. Convinced that the key to the white man's power lay in his possession of a written language, he set about bringing this secret to his own people. In 1821, after twelve years of work, he produced a syllabary of 86 characters, representing every sound in the Cherokee language. The system was quickly mastered by thousands of Cherokees and within three years a newspaper began to be published, and a constitution for the Cherokee Nation was drawn up in the Cherokee language.

Sequoyah borrowed many of his characters from English, but since he actually neither spoke nor read English, they represent completely different sounds in the two languages. The letter *D*, for example, is pronounced *a*, while *h* is pronounced *ni*, *W* is pronounced *la*, and *Z* is pronounced *no*. But the Sequoyah syllabary has remained in use to the present day, with no modifications considered necessary in 150 years. That an unlettered hunter and craftsman could complete a task now undertaken only by highly trained linguists must surely rank as one of the most impressive intellectual feats achieved by a single man.

Sioux

Ehanni, kangi kin zintkala ata ska heca. Nahan tatanka ob lila kolaw-icaye lo. Lakota kin tatanka wicakuwapi na wicaktepi iyutapi cannas, kangi kin u kte na tatanka kin iwahowicaye s'a. Heon Lakota kin lila acanzekapi. Hankeya, Lakota kin kangi kin oyuspapi. Iyopeyapi kta on, can hanska wan oinkpa el kaskapi na kuta peta tanka wan ilegyapi. Sota lila sapa ca wankatakiya iya icunhuh, kangi kin ata sapa hingle. Hankeya, peta kin wikan kin kihugnage naha kangi kin kinyan kigle – tka itahena ata sapa heca.

A long time ago, the crow was a bird that was completely white. He was also a very good friend of the buffalo. When the Indians would try to catch and kill the buffalo, the crow would come and warn them. For this reason, the Indians were very angry at the crow. Finally, the Indians caught the crow. In order to punish the crow, they tied him to the top of a tall pole and built a big fire under him. As the black smoke rose, the crow became completely black. Finally, the fire burned the rope in two and the crow flew away – but he has been black ever since.

How the Crow Became Black

Sioux, also known as Dakota, is spoken both in the United States and Canada. There are about 15,000 speakers in the United States, principally in South Dakota, though there are some in North Dakota, Montana, and Nebraska. In Canada there are about 4,000 speakers: 3,000 in Alberta, 700 in Manitoba, and 300 in Saskatchewan.

Sioux is the most important language of the Siouan family, which includes Winnebago, Crow, and a number of other languages. The name Dakota is a Sioux word meaning "friends" or "allies."

Blackfoot

A-chim-oo-yis-gon.
e-spoo-ta kin-non-a na-do-wa-bis
ke-ta-nik-goo-ye
oo-da-keen-non. ke-sto-wa a-ne-chiss
ke-che-sta-ne a-nom cha-koom-ma
e-spoo-che-ka ne-too-ye a-ne-chiss
kip-pe-soo-kin-on na-pa-yen
ee-seen-mo-kin-on ke-che-na-pon-sa-ko
da-ke-boo-che-kim-ma ma-da-pee-wa.
moo-ka-mo-che-pew-kin-on ka-mo-che-pew-kin-on
ma-ka-pe-ye nee-na-kee-sta-ta-poo. Kin-na-ye.

Lord's Prayer.
Our Father who art in heaven
hallowed
be thy name. Thy kingdom come
Thy will be done on earth,
as it is in heaven.
Give us this day our daily bread.
And forgive our debts,
as we forgive our debtors.
And lead us not into temptation,
but deliver us from evil. Amen.

The Blackfeet Indians live principally in the Canadian province of Alberta, as well as in the U.S. state of Montana. In Alberta they number about 3,500, living on three reservations in the southeastern part of the province. In Montana they number about 1,000, most of them living on a reservation near the town of Browning, just east of Glacier National Park. The Blackfoot language is of the Algonkian family.

Crow

Ush-ke-she-de-sooua bob-ba-sah uh-caw-sha-asede Usha-esah-ughdia be-lay-luc Ugh-ba-dud-dia coush aho-hake. Ish-gawoun besha-ahsoua-luc, dagh-gosh-bosho-luc, bah-couh-we-sha cou-cwah ah-cou-duke. Usha-esah-ughdia esa-ba-lay-duc, acouh-bah-goo-sa e-gee-lay-duc. Oogah chia-luc, hish-sha-luc, she-lay-luc, e esa bah-lah-gic. Oogah-luc, alah-coo-sio-luc, ewah-ah-cou-dua-luc, cou-cwah ushuma-la-chia ala-whoua-lawah cone bah-quoc.

On the first day of the sun dance as the sun breaks over the horizon, the sponsor enters the lodge and begins his fast which is in appreciation of past favors by the Great Spirit. Inside the lodge are a buffalo head and eagle feathers which are symbols of all the animals and birds that live on the great plains and in the Rocky Mountains. The sponsor is bare-footed and is uncovered above the waist. His face is painted with white, red, or yellow clay. The color of the paint, the application, and the symbols are handed down from generation to generation by each clan.

Crow is a Siouan language, once spoken over a large area of Montana and Wyoming, between the Yellowstone and Platte rivers. Today almost all the Crow Indians, numbering about 4,000, live on the Crow Indian Reservation, near the town of Hardin, Montana.

wayatihāē' ne nyakwai' khuh ne tyihukwaes. ne' nyakwai' thutēcunih
tyawe'ūh teyucūtaikūke'ū thutēcunih. taneke'ū tyihukwaes neke'ū
ēyuhēsek. teyu'kœhtūk, teyu'kœhtūk, teyu'kœhtūk. tyihukwaes wāē':
ēyuhēsek, ēyuhēsek, ēyuhēsek. tanenekyū' tyihukwaes waatkwenii'.
tanekyū' kayūnih ne' unēh wa'uhēt wa'u'kœ khuh. tanenēhke'ū
waunū'khwē' ne nyakwai', taneke'ū uthuchiyuu' ne tyihukwaes
haswe'nūkeh. tanenē'kyū' kayūnih sēniyū tetya'tetanū haswe'nūkeh ne'
tyihukwaes.

The Bear and the Chipmunk quarreled. The Bear wanted it to be night
all the time, it is said. The Chipmunk, it is said, wanted it to be day and
night. (The Bear said) "Dark all the time, dark all the time, dark all the
time" (faster and faster). The Chipmunk said, "Day and night, day and
night, day and night" (faster and faster). Then, it is said, the Chipmunk
won. That is why it now dawns and grows dark. Then, it is said, the
Bear got angry. He scratched the Chipmunk on his back. That is why
the Chipmunk has three stripes down his back.

The Seneca Indians lived for centuries in the western third of New York
State, being one of the Five Nations that formed the League of the Iroquois.
Today about 1,000 Senecas live on two reservations in western New York,
the Cattaraugus Reservation near the town of Irving, and the Allegany
Reservation near Salamanca. The Seneca language belongs to the Iroquoian
family. The alphabet consists of only 15 letters (*a*, *ã*, *c*, *e*, *ẽ*, *h*, *i*, *k*, *n*, *s*, *t*,
u, *ū*, *w*, *y*) plus the additional vowel *œ*.

Mohawk

Niyawehkowa katy nonwa onenh skennenji thisayatirhehon. Onenh
nonwa oghseronnih denighroghkwayen. Hasekenh thiwakwekonh
deyunennyatenyon nene konnerhonyon, "Ie henskerighwaghtonte."
Kenyutnyonkwaratonnyon, neony kenyotdakarahon, neony
kenkontifaghsoton. Nedens aesayatyenenghdon, konyennedaghkwen,
neony kenkaghnekonyon nedens aesayatyenenghdon,
konyennethaghkwen, neony kenwaseraketotanese kentewaghsatayenha
kanonghsakdatye. Niyateweghniserakeh yonkwakaronny; onidatkon
yaghdekakonghsonde oghsonteraghkowa nedens aesayatyenenghdon,
konyennethaghkwen.

Great thanks now, therefore, that you have safely arrived. Now, then, let
us smoke the pipe together. Because all around are hostile agencies
which are each thinking, "I will frustrate their purpose." Here thorny
ways, and here falling trees, and here wild beasts lying in ambush. Either
by these you might have perished, my offspring, or, here by floods you
might have been destroyed, my offspring, or by the uplifted hatchet in
the dark outside the house. Every day these are wasting us; or deadly
invisible disease might have destroyed you, my offspring.

The Iroquois Book of Rites

The Mohawk Indians lived originally in the Mohawk Valley of New York
State, between the modern cities of Schenectady and Utica. The easternmost
of the Five Nations that formed the League of the Iroquois, they sided with
the British during the Revolutionary War and were forced after the
Revolution to flee to Canada. Today the largest concentration of Mohawks
(about 1,500) is on the St. Regis Indian Reservation in St. Regis, New York,
facing the St. Lawrence River and bordering Canada. A few hundred more
live in various parts of Ontario and some are to be found in Quebec. The
Mohawk language is of the Iroquoian family.

Choctaw

ATIKEL I.

Aivlhpiesa Makosh Ulhpisa

Nana isht imaivlhpiesa moma ishahli micha, Kʋfamint yoka keyu hosh ilʋppa ka tokma atobacha aivlhpisa chi mako yakohmashke.

SEK. 1. Hattak yuka keyu hokʋtto yakohmit itibachʋfat hieli kʋt, nan isht imaivlhpiesa atokmʋt itilawashke; yohmi ka hattak nana hohkia, keyukmʋt kanohmi hohkia okla moma nana isht aim aivlhpiesa, micha isht aimaivlhtoba he aima ka kanohmi bano hosh isht ik imaivlhpieso kashke. Amba moma kʋt nana isht imachukma chi ho tuksʋli hokmakashke-

SEK. 2. Oklah moma hatokmʋt, nana kʋt aivlpiesa hinla kʋt afoyoka ho mʋhli hatokma ko, nana kʋt ʋlhpisa na Okla moma kʋt isht imachukma chi ka apisa he ʋt imaivlhpiesa cha Kafanmint yuka keyu ikbashke, yohmi tok osh ishahlit isht a mahaya hinla kʋt otani hokma, nittak nana hohkia nana ho apihinsa tok ʋt kobafi, keyukmʋt mosholichi cha ila chit ikbi bʋnna hokmʋt imaivlhpiesashke.

ARTICLE I

Declaration of Rights

That the general, great and essential principles of liberty and free government may be recognized and established, we declare:

Sec. 1. That all free men, when they form a social compact, are equal in rights, and that no man or set of men are entitled to exclusive, separate public emolument or privileges from the community, but in consideration of public services.

Sec. 2. That all political power is inherent in the people, and all free governments are founded on their authority and established for their benefit, and therefore they have at all times an inalienable and indefeasible right to alter, reform, or abolish their form of government in such manner as they may think proper or expedient.

Constitution of the Choctaw Nation

The Choctaw Indians lived originally in southern Mississippi, but in the 1830s they were forced to cede their lands to the United States government and move to what is now Oklahoma. There, together with the Chickasaws, Seminoles, Creeks, and Cherokees, they formed the so-called Five Civilized Tribes, each with its own territory, government, and code of laws. This independent status continued until 1907, when Oklahoma was admitted to the Union as a state.

Speakers of Choctaw today number about 9,000. About three-fourths live in southeastern Oklahoma, the rest on a reservation in central Mississippi. The Choctaw language is most closely related to Chickasaw, the two belonging to the Muskogean family. The name Oklahoma means "red people" in Choctaw.

Chickasaw

Chikasha, Chahta, Mushkoki Micha Chukhoma mọt Mushkoki aiọchololi achi cha tok.

Yakni aiasha yummut Oshapani i Okhata ọ hekia cha Hushi Akocha Bok Misha Sipokni onna mut Fulummi pila ọ aiya ot Bok Fulummi abuiydchit ulhchuba Bok tuklo ittịtukla aiya ot Hushi Akocha Okhata Ishto ot talhi tok.

Chikasha hatuk owutta ulheha mut mona impona kut immaiya tok, nunna aiyaka tawạ. Ikimmilho cha immaiyachit ik tikabo ot unoa mah momut aiyukpachit isht anumpoli cha tok.

Chepota ịki keyuk mut ishki ot illi hokma i kanomi fehna kut himmonali i chuka achufa ikbi cha i hullo kut immi che yummushchi cha tok.

The Chickasaws are of the Muskogean family, whose principal nations were the Chickasaw, Choctaw, Creek, and Chockhoomas. The country occupied by them extended from the Gulf of Mexico up the east side of the Mississippi River, then up the Ohio to the dividing ridge between the Tennessee and Cumberland rivers and on eastward to the Atlantic Ocean.

As trackers and hunters the Chickasaws had no superiors. They were celebrated for their personal bravery and indomitable spirit and had almost endless endurance. There were no Chickasaw orphans. If the mother or father died, or the father was slain in battle, the child was immediately placed with a near relative able to care for him and was thereby adopted into the new family and no differences were shown in the children.

The Chickasaw Indians lived originally in Mississippi, just north of the Choctaws, to whom they are linguistically related. About 1830 they were moved to what is now Oklahoma, where today they number about 5,000. Most of them live near the town of Ardmore, in the southernmost part of the state. About 2,500 people are still able to speak the language. Chickasaw belongs to the Muskogean family.

Fox

Neni′w ä‘kī′wānī^dtc ä′‘cī‘cā^dtc^{ıt}, ä‘pe‘cege‘siwe‘ci‘ₐg^{kıt}. Ä‘ₐ‘cki′-megu‘u′wīwi^dtc ä′nawäneni′‘ä‘i^dtc^{ıt}. Ī′nₐ nä′‘k i‘kwäw ä‘wäwe′-ne‘si^dtc^{ıt}. Tcäwī‘cwi′megu ä‘wäwene′‘siwä^dtc^{ıt}. Ä‘tₐgwāgī′‘inig ä‘uwīwe′tīwä^dtc^{ıt}. Nōmₐgä′w uwīwe′tīwä^dtc īni^dtcä′‘ip ä‘mawi-kīwānī^dtc^{ıt}. Kₐbōtwe′mcgu ä‘pōnike‘kä′netₐgi wä′^dtcīgwän^{nıt}. Kcyä‘ₐpₐgä′‘ipi kī‘ce‘sōn ᴀiyāpōtānₐgīgwänegu′te‘e wä^dtcipwäwi′-meguke‘kä′netₐgi wä′^dtcīgwän^{nıt}. Ä‘kī‘cāgu^dtci′tä‘ä^dtc ä‘kī′-wānī^dtc^{ıt}. Ä‘wₐ′ni‘e^dtc^{ıt}.

A man was lost when hunting, when hunting deer. He had just been married and he was a fine-looking man. And the woman was beautiful. Both were beautiful. It was in the fall when they married. When they had been married a short time, then it is said he went out and was lost. Soon he ceased to know whence he had come. It is a fact, so it is said, that the reason why he did not know whence he had come was because his eyes had been turned upside down by the moon. He felt terrible when he was lost. He was missed.

The One Whom the Moons Blessed

The Fox Indians, who number only about 500, live on a reservation in eastern Iowa, near the village of Tama. About two centuries ago they merged with the neighboring Sac (or Sauk) tribe, who spoke the same language, and thus the language is sometimes referred to as Fox and Sac. The Sac Indians now live in central Oklahoma and number about 1,000. The Fox language is of the Algonkian family.

Creek

Ma-ómof fú'suă ok'holátid 'lákid á'latis ; ihádshî tcháp-
gĭd, ímpafnita lámhi imántalidshid. Níta umálgan alágit
ístin pasátît pápît á'latis. Hókti ahákin háhit, hía fúsuă
á'latin ihuiläidsháɤadis. Hía fúsua ma nákî inhahóyadi
i'hsit isayipatítut, hofónen i'lisaláɤatīs. Ódshipin ómad ná-
kitäs hítchkuidshi wäitis kómakatis. Hofóni hákin tchíssi
tchátit hi'tchkatis ; mómen ma fúsuat i lkitó-aitis kómaɤatis.
Ma tchíssin itimpunayágit istumidshakátit í'lgi imilid-ha-
gi-táyad itimpunäyákatis. Ma fúsuă ítcha⸗kuadáksin ín'li
apákin ō'dshid ómatis. Mómen ma tchí'ssit ítsa⸗kuadáksi
îfákan kalágit intádshatis, istómit issi-imanäítchiko-tidáyin
háyatis ; mómen man ilidsháɤatis. Ma fúsuă fúsuă ómal
immíkkun käidsháɤatis. Lámhi-u míkko 'lákid ō'mis kóma-
gid ómis ; mómiga hú'lidäs apíyis, adám hí'lka hákadäs
fúllis mómof lámhihádshi ko'htsaktsahídshid isfúllid ómis.
Tchátad hó·lit ómin, hátgátît hí·lka ahopákat ómis. Ihú·lit
táfa hátkin isnihäídshit idshú'kuan hatídshit awolä'dshit
lámhi ókit hákin ómat, istófan ilí'htchikos.

At that time there was a bird of large size, blue in color, with a long tail,
and swifter than an eagle, which came every day and killed and ate their
people. They made an image in the shape of a woman, and placed it in
the way of this bird. The bird carried it off, and kept it a long time, and
then brought it back. They left it alone, hoping it would bring something
forth. After a long time a red rat came forth from it, and they believe
the bird was the father of the rat. They took counsel with the rat how to
destroy its father. Now the bird had a bow and arrows; and the rat gnawed
the bowstring, so that the bird could not defend itself, and the people
killed it. They called this bird the King of Birds. They think the eagle
is also a great King; and they carry its feathers when they go to War or
make Peace: the red mean War; the white, Peace. If an enemy approaches
with white feathers and a white mouth, and cries like an eagle, they dare
not kill him.

The Migration Legend of the Kasi'hta Tribe

The Creek Indians lived originally in Georgia and Alabama. Frequent clashes with advancing white settlers eventually led to the Creek War of 1813–14, in which the Creeks were decisively defeated and forced to cede more than half their land to the United States. In the 1830s they were forced to move to Oklahoma, where today they number about 15,000. Most of them live near the town of Okmulgee, which lies due south of Tulsa. Probably not more than 4,000 still speak the Creek language. Creek is closely related to Seminole, both of them belonging to the Muskogean family.

E'-dsi xtsi a', a bin da, ţsi ga,
U'-ba-mon-xe i-tse-the a-ka', a bin da, ţsi ga,
E'-dsi xtsi a', a bin da, ţsi ga,
Da'-ḳ'o i-the ga-xe a-ka', a bin da, ţsi ga,
O'-da-bthu i-the ga-xe a-ka', a bin da, ţsi ga,
Mon'-xe a-tha ḳ'a-be don a', a bin da, ţsi ga,
Da'-zhu-dse i-non-the a-ka', a bin da, ţsi ga,
He'-dsi xtsi a', a bin da, ţsi ga,
Zhin'-ga ḳi-non gi-the ţse a-tha e-ḳi-a bi a', a bin da, ţsi ga,
He'-dsi xtsi a', a bin da, ţsi ga,
Ţsi'-zhu U-dse-the Pe-thon-ba', a bin da, ţsi ga,
U'-ça-ḳa thin-ge i-he-the a-ka', a bin da, ţsi ga.

Verily, at that time and place,
They placed beneath the pile of stones and in the spaces
    between them the dry branches.
Verily, at that time and place,
They set fire to the dead branches placed within and about the
    pile of stones,
And the flames leaped into the air with vibrating motions,
Making the walls of the heavens
To redden with a crimson glow.
Verily, at that time and place,
They said to one another: Let the reflection of this fire on yonder
    skies be for the painting of the bodies of the little ones.
Verily, at that time and place,
The bodies of the people of the Tsi-zhu Fireplaces
Became stricken with the red of the fire, leaving no spot
    untouched.

                    Painting Ritual of the Osage War Ceremony

The Osage Indians lived originally in Missouri, but in 1872 were settled on the Osage reservation in northeastern Oklahoma. The reservation has the same boundaries as Osage County, with tribal headquarters in the town of Pawhuska. The Osage language is of the Siouan family. Only a few hundred speakers remain today.

Delaware

yukwi′n·ek·e^ɛ k^{ɛʷ}tcu′k^ɛhɔk·e^ɛhel·a^ʷk·e lowe^ɛ′n ga′ci·k^ɛtu′he^ɛ nun·-hu′k·we yut·a′ lamha′k·i·ye^ɛ. ɔk^ɛ pe′tci k^ɛtale^ɛ′tan pu′ŋg^ʷ ɔk kwe^ɛ-c^ɛha′t·e^ɛk ɔk aha′m·e^ɛni·^l pe′tci k^ɛtal·e^ɛ′tan ke^ɛ′ko ma′l·aci· kaª′nosli-na′k·wat^ɛ suk^ɛpe^ɛ′k·at^ɛ nen·i·ke^ɛ′ko ge^ɛt^ɛpe^{′ɛ}hel·a^ªt^ɛ la^ªmha′ki·ye·ne′n·i ə′nda^ɛ ama′ŋgi tu^{ᵘ′}χk^ɛhak·i·e′^ɛhel·ak^ɛ yu′endalausi·′eŋg^ɛ ga^ɛhe^ɛ′sə·n·a oto^ɛhe^ɛ′p·iŋ.

yuk·we pe′tci ako′^ᵘ wa^ɛk·ɔt·u′^ᵘwi ke^ɛ′ko e^ɛli·mgɔ′t·uk^ɛ ne^ɛ suk^ɛpe^ɛ′k·a ke^ɛ′ko ge^ɛt·ala^ʷ′mwiŋg^ɛ. ne^ɛ ə′nda^ɛ ki·^{l′}skak·e′^ɛhel·a^ᵃk ha′k·i· ɔk ən·en·^{lʲɛ} ənda′n·e^{ɛɛ}gɔ′t·ək^ɛ pu′ŋg^ɛ ɔk kwe^ɛc^ɛha′t·e^ɛk^ɛ lo′we^ɛn nale′tən·en ule^ɛχ-e^ɛ′yan ma^ɛta′n·t^ɛo.

Now at the time when the earth quaked, so it is said, a great cracking, rumbling noise arose here from down in the ground below. And there came rising dust and smoke, while here and there came rising something sticky, looking like tar, a black fluid. That substance overflowed down into the earth. That was when the great gaps opened in the ground, here where we dwell upon our mother's body.

So even it was not known what purpose was intended for the black fluid substance blown forth from below. There the earth lay gaping open and when the dust and smoke were seen, it was said to be the breath of the Evil Spirit.

The Delaware Indian Big House Ceremony

In early colonial times the Delaware Indians inhabited the Delaware Valley, in the states of New Jersey, New York, Pennsylvania, and Delaware. Beginning about 1720 they were gradually driven westward, first by the hostile Iroquois, later by the white man. Today they number less than 1,000, most of whom live in Oklahoma, near the town of Anadarko, the rest in southern Ontario, near the city of Brantford. The Delawares call themselves Lenape, "The People." Their language is of the Algonkian family.

Papago

Sh am hebai ha'i o'odhamag g kakaichu. Kutsh e a'ahe matsh wo u'io g ha'ichu e-hugi. Atsh am e nahto wehsijj, k am hihih gam huh mash a s-mu'ij, k gam huh dada k am u'u hegai. Tsh g wisag am hahawa wabsh jiwia, ash hegam si ha gewichshulig kakaichu. Kutsh ga huh amjeD s-kuhkim wo i him k am wo si e wamigid k ia huh he'ekia wo ha gewichshul, hab e juhka'i. T wabshaba hemako al kakaichu gam huh si e ehsto sha'i wecho. Atsh heg al i wih. Tsh im hab wa ep wehs ha hugio hegam kakaichu. Kutsh heg am ta'iwuni k meh am uhpam. K ash im huh meD e-kih wui, ch ash hab kaijhim: "Wahm att ha'ichu am chum ko'itohio. T g ohbi am jiwia. Wehs t-hugio! Wehs t-hugio!"

It is said that somewhere there lived some quail. The time came to go for their food. They all got ready, and went to the place where it was abundant, and arrived there and were taking it. Then the hawk came, striking down those quail. He would swoop down from above and raise himself and strike down a number of them in this manner. But one little quail completely hid himself under the brush. He was the only one that was left. The hawk destroyed all the rest of the quail. And he [the quail] rushed out and ran back. And he was running to his home saying: "We just went to try to get something to eat. The enemy came. Destroyed us all! Destroyed us all!"

Papago, pronounced POP-a-go, is spoken by about 8,000 people in southern Arizona and about 1,000 more in the province of Sonora in northern Mexico. It is closely related to Pima, which has about 5,000 speakers in southern Arizona; in fact, the two are really dialects of the same language. They are sometimes referred to collectively as O'odham, the Papago and Pima word for "people." Papago belongs to the Uto-Aztecan family of languages.

Nahuatl

Manoce ca ye cuel nelti muchiua
in quimattiuitze ueuetque, ilamatque in quipixtiuitze:
in ualpachiuiz topan mani,
in ualtemozque tzitzitzimi
in quipoloquiui tlalli, in quiquaquiui maceualli,
inic cemayan tlayouaz tlalticpac: in acan yez tlalticpac:
in quimattiuitze, in quipixtiuitze,
in cultin, in citi in inpial yetiuitze,
in muchiuatiuh, in neltitiuh.

Perhaps now is coming true, now is coming to pass,
what the men and women of old knew, what they handed down:
that the heavens over us shall sunder,
that the demons of the air shall descend
and come to destroy the earth and devour the people,
that darkness shall prevail, that nothing be left on earth.
Our grandmothers and grandfathers knew it
they handed it down, it was their tradition
that it would come to pass, that it would come to be.

A Prayer to Tlaloc

Nahuatl, with the stress on the first syllable, was the language of the great empire of the Aztecs. At one time spoken over all of present-day Mexico, it is still the most important Indian language in the country. Its 1½ million speakers live mainly in the states of Puebla, Veracruz, Hidalgo, and Guerrero, to the north, east, and south of Mexico City. Nahuatl belongs to the Uto-Aztecan family, which also includes a number of languages of the western United States. English words of Nahuatl origin include *tomato*, *chocolate*, *cacao, avocado*, *coyote*, and *ocelot*.

At the time of the Spanish conquest Aztec writing was entirely pictographic. The Spanish introduced the Roman alphabet and soon recorded a large body of Aztec prose and poetry. The full text of the prayer to Tlaloc, the god of rain, runs to about 200 lines.

C'ä c'ä tz'ininok, c'ä c'ä chamamok, cätz'inonic, c'ä cäsilanic, c'ä cälolinic, c'ä tolonna puch upacaj.

Wae' c'äte' nabe tzij, nabe uch'an: Majabi' jun winak, jun chicop, tz'iquin, cär, tap, che', abaj, jul, siwan, c'im, c'iche'laj; xa u tuquel caj c'olic. Mawi k'alaj uwächulew, xa u tuquel remanic palo, upacaj ronojel. Majabi' nac'ila' cämolobic, cäcotzobic, jun-ta cäsilobic cämalcaban-taj, cäcotzcaban-taj pa caj, x-ma gkowi nac'ila' c'olic yacalic.

Xa remanic ja', xa lianic palo, xa u tuquel remanic; x-ma c'o-wi nac'ila' lo c'olic. Xa cächamanic, cätz'ininic chi k'ekum chi akab.

This is the account of how all was still, the waters lay calm, there was no wind, and the expanse of the sky was empty.

This is the first account, the first narrative. There was neither man nor animal, birds, fish, crabs, trees, stones, caves, ravines, grasses, nor forests; there was only the sky. The surface of the earth had not appeared, there was only the calm sea and the great expanse of the sky. There was nothing brought together, nothing which could make a noise, nor anything which might move, or tremble, or fly, nor was anything standing.

There was only the calm water, the placid sea, alone and tranquil; nothing whatever existed. Only the expanse of water, and tranquillity in the darkness, in the night.

Popul Vuh

Maya, the language of the great Maya civilization that flourished more than a thousand years ago, is still spoken in various forms by several million people in Mexico, Guatemala, and Belize. Since earliest times the Maya language has contained numerous dialects, which today are sufficiently different to be regarded as separate languages. There are about eight such languages in Mexico and more than a dozen in Guatemala.

Maya proper, sometimes called Yucatec, is spoken by about one million people on the Yucatán Peninsula of eastern Mexico, as well as in northern Belize. In the states of Chiapas and Tabasco, there are Tzeltal (400,000 speakers), Tzotzil (350,000), Chol (150,000), and Chontal (50,000). Farther up the coast, in Veracruz, and inland in San Luis Potosí, Huastec is spoken by about 150,000 people. In Guatemala, which has about 3 million Maya Indians, the big four languages are Quiché (1,250,000 speakers), Cakchiquel (one million), Kekchi (500,000), and Mam (300,000). Kekchi is also spoken in southwestern Belize.

Alone among the Indians of America, the Mayas possessed a fully developed system of writing. The distinctive Maya glyphs, a sample of which appears at the right, have posed a formidable challenge to scholars and linguists ever since they were first discovered by the Spaniards in the 16th century. At first they were thought to be exclusively pictographs, but later they were found to be an extremely complex syllabary, formed by combinations of ideographs, phonetic signs, and also rebus writing, in which a ideograph is used to represent another word which happens to have the same pronunciation. (As if in English the sign for "eye" were used to represent the pronoun "I.") The first to be deciphered were those dealing with the calendar and astronomy, and considerable progress has been made in recent decades in unraveling the rest of the system. As many as 85 percent of the glyphs have now been more or less deciphered, and the work goes on.

The *Popul Vuh*, the sacred book of the Mayas, is a stirring account of Maya history and traditions, beginning with the creation of the world. The most outstanding example of native American literature that has survived the passing of centuries, it was first reduced to writing (in the Roman alphabet) in the middle of the 16th century.

MAYA GLYPHS

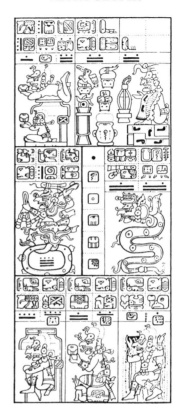

Zapotec

Zapandú ne ziña yáa
Gudindeca pur tu jma rindá naxhi
Ziña yáa na rindá naxhi
Xhpandaga, xquié ne xhquana naxhi.
Zapandú na rindá naxhi xhcú,
Napa xhope guibá, xhop guxhu bidó
Xhi gúxhu bidó rabi ziña yáa zapandú,
Líi nga ti xhcú canarenda rua nisadó.
Ngué bina ti gusugú
Rabi laacabe lachoxhí, xhi para guiete
Cica rindá ni nóo luguiá, rindá ni nóo xhaguete.
Purti nin que negue, nin que nase
Xhó ca naquíchí nga napa naiase.
Ora bina ziña yáa ne zapandú
Ni náa gusugú,
Náaca uandí, zacanga guidxhi layú.
Cica rindá ziña yáa, rindá zapandú.

The chintul [a tree native to Oaxaca] and the palm tree were discussing the question of aroma.

The palm tree said that the aroma of its leaves, flowers, and fruits are better. The chintul replied that its roots smell better, that they have the smell of the sky and of incense.

"What odor of incense?" replied the chintul to the palm tree. "You are refuse on the seashore."

This was heard by the dove who interjected, "Calm down, let no one be angry. The aroma above and the aroma below are equal. Because it is not just yesterday, nor the day before yesterday, that the smell of something white is the same as something black."

When the palm tree and the chintul heard what the dove had said, they agreed, "That is the way the earth is: the palm tree smells the same, the chintul smells the same."

The Chintul and the Palm Tree

Zapotec is spoken in southern Mexico, principally in the state of Oaxaca, by about 500,000 people. Like Mixtec, also spoken in Oaxaca, it is a member of the Oto-Manguean family of languages. There are actually more than 50 separate dialects of Zapotec; some are so different from each other that they are sometimes grouped into what are called the Zapotecan languages.

The Zapotec capital was Monte Albán, a great hilltop metropolis overlooking the Oaxaca valley and dating back to about 500 BC. After reaching its zenith about 500 AD, Zapotec culture went into a gradual decline and in 900 Monte Albán was abandoned.

Katiñi cha´nu vati tacha ndu naa nuura nikandi tacha koo iin soko nuura ta chi´i nuura vati kue´e cha´ni nuu chira, ra´ya ku´i xi´na kuii tasa va nuu ndi´i kue´eya nuu ñu´un ñuñivi. Ra´ya chani kati tu´un vati kua´a nuu kue´e va koo ta siin ñava koo va´a chani tachira nda´vi tara an va netichi an va ta´yuchi chava kuun kua´a savi. Tacha chi´i nuu ra nikandi kue´e xaan nuu.

Vati kue´e cha cha´ni nuu chira nikandi kue´e xaan kuuchi chakan ñi cha´nu katiñi vati yoni kuu kee tichi ve´e tacha ya´a che´e ndava cha ndu na´an chani kuu che´e tasa kuu kee ndikoñi nuu indiñi. Tacha chi´i ri´a ñava´a su´a kuni ñivi, vati sama tati xitayo chakan ñi cha´nu katiñi vati ñavi kue´e va´a ni ndoo nuu ñu´un ñuñivi.

When there is an eclipse of the sun the Mixtecs do not go out of their houses, because the elders say that the sun had fainted because of a very serious illness.

All of this illness comes down to the earth and causes great harm: the harvests dry up, and many children die since they are stricken with the illness that caused the sun to faint.

If the sun faints because of this illness, which is not of our making, then we die the way fish die when they are taken out of water.

The elders used to help the sun to wake up from its fainting spell by banging a tray with two sticks; the tray is turned face up and is struck many times.

To this day this method is used when little chickens faint; they put them inside the tray and beat it until the chickens are all right.

When the Sun Faints

Mixtec, like Zapotec, is an Oto-Manguean language spoken in Oaxaca, Mexico, by about 500,000 people. When the Zapotecs abandoned their capital of Monte Albán in 900, the Mixtecs, a more warlike people, took over the site and used it as a burial ground. In succeeding centuries the two fought many wars, but eventually they united to resist the encroachments of the Aztecs.

Papiamento

Despues cu e navegante spañó Alonso de Ojeda a bandona Curaçao cu destino pa Santo Domingo, el a discubri dia 15 di Agosto 1499 un cabo, cu el a yama San Román i dia 24 di mes luna el a hayé den un puerto i un lago grandísimo, cu el a duna nomber di San Bartolomeo, cuyo nomber despues tabata cambiá pa Maracaibo, na honor di un cacique riquísimo, biba cerca di e lago. Mui probable cu den e travesía Ojeda lo a toca Aruba, i casi sigur lo por yamé descubridor di e isla.

Tanto durante e tempo despues di descubrimento bao di dominio spañó, i despues di 1634 bao di poder holandes, nunca Aruba tabatin un propia historia. E gran distancia for di Curaçao, e corriente fuerte entre costa venezolana i e isla, e remontamento sin fin contra un biento fortísimo, i den un tempo cu lamar rondó di e islanan tabata cruzá cu frecuencia pa piratanan, a haci un comunicacion ligé i regular cu Curaçao mashá dificil pa veleronan.

After the Spanish navigator Alonso de Ojeda left Curaçao bound for Santo Domingo, he discovered on August 15, 1499 a cape which he called San Román. On the 24th of the same month he found himself in a port and huge lake, to which he gave the name of San Bartolomeo. This name was later changed to Maracaibo, in honor of a rich Indian chief living near the lake. It is most probable that en route Ojeda touched Aruba: it is fairly certain that he is the island's discoverer.

A period of Spanish rule followed the discovery of the island, and after 1634 it came under the dominion of the Dutch. But Aruba never had much of a "history." Its distance from Curaçao, the strong current between the Venezuelan coast and the island, its constant exposure to the relentless trade winds, the seas roundabout infested with pirates – all made rapid and regular communication very difficult for sailing vessels.

Papiamento, also spelled Papiamentu, is the native, though unofficial, language of the three Dutch islands in the southern Caribbean: Curaçao, Aruba, and Bonaire. It is a creole language with Spanish as its base, the only such language in the Caribbean. It also contains numerous words from Dutch, English, Portuguese, French, and several other languages. There are about 200,000 speakers.

Guarani

Ayajhe'óta pende apytepe
narötivéigui che vy' a y
ajhypyimita co pyjarepe
che resaype Paraguahy.
Che momoräva cu umi burrera
ipymandí jha jhesá jhovy
che py'apypente añopü jhera
jha che ajhogata co tesay.
Purajhei pope co che amocäva
yeroky jharupi che resay,
jha ñasaindyro romonguetava
che novia raicha, Paraguahy.

Let me relate to you
The sorrow that oppresses me,
And sprinkle the night with my tears
For my beloved Asunción.

I recall the women selling produce
With bare feet and blue eyes,
My bosom is burdened with anguish
And is choked with my crying.

Only the music can relieve
With its sweet notes my sadness,
And under a full moon will I declare
The love that I feel for you, Asunción.

MANUEL ORTIZ GUERRERO, *Asunción*

Guarani, with the stress on the final syllable, is, together with Spanish, one of the two official languages of Paraguay. It is the mother tongue of about 2 million people there, but it is estimated that as much as 80 percent of the country's population of 5 million is fluent in the language. No other Indian language is so widely used by all classes of society in a given country. There are also about 50,000 speakers in both Brazil and Bolivia.

Guarani is the most important member of the Tupian family of languages. The English words *petunia*, *jaguar*, *cougar*, and *toucan* all come from languages of this family. The name Paraguay is a Guarani word meaning "place of great water."

Quechua

Pitu Salla, millay cutin
Chayllatatacc, chayllatatacc
Cunahuanqui ñoccaracctacc
Rimarisacc chaymi sutin
Anchatan checnipacuni
Cay canchata cay huasita
Caypi caspa cay ccasita
Ppunchau tuta ñacacuni
Cay payacunacc uyanta
Ancha aputa ccahuascani
Payllatatacc ricuscani
Chay ccuchu tiascaymanta
Manan cusi caypi canchu
Hueqquen uyancupi caicca
Munaiñimpi canman chaicca
Manan pipas tianmanchu
Ccahuani puriccunata
Asicuspan ccuchicuncu
Maquincupi apacuncu
Llipipas samincunata
Ñoccallachu huisccacusac
Mana Mamay casccan raycu
Ccapac ttalla canay raycu
Cunanmanta qquesacusacc

Pitu Salla, many times,
Only this, only this,
You say to me.
Now I will speak
The very truth.
This court, this house,
The useless life,
Days and nights I hate.
The faces of the old women
Above all I detest.
That is all I can see
From the corner where I sit.
In this place there is no joy,
Only tears to weep.
Your wish would be
That none should live here.
They all walk, as I see,
Between laughing and crying,
Their fate in their hands,
Full of anxiety.
I am shut up here,
Because I have no mother.
Having no good nurse to tend me,
I have been to seek for one.

Ollantay

Quechua, pronounced (and sometimes spelled) Kechua, is the most widely spoken Indian language of South America. Its roughly 7 million speakers are located mainly in Peru (4 million), Bolivia (2 million), and Ecuador (750,000). It is a member of the Andean family of languages.

Quechua was the language of the great Inca Empire, which at its zenith in the late 15th century extended from Ecuador in the north to central Chile in the south. The Spanish conquest of the 16th century did not diminish the importance of Quechua, for the new conquerors continued its use throughout the area, and in fact extended it to other areas not part of the original empire. In succeeding centuries many Indian languages of the area have died out, the natives adopting Quechua in some cases, Spanish in others. There are more speakers of Quechua at present than at the time of the Spanish conquest, and the number is still increasing.

For all their great technological skills, the Incas never developed an alphabet. What written records there were, were kept by means of a quipu (the Quechua word for "knot"), an arrangement of cords of various colors which were knotted in different ways. All literature prior to the Spanish conquest was handed down by oral tradition. The Spanish introduced the Roman alphabet, but to this day the spelling has not been standardized. Quechua grammar, however, has been found to be extremely regular and consistent. English words of Quechua origin include *llama*, *puma*, *vicuña*, *condor*, *quinine*, *coca*, and *guano*.

Ollantay, a drama of life at the Inca court, is perhaps the best-known work of Quechua literature. It was composed by an unknown author about 1470.

Aymara

Aimaranacaja ayllunacana utjapjataina. Jacha ayllunacaja ackam sutinip-jatainau: Urus, Parias, Umasuyos, Pacajis, Sicasicas, Karankas, Yuncas, Laricajas. Aca ayllunacaja janira catocktasa Perú marcanacata jakenacan lurapjatapata ni jupanacap oracke yapuchiripjataynau, ucatsi ckori, colcke, cunaimanaca kollunacata apsuña yatipjataina.

Ukamaraqui, jacha ayllunaca utjataina, ackama sutichata: Charcas, Chichas, Kochapampas, Atacamas, Yuras, Killacas, cunaimananaca. Tapacha aca ayllunacaja yatipjatainau tacke casta parlasiñanaca; jichu-runa armthata, incanacan juchapata, quitinacateja kechua parlaña yatichapjataina.

Aimaranacaja janiua mayasapa marcan jacapjatainati sapa aylloja maya jiscka marcanua, jiliri mallkuta apnackata. Jacha jiscka apnackeri jackenau utjataina jilacata sata.

Aca jackenacaja challua catuña huali yatipjana, ucatsti huyhua ahuatiña yatipjataina manckañataqui.

The Aymaras lived in tribes or families. The large tribes were as follows: Urus, Parias, Umasuyos, Pacajis, Sicasicas, Karankas, Yuncas, Laricajas. Before they learned the customs of the Peruvians, these people worked the soil and mined gold, silver, and other minerals from the bowels of the earth.

Other large tribes were called: Charcas, Chichas, Kochapampas, Atacamas, Yuras, Killacas, and more. All these tribes and families once spoke distinct dialects, which were forgotten when the Incas taught them to speak Quechua.

Each of the Aymara tribes was subject to the orders of a great chief called Mallku, to whom other authorities of lower rank, such as the Jilacatas, deferred.

These people were good fishermen and hunters, and also raised llamas and sheep for food.

Aymara, with the stress on the final syllable, is the second of the major Indian languages of western South America. There are about 2 million speakers, of whom about three-fourths live in Bolivia, the rest in Peru. Like Quechua, Aymara is a member of the Andean family of languages.

LANGUAGES OF AFRICA

Hausa

Wata rana ana ruwa, bushiya tana yawo, sai ta zo bakin ramin kurege.
Tace kai, ina jin sanyi. Ko da wurin da zan fake? Sai kurege ya amsa
mata 'Alhamdu Lillahi! To, shigo ga ɗan wuri. Suka zauna tare. Jim
kaɗan sai kurege ya ce da ita ke bushiya, zaman nan namu dake, ba shi
da daɗi, jikinki ya cika tsini. Sai ki sake wuri!' Sai Bushiya ta ce ashe?
Ni kuwa, daɗi nike ji. Duk wanda wurin nan bai gamshe shi ba, ai sai
ya sake wani.

One day it was raining. The hedgehog greeted the ground squirrel saying,
"How do you like the cold? Is there anywhere I can shelter?" The squirrel
replied, "I'm well, thank God. Here's a little place, enter!" They then
lived together, but after a while the squirrel said, "Hedgehog! This stay
of yours with me is unpleasant, your body is all prickles. Change your
abode!" The hedgehog said, "Is that so? As for me, I enjoy it. The one
whom his place doesn't suit, shouldn't he change it for another?"

The Ground Squirrel and the Hedgehog

Hausa is the most widely spoken language of West Africa. In Nigeria it is
the first language of about 25 million people, living mainly in the northern
half of the country. Probably another 25 million Nigerians are able to
converse in it. There are also about 5 million speakers in Niger to the north.
The largest Hausa-speaking city in Nigeria is Kano.

The Hausa are a Moslem people long renowned as traders. As a result
their language is not only the lingua franca of northern Nigeria, but is also
spoken in a number of other countries. At least half the population of Ghana
can converse in Hausa to some degree.

Hausa is by far the most important of the Chadic languages, which form
a branch of the Afro-Asiatic family. Beginning about 1800 it was written in
a variety of the Arabic script called Ajami, but in the early 20th century the
British introduced the Roman alphabet. The latter predominates today; it is
the language of instruction in the primary schools and newspapers, and most
books are published in it. But Ajami is still used in religious schools and is
preferred by many traditional Hausa poets. The language contains a great
number of words borrowed from the Arabic.

288

Fulani

Jemma go'o alkali heþti nder deftere komoi mari hore pẹtẹl be wakkude junde kanko woni pataɗo. Alkali, marɗo hore pẹtẹl be wakkude junde, ẉi'i nder yọnki mako, 'Mi wawata þesdugo mangu hore am, amma mi ustan wakkude am'. O ɗaþþiti mekesje amma o heþtai ɗe. Wala ferẹ sei o nangi reta wakkude nder jungo mako, o waɗi reta ferẹ ha pitirla, o wuli nde. Sa'i nde ɗemgal yite yotti jungo mako o yofti nde, wakkude fuh wuldama. Ni'i alkali lati semtuɗo gạm o gongɗini bindaɗum nder deftere.

One evening a judge found in a book that everyone who had a little head and a long beard was a fool. Now the judge had a little head and a long beard, so he said to himself, "I cannot increase the size of my head, but I will shorten my beard." He hunted for the scissors, but could not find them. Without further ado he took half of his beard in his hand and put the other half into the candle and burnt it. When the flame reached his hand he let go, and all of the beard was burned. Thus the judge felt ashamed, for he had proved the truth of what was written in the book.

Fulani, also known as Fula or Fulbe, is spoken over a large band of western Africa, roughly 2,000 miles from east to west and 500 from north to south. The largest concentration is in northern Nigeria, where approximately 12 million Fulani live. But some 10 million others are to be found in Guinea, Guinea-Bissau, Senegal, Gambia, Mauritania, Mali, Burkina Faso, Niger, and Cameroon.

The light-skinned Fulani, a nomadic cattle-herding people, are thought to be of great antiquity. Their ultimate origin is a source of much speculation, some even suggesting that they are one of the tribes referred to by biblical and classical writers. The Fulani Empire of the 19th century was a Moslem theocracy that dominated most of Nigeria for more than 50 years. The language is generally placed in the Atlantic branch of the Niger-Congo family, but its richness and sophistication seem to set it apart from the others of the region.

Malinke

Dounou gna dan kouma Allah fé, a ye san kolo dan, ka dougou kolo dan, ka kocodjie baou dan, ka badji lou dan, ka kolou dan, ka yirilou dan, ka sogolou dan, ka mogo lou dan. A ba fen toumani ka djiro kè, a ko sogo bè makal ki bolobiri i niè la. Sogobè ya bolo fla biri i niè la. N'ka ba yè kègouyakè: a ma son ka niè da tougoun ka gna: a y'a bolokoni nou so bo niokon na; o ya to a y'a yè Allah ba-kan ka fèn diougou lou kè djiro: Sadiougoulou minignam, ninikin-nankan, bamba, mali. Kabini ô kèra, ba tè son ban Kadjiguing djiro. Hali ni san-ya gossi, a bè koulé bahou a ba lon mi yè djiro.

When God had finished creating the sky and the earth, he put trees, animals, and human beings on the earth. Then, when he wanted to cover the surface with water (oceans, streams, and rivers), he told all the animals to close their eyes. Every animal closed its eyes except for the goat. The goat, instead of covering its eyes with its hands, as everyone else was doing, spread its fingers in order to look through them. Thus it observed God putting nasty fish into the waters, dangerous snakes, alligators, hippopotamuses, and monsters. Since that day the goat has lost confidence in the water, and does not dare, under any circumstances, to go into the water, because it knows what there is in it.

Malinke is another important language of West Africa, spoken by about 1½ million people in Guinea and another 1½ million in Senegal, Gambia, Guinea-Bissau, Mali, and Ivory Coast. It was the language of the great Empire of Mali, which reached its zenith in the 14th century and from which the name of the modern country of Mali is derived.

Malinke belongs to the Mande branch of the Niger-Congo family of languages. The variety spoken in Senegal and Gambia, known as Mandinka, is sometimes thought of as a separate language. Less closely related, but still quite similar, are Bambara, the principal language of Mali, and Dyula, of Mali, Ivory Coast, and Burkina Faso. The three are often combined under the single term Mandingo.

Wolof

Kocc Barma a ngi juddoo Ñjàmbur, booba ag léégi mat na ñeenti-téémééri at. Yàlla mayoon na ko xel moo xam né dafa waaroon ñépp, ci jamanoom. Jamano ju mettiwoon la ndax doolee fa doon dox. Foo tollu ñu naan la dooleey bërë. Kocc amoon na ay taalibé yu bari, yu mu daan jàngal wax xam-xam ag jamano ndax jamano mooy yee nit. Kocc angi ci kërëm di daas ay jumtuwaayam ngir dem tool, am kuko fa fekk né ko, "Kocc, dama ñëwoon seetsi la ngir di la tàggu ndax dama bëgg dem Waalo seeti fa ligééy, ndax fii ndox mi barwu fi." Kocc tontu, né ko, "Li ngay seeti Waalo am na fi: mbey ag suff. Soo demee, sa kër dina rën-rëni, sa njaboot torax. Nawet baa ngiy dikk, na nga ko waajal te xaar Yàlla."

Kocc Barma was born in Louga 400 years ago. God gave him an intelligence that astonished everyone at that time. Those were hard times, which required great strength. During that period great perseverance was needed to survive. Kocc Barma had many disciples, whom he taught to teach others that they might learn from their ancestors. Kocc was at home sharpening his tools to go to the field, when someone came by and said to him, "Kocc, I have come to see you to say goodbye, because I'm going to St. Louis* to look for work because there is so little water here." Kocc answered him by saying, "What you are looking for in St. Louis we have here: farming and land. If you go your house would be in disarray and your family would be destitute. The rainy season is coming; you should prepare and wait for God."

Kocc Barma at Home

Wolof is the principal language of Senegal, in westernmost Africa. There it is spoken by about 5 million people, mainly in the western part of the country. There are also about 150,000 speakers in both Gambia and Mauritania. Wolof belongs to the Atlantic branch of the Niger-Congo family of languages.

*A city in Senegal north of Dakar. In Wolof it is called Waalo.

Yoruba

Ajọ ìgbimọ ti awọn àgbàgbà ni imâ yan ọba lârin awọn ẹniti nwọn ní ìtan pàtàki kan ninu èjẹ. llana kan ti o ṣe ajeiì amâ ṣáju ìyan ti ọba. Awọn olori amâ dan agbara ti ìrọju rẹ̀ ati iṣẹ́ akoso ara rẹ̀ wò. Li ọjọ́ ti a yàn fun dide e li ade, awọn olori amâ lọ si âfin ọba, nwọn a mu u dani pẹlu agbara, nwọn a si nà á pẹlu pàṣán. Bi ọba ba faradà aje nâ lai sún ara ki, nigbanâ nwọn yio de e li ade; bi bệkọ, nwọn yio yàn ọba miràn.

The king is chosen by a council of elders from among those who have a certain blood descent. A curious ceremony precedes a king's election. His powers of endurance and self-restraint are tested by the chiefs, who, on the day appointed for the coronation, go to the king's palace, get hold of him forcibly, and flog him with a whip. If the ordeal is suffered without flinching, then the king is crowned; if not, another king is chosen.

A King's Election in Yoruba Land

Yoruba, with the stress on the first syllable, is one of the major languages of Nigeria. It is spoken by about 25 million people in the southwestern part of the country, whose principal city is Ibadan. There are also about 750,000 speakers in Benin.

In earlier systems of classification Yoruba was included in the Kwa branch of the Niger-Congo family, but it is now considered part of the Benue-Congo branch. It was the language of the great Oyo empire of Nigeria, which at its zenith in the early 18th century included much of present-day Benin.

The Yoruba alphabet was largely the creation of Samuel Crowther, a freed Yoruba slave who later became a Christian missionary. It includes the letters ẹ, pronounced as in "bet" (e.g., èjẹ – blood), ọ pronounced as in "ought" (ọba – king), and ṣ, pronounced *sh* (*erekuṣu* – island). All three appear in the word *ọṣẹ*, which means "soap." The grave and acute accents do not indicate stress, but rather the rise and fall of the voice.

Ibo

Chukwu-Okike m, na ndị Nna-nna m,
Ekene m unu
Makana unu melụ m ji whụ ụbọshị tá
Ka m whụkwa ụbọshị ọzọga
Lue mgbe ishi m ga-aca ọca;
Menụ ka ọgụ ghalụ igbuji m ọkpa
Cebe nu mụ na ezin'ụnọ m
Kwaalụ m nụ ajọ madụ na ajọ maa;
Anaghị m evulu madụ ọbụna ajọ obi,
Ma onwe onye celụ na m adịghelụ ndụ
Mee ka onye ahụ vulu m ụzọ malụ
Ka obodo ndị nwụlụ anwụ shi dị;
Eji-m-ọwhọ
Anaghị atọ n'ụzọ.

My God and ancestors,
I thank you
For letting me see this day;
May I continue to see more
Till my hair becomes white;
May the hoe never cut my feet;
Protect me and my household
From evil men and spirits;
I wish no man evil,
But if anyone says I have lived too long,
Let him go before me to see
What it is like in the land of the dead;
The man who holds on to *ọwhọ**
Cannot get lost in his journey.

Ibo, also known as Igbo, is one of the major languages of Nigeria. It is spoken by about 20 million people, mainly in the southeastern part of the country. Like Yoruba, it is now considered part of the Benue-Congo branch of the Niger-Congo family of languages.

*A sacred staff which symbolizes righteousness

Mende

Kwaa tia ndokulo mia wɔɔ ti yɛ ndiamɔ yei hun. Folo yila ma, ti yɛ lima njia-hun lɔ kɛ ti foo nga mbaa-ti loi ma. Sia leke kwaa tɔni, kɛ i lɛnga yee tɔkpoi hun i yee ndoi gbɔle. Ji ndɔ-blaa ti wani ti mɔli, kɛ kwaa ndenga yɛ ndɔ-gboi mui a hɔ-hɔ lɔ hun i yaa jia ma. Kɛ ti gula ndokulo ma ti ngi lewe panda-wanda.

Ti yɛ bɔma limaa kɛ ti fonga mbaa-ti gbalei ma, nahin ii yaa a be-ni panda. Ndokulo bɛ kɛ i ya i wa a gɔmbui i kula yee kpalei na hun, kɛ i gbeelu-nga. Ji nunga ti wani ti mɔli, kɛ ndokulo bɛɛ i ndenga yɛ kpala-mɔ mui lokui-ya kɛ ngi yamei lɛli-ngɔ a yɛ la. Nunga ti kwaa gbee, ngi yeya kɛ ngi yama lɛli-ngɔ. Kɛ ti hou-nga ti ndewe nyɛgbɛlii.

Kɛ kwaa wote-nga ndokulo-gama yɛ gbei bi nji wie-ni a nge? Ndokulo kpɛmbui lɔ yɛ "hinda a wa a hinda: ndɔ-gboi lewe mia a wa a kpaa-mɔ lewe."

The monkey and the chameleon were friends. One day they were on a trip when the monkey saw palm wine on a tree that belonged to someone else. He immediately climbed the palm tree and drank the wine. When the owners arrived and asked who had drunk the wine, the monkey was quick to reply that a person who drinks staggers when he walks. Upon looking, the people saw the chameleon staggering. So they caught him and gave him a sound thrashing.

After that, they next came to a brushed farm that was not yet properly dry for burning. The chameleon saw his chance to get revenge and went and set fire to the farm. When the farm owners came and asked who had done it, the chameleon replied that a person who sets fire to a farm has his hands and eyes black with fire coal. The people checked the monkey's hands and this description was perfect. So they seized him too and flogged him mercilessly.

The monkey turned to the chameleon and said, "Why have you done this to me?" The chameleon replied: "Something is always caused by something. It is wine-drinking flogging that causes farm-burning flogging."

Mende is the most important native language of Sierra Leone, on the west coast of Africa. It is spoken by about 1½ million people, mainly in the south-central part of the country. Mende is a member of the Mande branch of the Niger-Congo family of languages.

Kpelle

Nuahn dah ga nahn
Defa welle de teka,
Kenoh dee a gba gbeyh
Dah nwehyn kashu.
Defa wolloh shungh nella
Ka shaangh quai gah
Dah welle shungh kela
A kur baddae gah de kleema.

Some stand and look while others do
Then come and say what ought to be,
To them the world is never right
For all is wrong that they can see.

They never see the good in things
That you and I would like to see
They seem to think whatever they say
Is just the thing that ought to be.

BAI T. MOORE, *Some People*

Kpelle is the most important of the many languages of Liberia. It is spoken by about 750,000 people, or one-fourth of the total population. Kpelle belongs to the Mande branch of the Niger-Congo family of languages.

Akan

Da bi Kweku Ananse Kaa Kyerɛ no ho dɛ Obɔboaboa wiadze nyansa nyinara dze ahyɛ Kutu mu na ɔdze akesi dua bi do a Obiara nkohu. Nna nadwen nye dɛ sɛ Otum yɛ dɛm a, ɔno nkotonoo na ɔbɛyɛ nyansafo wɔ wiadze nyina.

Ampa, Kweku Ananse boaboa wiadze nyansa nyina dze guu Kutu mu, na ɔdze Kutu yi too ne yefun do dɛ ɔdze refow dua dze akesi dua no do. Ɔperee, peree, na woentum annfow dua no ankɔ nenyim ahen biara, Osiandɛ, nakutu no da ne yefun do.

Ɔreyɛ dɛm nyina, na ne ba a wɔfre no Kweku Tsen gyina dua no ase rohwɛ no. Ma Kweku Ananse tsee ara nye dɛ, Paapa sɛ edze Kutu yi too wo ekyir a, nkyɛ ebotum dze afow dua yi.

Kwaku Ananse tsee dza ne ba no kǎe no. Ɔhun dɛ woentum akyekyer wiadze nyansa nyina dɛ mbrɛ ɔpɛɛ dɛ ɔbɛyɛ no. Ntsi ɔdze enyito gyaa Kutu no mɔ bɔɔ famu ma ɔbɔe. Nyansa a ɔboaboa a no wɔ mu no nyina petsee. Dɛm ntsi na nyansa wɔ wiadze nyina.

Once upon a time Kwaku Ananse told himself that he would gather all the wisdom in the world into a pot and hide it on top of a tree where no one could ever see it. He thought that by so doing he would be the only person on earth to have all the world's wisdom.

Indeed, Kwaku Ananse gathered all the wisdom in the world into a pot and placed the pot on his stomach to climb to the top of the tree. It really became difficult for Kwaku Ananse to reach the top of the tree because he had placed the pot on his stomach.

While he was struggling to get to the top, his son, Kwaku Tsen, spotted his father struggling to climb the tree. Kwaku Tsen then got closer and told his father that he could climb the tree only if he placed the pot behind him.

Hearing this from his son, Kwaku Ananse realized that he had not gathered all the world's wisdom as he promised. Out of shame he dropped the pot and it shattered and all the wisdom he had gathered scattered. This is why we have wisdom all over the world.

Akan (pronounced *ah-KAHN*) is the principal native language of Ghana, spoken there by about 10 million people or half the total population. It is actually a group of closely related languages, of which the two most important are Twi and Fante. Twi, the language of the great Ashanti Empire of the 18th and 19th centuries, is spoken by today's Twi tribe, as well as by the Ashantis, throughout most of the southern half of the country. (Twi is often referred to as Akan). Fante is spoken in the coastal districts just to the west of Accra. Akan belongs to the Kwa branch of the Niger-Congo family of languages. The frequently occurring letter ɔ in the passage above is a vowel, pronounced approximately *aw*.

Fon

Dantɔkpa sin axi ɔ, axi dé we nyi bo nɔ jè azan atoon atɔɔn gbé. Axi neɔ zan ɔ, azan daxo dé we nyi nu Kutɔnu To ɔ bisésé.

D'axi ne zan gbé ɔ, é nɔ mɔ me le gosin file bi, sin to le bi me bo nɔ wa axi ne mè. Axiɔ nɔ jé desú! Gbetɔ nɔ súkpɔ désú. Axiɔ lɔ ká nyɔ dekpe désú. Núsatɔ súnú kpó nyɔnú kpán bi we dó ten yéton yéton cobɔ nú sísá lè lɔ mɔ dó ten yéton. Nú ámɔ avɔsatɔ lè dófidéɔ, á ná mɔ núsau sátɔ lè dó malin malin me. A seyi zaan déɔ, a nan mɔ afɔkpa sátɔ lee dó fine. Amasin satɔ lee lɔɔ dó ten yéton mè; Yovo masin kpo Mewi ton kpan bi we dó fine. Núdúdú leɔ, ésɔ nɔ dɔ xó yéton á: tévi, aziin, ayikun, agbadé. Esixu xa bi a.

Edó mɔ có é ka si gan dé nú axi; éyin nú kpúkpɔ bawe jen ádeɔnè. Loɔ, áká do ná disa kpèdé.

Dantɔkpa xiɔ we nyi Axɔsú nú axi lè bi.

Dantokpa is a market which is held every five days. The day of this market is a big day for everyone who lives in Cotonou, the capital city.

On that day people come from everywhere, from many countries, to attend the market. There are always a lot of people. The market is also very beautiful. Both men and women are assigned various spots based upon the goods they offer. People selling various fabrics are located close to those selling body lotions. A little farther away are those selling various shoes. A little farther, you find both traditional and modern medicines. You also find a variety of foods: yams, peanuts, beans, corn, etc. . . .

The best thing is that you can get very good deals if you know how to bargain. You just need to be a little patient.

Dantokpa is simply the king of all markets.

Fon is the most important native language of Benin, on the southern coast of West Africa. It is spoken there by about 2½ million people, mainly in the south-central part of the country around the city of Abomey. In the country's two main cities, Porto-Novo and Cotonou, both on the coast, a slightly different dialect known as Gu is spoken.

Fon is one of the Kwa languages, a branch of the Niger-Congo family. Its native name is Fon-Gbe, *gbe* being the word for "language." Fon, strictly speaking, refers to the people.

Ewe

'Mise alobalo loo!' 'Alobalo neva!' 'Gbe ɖeka hɔ̃ va fo fiavinyɔnu dzetugbea ɖe yi ɖada ɖe koa ɖe dzi le tɔ dome. Fia di amewo be, woaxɔ ye vi la le hɔ̃ si vɛ na ye. Enumake fiafitɔ, adela kple nuhela wova. Fiafitɔ be, yeate ŋu afi nyɔnuvi la le hɔ̃ fe fego me. Adela be, ne hɔ̃ la kpɔ yewo be, yeagaxɔ nyɔnuvi la, yeafo tui, wòaku enumake. Nuhela be, ne hɔ̃ ge dze vɔua me wòfe la, yeagahee keŋkeŋ.'

'Wodze mɔ dzi ko la, eye fiafitɔ ɖafi nyɔnuvi la. Esi wova ɖo tɔ titina la, hɔ̃ la va be, yeafo nyɔnuvi la. Tete adela fo tui wòku hege dze vɔua me, wòfii tsayatsaya. Nuhela he vɔua enumake, eye wova afe dedie. Ame etɔ̃ siawo dometɔ ka wɔ wu, ne fia la nakatu?'

"Hear a parable!" "May the parable come!" "One day an eagle swooped down upon the beautiful daughter of a chief and carried her to an island in the river. The chief looked for people to fetch his daughter away from the eagle. A thief, a hunter, and a mender came at once. The thief said he could steal the girl from the talons of the eagle. The hunter said that should the eagle see them and try to recapture the girl, he would shoot him, so that he would die at once. The mender said that should the eagle (having been shot) fall into the boat and break it, he would patch it up.

"As soon as they had started off, the thief stole the girl. As they reached the middle of the river, the eagle came to take the child. Then the hunter shot him, so that he fell into the boat, which was shattered into a thousand pieces. The mender immediately patched the boat, so that they reached home safely. Which of these three people did the most, thereby gaining the praise of the chief?"

Ewe, pronounced *ay-way* or *ay-vay*, is spoken on the southern coast of West Africa between the Volta River in Ghana and the Mono River in Togo. There are about 2 million speakers in each country. Ewe belongs to the Kwa branch of the Niger-Congo family. The English word *voodoo* is of Ewe origin.

Mossi

Sõñg f mẽñga ti Wennam sõñg fo. Ti bakargo n bâs a mẽñga, dar a yemre, ti taõñg ñyok a la ra ka niñg pãñg n pam a mẽñg ye, a da kosda Wennam a sõñgre, la Wennam sẽ da logĕd a segẽ yela la woto: "Niñg pãñga bilfu t m sõñg fo." Ti a yaol n man dabar bilfu ti winri kaoge. Ren yeta neba sẽ zindb zalĕm la b yetẽ dar fã: "Wennam waoga; a nã kõ ma m sẽ date!" Wennam kõ kõ ba bumbu, b sã deñge n sõñg b mense, ye.

Help yourself and Wennam will help you. One day a hen fell into a trap but made no effort to extricate herself. She begged Wennam for help but Wennam, who was passing by, said, "First make an effort yourself and then I will come to your aid." The hen then made a slight motion and the rope snapped. This is addressed to all those who sit idly and repeat endlessly, "Wennam is great; he will grant my any wish." Wennam will not give them anything unless they begin by helping themselves.

Mossi, also known as Moré, is the principal language of Burkina Faso (formerly Upper Volta), in West Africa. There it is spoken by about 6 million people, or half the total population. Mossi belongs to the Gur, or Voltaic, branch of the Niger-Congo family of languages. The powerful Mossi kingdom of Ouagadougou, founded in the 15th century, ruled Upper Volta until 1896, when it was subdued and overthrown by the French.

Fang

E n'aboa na Ku ba Fifi vœlar angom; bœnga to ki dzal avori. Ni mbu mœtsi o nga so, Ku vœ zo Fifi na: "A monœdzãn, ma komœna o kœm mœlœr a tsi." Edo Fifi œnga zo Ku na: "A mi, ma kon va abi, nlo wa sim mœna bim, bim, bim! mœkoe lœr dzo afoe." Edo Ku œnga kœe tam afan eti. A so anga so ngoɨ a sœ, an' anga kwè Fifi z'abom mbè. A n'anga silœ nœna: A mi, yœ nkokon w'abobom mbè? Edo anga kœ adzira yœ nœ, yœ domœ nœ. Nnœangom Ku ba Fifi e nga wu valœ.

Once upon a time the hen and the cockroach, who were good friends, lived in the same village. During the season when all the inhabitants of the village were engaged in working in the fields, the hen invited her friend with these words: "Friend, come with me into the forest to help me clear my field." The lazy cockroach excused himself saying: "Friend, I really cannot accompany you today, I have been having violent headaches; I will go another time." The hen proceeded to the forest alone. Upon her return that evening she was astonished to find the cockroach playing the tom-tom. Becoming angry, she ran after him and began to peck him. That is why since that time hens cannot look at cockroaches without pecking them.

Fang is a major language of three countries on the west coast of Africa. It is spoken in southern Cameroon by about 1½ million people, in northwestern Gabon by about 400,000, and in mainland Equatorial Guinea by about 300,000. A Bantu language, it is closely related to two other languages of Cameroon, Bulu and Ewondo (Yaoundé).

Swahili

Mtego wanaotega, ninaswe nianguke,
Sifa yangu kuvuruga, jina liaibike,
Mungu mwema mfuga, nilinde lisitendeke,
Na wawekao kiaga, kudhuru watakasike.

Kwa wingi natangaziwa, maovu nisiyotenda,
Na habari nasikia, kila ninapokwenda,
Lakini Allah mwelewa, atalifanya kuwanda,
Jina wanalochukia, badala ya kukonda.

Badala ya kukonda, jina litanenepa,
Ugenini litakwenda, lisipopendeza hapa,
Kutafuta kibanda, ambako halitatupwa,
Huko wataolipenda, fadhili litawalipa.

A trap they set, for me to get caught,
My reputation they blemish, to spoil my name.
Oh, Lord the Keeper, save me from the plight,
And those who promise me harm, remove their aim.

Many slanderous charges are published against me,
And these I hear, wherever I go.
But God who understands, my name will clear,
The name they hate, He will surely emancipate.

Rather than wither, my name will thrive,
Abroad it will succeed, if here they will not heed.
Shelter it will find, where it will not be remiss,
Where those who care, it will reward and recompense.

SHAABAN ROBERT, *The Name*

Swahili, more correctly called Kiswahili, is the dominant language of East Africa. It is one of the official languages of both Tanzania and Kenya, and is also widely spoken in Uganda and Congo-Kinshasa. (In Congo-Kinshasa there is a separate dialect, known as Kingwana.) It also serves as a language of trade in Rwanda and Burundi. It is the mother tongue of only 5 million people, but perhaps as many 50 million others speak it fluently as a second language. No other native language of Africa can compare to Swahili in terms of number of speakers or in international standing.

Swahili is one of the Bantu languages, which form a branch of the Niger-Congo family. Its vocabulary has many words borrowed from Arabic. The name Swahili is derived from an Arabic word meaning "coastal," as the language developed among Arabic-speaking settlers of the African coast beginning about the 7th century. During the 19th century it was carried inland by Arab tradesmen, and later was made the language of administration in the German colony of Tanganyika. In 1964 Tanganyika, together with Zanzibar, became Tanzania.

The Swahili alphabet lacks the letters *c*, *q*, and *x* (though there is a *ch*), but it contains a number of its own. The letter *dh* is pronounced like *th* of "this" (e.g., *dhoruba* – hurricane), *gh* like the German *ch* (*ghali* – expensive), and *ng'* like the *ng* in "thing" but not as in "finger" (*ng'ombe* – cow). Whereas English grammatical inflections occur at the end of the word, in Swahili everything is done at the beginning. *Kitabu* is the Swahili word for "book" but the word for "books" is *vitabu*. This word falls into the so-called Ki Vi class, one of eight in the Swahili language. Others are the M Mi class (e.g., *mkono* – hand, *mikono* – hands; *mji* – town, *miji* – towns), and the M Wa class, used mainly for people (*mtu* – man, *watu* – men; *mjinga* – fool, *wajinga* – fools). These prefixes are also carried over to verbs of which the noun is the subject, as well as to numerals and modifying adjectives. Thus "one big book" in Swahili is *kitabu kimoja kikubwa* ("book-one-big"), but "two big books" is *vitabu viwili vikubwa*.

Amharic

፩ዲት ፡ ቊንተል ፡ ከአንድ ፡ ሀገር ፡ ሌላ ፡ አውሬ ፡ ሳታይ ፡ ትኖራ
ለች ፡ ለባልንጀራዋ ፡ እንዲህ ፡ አለቻት ፤ እኔን ፡ የሚያህለኝ ፡ ትልቅ ፡
አውሬ ፡ የለም ፡ በድምጽም ፡ የሚተከለኝ ፡ የለም ። አዎን ፡ እውነት ፡
ነው ፡ አለቻት ፤ ፪ቱም ፡ አላዩምና ፡ ሌላ ፡ ነገር ። ቀንም ፡ አንበሳ ፡
ሲጮህ ፡ ሰምታ ፡ እኔም ፡ እንደርሱ ፡ እጮህለሁ ፡ አለቻት ። ባልንጀ
ራዋ ፡ ግን ፡ እንዲህ ፡ አለቻት ፤ እኔ ፡ ፪ ታችሁንም ፡ እሰማለሁ ፡
ጩሂ ፡ አለቻት ። ያችም ፡ ቊንተል ፡ ስሚኝ ፤ ብላ ፡ ሆዷን ፡ ነፍታ ፡
ጮኸች ፡ ባልንጀራዋም ፡ እንዲህ ፡ አለች ፤ ያንበሳው ፡ ድምጽ ፡ ትልቅ ፡
ነው ፡ ያንችስ ፡ ድምፅ ፡ አይሰማም ፡ አለቻት ። ፪ተኛ ፡ ተናደደችና ፡
ስሚኝ ፡ ስጮህ ፡ አለች ። ከዚህ ፡ በኋላ ፡ ቊንተል ፡ እንደ ፡ አንበሳ ፡
እጮህለሁ ፡ ብላ ፡ ከ፪ት ፡ ተሰንጥቃ ፡ ሞተች ። እንደዚህም ፡ ሁሉ ፡
ከባለጸጋ ፡ ጋራ ፡ የሚጣላን ፡ ደሀ ፡ ደሀችን ፡ ያገኜ ፡ መከራ ፡ ያገኘዋል ።

A hare lived in a country where there was no other kind of animal. "There is no animal as big as I and none whose voice can equal mine," he said to one of his friends. "That is true," replied the other, for they had never seen another. One day, hearing a lion roar, the first hare said, "I shall cry like him." "Good. I'll stay to hear you. Cry!" said his friend. "Listen," said the hare, and, swelling his chest, he cried. His friend said to him, "The lion's voice is strong; yours, on the other hand, cannot be heard." The hare became very angry and said a second time, "Watch and listen how I cry." And under the illusion of roaring like a lion, he split in two and died. The same fate awaits the poor man who vies with the rich.

Amharic fable

Amharic is the national language of Ethiopia. It is the mother tongue of about 20 million people (one-third of the country's population), living mostly in the vicinity of the capital, Addis Ababa, and in the area to the north. About 30 million others speak it as a second language.

Amharic is one of the Semitic languages, which form a branch of the Afro-Asiatic family. It belongs to the Ethiopic branch of Semitic, as opposed to Arabic and Hebrew, which belong to other branches. The Semitic languages were brought to Ethiopia perhaps as early as 1000 BC. Speakers of a south Arabian dialect from the kingdom of Saba (the biblical Sheba) in southwest Arabia crossed the Red Sea and settled in the highlands of Ethiopia. From the 4th century AD onward the principal language of the country was Ge'ez, the forerunner of all the Ethiopic languages and still the language of the Ethiopian Coptic Church.

Amharic is written in the Ethiopic alphabet that was used to write Ge'ez, and which had its origin in the south Arabian writing system. Originally written from right to left, it eventually switched, probably under Greek influence, from left to right. There are 32 characters, each representing a consonant, but each has seven slightly different forms to reflect the vowel sound that follows. Two dots are placed after each word to separate it from the next.

Oromo

Hiriyoota lamatu imala dheeraa wajjiin jalqabe. Otuu deemanuu karatti aduun itti dhiite. Dhiibuu bosonaa malee nannoo gandi jiruu miti. Kanaafuu, muka gubbaa buluuf mala baafatan. Garuu, yoo hirriibni isaan qabe, muka irraa kuufuun isaanii akka malu sodaatuu dhaan, hundee muka guddaa jala buluu murteeffatan. Bineensi akka isaan hin nyaannes jabaatanii wal irraa eeguu dhaaf waadaa walii seenan. Isaan keessaa tokko gamna, kuun immoo dabeessa ture. Gamnichi sagalee wahii dhageenyaan hasaasee, "Maaltu waa nyaataa jira?" Jedhee gaafate. Dabeessichi: "Cal-jedhi, waraabessatu miila koo nyaataa jiraa," jedhee deebiseef jedhan.

Once upon a time two friends began a long journey together. As night was falling they began looking for a place to spend the night. There was no village around, only dense forest. So they decided to spend the night in a tree. But they were afraid they might tumble from the tree if they fell asleep and then be eaten by wild animals. Finally they decided to sleep at the foot of a large tree, promising each other to watch for any animal that might come to attack them. One of them, who was brave, heard a strange noise and whispered to the other, who was a coward, "I hear someone chewing something, what's going on?" The coward replied, "Just keep quiet! A hyena is eating one of my legs."

Oromo, formerly known as Galla, is one of the two major languages of Ethiopia. It is spoken mainly in the southern part of the country, and in small numbers across the border in Kenya. Although Amharic is considered Ethiopia's national language, Oromo, with its 20 million speakers, ranks among the top ten languages of Africa. The Voice of America broadcasts several hours a day in Oromo.

Oromo is one of the Cushitic languages, an important branch of the Afro-Asiatic family. Native speakers generally call it Oromiffa or Afaan Oromo. Though originally written in the Amharic script, it was never much used as a written language. But in the 1990s it was made the administrative language of all Oromo-speaking areas and also the language of instruction in the schools. At the same time the decision was made that henceforth it would be written in the Roman alphabet.

አድግን ከልብን ዖር ስራሕ ከቢዱና ብምባል ካብ ጎይቶኦም
ጠፊኦም ይኸዱ።ኣብ ጉዕዞ ከለው ይመስዮም እሞ ኣብ እግሪ ኦም
ይድቅሱ።ፍርቂ ለይቲ ምስ ኮነ ኣድጊ ተንሲኡ ከሃልል'የ
ይብል።ከልቢ ኣይፋልካን፤ኣራዊት በረኻ ድምፅኻ ሰሚዖም
ከይመፁና ግደፍ ይብሉ።ኣድጊ ግን ወይክ ፅን።ደጋጊሙ
ይሃልል።ኣንበሳን ዝብእን ድምፂ ሰሚዖም ይመፁ።ኣንበሳን ዝብእን
ኣነ'የ ዝበልዖ ኣይፋልካን ኣነ'ባ ይባሃሉ።ዝብኢ-መጀመርታ ድምፂ
ዝሰሚዕኩ ኣነ ስለዝኾንኩ ንዓይ'የ ዝግባእ ይብል።ኣንበሳ-ንልቢ
ሕደገለይ'ምበር ቀፅል ይብል።በዚ ይሰማምዑ።ዝብኢ ግን ልቢ
ከይሓደገ ንኹሉ'ቲ ኣድጊ ይበልዖ።ኣንበሳ-ኣበይ'ዳእ'ሉ ልቢ'ቲ
ኣድጊ ይብሉዎ፤ዝብኢ- ልቢ ኣይነበሮን፤ኣድጊ ልቢ እንተዝነብሮ'ዶ
ብለይቲ ሃሊሉ! ከብል ንኣንበሳ መሲሱሉ ይባፅል።

Once upon a time a donkey and a dog ran away from their owner complaining that he made them work too hard. As night was falling both slept under a tree. At midnight the donkey said to the dog, "I am going to heehaw." The dog, afraid of the beasts, said no. But the donkey did not listen and heehawed anyway. Unfortunately, a lion and a hyena heard the sound and came to attack them. Then the lion said, "The donkey belongs to me. I am going to eat it." But the hyena replied, "No, I was the first to hear the sound. I should be the first to eat it." Finally they agreed that the hyena would eat all of the donkey except its heart. But the hyena did not keep its word and ate the whole donkey including its heart. When the lion came and asked for the heart the hyena answered, "The donkey didn't have a heart. If he had a heart he would not have heehawed at night."

Tigrinya is spoken in Ethiopia and in neighboring Eritrea. In the former it is spoken about 4 million people, most of them in the northernmost province of Tigray. In Eritrea there are about 2 million speakers, or half the country's population.

Like Amharic, Tigrinya belongs to the Ethiopic branch of the Semitic languages. It is most closely related to Tigre, the other principal language of Eritrea. All three are written in the Ethiopic alphabet.

Somali

Sidii koorweyn halaad oo
Kor iyo Hawd sare ka timid
Kulayl badan baan qabaa

Shimbiro geed wada koraa
Midi ba cayn bay u cidaa
Carro ba waa camaladdeed
Illayn Lays ma cod yaqaan

Hal baa hilin igaga jaban
Hilbaha yaan ka ceshadaa
Habeenkii ka ma lulmoodoo
Dharaartii ka ma hadh galo

Sankaa qori igaga jabay
Sintaa midig baan ka jabay
Il baa sachar igaga dhacay
Haddana waan soconayaa

Like a she-camel with a large bell
Come from the plateau and upper Haud,
My heat is great.

Birds perched together on the same tree
Call each their own cries,
Every country has its own ways,
Indeed people do not understand each other's talk.

One of my she-camels falls on the road
And I protect its meat,
At night I cannot sleep,
And in the daytime I can find no shade.

I have broken my nose on a stick,
I have broken my right hip,
I have something in my eye,
And yet I go on.

Fortitude (anonymous)

Somali is the national language of Somalia, in easternmost Africa. It is spoken by virtually all of the country's 7 million people, and by another 4 million in Ethiopia. Smaller communities exist in Kenya and in Djibouti.

Somali is one of the Cushitic languages, which form a branch of the Afro-Asiatic family. Following Somalian independence in 1960 two alphabets were selected, from many contenders, for writing the language. One was Roman, the other Osmanian (named after its inventor), which contained elements of both Arabic and Ethiopic scripts. In 1973, however, when Somali was made the country's official language, the government decreed that it would be written in the Roman alphabet.

Kikuyu

Gikuyu ni gitikitie Ngai
mumbi wa Iguru na Thi,
na muheani wa indo ciothe.

Ngai ndarimuthia kana githethwa,
Ndari ithe kana nyina,
Ndataragwo na arutaga wira ari wiki.

Aikaraga Matu-ini
no ni ari mucii ungi bururi-ini wa Gikuyu
uria Ahurukaga riria okite gucera Thi;
mucii ucio uri Kirima-ini gia Kirinyaga.

Arathimaga Kana akaruma mundu
kana Kirindi, na
Aheanaga na agatunyana
kuringana na ciiko cia ciana Ciake.

Gikuyu ni kigocaga Ngai hingo ciothe
tondu wa uria anagitanahira muno,
ni gukihe bururi mwega
utagaga nyama, irio kana Mai.

The Kikuyu believe in God
the creator of heaven and earth,
the giver of all things.

God has no beginning nor end,
He has no father nor mother,
He takes no advice and works single-handedly.

He lives in heaven
but has another home in Kikuyuland,
where He rests when He visits earth;
this home is on Mount Kenya.

He blesses and curses individual
and society, and
He gives and withholds His gifts
according to the actions of His children.

The Kikuyu praise their God always
because of His genuine generosity,
in giving them fertile country
which lacks no meat, food, or water.

MAINA KAGOMBE, *The Kikuyu Concept of God*

The Kikuyu are the largest tribe in Kenya, numbering about 6 million people. They inhabit the fertile land around the slopes of Mount Kenya to the north of Nairobi. The Kikuyu language is of the Bantu family.

Luba

Muntu wakatompele mbao. Wafika katompa mbao, ino watana mulubao lumo lupye ntambo. Ino muntu wadi kāsake kumutapa; ntambo kānena'mba: Ngabule, kokantapa. Shi ubangabula nankyo nāmi nkakupa mpalo. Ino muntu wamwabula: ino kwadi'mba: Ke nkudi. Muntu amba: Nanshi e mo wadyumukila. Kwivwana padi mpuku mu lubao'mba: Iya bidi pano, ntambo; le kukīye? Nanshi umōngwelanga palubao.

Penepo ntambo'mbo: Mfwene; waponene mōnka mu lubao. Mpuku waita muntu amba: Iya umutape. Pēnepo muntu wafwena kāmutape, wamwipaya. Penepo ntambo pa kufwa kwadi muntu amba: Le nkupa ka, abe mpuku? Aye mpuku amba: Nsaka twisambe nōbe bulunda, unsele kōbe kunjibo, untule pa kapala. Nāndi wamusela wamutula pa kitala kāikele'tu nyeke.

A man went to examine his pit-traps. He came and looked at the traps, and found in one pit a lion. As the man was about to spear him the lion said, "Lift me out, do not spear me. If you lift me out, I will give you a reward." So the man lifted him out, but he said, "Now I will eat you." But hark, a rat in the pit said, "Come here, lion; why don't you come?" Now he was tricking him about the pit.

So the lion thought, "I will go near." So he fell once again into the pit. The rat called the man and said, "Come and spear him." So then the man came near and speared him, killing him. Then when the lion was dead, the man said, "What shall I give you, O Rat?" The rat replied saying, "I would like you to carry me home to your house, and put me on the tall food-rack." And as for the man, he carried him away and put him on the rack, and he lived there always.

Luba, also known as Chiluba, is one of the major languages of Congo-Kinshasa. It is spoken by about 10 million people, mainly in the southeastern part of the country. The language belongs to the Bantu family.

Lingala

Tokosepelaka míngi na botángi o kásá malúli ma báníngá baíké, bakoséngε te báléndisa bolakisi kóta ya Pútú o kelási ya baíndo. Yangó malámu míngi sɔ́lɔ́. Kási bandeko ba bísó bâná bakobósanaka te malúli ma pámba pámba makomɔ́nisa moto lokóla mwána moké. Mwána sɔ́kɔ́ azalí na límpa sikáwa, ekomɔ́nɔ yě sukáli, akobwáka límpa pé akolela sukáli. Loléngé lɔ́kɔ́ sɔ́kɔ́ bakolakisa bísó lingála, kiswahíli, kikɔ́ngɔ́, tsiluba, b.n.b., toébí naíno malámu té, tokoíbwáka pé tokolela français, flamand, anglais. Wâná níni? Tokomεmya kóta ya bísó té; tokoíbébisa bobébisi. Na yangó mindélé bakolomɔ́na bǒ bána bakê ba bilúlélá pé bakosεkε bísó.

We are pleased to read in the newspapers that many of our friends are pressing for the teaching of European languages in the schools for Blacks. This is an excellent idea. But our friends often forget that impractical ideas often make a man look like a small child. If the child who has, for example, a piece of bread, should see a piece of sugar, he will toss away the bread and take the sugar. It is the same with Lingala, Swahili, Kongo, Luba, etc., which we have not yet thoroughly mastered, but which we are discarding in favor of French, Flemish, and English. What then? We will no longer respect our own languages and can only debase them. Thus the whites look upon us as small children filled with vain desires and they make fun of us.

Lingala is the main lingua franca of northern Congo-Kinshasa, spoken (usually as a second language) by as many as 25 million people, or half the country's population. There are also about one million speakers in neighboring Congo-Brazzaville. Lingala is another of the Bantu languages.

Kongo

Kilumbu kimosi M'vangi wa vova kua bibulu. "Tuka ntama yitudi banza nani vakati kua beno yigufueti kala n'tinu, bubu nsoledi vo mbua sikakala n'tinu. Bonso luzeyi, mbua yi n'kundi wa unene wa muntu. Siyakubika n'kinzi, situa dia buna si tuayadisa mbua."

Kansi na nsiesi kazola yalua kua mbua ko. Mpimpa yina kaleka ko wabanze ye wa sosa nzila mu vunzakisa luzolo lua M'vangi. Kilumbu ki landa bibulu bia vuanda ga mesa, na nsiesi wa vuandila lukufi ye mbua. Buna wa geta kiyisi ga n'totu, muna ntangu yina mbua watimuka ye landa kiyisi. Bibulu biakulu biayituka mu mavanga ma mbua. Buna na nsiesi watelama ye vova, "Bue yani mbua kafueti yadila beto yani muntu gakena mavanga ka mazimbuka ko e?" Mbua kani yadisua kayala ko mu kilumbu kina, nate ye bubu M'vangi ukini sosa nani fueni gana kifulu kana kikala mbua.

Once upon a time the Creator said to the animals, "For a long time I've been thinking about who shall rule among you, and at last I've decided that it should be the dog. He is, after all, man's best friend. I invite each of you to a feast at which the dog will be crowned king."

But the hare could not stand the idea of being ruled by a dog. He lay awake all night thinking how to thwart the Creator's plan. The following day at the feast he sat next to the dog. Suddenly he threw down a bone, whereupon the dog leaped from the table to grab it. All the animals were shocked. Then the hare stood up and said, "How can the dog pretend to govern us if he is ignorant of the basic elements of good manners?" The crowning of the dog was, of course, canceled, and it is said that the Creator is still seeking a king for the animals.

Kongo, more correctly called Kikongo, is spoken principally in western Congo-Kinshasa. It is the native tongue of about 8 million people there and the second language of some 8 million more. There are also about one million speakers in Congo-Brazzaville and 1½ million in northern Angola. Kongo is another of the Bantu languages.

Ganda

Lumu ensolo zawakana okudduka nti anasooka okutuka kuntebe gyezali zitadewo yanaba omufuzi. Ngabulijjo wampologoma yeyasokayo, naye, teyamanya nti munne nawolovu yali yekwese mumukiragwe. Kale bweyali agenda okutula kuntebbe nawulira nga nawolovu amugamba nti, sebo tontuulako. Nawolovu ngayetwalira bufuzi. "Amagezi gakira amanyi."

The animals had no leader and decided to choose one. A race was held, and a chair was placed a long distance away. The first animal to reach the chair and sit on it would be the leader. As usual, the lion was the fastest, but he did not know that the chameleon was sitting behind his tail. As he sat on the chair, he heard a cry. He jumped up and was surprised to find the chameleon, who claimed he was first and therefore the leader. "Wisdom is better than strength."

Ganda, also known as Luganda, is the most important language of Uganda, in East Africa. Another of the Bantu languages, it is spoken by about 4 million people there, mainly in the southern region, which includes the capital Kampala. Ganda was the language of the powerful Kingdom of Buganda which ruled what is now Uganda until the end of the 19th century.

Ruanda

U Rwanda ni igihugu gito kiba muri Africa y'iburasirazuba. Gituwe n'amoko atatu ariyo: Abahutu, Abatwa, n'Abatutsi. Bose bavuga ururimi rumwe arirwo kinyarwanda. Mu mwaka w'i 1994 habaye mu rwanda itsembatsemba n'itsembabwoko ryahitanye abantu barenga miliyoni. U Rwanda rwabonye ubwigenge ku itariki ya 1 nyakanga 1962. Rutuwe na miliyoni zirindwi n'igice.

Rwanda is a small country in East Africa. It has three ethnic groups: the Hutus, Twa, and Tutsis. All the ethnic groups speak the same language, Kinyarwanda. In 1994 there was a genocide in Rwanda which left over one million people dead. Rwanda gained its independence on 1 July 1962. It has a population of 7½ million.

Ruanda, more properly known as Kinyarwanda, is an important language of east-central Africa. It is spoken by virtually all 7½ million people in Rwanda, including the bitterly hostile Hutus and Tutsis. There are also about 5 million speakers in neighboring Congo-Kinshasa. Ruanda is another of the Bantu languages.

Rundi

Kuva aho Uburundi bwikukiriye ibintu bitari bike vyarateye imbere mu gihugu. Kuva aho Republika ituvyagiriyemwo na ho, amajambere yarongerekanye muri vyinshi, cane cane mu butunzi bwa Leta. Mugabo ikinzindukanye aha lero, n'ukugira turabe aho ukurera abanyagihugu kugereye. Musanzwe muzi lero ko indero y'umuntu ihagaze kuri vyose: ari ku bwenge, ku magara, canke ku mutima. Rimwe narigeze kwandika muri *Ndongozi*, ko ubu hariko haraba ikirere amahanga hagati y'abize n'abatize. Na none birumvikana kuko bamwe baguma bikarihiriza ubwenge, abandi na bo bakaguma mu buhumyi bâmanye.

Since Burundi became independent, many things have improved within the country. And since the advent of the Republic, progress has been made in many fields, especially in the state's economy. But the reason I am writing today is to try to see how education has progressed. You already know that human progress depends on many things: on education, on health, on spiritual values. I once wrote in *Ndongozi* [a magazine] how the gap between the educated people and the illiterate is growing wider and wider. This is understandable, since the former continue to learn while the latter remain in their illiteracy.

Rundi, or Kirundi, is the national language of Burundi, just to the south of Rwanda. It is spoken by the entire population of the country, or some 6 million people, plus another 2 million in Congo-Kinshasa. A Bantu language, Rundi is closely related to Ruanda of Rwanda. The two are actually little more than dialects of the same language.

Nyanja

Kalekale Kunali munthu wina dzina lace Awonenji. Anzace Sanalikumuwelengela Koma iye Sanadzipatule. Tsiku lina pamene anawalondolela Ku ulenje, anthu odzikuzawo Sanawonjeko ndi maukonde awo. Pomwe analikubwelela Ku mudzi anakumana ndi njoru. Iwo anacha maukonde yawo. Njoru zitawonjedwa, zinazula mphompho zaukondewo ndi Kupitililabe. Awonenji anatemapo imodzi ndi buma mmaso ndipo imagma pansi ndi Kufa cifukwa inalikuphupha ndi infa. Awonenji amapha njoru ndi buma.

Once upon a time there lived a man whom his community generally regarded as an idiot. In spite of this he did not isolate himself. On a certain day he followed his companions on a hunting trip during which they did not kill any game. While returning home they met elephants which they trapped with nets that the elephants had tramped over. The idiot picked up a stone and struck one elephant in the eye. The elephant fell dead because it had already been very seriously wounded by a hunter. ... An idiot killed an elephant with a small stone.

Nyanja, more correctly known as Chinyanja, is the principal language of Malawi, in southern Africa. It is spoken there by over 6 million people or close to two-thirds of the population. There are an additional one million speakers in Zambia and about 500,000 in Mozambique. Nyanja is another of the Bantu languages. In Malawi it is generally referred to as Chewa.

Bemba

Calandwa ukutila indimi ishilandwa mu calo ca Africa shaba pakati kampendwa imyanda mutanda ne myanda cine konse konse. Cintu cayafya ukwishiba bwino impendwa ya ndimi ishilandwa ngatwati tweshe ukupatulula ululimi lumo lumo, mpaka fye ilyo lintu kukaba ifilangililo ifingi kabili ifyalondololwa bwino bwino. Kwena, impendwa ishilangilwe pamulu, shilelanga apabuta tutu ukutila indimi mu calo ca Africa shaba ishingi kabili ishalekana lekana, nokucila ku kuboko kwa kulyo ukwa ciswebebe ca Sahara.

The number of languages spoken on the African continent is estimated to be between six and eight hundred. Until more information is available, and until a more precise criterion as to what constitutes a separate language is agreed upon, no exact number can be given. The figures quoted, however, clearly indicate the great linguistic diversity of Africa, particularly that portion which lies south of the Sahara.

Bemba is the most widely spoken language of Zambia. Its 3 million speakers live mainly in the northeastern part of the country. Bemba is another of the Bantu languages.

Shona

Hwanzvo

Rudó nemwóyo wángu ndakákupá.
Simbá nemúrawo ndézvakó, mudíwa.
Iní kwángu kúíta kudá kwáko chéte.
Chipfúvá chángu, mudíwa wángu,
Chízeré nérufáro nerúnyemwerero.
Mudíwa, ndinókudáídzá kúti murúmé,
Así rúmwe rutivi urí amái kana babá.

Panéwé mudíwa, pfungwá yángu yáguma.
Ndavá kútomírírá zúvá gúrú,
Íro randíchashányirwá nérufú.
Ungátová ndíwo musí wandíchakúsíya,
Nokúti ndichátorwa, kana kubvutwa,
Muné ákó maókó usíkú kana masíkáti,
Pasíná aní angázvidzíve.

Chikomba

Mudíwa, usarwáré kana kutambudzika mumwoyo
Nazvósé zvinóbva mukanwa mevánhu,
Nokúti vakáipa vánotsvaga kuparadza.
Ndinófára nokúti wakátákura uyu mutóro,
Ukafámbá, nawó, ukasvika nawó pawáidá,
Pasíná kutsútsúmwá kana kutsóndórá,
Así bédzi kuónésá rudó rwáko kwandíri.

Zvandínazvó múmwoyo pamusóró páko,
Handígoné kuzvíbúrítsá ndikazvípédzá.
Mudíwa wángu, ndirí kuchémá misódzi
Minyóró némikúkútú pámusáná pókudáwé.
Ndinókuténda, mudíwa wángu,
Nokúti wakáfútidza mwotó úiné mvura mudámá,
Mwotóyo ukabvira zvinónwírwá mvúrá navánhu.

The Beloved

I gave you my love and my heart as well.
All power and authority are yours, my love.
Mine just to do your wish.
My breast, my beloved,
Is full of joy and laughter.
Beloved, I call you husband,
But you are also my mother or my father.

320

You are the bound of all my thought, my love,
There is only that solemn day that I must await,
The one when I shall be visited by death.
It will be only on that day that I will leave you,
Because I shall be taken, or rather snatched,
From your arms some night or day,
With no one able to prevent it.

The Lover
Beloved, do not sicken or suffer in your heart
From anything that comes from people's mouths,
Because, being evil, they seek to destroy.
I am glad because you have borne this burden,
And gone forward, and with it come to where you wanted,
Without growing unhappy or abandoning your trust.
Only showing your love to me.

What I have in my heart on your account,
I cannot express and utter all I would.
My love, I am weeping tears,
By turns both wet and dry through love of you.
I thank you, my beloved,
Because you blew up the fire, though with such difficulty,
And that fire flared up in such a wonderful way.

Dialogue Between Two Lovers

Shona is the principal language of Zimbabwe. It is spoken there by about 8 million people, or close to three-fourths of the native population. There are also about one million speakers in Mozambique and 200,000 in Botswana. Shona is another of the Bantu languages.

Afrikaans

Vanaand het ek weer so verlang,
in grondelose vrees
van eie gryse eensaamheid,
dat jy by my moet wees,

dat ek die wye koeltes van
jou stem om my kan voel,
soos die rimp'ling van die somerreën
vervlugtig oor my spoel.

En toe ek deur die duister wind
wat oor my huisie waai,
die knip hoor lig, het heel my hart
in vreugde opgelaai . . .

Nou sit ons voor die vuur en speel
die vlamlig deur ons hare . . .
Laag waai die reënwind buite deur
die afgevalle blare.

This evening once again I longed
in vague, abysmal fear
of my own old, grey loneliness
that you were with me here,

that the cool reaches of your voice
about me I were feeling,
like the rippling of the summer rain
so softly o'er me stealing.

And when above the dark, cold wind
that round my cottage blew
I heard the latch, my heart leapt up
with joy to welcome you . . .

And now we sit before the fire,
its flame-glow in our hair . . .
Meanwhile the rain-wind murmurs through
the fallen leaves out there.

W. E. G. LOUW, Quiet Evening

Afrikaans is one of the two official languages of the Republic of South Africa, the other being English. It is spoken by over 6 million people: the 3 million white Afrikaners, plus about 3 million "coloreds," or persons of mixed descent. The former live largely in Northern Province (formerly Transvaal) and in Free State (formerly Orange Free State), the latter mainly in the western part of Cape Province in the west. There are also about 50,000 speakers in Namibia.

Afrikaans is a development of 17th-century Dutch brought to South Africa by the first settlers from the Netherlands. The subsequent isolation of the people and their descendants caused increasing divergence from the original Dutch, so that Afrikaans may now be considered a separate language. Written Afrikaans can be most easily distinguished from Dutch by the indefinite article *'n*, which in Dutch is *een*.

Zulu

Ngimbeleni ngaphansi kotshani
Duze nezihlahla zomyezane
Lapho amagatsh' eyongembesa
Ngamaqaɓung' agcwel' uɓuhlaza.
Ngozwa nami ngilele ngaphansi
Utshani ngaphezulu ɓuhleɓa:
"Lala sithandwa, lal' uphumule."

Ngimbeleni endawen' enjena:
Laph' izinsungulo zezilimi
Zenkathazo zingenakuthola
Sango lokwahlukanis' umhlaɓa
Zingivus' eɓuthongwen' oɓuhle.
Uma wen' ofunda leminqana,
Ungifica, ungimbele lapho
Utshani ngaphezulu ɓuyothi:
"Lala sithandwa, lal' uphumule."

Bury me where the grasses grow
Below the weeping willow trees
To let their branches shed upon me
Leaves of varied greens.
Then, as I lie there, I shall hear
The grasses sigh a soft behest:
"Sleep, beloved one, sleep and rest."

Bury me in a place like this:
Where those who scheme and give their tongues
To plots and anger, never can
Displace the earth that covers me
Nor ever keep me from my sleep.
If you who read these lines should chance
To find me, O then bury me
Where grasses whisper this behest:
"Sleep, beloved one, sleep and rest."

BENEDICT WALLET VILAKAZI,
If Death Should Steal Upon Me

Zulu is one of the major Bantu languages of South Africa. The home of the Zulus, Zululand, is located in the historic region of Natal (now officially the province of KwaZulu-Natal) in the easternmost part of South Africa. The language is closely related to Xhosa, Swazi, and also Ndebele of Zimbabwe, the four belonging to the Nguni branch of the Bantu family. There are about 10 million speakers.

Xhosa

Nkosi, sikelel' i' Afrika
Malupakam' upondo Iwayo;
Yiva imitandazo yetu
Usisikelele

Yihla Moya, yihla Moya
Yihla Moya Oyingcwele

Sikelela iNkose zetu
Zimkumbule umDali wazo;
Zimoyike Zezimhlouele,
Azisikelele.

Lord, bless Africa
May her spirit rise high up;
Hear Thou our prayers
And bless us.

Descend, O Spirit
Descend, O Holy Spirit

Bless our chiefs;
May they remember their Creator,
Fear Him and revere Him,
That He may bless them.

Xhosa National Anthem

Xhosa is spoken principally in the historic region of Transkei (now Eastern Cape Province) in South Africa. It is another of the Bantu languages with about 8 million speakers. The *Xh* at the beginning of the name represents a "click" consonant which entered the language through contact with the Hottentot people, for whom these sounds are common.

Sotho

Le hoja 'muso ona o itlama ho sireletsa litokelo tsa botho tsa batsoali naheng ena, e leng tokelo ea ho nyalana le ho ba le bana, 'muso oa tlameha hape ho hopotsa baahi ba Lesotho ho hlokomela boikarabelo bo boholo ba sechaba ka kakaretso esitana le boiketlo ba sona ba nako e tlang. 'Muso ha o na ho kenakenana le taba ea hore na lelapa le be boholo bo bokae; 'muso ha o na ho seha moeli oa palo ea bana le hore na ba sieane ka lilemo tse kae, empa leha ho le joalo 'muso o kopa hore motho ka mong esitana le mekhatlo e ke e ele taba ena hloko le ho bona se tlisoang ke keketseho e potlakileng ena ea sechaba.

While this government does guarantee the protection of the human rights of every mother and father in the country, the right to marry and to procreate, it must remind the citizens of Lesotho to be aware of their great responsibility to the society as a whole, and to the future well-being of the entire nation. This government will not interfere with the size of anyone's family, it will not dictate any ideal number of children or the spacing of births, but it asks that private individuals and private organizations pay serious attention to all implications of the present rapid growth of our population.

Sotho, more correctly called Sesotho, is one of the major languages of southern Africa. Sotho proper refers to Southern Sotho, spoken by about 2 million people in Lesotho and another 3 million in the surrounding areas of South Africa. In its broader sense it includes:

(1) Northern Sotho, or Pedi, spoken in northern Transvaal, South Africa;
(2) Western Sotho, generally referred to as Tswana (see next page).

Sotho is another of the Bantu languages.

Tswana

Mmina-Photi wa bo khama le Ngwato-a-Masilo
Ka kala fela jaaka lenong Marung
Motseng gaetsho ka go tlhoka ke go lebile
Ke kwaletse tsala yame kele kgakala
"A pelo tsa lona di se fuduege
Mme dumelang mo Modimong."
Nna ke leje je le tlhaotsweng go – Nna Motheo wa kago.

I, descendant of Khama, and Nwato of the line of Masilo, whose
    totem is the duiker,
Hovered like a vulture, high up in the clouds.
Even as I looked, my home eluded my eyes.
I wrote to my friend from far away,
"Let not your hearts be troubled,
But trust in the Lord . . ."
I am a rock chosen to be the cornerstone of a people.

Tswana, more correctly called Setswana, is the national language of
Botswana and is also an important language of South Africa. In Botswana it
is spoken by about three-fourths of the population, or more than one million
people. In South Africa there are about 3 million speakers in the provinces
that border Botswana.

Tswana is the language of a people of the same name, from whom the
name Botswana is derived. Another of the Bantu languages, it is closely
related to Sotho, and is often referred to as Western Sotho.

Swazi

Nkulunkulu, mnikati wetibusiso temaSwati,
Siyatibonga tonkhe tinhlanhla;
Sibonga iNggwenyama yetfhu,
Live, netintshaba, nemifula.
Busisa tiphatshimandla takaNggwane;
Nguwe wedvwa Somandla wetfhu.
Sinike kuhlakanipha lokungenabucili;
Simise, usicinise, Simakadze.

O God, bestower of the blessings of the Swazi,
We are thankful for all our good fortune;
We give praise and thanks for our King,
And for our country, its hills and rivers.
Bless those in authority in our land;
Thou only art our Almighty,
Give us wisdom without guile;
Establish and strengthen us, Thou Everlasting.

Swazi National Anthem

Swazi, more correctly called Siswati, is the national language of the Kingdom of Swaziland in southern Africa. It is spoken by virtually the entire native population of the country, or about one million people, and another one million in South Africa. Swazi is one of the Bantu languages, closely related to Zulu and Xhosa, and in fact can be readily understood by speakers of these languages.

Hottentot

≠Kam /ŭi-aob gye //ĕib di gŭna /homi /na gye /ŭi hă i. /Gui tsĕb gye !gare-/uiĭ di /khareĭ ei heiĭ di somi /na gye ≠nŏa i, tsĭb gye //om tsĭ sĭgurase gye !gan-tana, tanaba ra /hororose. Ob gye //ĕib /gŭse gyere !ŭ beiraba /ŭi-aob ta /kamsa //goa bi, ti gye ≠ĕi. //Natib gye ≠nirase gye ≠homisęn, tsĭb gye //hei-≠nu ei bi nĭse !gŭn, tsĭ /ni dă-/haroroti gose gye ≠gai-/oa-/oasęn, tsĭb gye !ŭi-aob ei //hei-≠nŭ tsĭ //khŏse gye !khă bi.

Ob gye /ŭi-aoba //khŏse ≠kon ≠oms ăba χu ≠kei-≠keihe, tsĭ gye //gao tsĭb gye //eiχa hăse uri-khăi tsĭ beiraba gye !khŏ, tsĭ //năba gye /gŭse mă i tsouĭ /na gye /nami-//na bi. χawe //ndsan nĭ nou gŭna mŭ, tįmis /kan gye beiraba sau tsĭ tsoub /na gye uri-//gŏa tsĭ /khom-/khomsase !garegu ei gye ≠ku. //Natib gye !ŭi-aoba !gawrua-/na hăse /ŭn ăba ra tsuru-/ă gye ≠gei: „≠Kawa //eiba χu ≠gŏsęn tama is gye ≠khŏas tsĭ /am-≠gŏsęns tsĭna ra ŭ-hă."

One day a young shepherd was watching his sheep on a mountainside. While he was sitting on a rock in the shade of a tree, his head nodded forward and he fell asleep. A ram grazing nearby, seeing the shepherd lower his head, thought he was threatening to fight. So he got ready, and drawing himself back a few paces he launched himself at the shepherd and butted him severely.

The shepherd, thus rudely awakened from his sleep, arose angrily, caught the ram, and threw him into a well standing nearby. But the moment the other sheep saw their leader fall into the well, they followed him in and were dashed to pieces on the rocks. So the shepherd, tearing his hair, cried out: "What sorrow and trouble are brought about by useless anger!"

Hottentot, now generally referred to as Nama, is spoken in Namibia. Like Bushman, also spoken in Namibia, it stands apart from the rest of the languages of southern Africa, as it belongs to the tiny Khoisan family. The Hottentots and the Bushmen were the original inhabitants of southern Africa, but they were driven south by the more advanced Bantu sometime in the 1st millennium AD. There are about 200,000 speakers of Hottentot, more than twice that of any of the other Khoisan languages.

The most notable feature of the Khoisan languages is the use of the so-called "click" consonants, produced by drawing air into the mouth and clicking the tongue. When the earliest Dutch settlers in southern Africa first encountered this language, they described it as consisting of nothing more than the sounds *hot* and *tot*. Today the term Hottentot is considered derisive, and Nama is preferred.

Bushman

Kórokẹn ǁχau ǀki ǁkaúë, au ǁkaúëtẹn ǀkā wāï.
Kórokẹn ǀne ǁχeïǁχeī, haṅ ǀne taṅ-ī ǁkaúë aŭ wāïta
ă. ( ) Haṅ bọ́rǒ, haṅ taṅ-ī, aŭ haṅ tátti ẹ̄ kóro
ǀkŭ ẹ̄. Hẹ́ ti hiṅ ẹ̄, ha ǀkŭ bọ̄rǒ, haṅ ǁkwaṅ táṅ-ī,
haṅ tatti kóro ǀkú ẹ̄. Hẹ̄ ti hiṅ ẹ̄, ha ǀku bọ̄rǒ aŭ
ha táṅ-ī, haṅ ǁkwăṅ ká ǁkaúë ă ha ā, ha si hā̰, ha
si ǁχạm hā.

( ) Hẹ̄ ti hiṅ ē, ǁkaúëtẹn ǀne ǀkoeiṅ í, ǁkaúëtẹn
ǀne ǀkī ha, ǁkaúëtẹn ǀne ts'ī ǀkūkẹn ha, haṅ ǀne hō
ha, haṅ ǀne ǁaṅ ǀkí lē ha au ǀkúbbi; ( ) hē ti hiṅ
ē haṅ ǀne ǃnaú tī hă.

The jackal watches the leopard when the leopard has killed a springbok.
The jackal whines (with uplifted tongue), he begs the leopard for
springbok flesh. He howls, he begs, for he is a jackal. Thus he howls,
he indeed begs, because he is a jackal. Therefore he howls when he begs,
he indeed wants the leopard to give him flesh, that he may eat, that he
also may eat.

Then the leopard is angry, the leopard kills him, the leopard bites him
dead, he lifts him up, he goes to put him into the bushes; thus he hides
him.

Bushman, now known by its native name of San, is another of the Khoisan
languages. There are about 75,000 speakers today, two-thirds in western
Botswana, the rest in northern Namibia. Like the other Khoisan languages,
Bushman has numerous "click" consonants, represented by symbols such as
/, ≠, //, !, and #.

Malagasy

Aza anontaniana izay anton'izao
Fanginako lalina ary feno tomany!
Aza anontaniana, satria fantatrao
Fa fahatsiarovana no anton'izany . . .

Tsaroako ny tsikin'ny androko omaly,
Izay manjary aloka foana, indrisy!
Tsaroako! . . . Antsoiko ta tsy mba mamaly,
Ary toa manadino, ary toa tsy mba nisy!

You shall not ask what the present tears
From the deep of my silence mean!
You shall not ask because you know
They are memories of long ago!

I recall the joys of days gone by,
They waned alas to flit away!
I claim and call them forth in vain
As though oblivious and never again!

J. J. RABEARIVELO, Love Song

Malagasy, also known as Malgache, is spoken in the island nation of Madagascar. Its 15 million speakers include virtually all of the country's population.

It would be logical to assume that Malagasy belongs to one or another of the African language families, but that is not the case. It is actually one of the Austronesian languages, the rest of which are spoken thousands of miles to the east, mainly in Southeast Asia. It is most closely related to a group of languages spoken by the Dayak people on the island of Borneo (Kalimantan). The ancestors of today's inhabitants of Madagascar are thought to have arrived from Borneo some time before 500 AD.

Malagasy contains some words of Bantu, Arabic, French, and English origin. It has a soft, musical quality somewhat reminiscent of Italian.

AN ARTIFICIAL LANGUAGE

Esperanto

Ne provizu al vi trezorojn sur la tero, kie tineo kaj rusto konsumas, kaj kie ŝtelistoj trafosas kaj ŝtelas; sed provizu al vi trezorojn en la ĉielo, kie nek tineo nek rusto konsumas, kaj kie ŝtelistoj nek trafosas nek ŝtelas; ĉar kie estas via trezoro, tie estos ankaŭ via koro. La lampo de la korpo estas la okulo; se do via okulo estas sendifekta, via tuta korpo estos luma. Sed se via okulo estas malbona, via tuta korpo estos malluma. Se do la lumo en vi estas mallumo, kiel densa estas la mallumo!

Lay not up for yourselves treasures upon earth, where moth and rust doth corrupt and where thieves break through and steal; but lay up for yourselves treasures in heaven, where neither moth nor rust doth corrupt, and where thieves do not break through nor steal; for where your treasure is, there will your heart be also. The light of the body is the eye; if therefore thine eye be single, thy whole body shall be full of light. But if thine eye be evil, thy whole body shall be full of darkness. If therefore the light that is in thee be darkness, how great is the darkness!

Portion of the Sermon on the Mount, Matthew vi 19–23

Esperanto, the most important and influential of the so-called artificial languages, was devised in 1887 by Dr. Lazarus Ludwig Zamenhof of Warsaw, Poland. Based on the elements of the foremost Western languages, Esperanto is incomparably easier to master than any national tongue, as its grammar rules are completely consistent, and a relatively small number of basic roots can be expanded into an extensive vocabulary by means of numerous prefixes, suffixes, and infixes. The French Academy of Sciences has called Esperanto "a masterpiece of logic and simplicity."

The Esperanto alphabet consists of 28 letters: 22 English letters plus ĉ, pronounced *ch* (e.g., *ĉielo* – sky), ĝ, pronounced *j* (*aĝo* – age), ĥ, pronounced like the German *ch* but rarely used, ĵ, pronounced *zh* (*ĵurnalo* – newspaper), ŝ, pronounced *sh* (*fiŝo* – fish), and ŭ, used in forming diphthongs (*ankaŭ* – also). *C* is pronounced *ts* (*cento* – hundred), *j* is pronounced *y* (*jes* – yes), and *q*, *w*, *x*, and *y* are absent. Every word is pronounced exactly as it is spelled, with the stress always on the next to last syllable. There are no silent letters.

All nouns in Esperanto end in -*o*, adjectives in -*a*, adverbs in -*e*, and verb infinitives in -*i*. Notice the combination *varmo* (warmth), *varma* (warm), *varme* (warmly), and *varmi* (to warm). The suffix -*j* is added to nouns to form the plural and also to adjectives when the nouns they modify are plural. The present tense of a verb ends in -*as*, the past tense in -*is*, the future in -*os*, the conditional in -*us*, and the imperative in -*u*. No changes are made for person or for number. There is no indefinite article; the one definite article *la* stands for all numbers and genders.

Many Esperanto words are formed by the insertion of an infix into the middle of an already existing word. The infix *-in-*, for example, indicates the feminine form (e.g., *frato* – brother, *fratino* – sister; *koko* – rooster, *kokino* – hen). The infix *-eg-* indicates intensity (*pluvo* – rain, *pluvego* – downpour); *-ar-* indicates a collection of similar objects (*arbo* – tree, *arbaro* – forest); and *-er-* indicates a unit of a whole (*ĉeno* – chain, *ĉenero* – link).

From an examination of the passage above, it may be seen that all but a very few Esperanto words have been adopted from one of the major Western European languages.

Part III

Country-by-country survey

AFGHANISTAN (25 million). Pashto is the language of the largest ethnic group in Afghanistan, the Pashtuns, who number about 15 million. Most of the rest of the population, about 8 million people, speak Persian, known here as Dari. In the far north there are about 2 million speakers of Uzbek and 500,000 speakers of Turkmen. In the south about 250,000 people speak Baluchi.

ALBANIA (3 million). Albanian is spoken by virtually the entire population. There are about 100,000 speakers of Greek in the south.

ALGERIA (30 million). Arabic is spoken by about 85 percent of the population. Kabyle, a Berber language, is spoken by about 3 million people in the mountains east of Algiers. Far to the south, in scattered parts of the Sahara Desert, about 10,000 Tuaregs speak Tamashek. French is spoken by the dwindling European community and by many educated Algerians.

ANDORRA (65,000). The official language is Catalan, the native language of about 25 percent of the population. Spanish is spoken by about 30,000 people, Portuguese by 7,000, French by 5,000.

ANGOLA (11 million). The official language is Portuguese. The most important native language is Mbundu, a term that actually embraces two languages: Umbundu, with about 4 million speakers in central Angola, and Kimbundu, with about 2½ million speakers in the north. Kongo is spoken by about 1½ million people in the far north, Chokwe by about 500,000 people in the northeast, and Lwena (Luvale) by about 400,000 people in the eastern panhandle. Lunda, closely related to Chokwe, is spoken by about 100,000 people in the northeast.

ANTIGUA AND BARBUDA (75,000). English is the official language, but much of the population speaks an English creole.

ARGENTINA (35 million). Spanish is the official language, spoken by virtually the entire population. Italian speakers number about 500,000, German speakers 300,000, and Yiddish speakers 100,000. Toba, an Indian language, is spoken by about 20,000 people in the far north near the border with Paraguay.

ARMENIA (3½ million). Armenian is spoken by virtually the entire population. The dwindling Russian-speaking community is now down to only 10,000 people.

AUSTRALIA (20 million). English is spoken by everyone except for the aborigines, of whom about 30,000 speak one of 150 different languages.

These include Aranda (Arrernte) and Warlpiri, each with about 3,000 speakers in Northern Territory. In Western Australia there are Pitjantjatjara (2,000 speakers) and Walmajarri (1,000). In the far north, on the Torres Strait islands and also in Townsville, Queensland, about 3,000 people speak Kala Yagaw Ya.

AUSTRIA (8 million). German is spoken by virtually the entire population. There are about 150,000 speakers of Croatian, while in the southern province of Carinthia about 20,000 people speak Slovenian.

AZERBAIJAN (8 million). Azerbaijani is spoken by about 90 percent of the population, or close to 7 million people. The dwindling Russian- and Armenian-speaking communities are now down to about 150,000 each. There are also about 150,000 speakers of Lezgin.

BAHAMAS (300,000). English is the official language, but much of the population speaks an English creole.

BAHRAIN (600,000). Arabic is spoken by at least 80 percent of the population. Immigrant workers from Iran, India, and Pakistan speak Persian, Urdu and Punjabi.

BANGLADESH (125 million). Bengali is spoken by the vast majority of the population.

BARBADOS (250,000). English, the official language, is spoken by the entire population. However, in everyday speech the people generally revert to an English creole known as Bajan.

BELARUS (10 million). Belorussian is spoken by about two-thirds of the population. The remaining one-third speak Russian, which remains the principal working language of the country.

BELGIUM (10 million). Flemish, spoken in the north (the area known as Flanders), and French, spoken in the south (Wallonia), are Belgium's two official languages. The dividing line passes just south of Brussels, though Brussels itself is French-speaking. Flemish is native to about 6 million people and French to about 3½ million, with about one million Belgians bilingual. Near the German border about 100,000 people speak German.

BELIZE (250,000). English, the official language, is spoken by about three-fourths of the population, many of whom also speak an English creole. Spanish is the mother tongue of about 25 percent, many of whom speak English as well. Maya, or Yucatec, is spoken by about 15,000 people in the northern third of the country, while Kekchi, also of the Mayan family, has about 10,000 speakers in a small area of the southwest. About 15,000 people speak Black Carib, a language of the Arawakan family.

BENIN (6 million). The official language is French. Fon is the most important native language, with about 2½ million speakers in the southern half of the country. Yoruba is spoken by about 750,000 people along the eastern border, Bariba by about 500,000 people in the north.

BHUTAN (1½ million). The national language is known as Jonkha. It is based on a dialect of Tibetan and is written in the Tibetan script. Nepali is spoken in the southwest.

BOLIVIA (8 million). This country has the highest percentage of Indians of any in the hemisphere. Spanish, the official language, is the mother tongue of less than half the population. The two major Indian languages are Quechua, with about 2 million speakers, and Aymara, with about 1½ million, both of the Andean highlands. Guarani is spoken by about 50,000 people in the south. A minor language is Chiquitano, with about 20,000 speakers in Santa Cruz State.

BOSNIA AND HERZEGOVINA (4 million). The language spoken here is a form of Serbo-Croatian, officially known as Bosnian.

BOTSWANA (1½ million). The official language is English, but Tswana is spoken by nearly three-fourths of the population. Shona is spoken by about 200,000 people in the east. There are about 50,000 Bushman speakers in the west.

BRAZIL (165 million). Portuguese is spoken by the vast majority of the population. However, there are sizable colonies of speakers of German, Italian, and Japanese. Brazil's 200,000 Indians speak more than 100 different languages. Guarani is spoken by about 50,000 people in the southwest, Ticuna by about 25,000 people in the north, Kaingang by about 20,000 in the four southernmost provinces, Guajajara by about 10,000 in Maranhão state in the north, and Chavante by about 7,000 people in the state of Minas Gerais in the southeast.

BRUNEI (300,000). The official language is Malay, with about 250,000 speakers, but English is also widely spoken. There are also some speakers of Chinese.

BULGARIA (8 million). Bulgarian is spoken by about 90 percent of the population. The Turkish-speaking minority numbers about 750,000.

BURKINA FASO (12 million). The official language is French. The most important native language is Mossi (Moré), with about 6 million speakers. Other languages include Fulani (one million), Gurma (600,000), Dyula and Senufo (250,000 each), and Tuareg, or Tamashek (100,000).

BURMA (50 million). Burmese is spoken by about two-thirds of the population. Two other important languages are Shan, with about 4 million speakers in Shan State, east of Mandalay, and Karen, with about 3 million speakers in the south. Mon, once a major language of the region, now has about one million speakers in the panhandle near the city of Moulmein. Chin (one million) is spoken in the Chin Hills bordering southern Assam, India, while Arakanese (one million) is spoken in the southwest. Other languages include Kachin, or Chingpaw (500,000) of the extreme north, Palaung (350,000) of Shan State, and Wa, or Kawa (50,000), spoken along the Salween River as it enters Burma from China.

BURUNDI (6 million). Rundi is spoken by the entire population. It is co-official with French. Swahili serves as a commercial language.

CAMBODIA (12 million). The national language is Khmer, spoken by about 90 percent of the population. Chinese and Vietnamese are each spoken by about 500,000 people. Among native languages, Cham is the most important, with about 250,000 speakers.

CAMEROON (15 million). French and English are both official. Native languages number well over 100. Bantu languages predominate in the south, the most important being the closely related Fang, Bulu, and Ewondo (Yaoundé) languages, with a total of 3 million speakers. In the north the principal language is Fulani, with about 1½ million speakers. Also in the Bantu family is Duala (1½ million), spoken in and around the city of the same name. Mbum (200,000) is spoken in the central regions. A variety of Pidgin English is widely spoken along the coast.

CANADA (30 million). English and French are the two official languages. English is the mother tongue of approximately 18 million Canadians, French of approximately 7 million. Nearly 6 million of the 7 million French speakers live in the province of Quebec, where they outnumber speakers of English by eight to one. More than 5 million Canadians are bilingual, speaking both English and French with equal, or nearly equal, facility.

Some 5 million Canadians claim another language as their mother tongue. In the 1996 census Chinese was listed as the mother tongue of 736,000 people, Italian of 514,000, German of 470,000, Spanish of 228,000, Portuguese of 222,000, Polish of 222,000, Punjabi of 214,000,

Ukrainian of 175,000, Arabic of 166,000, and Tagalog of 158,000. Some of these numbers have increased significantly since then.

Many Indian languages are also spoken in Canada. The two most important are Cree (75,000 speakers) and Ojibwa, or Chippewa (25,000), both spoken mainly in central Canada. In eastern Canada there is Montagnais, spoken by about 8,000 people along the northern shore of the St. Lawrence River, Micmac, by about 7,000 mainly in Nova Scotia, and Algonquin, by about 2,000 in southwestern Quebec and adjacent areas of Ontario. Malecite, or Maliseet, is spoken by about 600 people in New Brunswick, Naskapi, closely related to Montagnais, by about 400 in Labrador, and Mohawk by about 300 in Quebec and Ontario.

In the Prairie Provinces there is also Sioux with about 4,000 speakers. Blackfoot (3,500) is spoken entirely in Alberta. Chipewyan (1,500) is spoken in the Prairie Provinces and also in the Northwest Territories. In the Northwest Territories there are also Dogrib (2,000), spoken in the area between the Great Slave and Great Bear lakes, and South Slave (2,000) and North Slave, or Hare (300), in the area west of these lakes. To the far north, in Yukon Territory, there is Gwich'in (400), with some additional speakers across the border in northeastern Alaska.

British Columbia has a large number of Indian languages, all with fewer than 2,000 speakers. Carrier (1,500) is spoken along the Fraser River, as are Shuswap (750) and Thompson (600). Chilcotin (700) is spoken along a river of the same name. Tsimshian, spoken in northern British Columbia, refers to a small group of three languages – Gitksan (1,200 speakers), Nishga (800), and Tsimshian proper (500). Nootka (600) is spoken on Vancouver Island, and Haida (250) on the Queen Charlotte Islands.

Canada's Eskimos, or Inuit, number about 25,000. Their language is known here as Inuktitut. About 18,000 live in the Northwest Territories and the new territory of Nunavut, the rest in northern Quebec.

CAPE VERDE (400,000). The official language is Portuguese. Most of the population speaks a Portuguese creole called Crioulo, which varies considerably from island to island.

CENTRAL AFRICAN REPUBLIC (3 million). The official language is French. Sango, originally the language of a single tribe living on the banks of the Ubangi River, has become the lingua franca of most of the country. Gbaya is an important language of the west, Banda of the central and eastern regions. Each has about 800,000 speakers.

CHAD (8 million). The official languages are French and Arabic. The most widespread native language is Sara, with about 2 million speakers in the southern half of the country. Arabic, spoken mainly in the north, has about one million. Maba is spoken by about 400,000 people in the area of the east known as Wadai, and Teda (Tibbu) by about 300,000 people in the northeastern desert.

CHILE (15 million). Spanish is spoken by the great majority of the population. There is one important Indian language: Araucanian, spoken by about 1½ million people in the area between Concepción and Valdivia.

CHINA (1¼ billion). All but about 100 million people in China, some 92 percent of the population, speak one or another of the dialects of Chinese. Of these, close to 75 percent, or nearly 900 million, speak the Mandarin dialect of the north. For a discussion of the other Chinese dialects see page 205.

Of China's many ethnic minorities the largest is the Chuang (Zhuang), who number about 15 million. Their language, which belongs to the Tai family, is spoken primarily in the Kwangsi Chuang (Guangxi Zhuang) Autonomous Region, which extends to the Gulf of Tonkin. Other major groups are the Uigurs (8 million), of the Sinkiang (Xinjiang) Uigur Autonomous Region, northwest China, who speak a Turkic language; the Miao (8 million), residing mainly in Kweichow (Guizhou) Province, south-central China, whose language belongs to a separate branch of the Sino-Tibetan family; the Yi, or Lolo (7 million), whose language, of the Tibeto-Burman family, is spoken in Yunnan Province, which borders the countries of Southeast Asia; and the Tujia (6 million), also Tibeto-Burman, of Hunan, Kweichow, and Hupei (Hubei). Other languages include Puyi, or Chungchia (2½ million), of Kweichow, which is of the Tai family; Dong, or Tung (3 million), a Tai language spoken in Kweichow and Kwangsi; Yao (2 million), related to the above-mentioned Miao, spoken in southeastern China; Bai (1½ million), a Tibeto-Burman language of northern Yunnan; Dai (one million), a Tai language of Yunnan; and Li (one million), a Tai language spoken on Hainan Island. Four languages of other countries are spoken by more than a million people in China: Tibetan (5 million), Mongolian (5 million), Korean (2 million), and Kazakh (one million).

Languages whose speakers in China number less than one million include:

(1) Lisu (500,000), a Tibeto-Burman language spoken in Yunnan;
(2) Wa, or Kawa (250,000), a Mon-Khmer language spoken in the Chinese-Burmese border area;
(3) Nung (170,000), a Tai language spoken in southeastern Yunnan near the border with Vietnam;
(4) three Tibeto-Burman languages spoken in Yunnan: Lahu (400,000), Naxi, or Moso (280,000), and Kachin, or Chingpaw (100,000), which is also spoken in Burma.

Among the many languages with fewer than 100,000 speakers there are Salar (75,000), a Turkic language of Tsinghai (Qinghai) Province in north-central China, and three Tungusic languages: Sibo (40,000), spoken in western Sinkiang near the border with Kazakhstan, Evenki (15,000), spoken in a number of settlements in northern China, and Hezhen (2,000), spoken in northeasternmost China near the Russian city of Khabarovsk. Evenki and Hezhen are also spoken in Russia, where the latter is known as Nanai.

COLOMBIA (40 million). Spanish is spoken by the vast majority of the population. The most widely spoken Indian language is Goajiro, of the Arawakan family, with about 100,000 speakers on the Guajira Peninsula on the Caribbean coast. Paez is spoken by about 50,000 people near the town of Popayán in the southwest.

CONGO (Brazzaville) (2½ million). The official language is French. The most important native languages are Lingala, of the north, and Kongo, of the south, each with about one million speakers. In the south Monokutuba, a creole language based on Kongo and close to Kituba of Congo-Kinshasa, serves as the lingua franca.

CONGO (Kinshasa) (50 million). The official language is French. The most important native languages are Luba, of the southeast (10 million speakers), Kongo, of the west (8 million), and Mongo, of the central regions (6 million). Others include Ruanda (5 million), of the east; Ngala (3 million), of the north; Zande (3 million), near the border with Sudan; Rundi (2 million), of the east; Chokwe (one million), of the southwest; and Mangbetu (750,000), of the north. Three languages serve as lingua francas throughout much of the country, with many people speaking more than one of them. Lingala, of the north, and Kingwana, a dialect of Swahili, of the east, are each spoken by at least half the population. And Kongo is spoken as a second language by another 8 million people in the west. Kituba, a creole language based on Kongo, is spoken in the westernmost part of the country near the mouth of the Congo River.

COSTA RICA (3½ million). Spanish is spoken by the vast majority of the population. Two Indian languages spoken here are Bribri, with about 6,000 speakers, and Cabecar, with about 4,000.

CÔTE D'IVOIRE. *See* Ivory Coast.

CROATIA (4½ million). Serbo-Croatian is spoken by the vast majority of the population, though the 4 million Croats may be said to speak Croatian, while the 500,000 Serbs may be said to speak Serbian.

CUBA (11 million). Spanish is spoken by almost everyone.

CYPRUS (750,000). Greek and Turkish are this island's two languages, the former with about 600,000 speakers, the latter with about 150,000, mostly in the northern third of the country.

CZECH REPUBLIC (10 million). Czech is spoken by virtually the entire population.

DENMARK (5 million). Danish is spoken by virtually everyone.

DJIBOUTI (500,000). The two principal languages here are Somali (250,000 speakers), of the Issa tribe, and Afar (200,000 speakers). The official languages are French and Arabic.

DOMINICA (75,000). On this island nation, lying between French-speaking Guadeloupe and Martinique, the official language (English) is spoken by most of the population. But in everyday speech the people generally revert to a French creole which they themselves call French patois.

DOMINICAN REPUBLIC (8 million). Spanish is spoken by virtually the entire population.

ECUADOR (12 million). The official language is Spanish. Quechua is the most important Indian language with about 750,000 speakers. Another Indian language is Jivaro (Shuar), with about 30,000 speakers.

EGYPT (65 million). Arabic is spoken by virtually the entire population.

EL SALVADOR (6 million). Spanish is spoken by the vast majority of the population.

EQUATORIAL GUINEA (500,000). The official languages are Spanish and (since 1997) French. In the mainland province of Río Muni (population 400,000) the principal language is Fang. On the island of Fernando Poó, or Bioko (population 100,000), the natives, who number about 40,000, speak Bubi. Much of the rest of the population consists of workers and settlers from Nigeria and Cameroon.

ERITREA (4 million). The two major languages here are Tigrinya, with about 2 million speakers, and Tigre, with about one million. Others include Afar (150,000) and Beja (125,000).

ESTONIA (1½ million). The native language, Estonian, is spoken by about two-thirds of the population, or one million people. The Russian-speaking population of 300,000 is concentrated most heavily in the east, though many Russians live in the major cities.

ETHIOPIA (65 million). Amharic, the national language, is the mother tongue of about 20 million Ethiopians but is spoken as a second language by perhaps 30 million others. Tigrinya (4 million speakers) is spoken in the northern province of Tigray, Gurage (3 million) southwest of Addis Ababa, and Harari (50,000) in the city of Harar. All of these languages are of the Semitic family and are descended from Ge'ez, the classical literary language of Ethiopia.

The other major languages are mainly of the Cushitic family. The most important is Oromo (20 million speakers), spoken to the west, south, and east of Addis Ababa. Sidamo (5 million) is spoken in the south, Somali (4 million) in the southeast, Afar (one million) in the northeast, and Hadiyya (one million) southwest of Addis Ababa. Another language of the south is Wolaytta (3 million speakers), which belongs to a separate group called the Omotic languages.

English is widely spoken in official circles, while Arabic and Italian are understood in a number of places.

FIJI (800,000). The indigenous language, Fijian, is spoken by only about half the population. The rest, mainly of Indian descent, speak Hindi. Much of the population also speaks English, which is the official language.

FINLAND (5 million). Finnish is spoken by over 90 percent of the population. There are about 300,000 Swedish speakers on the southwestern and southern coasts and on the Åland Islands in the Baltic Sea. Of Finland's 2,500 Lapps, about 2,000 speak the Lappish language.

FRANCE (60 million). French is the national language. In southeastern France, the region known historically as Provence, perhaps a million people speak Provençal in addition to French. Near the German border, in the region formerly known as Alsace-Lorraine, there are about one million speakers of German. In Brittany about 200,000 people speak Breton. Along the border with Spain there are 250,000 speakers of Catalan in an area near the eastern end, and 100,000 speakers of Basque in an area near the western end. On Corsica a dialect of Italian is spoken.

FRENCH GUIANA (175,000). French is the official language, but the majority speak a French creole.

GABON (1 million). The official language is French. About 40 Bantu languages are spoken, the most important being Fang, of the northwest, with about 400,000 speakers.

GAMBIA (1 million). The official language is English. Native languages include Malinke (400,000 speakers), Fulani (200,000), Wolof (150,000), and Dyola and Soninke (100,000 each).

GEORGIA (5 million). Georgian is spoken by about 80 percent of the population, or close to 4 million people. Armenian speakers number about 400,000, Azerbaijani speakers about 300,000, and Russian speakers about 150,000. About 125,000 speakers of Ossetian live in the South Ossetian Autonomous Region, in the north-central part of the country. In the extreme northwest there are about 100,000 speakers of Abkhazian.

GERMANY (80 million). German is the national language. The largest ethnic minority is now the Turks, numbering about 2 million and still speaking Turkish at home. Other émigré communities speak Italian, Greek, Serbo-Croatian, Polish, Russian, and Kurdish. Sorbian (Lusatian), a Slavic language, is spoken by about 50,000 people in the easternmost part of the county near the border with Poland and the Czech Republic. In the far north, near the border with Denmark, about 10,000 people speak Frisian.

GHANA (20 million). The official language is English. The most important native language is Akan, spoken by as many as 10 million people in the southern part of the country. Ewe has about 2 million speakers in the east, between the Volta River and the border with Togo. Closely-related Ga and Adangme are spoken by about 1½ million people in the south-eastern corner of the country. The two main languages of the north are Dagomba (Dagbane) with about two million speakers, and Gurma with about 500,000. As many as 10 million Ghanaians also have a working knowledge of Hausa.

GIBRALTAR (30,000). The official language is English. The permanent residents speak mainly Spanish, but most of them know English as well.

GREAT BRITAIN. *See* United Kingdom.

GREECE (10 million). Greek is spoken by virtually the entire population. Minority languages include Turkish (100,000 speakers), Macedonian (50,000), and Albanian (50,000).

GREENLAND (60,000). Eskimo, known here as Greenlandic, is the official language and is spoken by the great majority of the population. The 7,000 Danes in Greenland speak Danish.

GRENADA (100,000). English is the official language, but much of the population speaks an English creole.

GUATEMALA (12 million). The official language is Spanish. Indians, who constitute about 40 percent of the population, speak more than a dozen different languages of the Mayan family. The big four are Quiché (1¼ million speakers), Cakchiquel (one million), Kekchi (500,000), and Mam (300,000). About 25,000 people speak Black Carib, a language of the Arawakan family.

GUINEA (8 million). The official language is French. The major African languages are Fulani (3 million speakers), in central Guinea; Malinke (1½ million), in the north; and Susu (one million), in the southwest. Kissi (500,000) and Loma (250,000) are spoken near the border with Liberia and Sierra Leone.

GUINEA-BISSAU (1 million). The official language is Portuguese. Native languages include Balante (300,000 speakers), Fulani (250,000), and Malinke (100,000). A Portuguese creole called Crioulo serves as the lingua franca.

GUYANA (750,000). The official language is English. It is rapidly replacing Hindi and Tamil as the language of the large East Indian population. Virtually everyone also speaks a local English creole. There are about 2,000 speakers of Arawak.

HAITI (7 million). The language of everyday speech here is a French creole, generally referred to as Haitian Creole. It is co-official with French.

HONDURAS (6 million). Spanish is spoken by the vast majority of the population. There are about 75,000 speakers of Black Carib, an Indian language of the Arawakan family. Miskito, or Mosquito, is spoken by about 10,000 people along the eastern coast. On the Bahía (Bay) Islands off the coast the predominant language is English.

HUNGARY (10 million). Hungarian is spoken by virtually the entire population. There are some speakers of Romany, the Gypsy language.

ICELAND (275,000). Icelandic is the official and universal language.

INDIA (one billion). With twelve major languages and perhaps 150 lesser ones, India is probably the most linguistically diverse country in the world.

The most widely spoken language is Hindi, with about 400 million speakers in the north-central part of the country. To this may be added Urdu, which it closely resembles, with another 50 million. The two other most important languages of northern and central India are Bengali, spoken in West Bengal (80 million speakers), and Marathi, spoken in

Maharashtra (75 million). After that come Gujarati, spoken in Gujarat (50 million), Oriya, in Orissa (35 million), Punjabi, in the Punjab (25 million), Bhojpuri, in Bihar (25 million), Rajasthani, a collection of dialects spoken in Rajasthan (15 million), Assamese, in Assam (15 million), Maithili and Magahi, of Bihar (10 million each), Bhili, in west-central India (6 million), Sindhi, in western India (2½ million), Nepali, in West Bengal (2½ million), and Garhwali and Kumauni, in Uttar Pradesh (2 million each). All the above languages are descended from Sanskrit, and thus of the Indo-European family.

The southern third of India is the home of the Dravidian languages, totally unrelated to those of the north. The four major languages of this family are Telugu, spoken in Andhra Pradesh (75 million speakers), Tamil, in Tamil Nadu (65 million), Kannada, or Kanarese, in Karnataka (40 million), and Malayalam, in Kerala (35 million). Other Dravidian languages are Gondi (2½ million), Kurukh, or Oraon (1½ million), and Kui (500,000), all spoken in central India, and Tulu (1½ million), spoken in Karnataka.

A third group of languages, called the Munda languages, is spoken in scattered areas of northern and central India. The most important of these is Santali, with about 6 million speakers. Others are Mundari (one million), Ho (one million), Korku (500,000), and Savara, or Sora (300,000). The Tibeto-Burman family is represented by a great number of languages in the state of Assam: Meithei (1½ million), spoken in Manipur; Bodo (1½ million), spoken north of the Brahmaputra River; Garo (750,000), spoken in the Garo Hills; and Lushei (500,000), spoken in the southernmost districts. Finally, there is one Mon-Khmer language in India: Khasi, with about one million speakers in the Khasi Hills, west of the city of Shillong.

A major element in the Indian linguistic picture is a non-Indian language, English. Though understood by only a small percentage of the population, it is still the most likely means of communication between people from different parts of the country. Although the Indian constitution provided that Hindi would become the official language of India in 1965, it was decided in that year that English would continue for the time being as "associate official language."

INDONESIA (225 million). Indonesian is the national language. Though it is the native tongue of only 25 million people, it is spoken or understood by as much as three-fourths of the population. Other major languages are Javanese, spoken in central and eastern Java (80 million speakers), Sundanese, spoken in western Java (30 million), and Madurese, spoken on Java and also on the island of Madura (10 million). The large island of Sumatra has a number of important languages: Minangkabau (5 million), Batak (4 million), Aceh, or Achinese (3 million), Lampung (1½ million), and Rejang (one million). On Celebes (Sulawesi) there are

Buginese (4 million) and Makassar (2 million); on Bali there is Balinese (3 million); on Lombok there is Sasak (2 million); on Timor, Timorese (750,000); and in East Timor, Tetun (500,000). On Borneo (Kalimantan) there is Banjarese (3 million speakers), but the Dayak peoples, who number about one million, speak Sea Dayak, or Iban, and Land Dayak, the latter term also referring to a cluster of related languages. In Irian Jaya (formerly West Irian) on the island of New Guinea some fifty languages of the Papuan family are spoken. The most important is Dani, with about 250,000 speakers in the central highlands. Asmat is spoken by about 50,000 people on the southern coast.

IRAN (65 million). The national language is Persian, with more than 40 million speakers. In the province of Azerbaijan in the northwest there are about 10 million speakers of Azerbaijani. In the southwest about 3 million people speak Luri. Along the shores of the Caspian Sea there are Gilaki (3 million speakers) and Mazanderani (2 million). Kurdish-speaking Kurds number about 5 million. Baluchi is spoken by about one million people in the extreme southeast, near the border with Pakistan. Other languages include Arabic (one million), Turkmen (one million), Armenian (250,000), and Assyrian (100,000).

IRAQ (20 million). The national language is Arabic. There is a sizable Kurdish-speaking minority in the north, numbering about 4 million. Azerbaijani is spoken by about 250,000 people, Assyrian by 150,000, Armenian by 100,000.

IRELAND (3½ million). English and Irish (Gaelic) are the two official languages. The latter, however, is spoken by less than one-third of the population, all of whom speak English as well.

ISRAEL (6 million). The native-born citizens of Israel speak Hebrew. The many immigrants to the country speak a number of different languages (Russian, English, Polish, Romanian, Yiddish, German, Persian, Ladino, etc.), but most have mastered Hebrew, to some degree, since their arrival in Israel. Arabic, which is co-official with Hebrew, is spoken by the Arab minority of one million.

ITALY (60 million). Italian is the national language. In the region of Alto Adige, bordering Austria, German is spoken by about 300,000 people and is co-official with Italian. French is spoken by about 300,000 people in the region of Aosta in the northwest. In the extreme northeast, near the border with Austria and Slovenia, there are about 700,000 speakers of Friulian, a Rhaeto-Romanic dialect, and about 100,000 speakers of Slovenian. Another Rhaeto-Romanic dialect, Ladin, is spoken by about 30,000 people in eastern Alto Adige. In southern Italy there is an

Albanian minority of about 100,000, as well as about 25,000 speakers of Greek. On Sardinia about 1½ million people speak Sardinian.

IVORY COAST (15 million). The official language is French, spoken at least as a second language by more than half the population. More than 50 native languages are spoken here. Among the more important are the closely related Agni (Anyi) and Baule languages, with about 4 million speakers, mainly in the southeast. Dyula and Senufo are spoken in the north, Malinke in the northwest. and Bete in the southwest. Fully one-fourth of Ivory Coast's population are immigrants from other countries.

JAMAICA (2½ million). The official language is English. Much of the population, however, speaks a creole language generally referred to as Jamaican English.

JAPAN (125 million). Japanese is the national language. There are about 700,000 speakers of Korean. Ainu, apparently unrelated to any other language in the world, is now spoken by only a handful of people on Hokkaido and appears on the verge of extinction.

JORDAN (5 million). Arabic is spoken by virtually the entire population.

KAZAKHSTAN (15 million). The official language, Kazakh, is spoken by just over half the population, or about 8 million people. Russian, with about 5 million speakers, is the main language of Almaty, the largest city, and also of the northeastern part of the country. Other languages are Ukrainian (750,000), German (500,000), Uzbek (350,000), Tatar (300,000), and Uigur (150,000).

KENYA (30 million). The official language, Swahili, is spoken over much of the country, though usually as a second language. English is also widely used, especially for commercial purposes. Other major Bantu languages are Kikuyu, with about 6 million speakers just to the north of Nairobi; Luyia, with about 4 million speakers in the area adjacent to Lake Victoria; Kamba, with about 3 million speakers in the southeastern part of the country; Gusii or Kisii (2 million), in the southwest; and Meru (1½ million), in the east. Luo, a Nilotic language, is spoken by about 4 million people in the area adjacent to Lake Victoria. In a second branch of the Nilotic family there are Masai, with about 500,000 speakers along the border with Tanzania, and Turkana, with a like number in the northwestern corner of the country. In a third branch there are Kalenjin, with about 3 million speakers in west-central Kenya, and Suk (Pokot), with 100,000 speakers to the north, along the border with Uganda. Two Cushitic languages are spoken in the east and northeast: Somali, with about 300,000 speakers, and Oromo, with 100,000.

KIRIBATI (100,000). The language spoken in this new country (which includes the former Gilbert, Phoenix, and Line Islands) is Gilbertese. It is also known as Kiribati. The official language is English.

KOREA (70 million). Korean is the official and universal language in both South and North Korea.

KUWAIT (2 million). Arabic is spoken here.

KYRGYZSTAN (5 million). The official language, Kyrgyz, is spoken by close to two-thirds of the population, or more than 3 million people. Second place now goes to Uzbek, with 650,000 speakers. Russian ranks third with 600,000.

LAOS (5 million). Lao is spoken by about 80 percent of the population. Tribal languages include Miao, or Hmong, with about 200,000 speakers, and Yao, or Mien, with about 100,000. There are also some speakers of Vietnamese and Chinese. French is widely spoken in official circles.

LATVIA (2½ million). The native language, Latvian, is spoken by about 1,350,000 people, just over half the population. Russian speakers number about 750,000. There are also some speakers of Belorussian, Ukrainian, and Polish.

LEBANON (3½ million). Arabic is the official and dominant language, though French is also widely spoken. Armenian speakers number about 200,000. There are also about 15,000 speakers of Assyrian.

LESOTHO (2 million). Sotho is spoken by virtually the entire population. It is co-official with English.

LIBERIA (3 million). The official language is English. Of the native languages the most important is Kpelle, with about 750,000 speakers. Vai, with a script of its own dating back to the early 19th century, is spoken along the coast at the western end of the country. Also on the coast are Bassa, in central Liberia, and Grebo, in the southeastern corner. Kissi and Loma are spoken in the north, near the border with Guinea and Sierra Leone. A variety of Pidgin English serves as a lingua franca.

LIBYA (5 million). Arabic is spoken by the great majority of the population. There are some speakers of Tuareg (Tamashek) in the west.

LIECHTENSTEIN (30,000). German is spoken here.

LITHUANIA (3½ million). The native language, Lithuanian, is spoken by about 80 percent of the population. Russian speakers number about 300,000, Polish speakers about 250,000. There are also some speakers of Belorussian and Ukrainian.

LUXEMBOURG (400,000). The language of everyday speech here is Luxembourgian, but most of the population speaks French and German as well. While there is no "official" language, French is used for government documents and pronouncements.

MACEDONIA (2 million). Macedonian is spoken by about two-thirds of the population. There is a large Albanian-speaking minority of about 500,000, concentrated mainly in the west. Turkish, Serbo-Croatian, Bulgarian, and Greek are also spoken.

MADAGASCAR (15 million). Malagasy is spoken by virtually the entire native population. It is co-official with French.

MALAWI (10 million). Nyanja, known as Chewa in Malawi, is the most important language, with over 6 million speakers. It is co-official with English. Other languages include Lomwe (2 million), spoken in the south, Yao, with about one million speakers along the southern shore of Lake Nyasa, and Tumbuka, with about 500,000 speakers in the north.

MALAYSIA (20 million). The official language is Malay, spoken by about 10 million people. Chinese ranks second, with about 5 million, and Tamil third, with about one million. Malay and Chinese are also spoken in Sarawak and Sabah, but a number of languages are spoken by the Dayak peoples there. Sea Dayak, or Iban, has about 500,000 speakers; Land Dayak, spoken in southern Sarawak, has about 100,000.

MALDIVES (300,000). The language spoken here is Maldivian, an offshoot of Sinhalese. Locally it is known as Divehi.

MALI (10 million). The official language is French. Bambara is the most important native language, with about 3 million speakers in the eastern part of the southern portion of the country. Senufo (one million) is spoken in the south, near the border with Ivory Coast. Fulani (one million), Soninke (one million), and Malinke (700,000) are spoken in the west. Songhai has about one million speakers in the area near the town of Timbuktu. Tuareg, or Tamashek, a Berber language, is spoken by about 750,000 people in the eastern regions. Dyula (300,000) is spoken in the south.

MALTA (400,000). The native language is Maltese, though most people speak English as well. Both are official languages.

MARSHALL ISLANDS (65,000). The language spoken here is Marshallese. It is co-official with English.

MAURITANIA (2½ million). The official language is Arabic, spoken by about 85 percent of the population. The other languages, mainly of the south, are Wolof and Fulani, each with about 150,000 speakers, and Soninke, with about 100,000.

MAURITIUS (1 million). This racially diverse island presents a wide variety of languages. A French creole is the mother tongue of about 300,000 people; it is also the principal spoken language of 300,000 more and serves as the lingua franca for much of the country. Of the 700,000 people of Indian origin, about 30 percent speak Hindi, 30 percent Bhojpuri, 10 percent Urdu, 5 percent Tamil, the rest mainly French Creole. French speakers number about 50,000, Chinese about 15,000. The official language is English, but it is spoken very little.

MEXICO (100 million). Spanish, the official language, is spoken by the vast majority of the population. Speakers of Indian languages number about 8 million (three-fourths of whom also speak Spanish), most of them in the southern part of the country. The most important Indian language is Nahuatl, with about 1½ million speakers in the area north, east, and south of Mexico City. Second place goes to Maya, or Yucatec, with about one million speakers on the Yucatán Peninsula. In the state of Chiapas other Mayan languages are spoken: Tzeltal (400,000 speakers), Tzotzil (350,000), Chol (150,000), and Zoque (50,000), while in Tabasco there is Chontal (50,000). In Oaxaca there are Zapotec (500,000), Mixtec (500,000), Mazatec (200,000), Mixe (150,000), and Chinantec (150,000). Other languages include Otomi, spoken chiefly in México and Hidalgo (400,000); Totonac, of Veracruz and Puebla (300,000); Mazahua, of México (200,000); Huastec, of Veracruz and San Luis Potosí (150,000); and Tarasco, of Michoacán (100,000). In northern Mexico the most important Indian languages are Tarahumara, of Chihuahua, and Mayo, of Sonora and Sinaloa, each with about 50,000 speakers.

MICRONESIA (100,000). Each of the four main islands of this new country (the former Caroline Islands) has its own language. On Yap, farthest to the west, and the surrounding islands, the 10,000 people speak Yapese. On Truk, now known as Chuuk, the population of about 50,000 speaks Trukese. On Ponape, now known as Pohnpei, there are about 30,000 speakers of Ponapean. And on Kosrae the 8,000 inhabitants speak Kosraean. The official language is English.

MOLDOVA (4½ million). The official language is Moldovan, spoken by about 3 million people. Russian speakers, the majority of whom live east of the Dniester River, number about 500,000. There are also about 250,000 speakers of Ukrainian. In the southwest about 100,000 people speak Gagauz, a Turkic language.

MONACO (30,000). French is the major language, though there is also an Italian-speaking minority.

MONGOLIA (2½ million). Mongolian is spoken by the vast majority of the population. There are about 100,000 speakers of Kazakh in the west.

MOROCCO (30 million). Arabic, the official language, is spoken by about three-fourths of the population. The 7 million Berbers speak a number of different languages. Tachelhit, of the south, and Tamazight, of the central regions, each has about 3 million speakers. Riff is spoken by about one million people in the north. French and Spanish are widely spoken, the latter principally in the former Spanish zone.

MOZAMBIQUE (20 million). The official language is Portuguese. The most important native languages are Makua, of the north (5 million speakers), Tsonga, of the south (2½ million), Lomwe, of the north (1½ million), and Sena, of the central provinces (1½ million). Numbering about one million speakers are Shona, in the provinces bordering Zimbabwe; Tswa, of the coastal province of Inhambane in the south; and Chuabo, of the central coastal area. Other languages with roughly 500,000 speakers are Ronga, of the extreme south near the capital of Maputo; Nyungwe, along the Zambezi River; and Marendje, Nyanja, Makonde, and Yao, all of the north in the provinces bordering Tanzania.

MYANMAR. *See* Burma.

NAMIBIA (1½ million). The official language is English. The most important native language is Ambo, spoken by the 850,000 Ovambos of the northern part of the country. Herero is spoken by about 150,000 people in the east and central regions. Two languages of the Khoisan family are spoken in Namibia: Hottentot, or Nama, with about 200,000 speakers, and Bushman, or San, with about 25,000. Among the whites about 50,000 speak Afrikaans, 30,000 speak English, and 15,000 speak German.

NAURU (10,000). On this small island nation, just to the west of the Gilbert Islands, the principal language is Nauruan. There are also some speakers of Gilbertese.

NEPAL (25 million). The official language is Nepali, the mother tongue of about 15 million people in Nepal, with an additional 2 million speaking it as a second language. Maithili is spoken by about 3 million people, Bhojpuri by 1½ million. In the Katmandu Valley there are some one million speakers of Newari. Over one million Nepalese speak Tibetan as a second language.

NETHERLANDS (15 million). Dutch is spoken by the entire population. In the northern province of Friesland about 400,000 people speak Frisian in addition to Dutch.

NETHERLANDS ANTILLES (200,000). The official language is Dutch, but on the larger southern islands of Curaçao and Bonaire the language of everyday use is Papiamento.

NEW ZEALAND (4 million). English is spoken by the vast majority of the population. Maori, the language of New Zealand's indigenous inhabitants, the Maoris, is spoken by about 100,000 people. In 1987 it was made co-official with English.

NICARAGUA (5 million). Spanish is spoken by the vast majority of the population. Miskito, or Mosquito, an Indian language, is spoken by about 100,000 people along the eastern coast.

NIGER (10 million). The official language is French. The most important native language is Hausa, with about 5 million speakers in the central and southeastern parts of the country. Djerma (1½ million) is spoken in the southwest, in the area that includes Niamey, the capital. Fulani (one million) and Tuareg, or Tamashek (one million) are spoken in the north and central regions. Kanuri (500,000) is spoken in the south, Songhai (500,000) in the southwest, and Teda, or Tibbu (50,000) in the northeast.

NIGERIA (120 million). This, the most populous nation in Africa, also has the greatest number of languages (about 250), though only four account for over two-thirds of the population. Hausa, of the north, is the mother tongue of about 25 million people, but is spoken by over 50 million in all. Yoruba is spoken by about 25 million in the southwest, Ibo by about 20 million in the southeast, and Fulani by about 12 million also in the north. Other languages are Kanuri (5 million), of Borno State in the northeast; the closely related Efik and Ibibio languages (5 million), the former spoken in and around the town of Calabar in the southeast, the latter adjacent to it on the west; Edo (4 million) in Bendel (now Edo) State near Benin City; Tiv (2½ million), in Benue and Plateau states, central Nigeria; and Ijo, or Ijaw (2 million) in the Niger River delta.

357

Urhobo is spoken by about 500,000 people in Edo State south of Benin City, Nupe by 1½ million near the junction of the Niger and Kaduna rivers, and Idoma by 250,000 in Benue State. The official language is English.

NORWAY (4 million). Norwegian is spoken by virtually the entire population. Most of the country's 20,000 Lapps speak Lappish.

OMAN (2½ million). Arabic is spoken by the indigenous population, which, however, constitutes only 75 percent of the total. The rest are mainly Urdu speakers from India, Baluchi speakers from Pakistan, and Bengali speakers from Bangladesh.

PAKISTAN (150 million). The official language is Urdu. It is the mother tongue of only 10 million people but is spoken as a second language by as much as two-thirds of the population. The other major language is Punjabi, with about 75 million speakers. Sindhi is spoken by about 15 million people in the province of Sind, while Pashto is spoken by about 20 million in the North-West Frontier Province. In the province of Baluchistan in the southwest there are about 4 million speakers of Baluchi, an Iranian language, and 2 million speakers of Brahui, a Dravidian language.

PALAU (20,000). On this small island nation, lying due east of Mindanao in the Philippines, the native language is Palauan. It is co-official with English.

PANAMA (3 million). Spanish is the national language, though a number of minor Indian languages are also spoken. The two most important are Guaymi, with about 150,000 speakers in the northwest, and Cuna, with about 50,000 speakers on the islands of the San Blas Archipelago.

PAPUA NEW GUINEA (5 million). More than 500 languages are spoken here. The majority are of the Papuan family, though a number of Oceanic languages are spoken in the coastal areas and on the outlying islands. In New Guinea, the northern half of the country, the three most important languages are Enga (150,000 speakers) and Chimbu (75,000), each spoken in a province of the same name, and Hagen (75,000), spoken in Western Highlands Province. Kamano, of Eastern Highlands Province, and Wahgi, of Western Highlands Province, each has about 50,000 speakers. In Morobe Province on the Huon Peninsula there is Kâte, a Papuan language with 6,000 native speakers, and Yabim, an Oceanic language with 2,000, but each is used as a religious language for about 75,000 others.

In Papua, the southern half of the country, Orokaiva is spoken by about 25,000 people on the east coast, Toaripi by 25,000 on the west coast, and Motu by about 15,000 people in and around Port Moresby. On the island of New Britain Tolai is spoken by about 60,000 people. On the Admiralty Islands, north of New Guinea, some 30 Oceanic languages are spoken. On Bougainville, the westernmost of the Solomon Islands but part of Papua New Guinea, at least six different Oceanic languages are spoken.

The major lingua franca of Papua New Guinea is Tok Pisin, a variety of Pidgin English now spoken by as many as 3 million people. Hiri Motu (formerly known as Police Motu), a simplified form of Motu, is spoken by about 250,000. Both languages have official status in the country.

PARAGUAY (5 million). Spanish, the official language, is spoken by about 60 percent of the population, or 3 million people. Guarani, an Indian language, has about 2 million speakers, mostly in the rural areas. About half the country's population is bilingual.

PERU (25 million). The official language, Spanish, is spoken by about 80 percent of the population. Indian languages predominate in the highlands; Quechua, which is co-official with Spanish, has about 4 million speakers, Aymara about 500,000. Among minor languages, Aguaruna is spoken by about 25,000 people, Cocama by about 15,000, Shipibo by about 12,000, Ticuna by about 6,000.

PHILIPPINES (75 million). Tagalog, the language of southern Luzon (where the capital, Manila, is located), has been declared the national language and given the name of Pilipino. It is the mother tongue of about 20 million people, but is now spoken by about as much as three-fourths of the population. Also on Luzon are Ilocano, with about 6 million speakers in the far north, Bikol (4 million) on the Bikol peninsula at the southeastern end of the island, and Pampangan (2 million) and Pangasinan (1½ million), both spoken to the north and west of Manila. On the middle islands there are the three Visayan languages, Cebuano (15 million speakers), Hiligaynon (6 million), and Waray-Waray (Samaran) (3 million). Among the Moros, a Moslem people of the southern Philippines, there are Maranao and Maguindanao, each with about one million speakers on Mindanao, and Tausug, spoken by about 800,000 people on Jolo Island of the Sulu Archipelago, which extends close to Sabah, Malaysia. At least 40 million Filipinos speak English fluently as a second or third language.

POLAND (40 million). Polish is practically universal. Kashubian, considered by some a separate language, by others a dialect of Polish, is spoken by about 100,000 people in the province of Gdansk.

359

PORTUGAL (10 million). Portuguese is spoken almost universally.

PUERTO RICO (4 million). Spanish is spoken everywhere, but English is taught as a second language and is commonly heard in the cities.

QATAR (600,000). Arabic, the official language, is the mother tongue of less than half the population. The rest, immigrant workers from India and Pakistan, speak Urdu, Punjabi, Persian, and a number of other languages.

ROMANIA (22 million). Romanian is spoken by about 90 percent of the population. In Transylvania, the northwestern part of the country, the predominantly Hungarian population of 1½ million speaks Hungarian. Romania also has many Gypsies who speak the Romany language.

RUSSIA (145 million). Russian, the official language, is spoken by more than 85 percent of the population, or 125 million people. With the breakup of the Soviet Union, it is one of the few remaining Indo-European languages spoken in the country. Another is Ossetian, an Iranian language spoken by about 500,000 people in the Caucasus. Yiddish, historically the language of Russia's Jewish population, is rapidly dying out.

Four Finno-Ugric languages are spoken in central European Russia. Mordvin (750,000 speakers) is spoken in the republic of Mordovia; Udmurt (500,000) in the republic of Udmurtiya; Mari (500,000) in the republic of Mari-El; and Komi (350,000) in the Komi Republic. Two Ugric languages, of the family that includes Hungarian, are Khanty (15,000) and Mansi (4,000), both spoken in the Ob River basin of Western Siberia. Combining with the Finno-Ugric languages to form the Uralic family are the four Samoyed languages of northernmost Russia: Nenets (35,000), Selkup (2,000), plus Nganasan and Enets, each with fewer than 1,000 speakers.

About 20 languages of Russia are of the Altaic family. The largest subgroup is the Turkic, which includes Tatar (6 million speakers), Chuvash (1½ million), and Bashkir (one million), all spoken in European Russia; as well as Kumyk (250,000), Karachai (150,000), Balkar (80,000), and Nogai (75,000), spoken in the Caucasus; and Yakut (300,000), Tuvinian (200,000), Khakass (80,000), and Altai (75,000), spoken in Siberia. Two Mongolian languages are Buryat (375,000) and Kalmyk (150,000). The Tungusic subgroup of the Russian Far East includes Evenki (15,000), Even (7,000), and Nanai (7,000).

Still another language family of Russia is the Caucasian, located in the Caucasus between the Black and the Caspian seas. These languages number about 40, three-fourths of them spoken in the single republic of

Dagestan. Those that have been reduced to writing are Chechen (one million speakers), Avar (600,000), Kabardian (375,000), Dargwa (350,000), Lezgin (300,000), Ingush (200,000), Adygei (125,000), Lak (100,000), Tabasaran (100,000), and Abazinian (25,000).

The tiny Paleo-Asiatic family of northeastern Siberia consists of Chukchi (12,000 speakers), Koryak (6,000), Nivkh (2,000), Ket (1,000), and Itelmen and Yukagir, each spoken by only a few hundred people. Lastly there are 2,000 speakers of Lappish on the Kola Peninsula, 1,000 speakers of Eskimo in northeastern Siberia, and a few hundred speakers of Aleut on the Commander Islands.

RWANDA (7½ million). Ruanda is spoken by virtually the entire population. It is co-official with French and English. Swahili is used for commercial purposes.

SAINT KITTS AND NEVIS (40,000). English is the official language, but the majority of the population speaks an English creole.

SAINT LUCIA (150,000). Virtually everyone on this island speaks English, which is the official language. But in everyday speech the people prefer a French creole which they themselves call French patois.

SAINT VINCENT (100,000). English, the official language, is spoken by virtually the entire population. However, an English creole is the language of everyday use.

SAMOA (200,000). Samoan is spoken by virtually the entire population. It is co-official with English.

SAN MARINO (25,000). Italian is spoken here.

SÃO TOMÉ AND PRÍNCIPE (150,000). The official language is Portuguese but a Portuguese creole called Crioulo is spoken by most of the population.

SAUDI ARABIA (20 million). Arabic is spoken everywhere.

SENEGAL (10 million). The official language is French. Wolof is the most important native language, with about 5 million speakers mainly in the western part of the country. Other languages include Fulani (2 million speakers), Serer (one million), Dyola (500,000), and Malinke (350,000).

SEYCHELLES (80,000). The official language is English but French is also widely spoken. A French creole is the language of the home and street.

SIERRA LEONE (5 million). The official language is English. Krio, an English creole, is the day-to-day language in Freetown, the capital, and serves as the lingua franca of much of the rest of the country. The two principal native languages are Mende, a Mande language of south-central Sierra Leone, and Temne, an Atlantic language of the central and north-western districts. Each has about 1½ million speakers. Limba is spoken by about 400,000 people in the north-central area. Vai is spoken along the coast near the border with Liberia, Kissi in the interior near the border with Liberia and Guinea.

SINGAPORE (3½ million). Chinese is spoken by nearly three-fourths of the population, or 2½ million people. Malay speakers number about 500,000, Tamil about 250,000. Malay has been designated the "national language," while English, Chinese, Tamil, and also Malay are known as "official languages."

SLOVAKIA (5 million). Slovak is spoken by about 90 percent of the population. There is a large Hungarian-speaking minority of 500,000 people in the south. Slovakia also has many Gypsies who speak the Romany language.

SLOVENIA (2 million). Slovenian is spoken by about 90 percent of the population. Most of the rest speak Serbo-Croatian. There are some speakers of Hungarian in the northeast, and of Italian along the Adriatic coast.

SOLOMON ISLANDS (500,000). Over 50 Oceanic and five Polynesian languages are spoken here, none by more than five percent of the population. There are about 10 on Malaita Island, 8 each on Guadalcanal, New Georgia and Santa Isabel, 5 on San Cristobal (Makira), 4 on Choiseul, and still others on the smaller islands. An English creole known as Pijin is the mother tongue of a few thousand people, but is spoken as a second language by about one-third of the population. The official language is English.

SOMALIA (7 million). Somali is spoken by virtually the entire population. Arabic is widely understood in the cities.

SOUTH AFRICA (45 million). The official languages are Afrikaans and English, the former spoken by about 6 million people, the latter by about 4 million. Of the native languages the most important are Zulu, spoken principally in Natal (10 million speakers); Xhosa, spoken mainly in Transkei (8 million); Pedi, in Transvaal (4 million); Tswana, near the border with Botswana (3 million); Sotho, near the border with Lesotho (3 million); and Tsonga, also of Transvaal (2 million). Swazi (one million) is spoken in the area adjoining Swaziland, while Venda (one million) and Ndebele (800,000) are both spoken in northern Transvaal. Fanakalo, a jargon based on Zulu with numerous English and some Afrikaans words added, is spoken among workers in the mines.

SPAIN (40 million). Spanish is the national language. Catalan, however, is spoken by about 6 million people in the northeastern provinces and by another 500,000 in the Balearic Islands. In northwestern Spain about 3 million people speak Galician, a dialect of Portuguese. Near the French border, in the provinces facing the Bay of Biscay, there are about 600,000 speakers of Basque.

SRI LANKA (20 million). Sinhalese and Tamil, completely unrelated to each other, are this country's two languages, with about 2½ million people fluent in both. About 12½ million speak only Sinhalese, while about 5 million people, living mainly in the north and on the east coast of the island, speak only Tamil.

SUDAN (35 million). Arabic, the official language, is spoken by about half the population, mainly in the northern two-thirds of the country. Also in the north is Nubian, one dialect of which is spoken by about 2 million people in the central state of Kordofan, another by about 500,000 people in Northern State. Beja is spoken by about 2 million people in the state of Kassala facing the Red Sea, Fur by about 500,000 in the western state of Darfur. Of the dozens of languages of the south the two most important are Dinka (4 million speakers) and Nuer (1½ million). Zande (one million) is spoken near the border with Congo-Kinshasa, Shilluk (500,000) in Upper Nile State, and Bari (750,000) and Lotuko (500,000) near the border with Uganda.

SURINAME (400,000). The official language is Dutch, but the language of the streets is an English creole known as Sranan, or Taki-Taki. It is the mother tongue of nearly half the population and is spoken as a second language by perhaps 80 percent. Another English creole, Saramacca, is spoken by the 20,000 Bush Negroes of the interior. Hindi and Javanese each have about 50,000 speakers. Among Suriname's tiny Indian tribes about 2,500 people speak Carib and 1,000 speak Arawak.

SWAZILAND (1 million). Swazi is spoken by virtually the entire African population. The official language is English.

SWEDEN (9 million). Swedish is the national language. The Finnish-speaking minority numbers about 200,000. In the far north about 10,000 people speak Lappish.

SWITZERLAND (7 million). Switzerland has four official languages. German ranks first with about 5 million speakers. Standard German is the written language and is used in the parliament, universities, courts, and churches, but Swiss German, a distinctly different local dialect, is used in everyday speech. French is spoken by about 1½ million people in the west, in an area that includes Geneva. Italian is spoken by about 500,000 people living mainly in the canton of Ticino in the southeast. Romansch, a Rhaeto-Romanic dialect, is spoken by about 50,000 people in the canton of Graubünden in easternmost Switzerland.

SYRIA (15 million). Arabic is spoken by the vast majority of the population. French is spoken by many people as a second language. Other languages include Kurdish (one million speakers), Armenian (250,000), Circassian (50,000), Assyrian (15,000), and Aramaic (2,000).

TAIWAN (22 million). Chinese is the national language, the Mandarin dialect being official. Among the 17 million native Taiwanese, about 15 million speak the Amoy dialect, while about 2 million speak Hakka. The island's 300,000 aborigines speak about ten different languages, which constitute a separate branch of the Austronesian family.

TAJIKISTAN (6 million). The official language is Tajik, spoken by about 5 million people. The second language is Uzbek, with about 1½ million speakers. The number of Russian speakers has declined to less than 100,000.

TANZANIA (35 million). About 120 languages are spoken here. Swahili is the language of administration and is spoken by most of the population, usually as a second language. English is also widely used, especially for commercial purposes. Most of the native languages are of the Bantu family, the most important being Sukuma, spoken in the northwest (6 million speakers), and closely related Nyamwezi, spoken mostly in Tabora Province in west-central Tanzania (one million). Makonde (2 million) is spoken in the extreme south, Haya (2 million) in Kagera (formerly West Lake) Province in the extreme northwest, Nyakyusa (2 million) at the north end of Lake Nyasa, Chagga (1½ million) on the slopes of Mt. Kilimanjaro, Ruguru or Luguru (1½ million) in the area just west of Dar es Salaam, Shambala (1½ million) in Tanga Province in the northeastern corner of the country, Gogo (1½ million) in central Tanzania, Ha (one million) in Kigoma Province bordering Burundi, Hehe (one million) in Iringa district in south-central Tanzania, and Yao (750,000) near the border with Mozambique. Masai, a Nilotic language, is spoken by about 300,000 people near the border with Kenya. In the Khoisan family are Sandawe (75,000), spoken near the town of Kondoa, and Hatsa, or Hadzapi, with only a few hundred speakers around the perimeter of Lake Eyasi. On Zanzibar Swahili is the dominant language, though Arabic and a number of Indian languages are also spoken.

THAILAND (60 million). Thai is spoken by about 35 million people. Lao, the language of neighboring Laos, is spoken by about 15 million people in the east near the Mekong River. Speakers of Chinese number about 7 million. Other languages include Malay, with about 2 million speakers in the extreme south, and Khmer, with about 750,000 speakers in the southeast. Among native languages the most important are Mon (75,000), spoken near the western border, and Karen (75,000) and Miao (50,000), spoken in the north.

TOGO (5 million). The official language is French. More than 30 native languages are spoken here, those in the south belonging to the Kwa branch of the Niger-Congo family, those of the north belonging to the Gur (Voltaic) branch. Ewe, of the former, is by far the most important with about 2 million speakers. The major languages of the north are Kabre and Gurma.

TONGA (100,000). The language spoken here is Tongan. It is co-official with English.

TRINIDAD AND TOBAGO (1,250,000). The official and dominant language is English. A French creole, once widely spoken, is still heard in scattered areas. The many descendants of immigrants from India speak Hindi, Tamil, and a number of other languages in addition to English.

TUNISIA (10 million). Arabic is spoken by the vast majority of the population. Many people also speak French.

TURKEY (65 million). Turkish is spoken by about 90 percent of the population. Kurdish-speaking Kurds of southeastern Turkey form the largest minority, numbering about 8 million. Other languages include Arabic (one million speakers), Circassian (75,000), Armenian (50,000), Greek (50,000), Georgian (50,000), Ladino (20,000), and Aramaic (1,000).

TURKMENISTAN (5 million). The official language is Turkmen, spoken by about 3½ million people. Speakers of Uzbek number about 400,000, of Russian about 250,000.

TUVALU (10,000). The language spoken in this new country (the former Ellis Islands) is Tuvaluan. The official language is English.

UGANDA (25 million). The official language is English. Among native languages the most important is Ganda, or Luganda, a Bantu language with about 4 million speakers in an area that includes Kampala, the capital. Other Bantu languages are Nkole, or Nyankole (2½ million speakers), of the southwest near Tanzania; Chiga, or Kiga (2 million), of the extreme southwest; Soga (2 million), of the south; Gisu (one million), of the southeast; Toro (500,000), of the southwest; and Nyoro (500,000), spoken east of Lake Albert. In the Nilotic family are Teso (1½ million) and Karamojong (500,000), both spoken in the northeast, while Lango and Acholi (one million each), are spoken in north-central Uganda, and Alur (500,000) in the northwest. In the Central Sudanic family are Lugbara (one million) and Madi (250,000), both of the northwest. Swahili is spoken as a second language by as much as a third of the population.

UKRAINE (50 million). Ukrainians make up about three-quarters of the population; Russians, living predominantly in the east and on the Crimean Peninsula, about one-quarter. Although the official language is Ukrainian, many Ukrainians consider Russian to be their first language.

UNITED ARAB EMIRATES (2½ million). The indigenous (and official) language, Arabic, is actually spoken by less than half the population. The remainder speak Persian and a number of languages of India and Pakistan.

UNITED KINGDOM (60 million). English is spoken universally. About 600,000 people in Wales speak Welsh, 100,000 in Northern Ireland speak Irish, and 75,000 in Scotland speak Scottish Gaelic, but all these people speak English as well.

UNITED STATES OF AMERICA (280 million). English is the national language, spoken by the vast majority of the population. However, the continuous arrival of immigrants in America, representing virtually every country in the world, has resulted in dozens of other languages being spoken. According to the 2000 census, some 45 million Americans, or 17 percent of the population, speak a language other than English at home. Sixty percent of this total, or 27 million, speak Spanish. The rest speak Chinese, Japanese, Korean, Vietnamese, Khmer, Russian, Polish, Italian, French, German, Portuguese, Greek, Persian, Arabic, Hindi, Thai, Tagalog, Yiddish, and many other languages. Some 10 million people living in the United States are reported to have little or no knowledge of English at all.

According to the 1990 census, of America's 1,800,000 Indians, 430,000, or about one-fourth, speak an Indian language at home. The most important by far is Navajo, with about 150,000 speakers in Arizona, New Mexico, and Utah. Next in line come Sioux, or Dakota (15,000), spoken in the northern midwest; Cherokee, with about 10,000 speakers in Oklahoma and 1,000 in North Carolina; Apache (10,000), of Arizona; Choctaw (9,000), of Oklahoma and Mississippi; Papago (8,000), of Arizona; Keresan (8,000) and Zuñi (6,000), of New Mexico; Ojibwa, or Chippewa (5,000), of the northern Midwest; and Pima and Hopi (5,000), both of Arizona. Also in Oklahoma are Creek (4,000), Chickasaw (3,000), Kiowa (1,000), Comanche (1,000), and Caddo, Pawnee, Osage, and Delaware, each with only a few hundred speakers. Cheyenne (1,500) is divided between Oklahoma and Montana, Arapaho (1,000) between Oklahoma and Wyoming, and Fox (500) between Oklahoma and Iowa.

In Montana there are also Crow (4,000 speakers), Blackfoot (1,000), and Flathead (1,000). In New Mexico there are also Tiwa, spoken by the Taos and Isleta Indians (4,000), Tewa, spoken by the San Juan and Santa Clara Indians (3,000), and Towa, spoken by the Jemez Indians (1,400). Ute is spoken by about 2,000 people in Utah and Colorado. Shoshone (2,000) and Paiute (1,500) are spoken in a number of Western states. In the Midwest there are also Winnebago, with about 750 speakers in Wisconsin and Nebraska, and Omaha, with about 500 speakers in Nebraska. In Arizona there are also Yuma and Mohave, each with fewer than 500 speakers. Yakima is spoken by about 1,000 people in Washington, Nez Perce by a few hundred in Idaho, and Klamath by fewer than 100 in Oregon. In New York there are Mohawk (1,500), Seneca (800), and Oneida (300), which also has some speakers in Wisconsin. In Florida, Seminole is spoken by about 2,000 people, while in Rhode Island about 800 people speak Passamaquoddy.

In Alaska there are about 20,000 speakers of Eskimo, as well as 1,000 speakers of Tlingit and a hundred or so speakers of Haida, both in the panhandle. In the Aleutian Islands there are about 1,000 speakers of Aleut. In Hawaii about 15,000 people speak Hawaiian.

URUGUAY (3 million). Spanish is spoken by virtually the entire population.

UZBEKISTAN (25 million). The official language is Uzbek, spoken by about 18 million people. Russian speakers number about one million. There are also about one million speakers each of Tajik and Kazakh. Kara-Kalpak is spoken by about 500,000 people in the republic of the same name in the westernmost part of the country. Some 400,000 Crimean Tatars speak the Tatar language.

VANUATU (200,000). On this nation of some 80 islands (the former New Hebrides), which lie to the west of Fiji, more than 100 different Oceanic languages are spoken. An English creole known as Bislama serves as the lingua franca.

VENEZUELA (25 million). Spanish is spoken by the vast majority of the population. Indian languages include Goajiro (100,000) near the Guajira Peninsula of Colombia, and Warao (30,000), Piaroa (12,000), and Carib (10,000) spoken in the delta of the Orinoco River.

VIETNAM (80 million). Vietnamese is spoken by about seven-eighths of the population. Chinese, Thai, and Khmer each have about one million speakers. Dozens of native languages are also spoken. In the north there are Tho, or Tay (1½ million speakers), Muong, the only language definitely related to Vietnamese (one million), as well as Nung (750,000), Miao, or Hmong (500,000), and Yao, or Mien (500,000). In the south the various Montagnard peoples speak Jarai (250,000), Rhade (200,000), Bahnar (150,000), Sedang (100,000), and many other languages. In the lowlands there is Cham, with about 100,000 speakers.

YEMEN (15 million). Arabic is spoken by virtually the entire population.

YUGOSLAVIA (10 million). Serbian is spoken by about 80 percent of the population. In Kosovo about 1½ million people speak Albanian. In the north, in the province of Vojvodina, there are about 400,000 speakers of Hungarian.

ZAÏRE. *See* Congo (Kinshasa).

ZAMBIA (10 million). The official language is English. Bemba is the most important native language, with about 3 million speakers in the northeastern part of the country. Tonga, of the south, and Nyanja, of the east and central regions, are each spoken by about one million people. Lozi is spoken by about 500,000 people in the southwest, Nsenga by about 400,000 in the southeast, and Tumbuka by about by 300,000 in the east. Lwena (Luvale) and Lunda, of the northwest, and Kaonde, of central Zambia, each have about 200,000 speakers.

ZIMBABWE (11 million). The official language is English, spoken by the country's 200,000 whites and about half of the rest of the population. Shona is the principal native language, with about 8 million speakers. Ndebele is spoken by about 2 million people in the southwest.

Sources of individual passages

Afrikaans   Translation by C. J. D. Harvey, in *Afrikaans Poems with English Translations*, ed. by A. P. Grové and C. J. D. Harvey, Oxford University Press, Cape Town and New York, 1962.

Albanian   Stuart Edward An, *Albanian Literature,* B. Quaritch, London, 1955.

Aleut   Richard Henry Geoghegan, *The Aleut Language*, U.S. Department of the Interior, 1944.

Amharic   Martino Mario Moreno, *Cent Fables Amhariques*, Imprimerie Nationale, Paris, 1947.

Aranda   Transcribed by Jennifer Inkamala, Yiprinya School, Alice Springs, Australia, 2000.

Avar   A. Akhlakov, *Heroic-Historic Songs of the Avars*, Makhachkala, U.S.S.R., 1968.

Basque   Resurrección María de Azkue, *Euskaléraren Yakintza*, Espasa-Calpe, S.A., Madrid, 1942.

Batak   H. N. van der Tuuk, *Bataksch Leesboek*, Frederik Muller, Amsterdam, 1860.

Belorussian   Serialized in the magazine *Polymya*. This extract appeared in the issue of November 1968.

Bengali   *Collected Poems and Plays of Rabindranath Tagore*, Macmillan Company, London, 1936.

Breton   Ronan Huon, *An Ivan Glas*, Al Liamm, Brest, 1971.

Bulgarian   Translation by Marguerite Alexieva and Theodora Atanassova, Narodna Kultura, Sofia, 1955.

Burushaski   D. L. R. Lorimer, *The Burushaski Language*, H. Aschehoug, Oslo, 1935.

Buryat   T. A. Bertagaev and Ts. B. Tsydendambaev, *Grammatika Buryatskogo Yazyka* ("Buryat Grammar"), Oriental Literature Publishing House, Moscow, 1962.

Bushman   W. H. I. Bleek and L. C. Lloyd, *Specimens of Bushmen Folklore*, C. Struik, Cape Town, 1968.

Chamorro	Donald M. Topping, *Spoken Chamorro*, University of Hawaii Press, Honolulu, 1969.
Chechen	N. F. Yakovlev, *Sintaksis Chechenskogo Yazyka* ("Chechen Syntax"), Academy of Sciences of the U.S.S.R., 1940.
Chinese	Translation by Mabel Lee, HarperCollins, New York, 2000.
Chuang	A. A. Moskalev, *Grammatika Yazyka Chzhuan* ("Chuang Grammar"), Nauka, Moscow, 1971.
Coptic	*Coptic Texts*, ed. by William H. Worrell, University of Michigan Press, Ann Arbor, 1942.
Cree	*The Cree Language Is Our Identity*, The La Ronge Lectures of Sarah Whitecalf, edited and translated by H. C. Wolfart and Freda Ahenakew, University of Manitoba Press, Canada, 1993.
Creek	*Tchikilli's Kasi'hta Legend*, with a commentary by Albert S. Gratschet, Academy of Science of St. Louis, 1888.
Croatian	Translation by Zora G. Depolo, Lincoln-Prager Publishers, London, 1959.
Czech	Translation by M. and R. Weatherall, George Allen & Unwin, London, 1948.
Danish	*Andersen's Fairy Tales*, Macmillan, New York, 1966.
Delaware	Frank G. Speck, *A Study of the Delaware Indian Big House Ceremony*, Pennsylvania Historical Commission, Harrisburg, 1931.
Dutch	Translation by B. M. Mooyaart-Doubleday, Doubleday & Company, Garden City, New York, 1952.
English (Old)	Translation by Seamus Heaney, W. W. Norton, New York, 2000.
English (Middle)	Vincent F. Hopper, *Chaucer's Canterbury Tales, An Interlinear Translation*, Barron's Educational Series Inc., Woodbury, N.Y., 1948.
Eskimo	*Inuktitut* Magazine, issue of September, 1983, entitled "Writing Systems and Translations." Introduction (from which this passage was taken) by Mark Kalluak, Indian and Northern Affairs Canada, Ottawa.
Estonian	William K. Matthews, *Child of Man*, Boreas Publishing, London, 1955.
Evenki	V. D. Kolesnikova, *Sintaksis Evenkiiskogo Yazyka* ("Evenki Syntax"), Nauka, Moscow, 1966.
Ewe	Diedrich Westermann, *A Study of the Ewe Language*, Oxford University Press, London, 1930.
Faroese	William B. Lockwood, *An Introduction to Modern Faroese*, E. Munksgaard, Copenhagen, 1955.

Fijian	G. B. Mimer, *Fijian Grammar*, Government Press, Suva, Fiji.
Finnish	Translation by Naomi Walford, G. P. Putnam's Sons, New York, 1949.
Flemish	Translation by C. B. Bodde, Harper & Bros., New York, 1924.
Fox	Truman Michelson, *Fox Miscellany*, Smithsonian Institution, Bureau of American Ethnology, Bulletin 114, Washington, 1937.
French	Translation by Eleanor Marx Aveling, Dodd, Mead, New York.
Frisian	"The Literature of Frisian Immigrants in America," *De Tsjerne*, Volume V, 1950.
Fulani	Frank William Taylor, *A First Grammar of the Adamawa Dialect of the Fulani Language*, Clarendon Press, Oxford, 1921.
Gaelic	*Short Stories of Padraic Pearse*, selected and adapted by Desmond Maguire, Mercier Press, Cork, 1968.
Georgian	Translation by Marjory Scott Wardrop, Co-operative Publishing Society of Foreign Workers in the U.S.S.R., Moscow, 1938.
German	Translation by H. T. Lowe-Porter, Alfred A. Knopf, New York, 1958.
Greek (Classical)	Translation by Seth G. Benardete, in *The Complete Greek Tragedies*, ed. by David Grene and Richmond Lattimore, Modern Library, New York, 1956.
Greek (Modern)	Translation by Jonathan Griffin, Simon and Schuster, New York, 1966.
Hawaiian	*The Echo of Our Song*, translated and edited by Mary K. Pukui and Alfons L. Korn, University of Hawaii Press, Honolulu, 1973.
Hottentot	D. M. Beach, *The Phonetics of the Hottentot Language*, Cambridge University Press, Cambridge, 1938.
Hungarian	Translation by Frances A. Gerard, Harper & Bros., New York, 1896.
Ibo	Translated by Romanus N. Egudu and Donatus I. Nwoga, Nwankwo-Ifejika (Publishers), Enugu, 1971.
Icelandic	Hallberg Hallmundsson, *An Anthology of Scandinavian Literature*, Macmillan, New York, 1965.
Indonesian	A. Teeuw, *Modern Indonesian Literature*, Martinus Nijhoff, The Hague, 1967.
Italian	Translation by Eric Mosbacher, Grove Press, New York, 1953.
Japanese	Translation by John Bester, Kodansha International, Tokyo, New York, 1974.

Kalmyk	*Yazyki Narodov SSSR* ("The Languages of the Peoples of the U.S.S.R."), Nauka, Leningrad, 1968.
Kashmiri	*Paramananda-Sukti-Sara*, edited and translated by Zinda Kaul, Durga Press, Srinagar, 1941.
Kazakh	Translation by Lev Navrozov, Foreign Languages Publishing House, Moscow.
Khanty	János Gulya, *Eastern Ostyak Chrestomathy*, Indiana University, Bloomington, Indiana, 1966.
Khmer	*Cambodia's Lament, A Selection of Cambodian Poetry*, edited and translated by George Chigas, Millers Falls, Massachusetts, 1991.
Korean	*A Pageant of Korean Poetry*, selected and translated by In-Sŏb-Zŏng, Eomun-Gag, Seoul, 1963.
Lao	*Chansons Lao*, Ministère des Beaux Arts, Kingdom of Laos.
Lappish	Björn Collinder, *The Lapps*, Princeton University Press, Princeton, New Jersey, 1949.
Latin	Norbert Guterman, *A Book of Latin Quotations*, Anchor Books, Garden City, New York, 1966.
Latvian	Juris Silenieks, in *Quinto Lingo*, February, 1969.
Lingala	L. B. de Boek, *Manuel de Lingála*, Éditions de Scheut, Brussels, 1952.
Luba	H. W. Beckett, *Hand Book of Kiluba*, produced under the supervision and direction of Chevalier John Alexander Clarke, Garenganze Evangelical Mission, Mulongo, D.P. Lubumbashi, 1951.
Maithili	*The Songs of Vidyapati*, ed. by Subhadra Jha, Motilal Banarasidass, Banaras, India.
Malay	M. B. Lewis, *Teach Yourself Malay*, English Universities Press, London, 1947.
Maori	*The Maori Song Book*, English lyric and arrangement by Sam Freedman, Seven Seas Publishing, Wellington, 1966.
Marathi	T. E. Katenina, *Yazyk Maratkhi* ("The Marathi Language"), Nauka, Moscow, 1967.
Marshallese	Byron W. Bender, *Spoken Marshallese: An intensive language course with grammatical notes and glossary*, University of Hawaii Press, Honolulu, 1969.
Maya	Text by R. P. F. Ximenez with Spanish translation by Dora M. de Burgess and Patricio Xec, Quezaltenango, Guatemala City, 1955.
Mixtec	Alejandra Cruz Ortiz, *El nudo del tiempo*, Centro de Investigaciones y Estudios, Tlalpan, 1998.
Mohawk	*The Iroquois Book of Rites*, edited by Horatio Hale, reprinted by University of Toronto Press, Toronto, 1963.

Moldovan	Translation by Corneliu M. Popescu.
Mossi	F. Froger, *Manuel Pratique de Langue Môré*, L. Fournier, Paris 1923.
Nahuatl	Translation by Thelma D. Sullivan, in *Estudios de Cultura Náhuatl*, Volume V, 1965.
Nakhi	Joseph F. Rock, *The Zhi ma Funeral Ceremony of the Na-Khi of Southwest China*, St. Gabriel's Mission Press, Vienna, 1955.
Nenets	Z. N. Kupriyanova, L. V. Khomich, A. M. Shcherbakova, *Nenetsky Yazyk* ("The Nenets Language"), State Educational-Pedagogical Publishers, Leningrad, 1957.
Nepali	Nikolai I. Koroliov, *Yazyk Nepali* ("The Nepali Language"), Nauka, Moscow, 1965.
Norwegian	*Aku Aku*, Rand McNally, Chicago, 1958.
Ojibwa	Leonard Bloomfield, *Eastern Ojibwa*, University of Michigan Press, Ann Arbor, 1957.
Oriya	Boris M. Karpushkin, *Yazyk Oriya* ("The Oriya Language"), Nauka, Moscow, 1964.
Osage	Francis La Flesche, *War Ceremony and Peace Ceremony of the Osage Indians*, Smithsonian Institution, Bureau of American Ethnology, Bulletin 101, 1939.
Papiamento	W. M. Hoyer, *A Brief Historical Description of the Island of Aruba*, Boekhandel Bethencourt, Curaçao, 1945.
Pashto	Translation by Olaf Caroe, in *The Poems of Khushhal Khan Khatak* by Evelyn Howell and Olaf Caroe. Distributed by Oxford University Press for the Pashto Academy, University of Peshawar, Peshawar, 1963.
Polish	*The Separate Notebooks*, translated by Robert Hass and Robert Pinsky with the author and Renata Gorczynski, The Ecco Press, New York, 1984.
Portuguese	Translated by Mary Jull Costa, Harcourt, 1999.
Provençal	Translation by Maro Beath Jones, Saunders Studio Press, Claremont, California, 1937.
Quechua	Translation by Clements R. Markham, Trübner, London, 1871.
Romanian	*Introduction to Rumanian Literature*, ed. by Jacob Steinberg, Twayne Publishers, New York, 1966.
Romany	Jan Kochanowski, *Gypsy Studies*, International Academy of Indian Culture, New Delhi, 1963.
Russian	Translation by Max Hayward and Manya Harari, Pantheon Books, New York, 1958.

Samoan	C. C. Marsack, *Teach Yourself Samoan*, English Universities Press, London, 1962.
Sanskrit	Charles Rockwell Lanman, *Sanskrit Reader*, Ginn, Boston, 1888.
Seneca	Nils M. Holmer, *The Seneca Language*, Upsala Canadian Studies, Lund, 1954.
Serbian	Translation by Drenka Willen, Harcourt, Brace & World, New York, 1962.
Shona	*Shona Praise Poetry*, compiled by A. C. Hodza, edited by G. Fortune, Oxford University Press, Oxford, 1979.
Sinhalese	Translation by S. Radhakrishnan, Oxford University Press, London, 1950.
Slovak	Translation by Jean Rosemary Edwards, Artia Prague, Prague, 1961.
Slovenian	Translation by Sidonie Yeras and H. C. Sewell Grant, Pushkin Press, London, 1930.
Somali	B. W. Andrzejewski and I. M. Lewis, *Somali Poetry*, Clarendon Press, Oxford, 1964.
Spanish	Translation by John Ormsby, Heritage Press, New York.
Swedish	Translation by Leif Sjöberg and W. H. Auden, Alfred A. Knopf, New York, 1964.
Syriac	*The New Testament and Psalms in Syriac*, British and Foreign Bible Society, London, 1919.
Tagalog	E. San Juan Jr., *Rice Grains*, International Publishers, New York, 1966.
Tahitian	R. D. Lovy and L. J. Bouge, *Grammaire de la langue tahitienne*, Publications de la Société des Océanistes, Musée de l'Homme, Paris, 1953.
Tamil	J. M. Somasundaram Pillai, *Two Thousand Years of Tamil Literature*, Madras, 1959.
Telugu	Translation by Charles Philip Brown, College Press, Madras, 1829.
Tibetan	George N. Roerich, *Selected Works*, Nauka, Moscow, 1967.
Tongan	E. E. V. Collocott, *Tales and Poems of Tonga*, The Museum, Honolulu, 1928.
Turkish	*Fazil Hüsnü Dağlarca, Selected Poems*, translated by Talât Sait Halman, University of Pittsburgh Press, Pittsburgh, 1969.
Uigur	E. N. Nadzhip, *Sovremenny Uigurski Yazyk* ("Modern Uigur"), Oriental Literature Publishing House, Moscow, 1960.

Ukrainian	*The Poetical Works of Taras Shevchenko*, translated by C. H. Andrusyshen and Watson Kirkconnell, University of Toronto Press, Toronto, 1964.
Urdu	Muhammad Sadiq, *A History of Urdu Literature*, Oxford University Press, London, 1964.
Vietnamese	Translation by Huỳnh Sanh Thông, Yale University Press, New Haven, 1983.
Visayan	John U. Wolff, *Beginning Cebuano*, Yale University Press, New Haven, 1966.
Welsh	J. Gwilym Jones, *William Williams Pantycelyn*, University of Wales Press, Cardiff, 1969.
Yiddish	*In My Father's Court*, Jewish Publication Society of America, Philadelphia, 1966.
Yoruba	J. A. de Gaye and W. S. Beecroft, *Yoruba Composition*, Routledge & Kegan Paul, London, 1951.
Zapotec	*Relatos Zapotecos*, Dirección General de Culturas Populares, Mexico City, 1997.
Zulu	*Zulu Horizons*, The Vilakazi Poems rendered into English by D. McK. Malcolm and Florence Louie Friedman, Howard Timmins, Cape Town, 1962.

Index